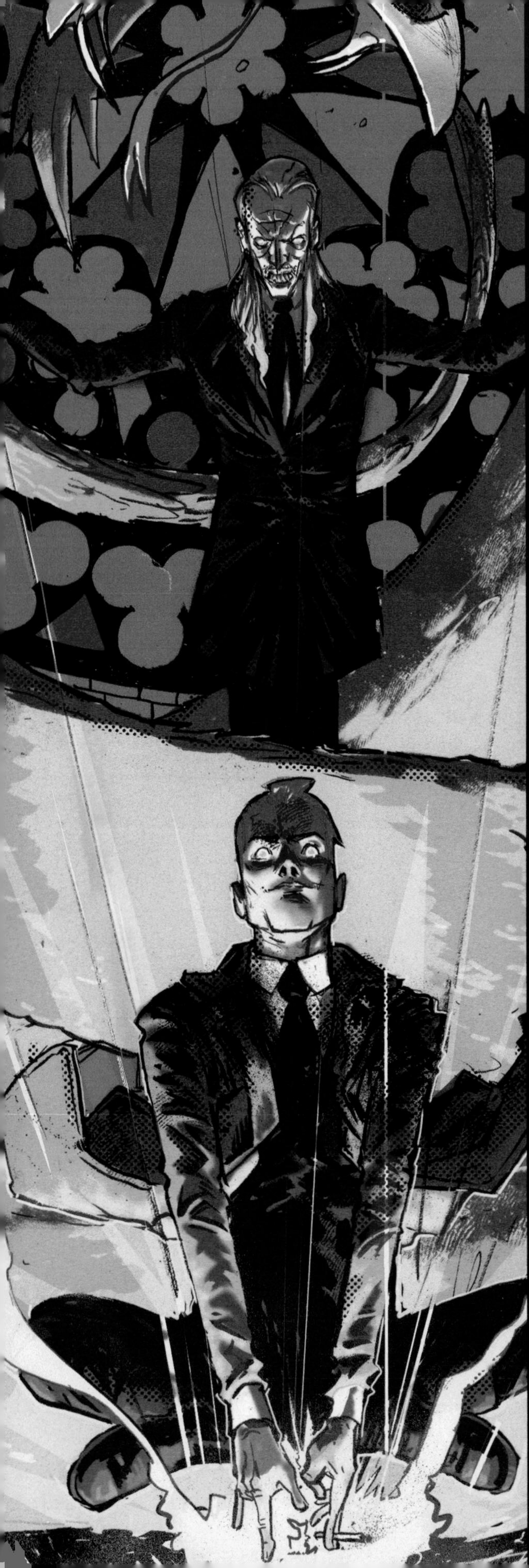

VOLUME 2
# THE ART OF THE DEAL

# CONSTANTINE THE HELLBLAZER

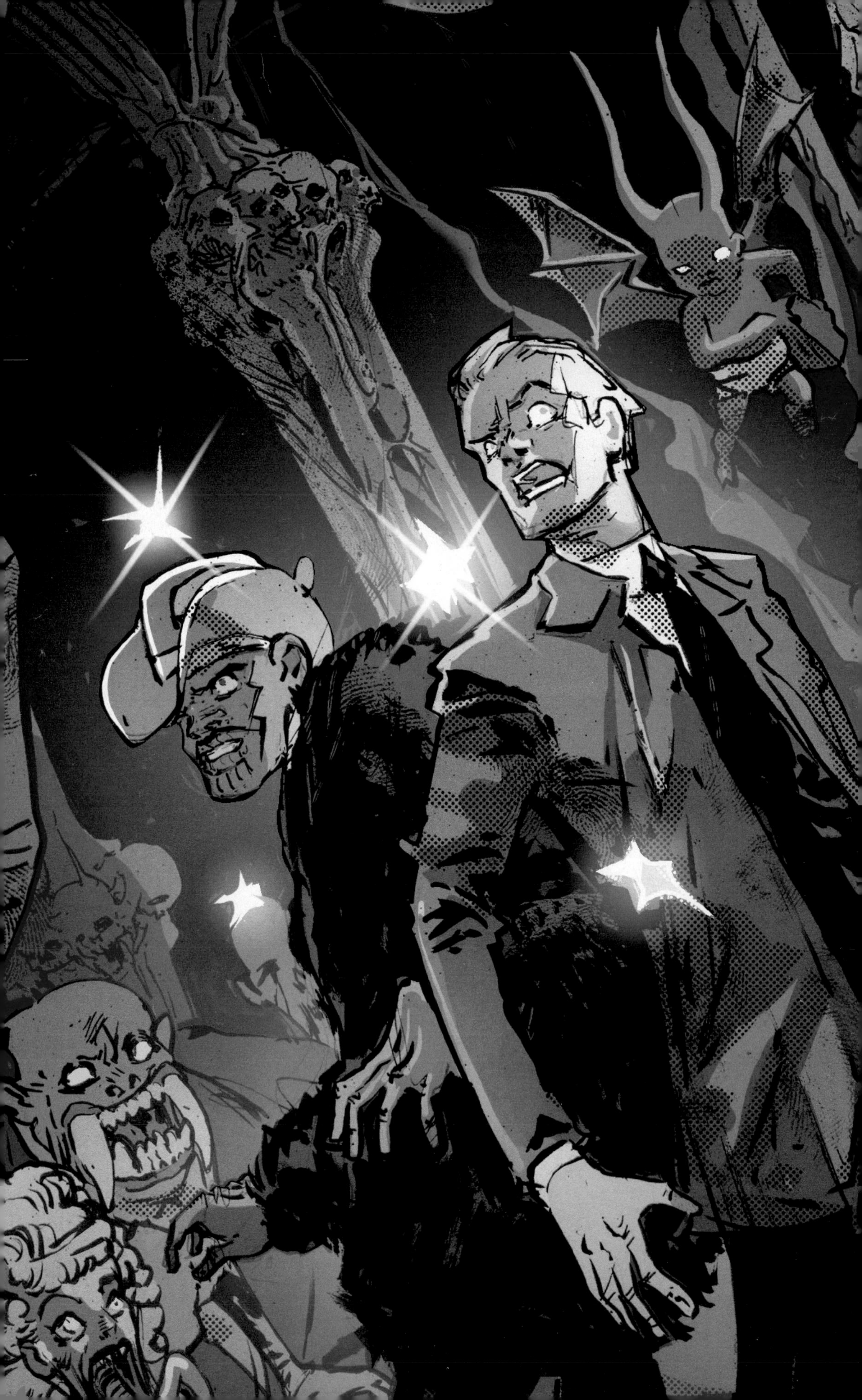

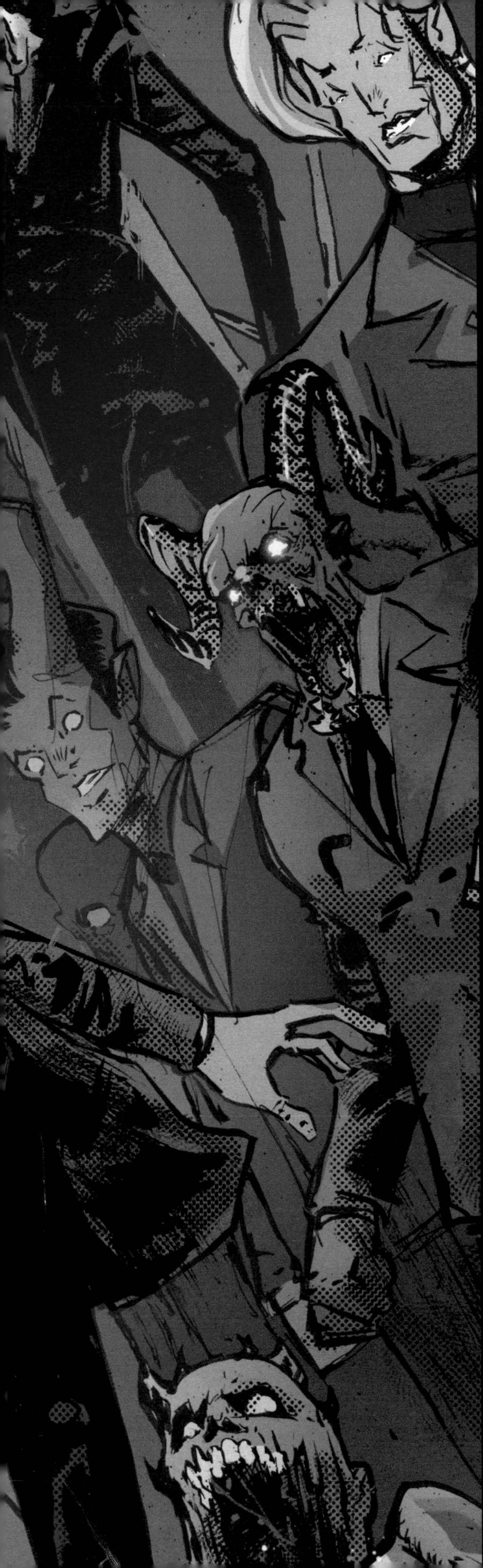

# CONSTANTINE THE HELLBLAZER

## VOLUME 2
## THE ART OF THE DEAL


WRITTEN BY
MING DOYLE
JAMES TYNION IV

ART BY
RILEY ROSSMO
TRAVEL FOREMAN
ERYK DONOVAN
BRIAN LEVEL
JOSEPH SILVER

COLOR BY
IVAN PLASCENCIA
KELLY FITZPATRICK

LETTERS BY
TOM NAPOLITANO

COVERS BY
RILEY ROSSMO

JOHN CONSTANTINE CREATED BY
ALAN MOORE,
STEVE BISSETTE,
JOHN TOTLEBEN AND
JAMIE DELANO
& JOHN RIDGWAY

ANDY KHOURI AMEDEO TURTURRO KRISTY QUINN Editors - Original Series
JEB WOODARD Group Editor - Collected Editions
ROBIN WILDMAN Editor - Collected Edition
STEVE COOK Design Director - Books
DAMIAN RYLAND Publication Design

BOB HARRAS Senior VP - Editor-in-Chief, DC Comics

DIANE NELSON President
DAN DIDIO and JIM LEE Co-Publishers
GEOFF JOHNS Chief Creative Officer
AMIT DESAI Senior VP - Marketing & Global Franchise Management
NAIRI GARDINER Senior VP - Finance
SAM ADES VP - Digital Marketing
BOBBIE CHASE VP - Talent Development
MARK CHIARELLO Senior VP - Art, Design & Collected Editions
JOHN CUNNINGHAM VP - Content Strategy
ANNE DEPIES VP - Strategy Planning & Reporting
DON FALLETTI VP - Manufacturing Operations
LAWRENCE GANEM VP - Editorial Administration & Talent Relations
ALISON GILL Senior VP - Manufacturing & Operations
HANK KANALZ Senior VP - Editorial Strategy & Administration
JAY KOGAN VP - Legal Affairs
DEREK MADDALENA Senior VP - Sales & Business Development
JACK MAHAN VP - Business Affairs
DAN MIRON VP - Sales Planning & Trade Development
NICK NAPOLITANO VP - Manufacturing Administration
CAROL ROEDER VP - Marketing
EDDIE SCANNELL VP - Mass Account & Digital Sales
COURTNEY SIMMONS Senior VP - Publicity & Communications
JIM (SKI) SOKOLOWSKI VP - Comic Book Specialty & Newsstand Sales
SANDY YI Senior VP - Global Franchise Management

CONSTANTINE: THE HELLBLAZER VOLUME 2—THE ART OF THE DEAL



DC Comics, 2900 West Alameda Ave., Burbank, CA 91505
Printed by RR Donnelley, Salem, VA, USA. 8/19/16. First Printing.
ISBN: 978-1-4012-6371-3

Library of Congress Cataloging-in-Publication Data is available.

PEFC Certified
Printed on paper from sustainably managed forests and controlled sources
PEFC
PEFC/29-31-75
www.pefc.org

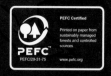

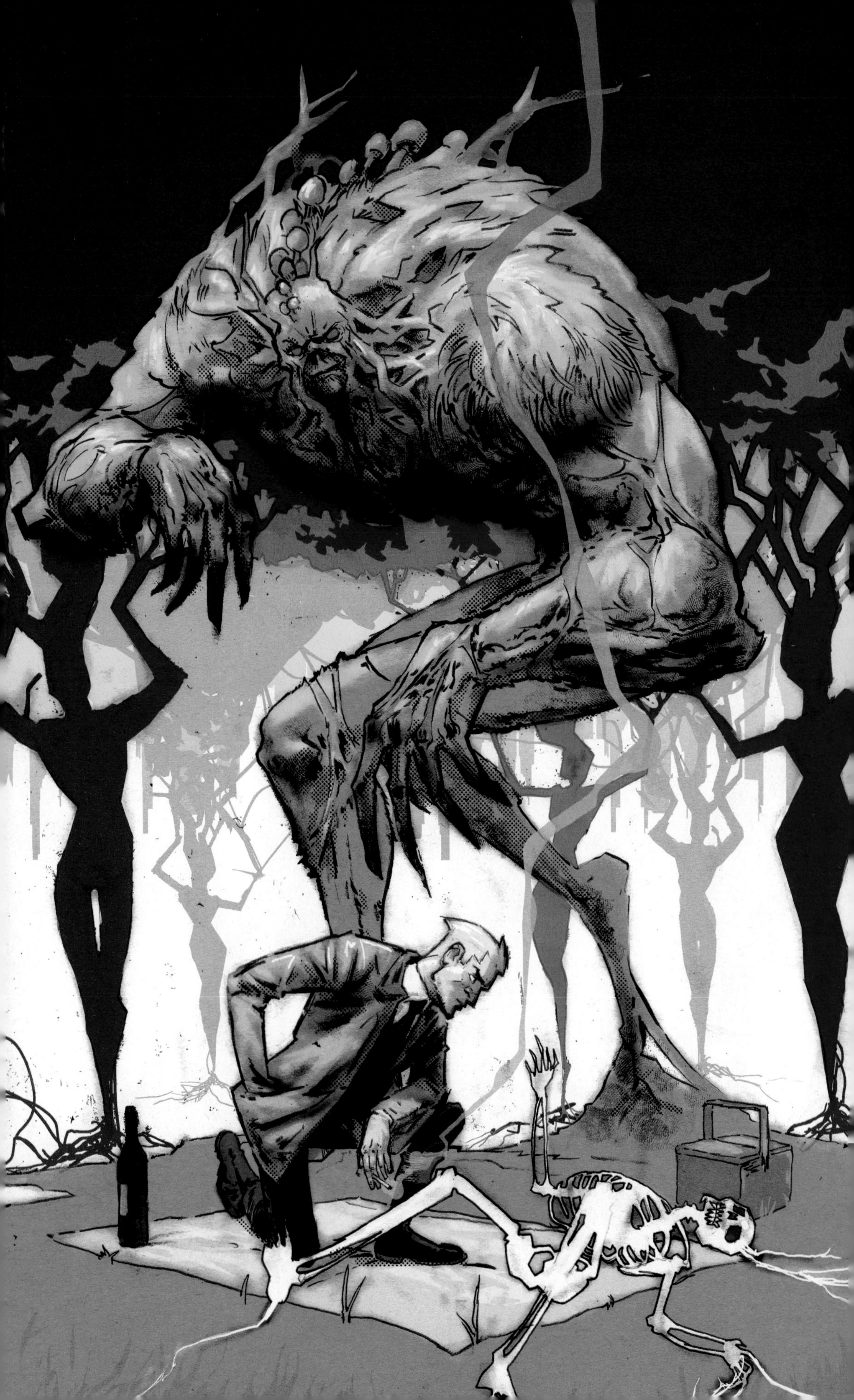

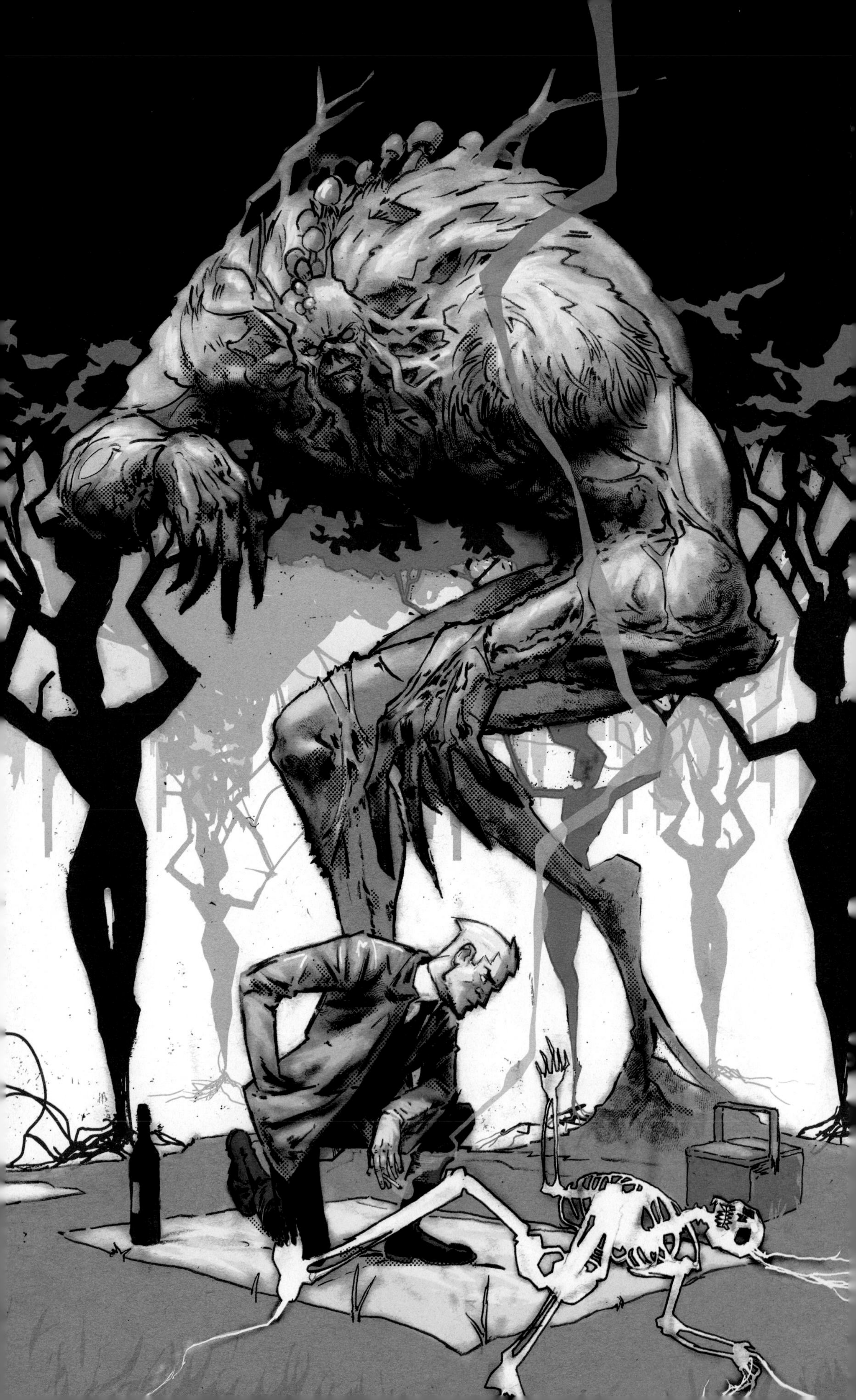

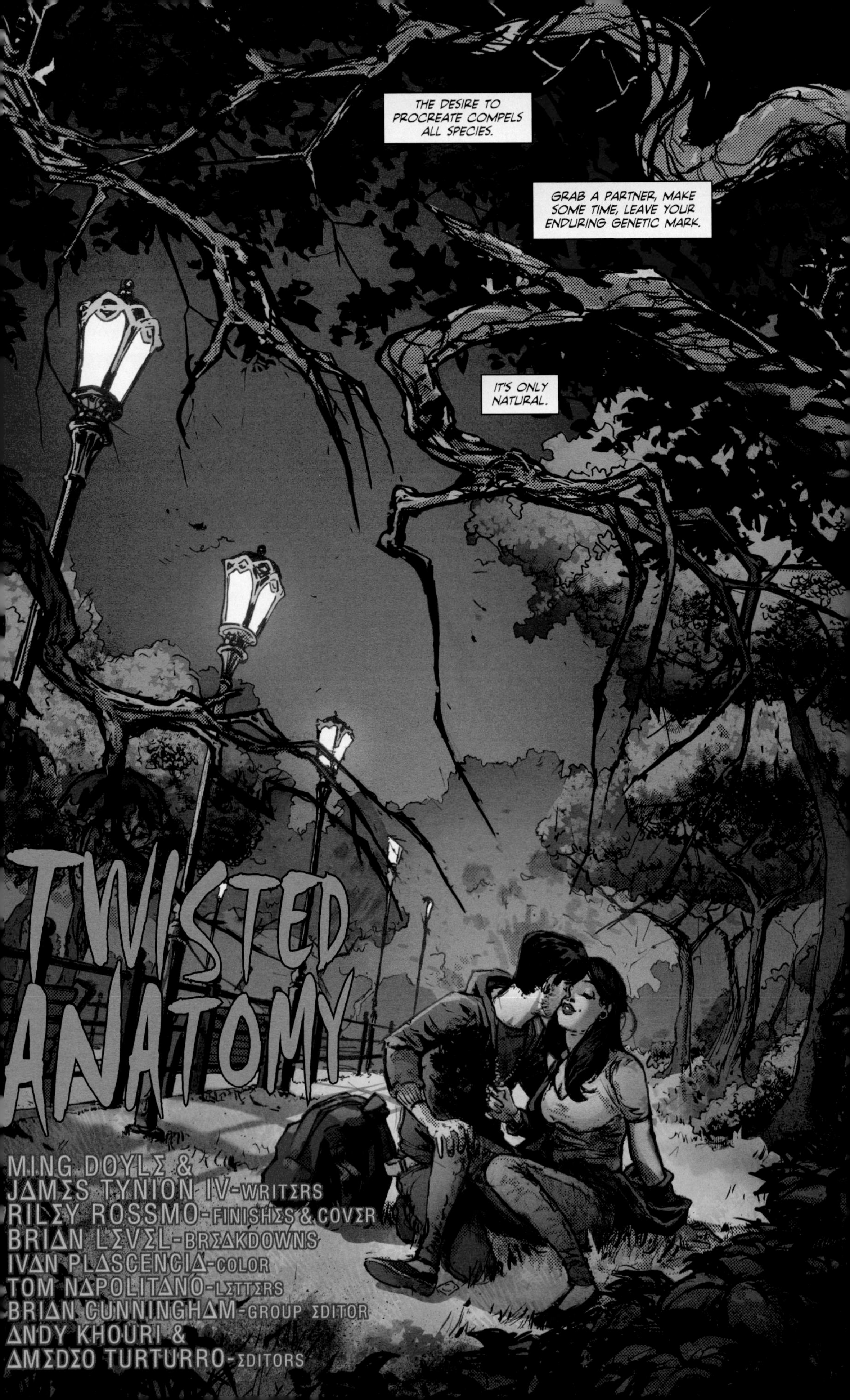
THE DESIRE TO PROCREATE COMPELS ALL SPECIES.
GRAB A PARTNER, MAKE SOME TIME, LEAVE YOUR ENDURING GENETIC MARK.
IT'S ONLY NATURAL.
TWISTED ANATOMY
MING DOYLE & JAMES TYNION IV-WRITERS
RILEY ROSSMO-FINISHES & COVER
BRIAN LEVEL-BREAKDOWNS
IVAN PLASCENCIA-COLOR
TOM NAPOLITANO-LETTERS
BRIAN CUNNINGHAM-GROUP EDITOR
ANDY KHOURI & AMEDEO TURTURRO-EDITORS

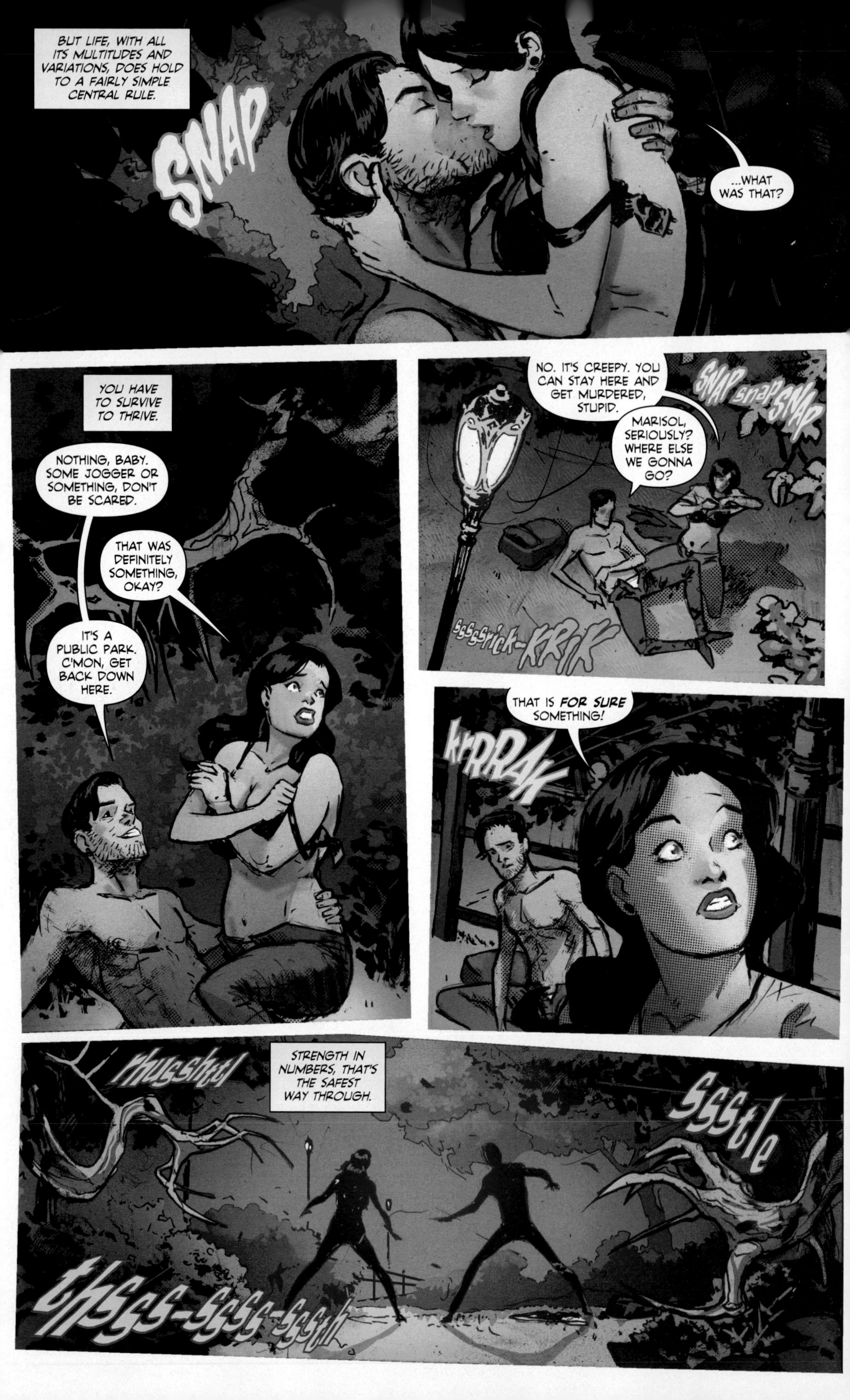
BUT LIFE, WITH ALL ITS MULTITUDES AND VARIATIONS, DOES HOLD TO A FAIRLY SIMPLE CENTRAL RULE.
SNAP
...WHAT WAS THAT?
YOU HAVE TO SURVIVE TO THRIVE.
NOTHING, BABY. SOME JOGGER OR SOMETHING, DON'T BE SCARED.
THAT WAS DEFINITELY SOMETHING, OKAY?
IT'S A PUBLIC PARK. C'MON, GET BACK DOWN HERE.
NO. IT'S CREEPY. YOU CAN STAY HERE AND GET MURDERED, STUPID.
MARISOL, SERIOUSLY? WHERE ELSE WE GONNA GO?
SNAP snap SNAP
sssssrick-KRIK
THAT IS FOR SURE SOMETHING!
krRRAK
STRENGTH IN NUMBERS, THAT'S THE SAFEST WAY THROUGH.
rhussht
ssstle
thsss-ssss-sssh

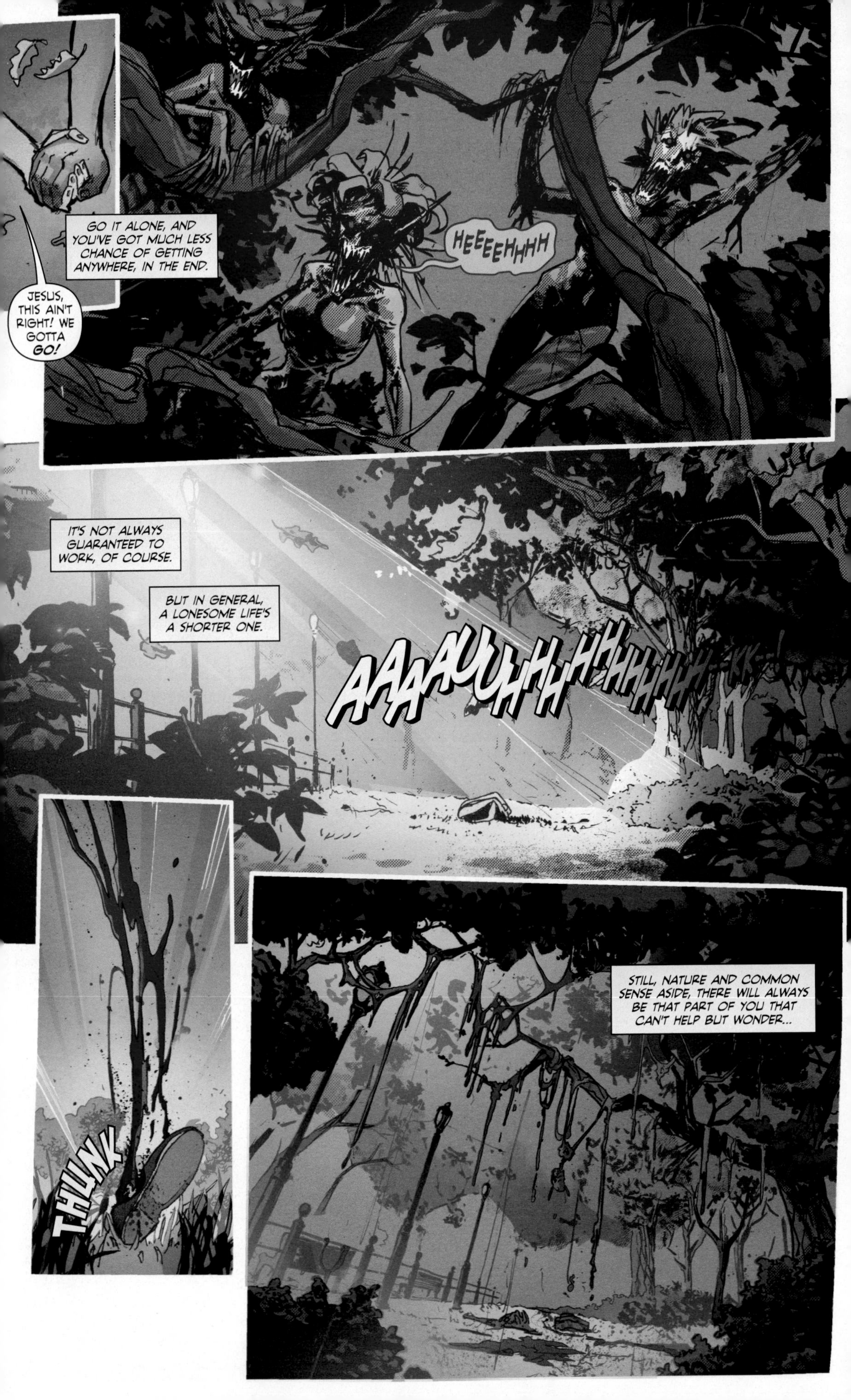
GO IT ALONE, AND YOU'VE GOT MUCH LESS CHANCE OF GETTING ANYWHERE, IN THE END.
JESUS, THIS AIN'T RIGHT! WE GOTTA GO!
HEEEEHHHH
IT'S NOT ALWAYS GUARANTEED TO WORK, OF COURSE.
BUT IN GENERAL, A LONESOME LIFE'S A SHORTER ONE.
AAAAUUHHHHHHHHHHHHHHHH
THUNK
STILL, NATURE AND COMMON SENSE ASIDE, THERE WILL ALWAYS BE THAT PART OF YOU THAT CAN'T HELP BUT WONDER...

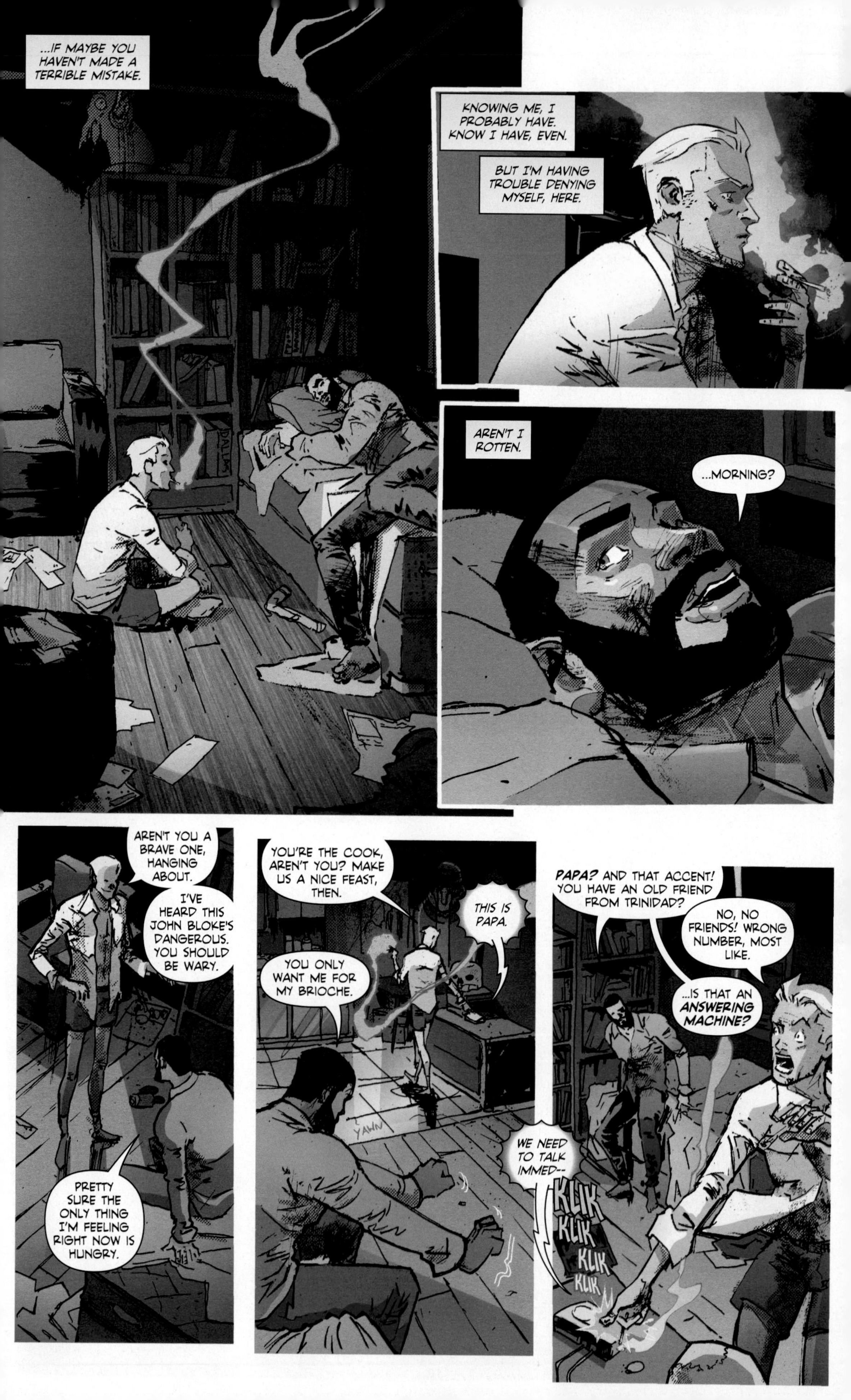
...IF MAYBE YOU HAVEN'T MADE A TERRIBLE MISTAKE.
KNOWING ME, I PROBABLY HAVE. KNOW I HAVE, EVEN.
BUT I'M HAVING TROUBLE DENYING MYSELF, HERE.
AREN'T I ROTTEN.
...MORNING?
AREN'T YOU A BRAVE ONE, HANGING ABOUT.
I'VE HEARD THIS JOHN BLOKE'S DANGEROUS. YOU SHOULD BE WARY.
PRETTY SURE THE ONLY THING I'M FEELING RIGHT NOW IS HUNGRY.
YOU'RE THE COOK, AREN'T YOU? MAKE US A NICE FEAST, THEN.
YOU ONLY WANT ME FOR MY BRIOCHE.
THIS IS PAPA.
YAWN
PAPA? AND THAT ACCENT! YOU HAVE AN OLD FRIEND FROM TRINIDAD?
NO, NO FRIENDS! WRONG NUMBER, MOST LIKE.
...IS THAT AN ANSWERING MACHINE?
WE NEED TO TALK IMMED--
KLIK KLIK KLIK KLIK

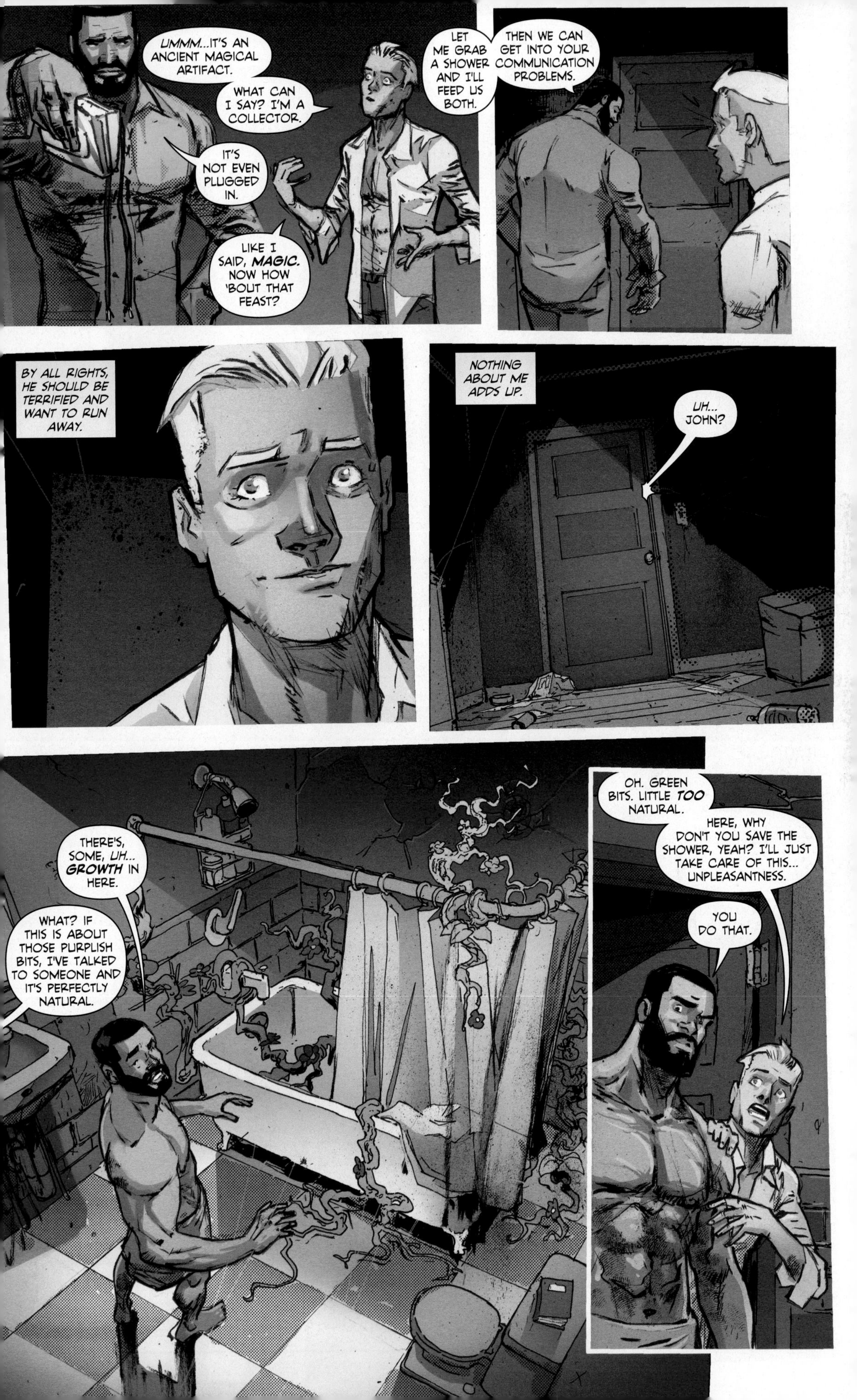
UMMM...IT'S AN ANCIENT MAGICAL ARTIFACT.
WHAT CAN I SAY? I'M A COLLECTOR.
IT'S NOT EVEN PLUGGED IN.
LIKE I SAID, *MAGIC.* NOW HOW 'BOUT THAT FEAST?
LET ME GRAB A SHOWER AND I'LL FEED US BOTH.
THEN WE CAN GET INTO YOUR COMMUNICATION PROBLEMS.
*BY ALL RIGHTS, HE SHOULD BE TERRIFIED AND WANT TO RUN AWAY.*
*NOTHING ABOUT ME ADDS UP.*
*UH... JOHN?*
THERE'S, SOME, *UH...* ***GROWTH*** IN HERE.
WHAT? IF THIS IS ABOUT THOSE PURPLISH BITS, I'VE TALKED TO SOMEONE AND IT'S PERFECTLY NATURAL.
OH. GREEN BITS. LITTLE ***TOO*** NATURAL.
HERE, WHY DON'T YOU SAVE THE SHOWER, YEAH? I'LL JUST TAKE CARE OF THIS... UNPLEASANTNESS.
YOU DO THAT.

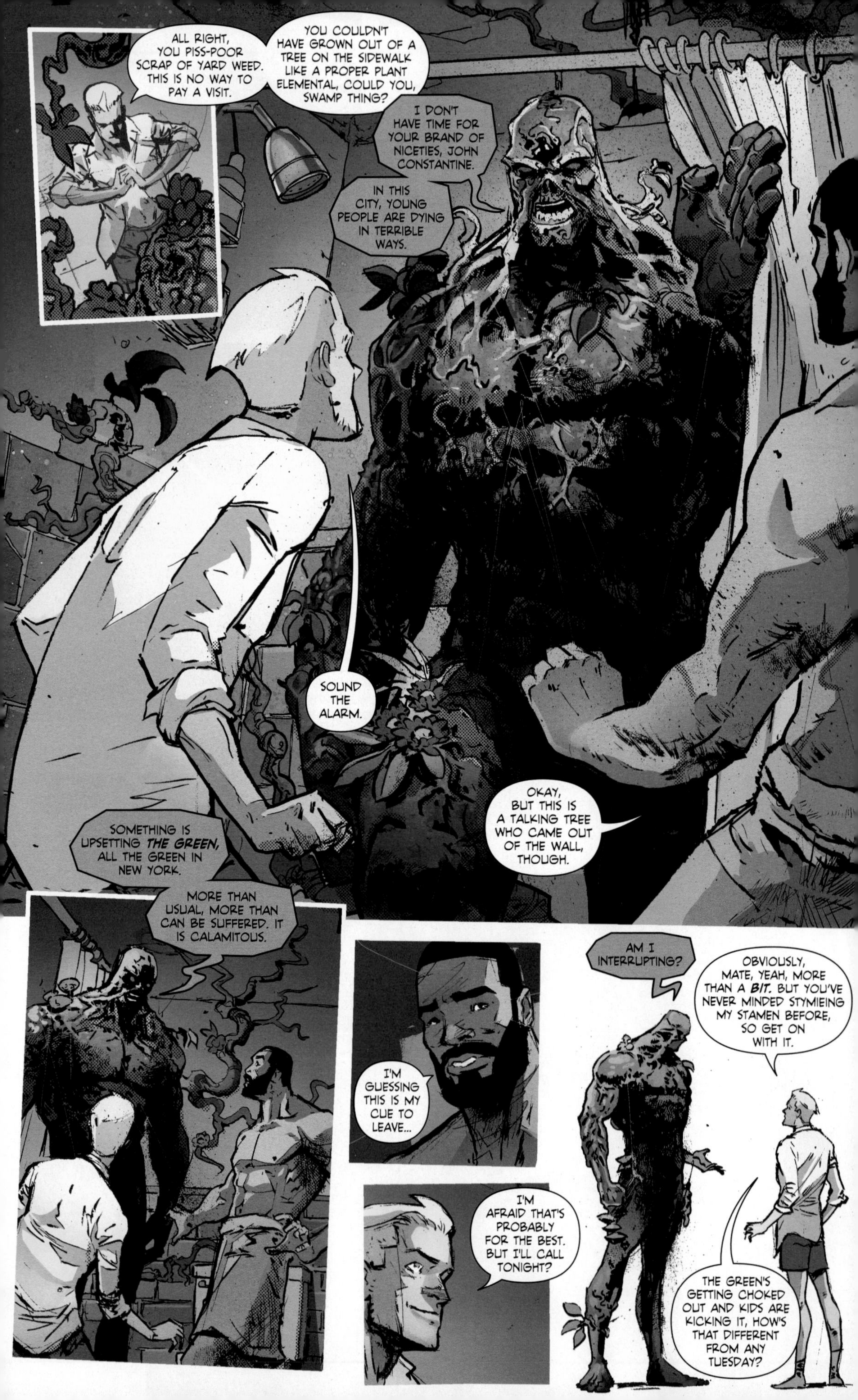
ALL RIGHT, YOU PISS-POOR SCRAP OF YARD WEED. THIS IS NO WAY TO PAY A VISIT.
YOU COULDN'T HAVE GROWN OUT OF A TREE ON THE SIDEWALK LIKE A PROPER PLANT ELEMENTAL, COULD YOU, SWAMP THING?
I DON'T HAVE TIME FOR YOUR BRAND OF NICETIES, JOHN CONSTANTINE.
IN THIS CITY, YOUNG PEOPLE ARE DYING IN TERRIBLE WAYS.
SOUND THE ALARM.
OKAY, BUT THIS IS A TALKING TREE WHO CAME OUT OF THE WALL, THOUGH.
SOMETHING IS UPSETTING *THE GREEN,* ALL THE GREEN IN NEW YORK.
MORE THAN USUAL, MORE THAN CAN BE SUFFERED. IT IS CALAMITOUS.
I'M GUESSING THIS IS MY CUE TO LEAVE...
I'M AFRAID THAT'S PROBABLY FOR THE BEST. BUT I'LL CALL TONIGHT?
AM I INTERRUPTING?
OBVIOUSLY, MATE, YEAH, MORE THAN A *BIT.* BUT YOU'VE NEVER MINDED STYMIEING MY STAMEN BEFORE, SO GET ON WITH IT.
THE GREEN'S GETTING CHOKED OUT AND KIDS ARE KICKING IT, HOW'S THAT DIFFERENT FROM ANY TUESDAY?

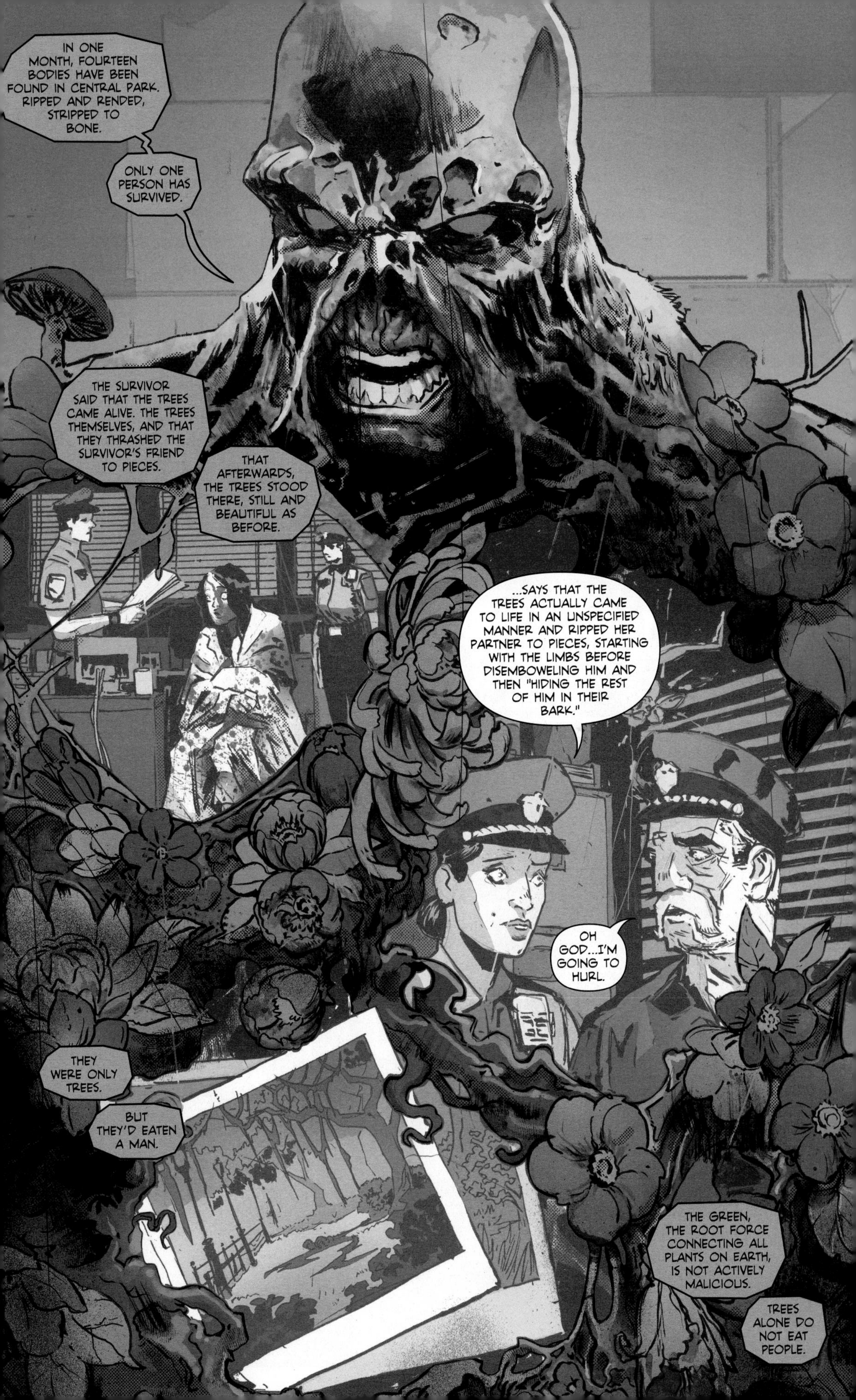
IN ONE MONTH, FOURTEEN BODIES HAVE BEEN FOUND IN CENTRAL PARK. RIPPED AND RENDED, STRIPPED TO BONE.
ONLY ONE PERSON HAS SURVIVED.
THE SURVIVOR SAID THAT THE TREES CAME ALIVE. THE TREES THEMSELVES, AND THAT THEY THRASHED THE SURVIVOR'S FRIEND TO PIECES.
THAT AFTERWARDS, THE TREES STOOD THERE, STILL AND BEAUTIFUL AS BEFORE.
...SAYS THAT THE TREES ACTUALLY CAME TO LIFE IN AN UNSPECIFIED MANNER AND RIPPED HER PARTNER TO PIECES, STARTING WITH THE LIMBS BEFORE DISEMBOWELING HIM AND THEN "HIDING THE REST OF HIM IN THEIR BARK."
OH GOD...I'M GOING TO HURL.
THEY WERE ONLY TREES.
BUT THEY'D EATEN A MAN.
THE GREEN, THE ROOT FORCE CONNECTING ALL PLANTS ON EARTH, IS NOT ACTIVELY MALICIOUS.
TREES ALONE DO NOT EAT PEOPLE.

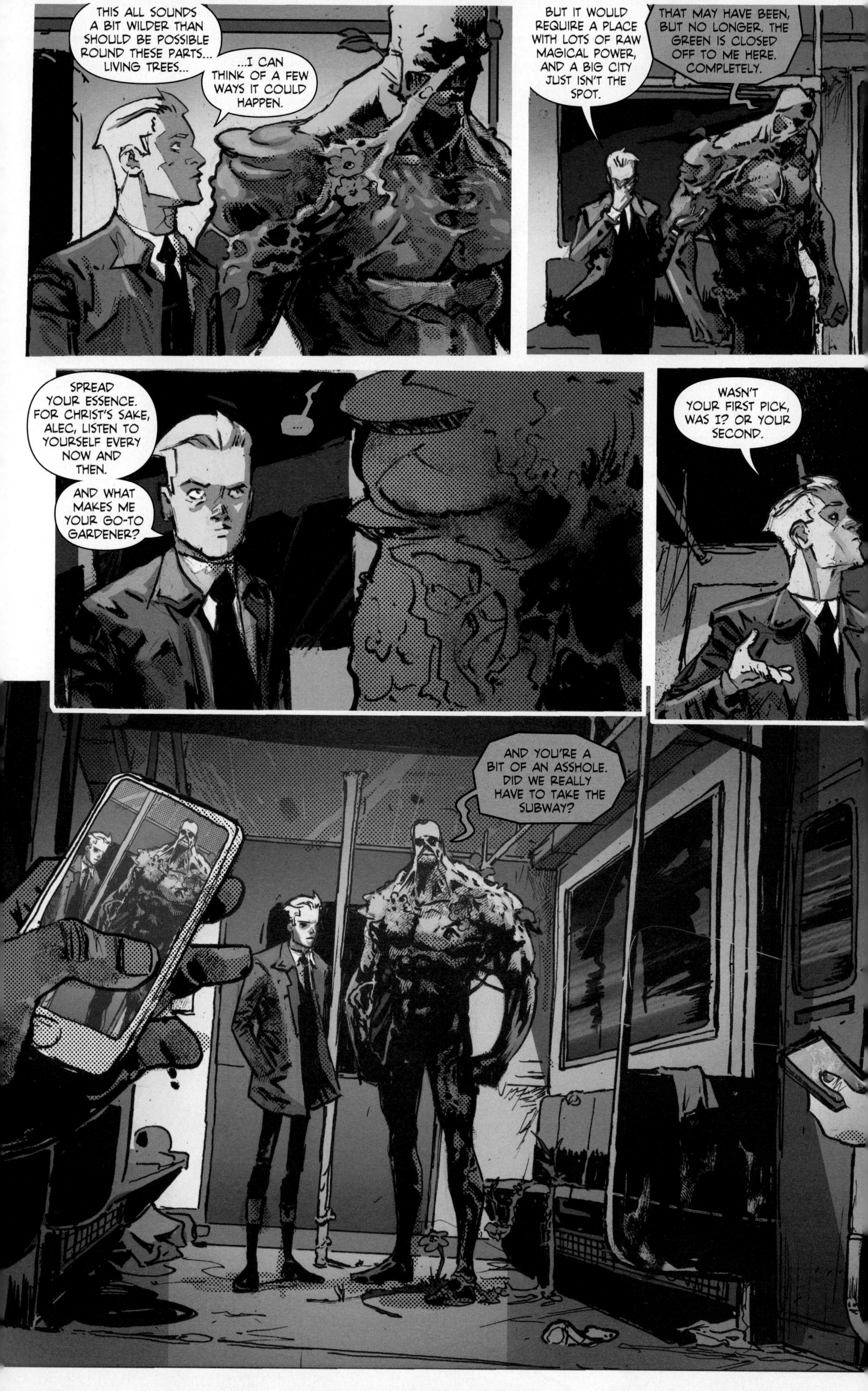
THIS ALL SOUNDS A BIT WILDER THAN SHOULD BE POSSIBLE ROUND THESE PARTS... LIVING TREES...
...I CAN THINK OF A FEW WAYS IT COULD HAPPEN.
BUT IT WOULD REQUIRE A PLACE WITH LOTS OF RAW MAGICAL POWER, AND A BIG CITY JUST ISN'T THE SPOT.
THAT MAY HAVE BEEN, BUT NO LONGER. THE GREEN IS CLOSED OFF TO ME HERE. COMPLETELY.
SPREAD YOUR ESSENCE. FOR CHRIST'S SAKE, ALEC, LISTEN TO YOURSELF EVERY NOW AND THEN.
AND WHAT MAKES ME YOUR GO-TO GARDENER?
...
WASN'T YOUR FIRST PICK, WAS I? OR YOUR SECOND.
AND YOU'RE A BIT OF AN ASSHOLE. DID WE REALLY HAVE TO TAKE THE SUBWAY?

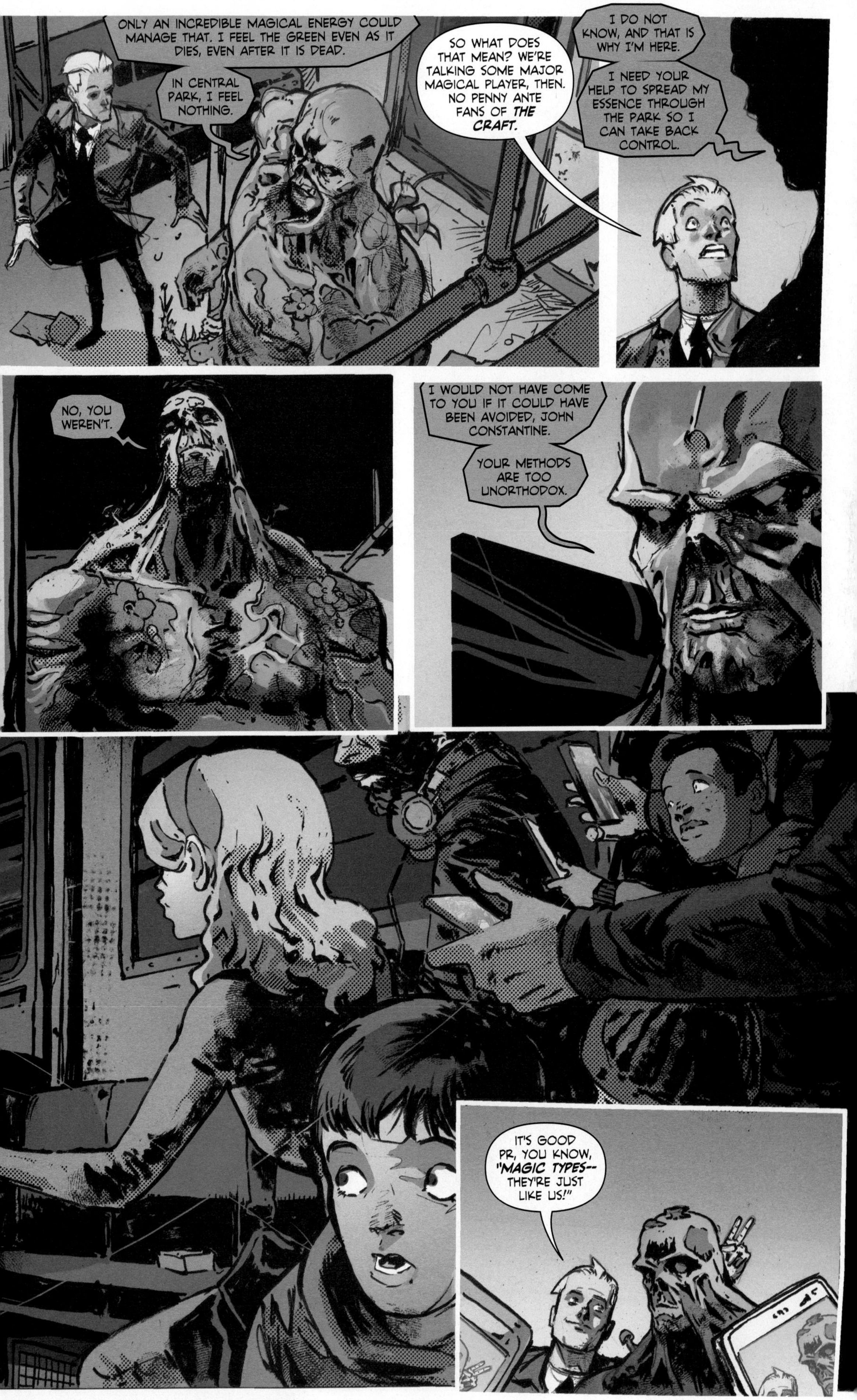
ONLY AN INCREDIBLE MAGICAL ENERGY COULD MANAGE THAT. I FEEL THE GREEN EVEN AS IT DIES, EVEN AFTER IT IS DEAD.
IN CENTRAL PARK, I FEEL NOTHING.
SO WHAT DOES THAT MEAN? WE'RE TALKING SOME MAJOR MAGICAL PLAYER, THEN. NO PENNY ANTE FANS OF *THE CRAFT.*
I DO NOT KNOW, AND THAT IS WHY I'M HERE.
I NEED YOUR HELP TO SPREAD MY ESSENCE THROUGH THE PARK SO I CAN TAKE BACK CONTROL.
NO, YOU WEREN'T.
I WOULD NOT HAVE COME TO YOU IF IT COULD HAVE BEEN AVOIDED, JOHN CONSTANTINE.
YOUR METHODS ARE TOO UNORTHODOX.
IT'S GOOD PR, YOU KNOW, "*MAGIC TYPES--* THEY'RE JUST LIKE US!"

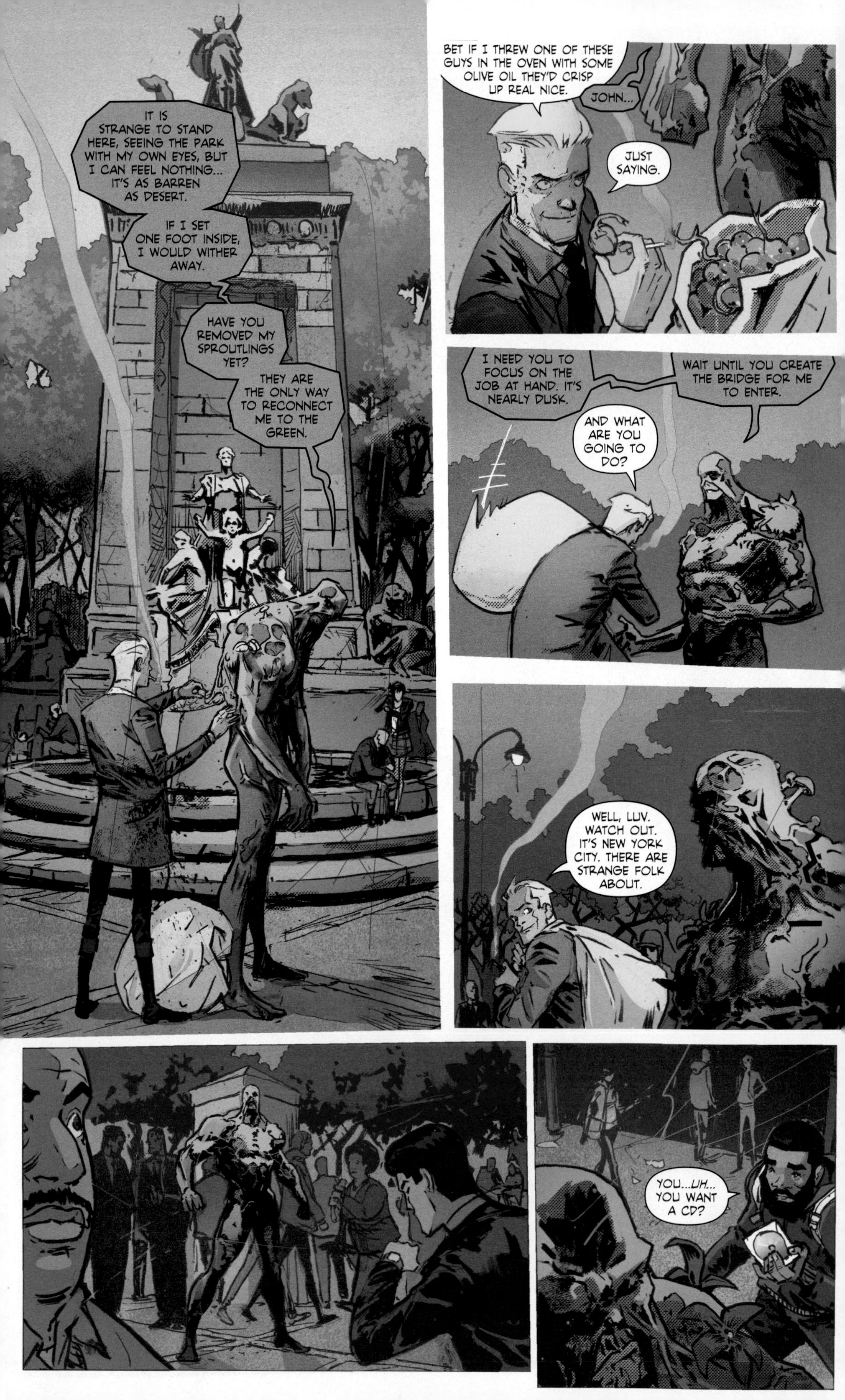
IT IS STRANGE TO STAND HERE, SEEING THE PARK WITH MY OWN EYES, BUT I CAN FEEL NOTHING... IT'S AS BARREN AS DESERT.
IF I SET ONE FOOT INSIDE, I WOULD WITHER AWAY.
HAVE YOU REMOVED MY SPROUTLINGS YET?
THEY ARE THE ONLY WAY TO RECONNECT ME TO THE GREEN.
BET IF I THREW ONE OF THESE GUYS IN THE OVEN WITH SOME OLIVE OIL THEY'D CRISP UP REAL NICE.
JOHN...
JUST SAYING.
I NEED YOU TO FOCUS ON THE JOB AT HAND. IT'S NEARLY DUSK.
WAIT UNTIL YOU CREATE THE BRIDGE FOR ME TO ENTER.
AND WHAT ARE YOU GOING TO DO?
WELL, LUV. WATCH OUT. IT'S NEW YORK CITY. THERE ARE STRANGE FOLK ABOUT.
YOU...*UH*... YOU WANT A CD?

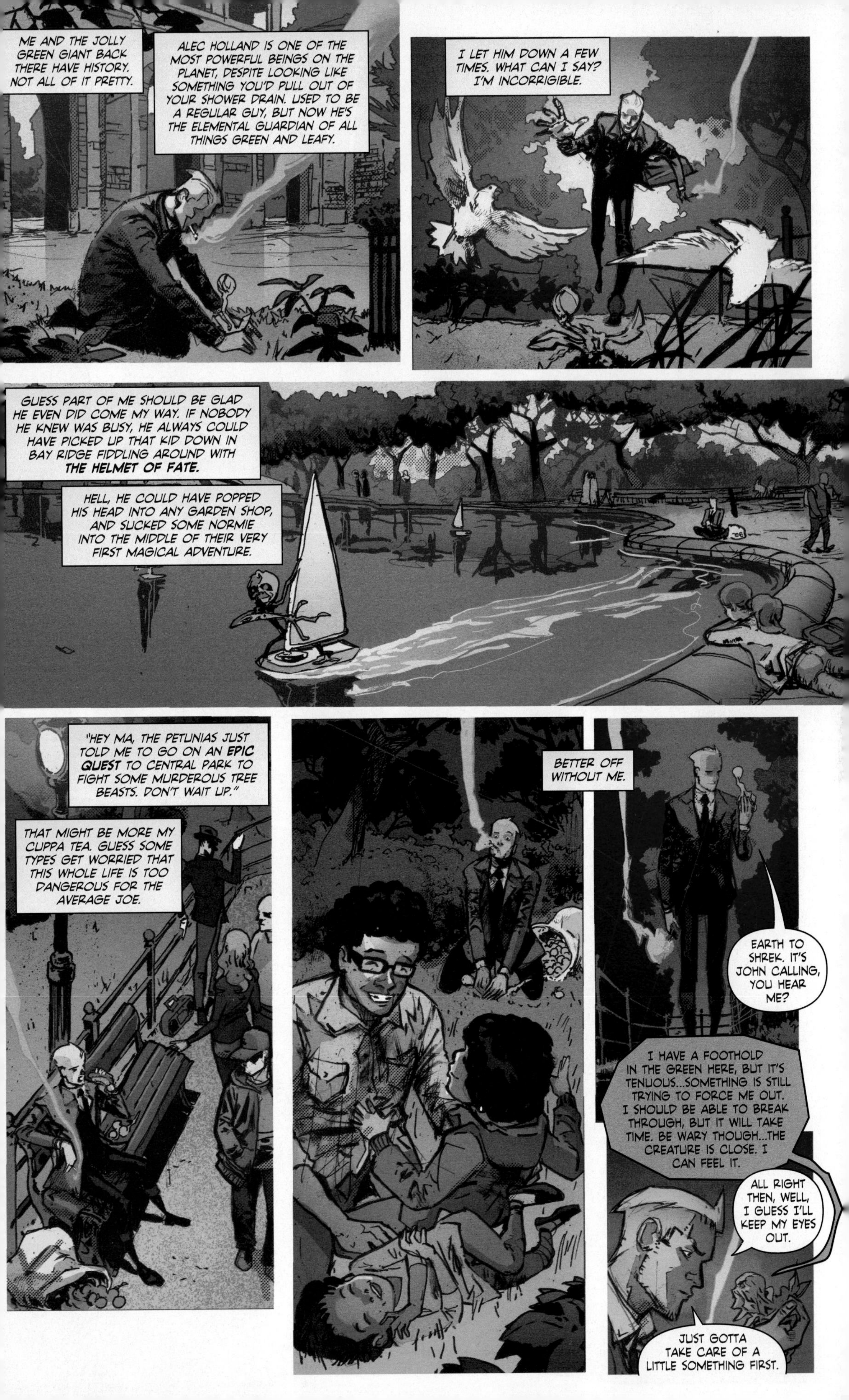

ME AND THE JOLLY GREEN GIANT BACK THERE HAVE HISTORY. NOT ALL OF IT PRETTY.
ALEC HOLLAND IS ONE OF THE MOST POWERFUL BEINGS ON THE PLANET, DESPITE LOOKING LIKE SOMETHING YOU'D PULL OUT OF YOUR SHOWER DRAIN. USED TO BE A REGULAR GUY, BUT NOW HE'S THE ELEMENTAL GUARDIAN OF ALL THINGS GREEN AND LEAFY.
I LET HIM DOWN A FEW TIMES. WHAT CAN I SAY? I'M INCORRIGIBLE.
GUESS PART OF ME SHOULD BE GLAD HE EVEN DID COME MY WAY. IF NOBODY HE KNEW WAS BUSY, HE ALWAYS COULD HAVE PICKED UP THAT KID DOWN IN BAY RIDGE FIDDLING AROUND WITH THE HELMET OF FATE.
HELL, HE COULD HAVE POPPED HIS HEAD INTO ANY GARDEN SHOP, AND SUCKED SOME NORMIE INTO THE MIDDLE OF THEIR VERY FIRST MAGICAL ADVENTURE.
"HEY MA, THE PETUNIAS JUST TOLD ME TO GO ON AN EPIC QUEST TO CENTRAL PARK TO FIGHT SOME MURDEROUS TREE BEASTS. DON'T WAIT UP."
THAT MIGHT BE MORE MY CUPPA TEA. GUESS SOME TYPES GET WORRIED THAT THIS WHOLE LIFE IS TOO DANGEROUS FOR THE AVERAGE JOE.
BETTER OFF WITHOUT ME.
EARTH TO SHREK. IT'S JOHN CALLING, YOU HEAR ME?
I HAVE A FOOTHOLD IN THE GREEN HERE, BUT IT'S TENUOUS...SOMETHING IS STILL TRYING TO FORCE ME OUT. I SHOULD BE ABLE TO BREAK THROUGH, BUT IT WILL TAKE TIME. BE WARY THOUGH...THE CREATURE IS CLOSE. I CAN FEEL IT.
ALL RIGHT THEN, WELL, I GUESS I'LL KEEP MY EYES OUT.
JUST GOTTA TAKE CARE OF A LITTLE SOMETHING FIRST.

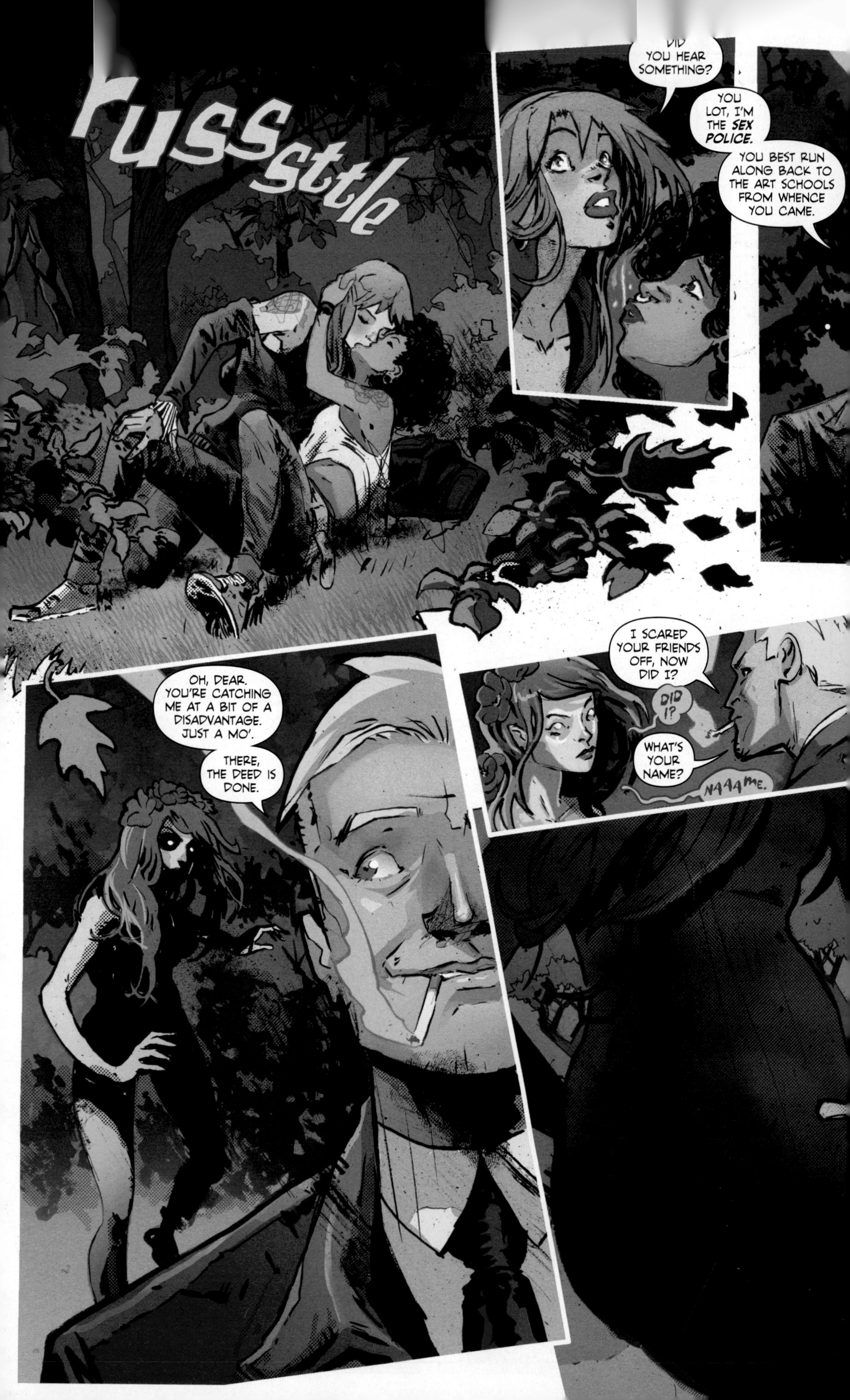
russsttle
DID YOU HEAR SOMETHING?
YOU LOT, I'M THE **SEX POLICE.**
YOU BEST RUN ALONG BACK TO THE ART SCHOOLS FROM WHENCE YOU CAME.
I SCARED YOUR FRIENDS OFF, NOW DID I?
DID I?
WHAT'S YOUR NAME?
NAAAME.
OH, DEAR. YOU'RE CATCHING ME AT A BIT OF A DISADVANTAGE. JUST A MO'.
THERE, THE DEED IS DONE.

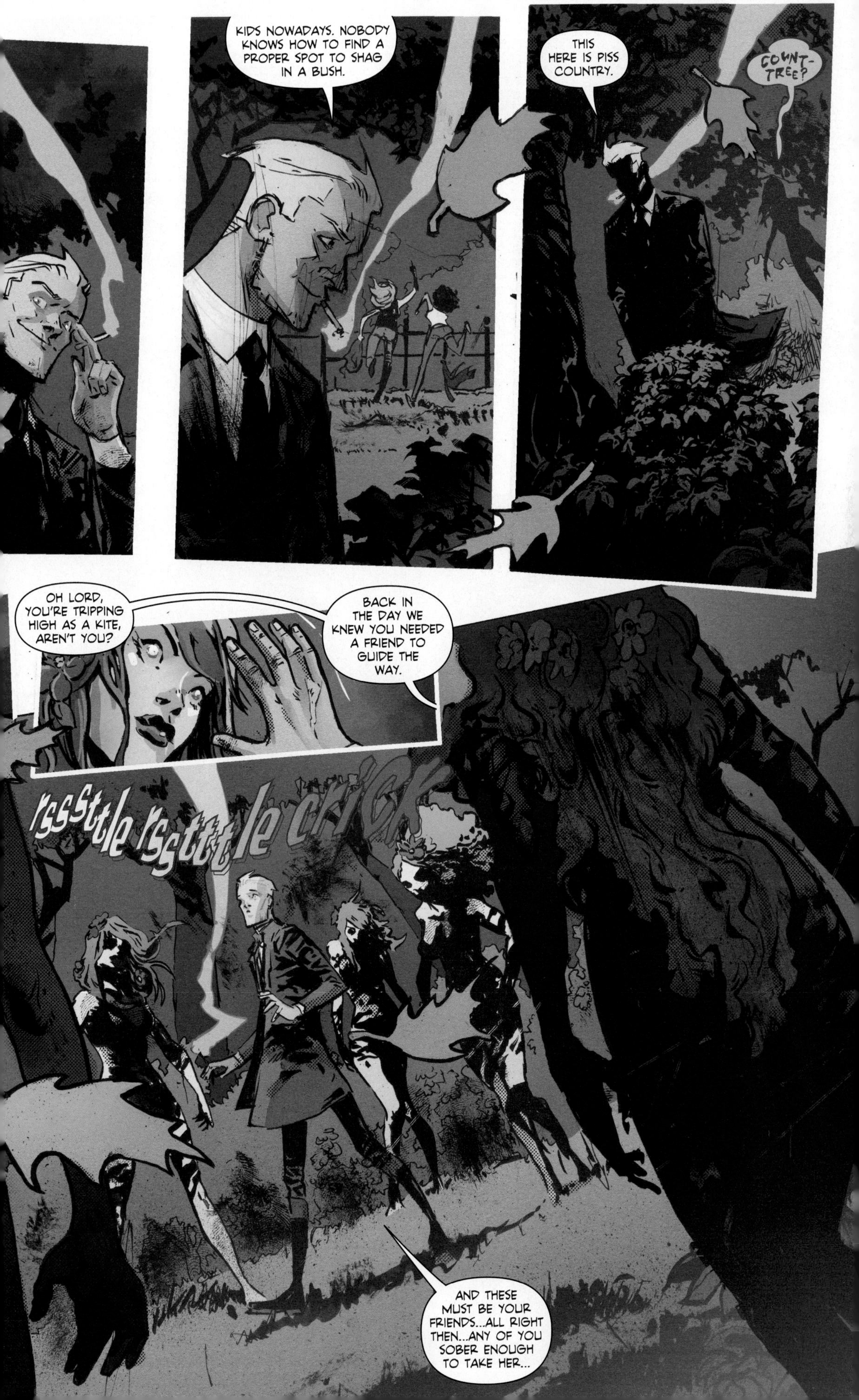
KIDS NOWADAYS. NOBODY KNOWS HOW TO FIND A PROPER SPOT TO SHAG IN A BUSH.
THIS HERE IS PISS COUNTRY.
COUNT-TREE?
OH LORD, YOU'RE TRIPPING HIGH AS A KITE, AREN'T YOU?
BACK IN THE DAY WE KNEW YOU NEEDED A FRIEND TO GUIDE THE WAY.
rsssttle rssttttle crick
AND THESE MUST BE YOUR FRIENDS...ALL RIGHT THEN...ANY OF YOU SOBER ENOUGH TO TAKE HER...

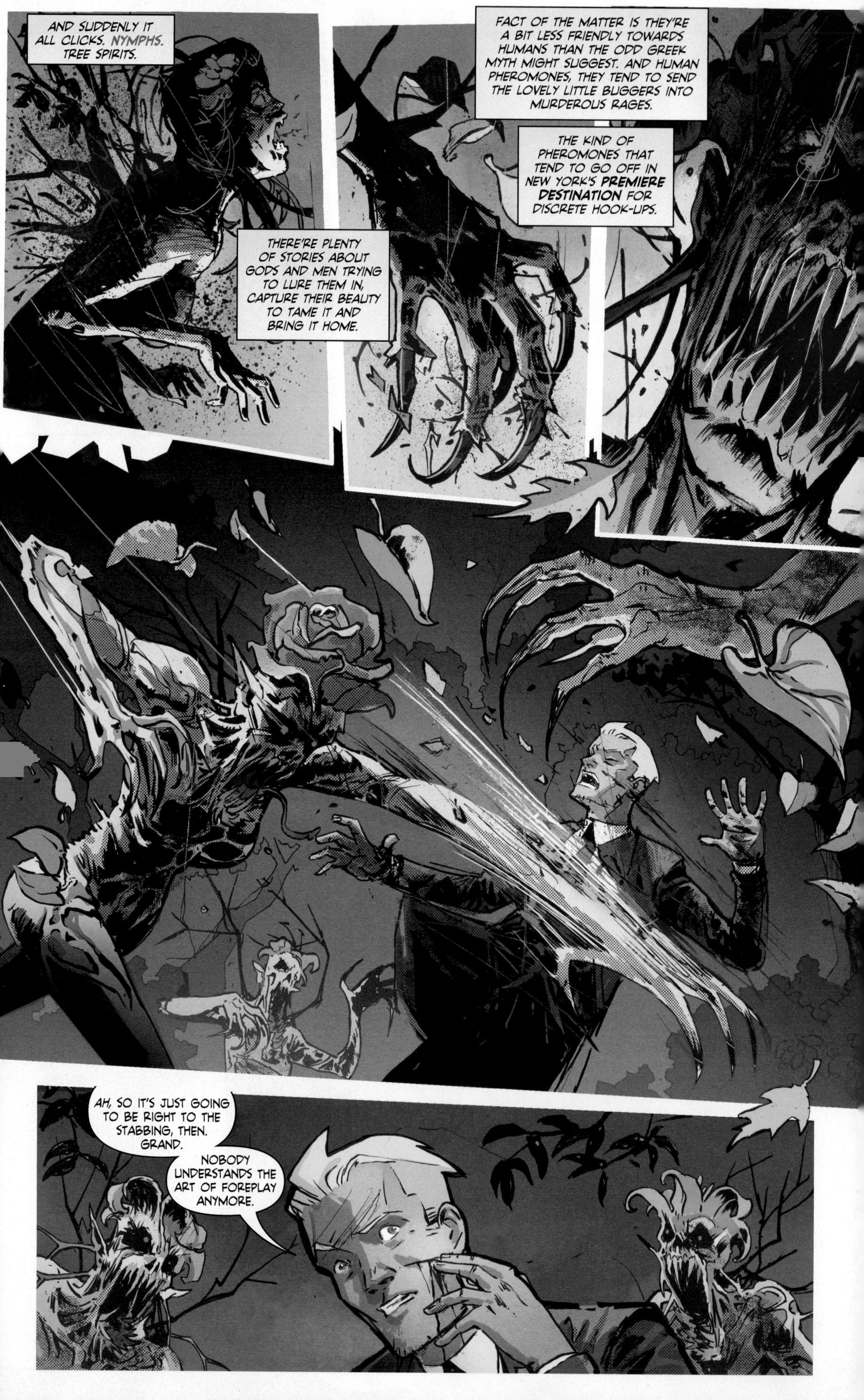
AND SUDDENLY IT ALL CLICKS. NYMPHS. TREE SPIRITS.
THERE'RE PLENTY OF STORIES ABOUT GODS AND MEN TRYING TO LURE THEM IN, CAPTURE THEIR BEAUTY TO TAME IT AND BRING IT HOME.
FACT OF THE MATTER IS THEY'RE A BIT LESS FRIENDLY TOWARDS HUMANS THAN THE ODD GREEK MYTH MIGHT SUGGEST. AND HUMAN PHEROMONES, THEY TEND TO SEND THE LOVELY LITTLE BUGGERS INTO MURDEROUS RAGES.
THE KIND OF PHEROMONES THAT TEND TO GO OFF IN NEW YORK'S PREMIERE DESTINATION FOR DISCRETE HOOK-UPS.
AH, SO IT'S JUST GOING TO BE RIGHT TO THE STABBING, THEN. GRAND.
NOBODY UNDERSTANDS THE ART OF FOREPLAY ANYMORE.

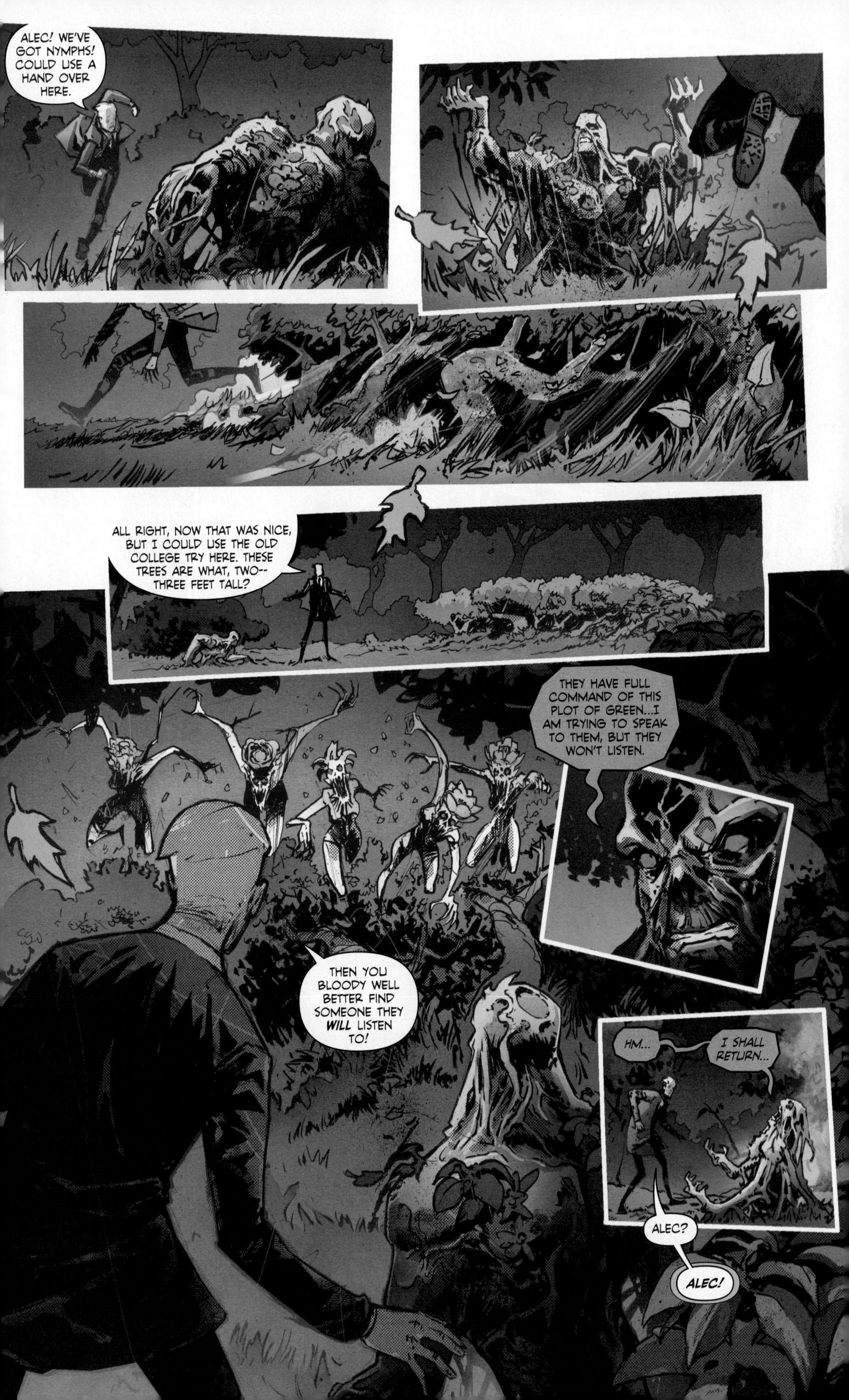
ALEC! WE'VE GOT NYMPHS! COULD USE A HAND OVER HERE.
ALL RIGHT, NOW THAT WAS NICE, BUT I COULD USE THE OLD COLLEGE TRY HERE. THESE TREES ARE WHAT, TWO-- THREE FEET TALL?
THEY HAVE FULL COMMAND OF THIS PLOT OF GREEN...I AM TRYING TO SPEAK TO THEM, BUT THEY WON'T LISTEN.
THEN YOU BLOODY WELL BETTER FIND SOMEONE THEY ***WILL*** LISTEN TO!
HM...
I SHALL RETURN...
ALEC?
***ALEC!***

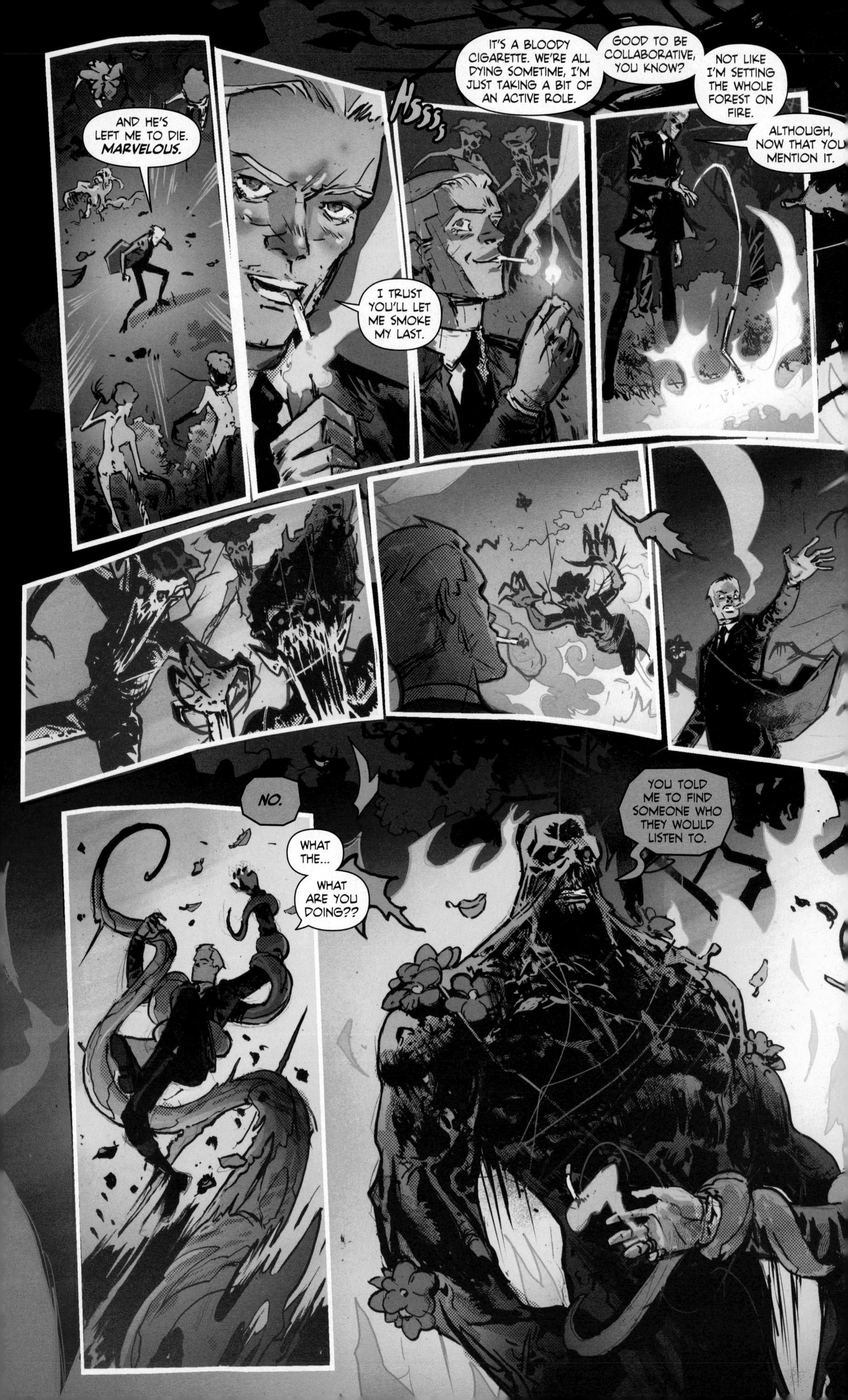
AND HE'S LEFT ME TO DIE. MARVELOUS.
I TRUST YOU'LL LET ME SMOKE MY LAST.
HSSSS
IT'S A BLOODY CIGARETTE. WE'RE ALL DYING SOMETIME, I'M JUST TAKING A BIT OF AN ACTIVE ROLE.
GOOD TO BE COLLABORATIVE, YOU KNOW?
NOT LIKE I'M SETTING THE WHOLE FOREST ON FIRE.
ALTHOUGH, NOW THAT YOU MENTION IT.
NO.
WHAT THE...
WHAT ARE YOU DOING??
YOU TOLD ME TO FIND SOMEONE WHO THEY WOULD LISTEN TO.

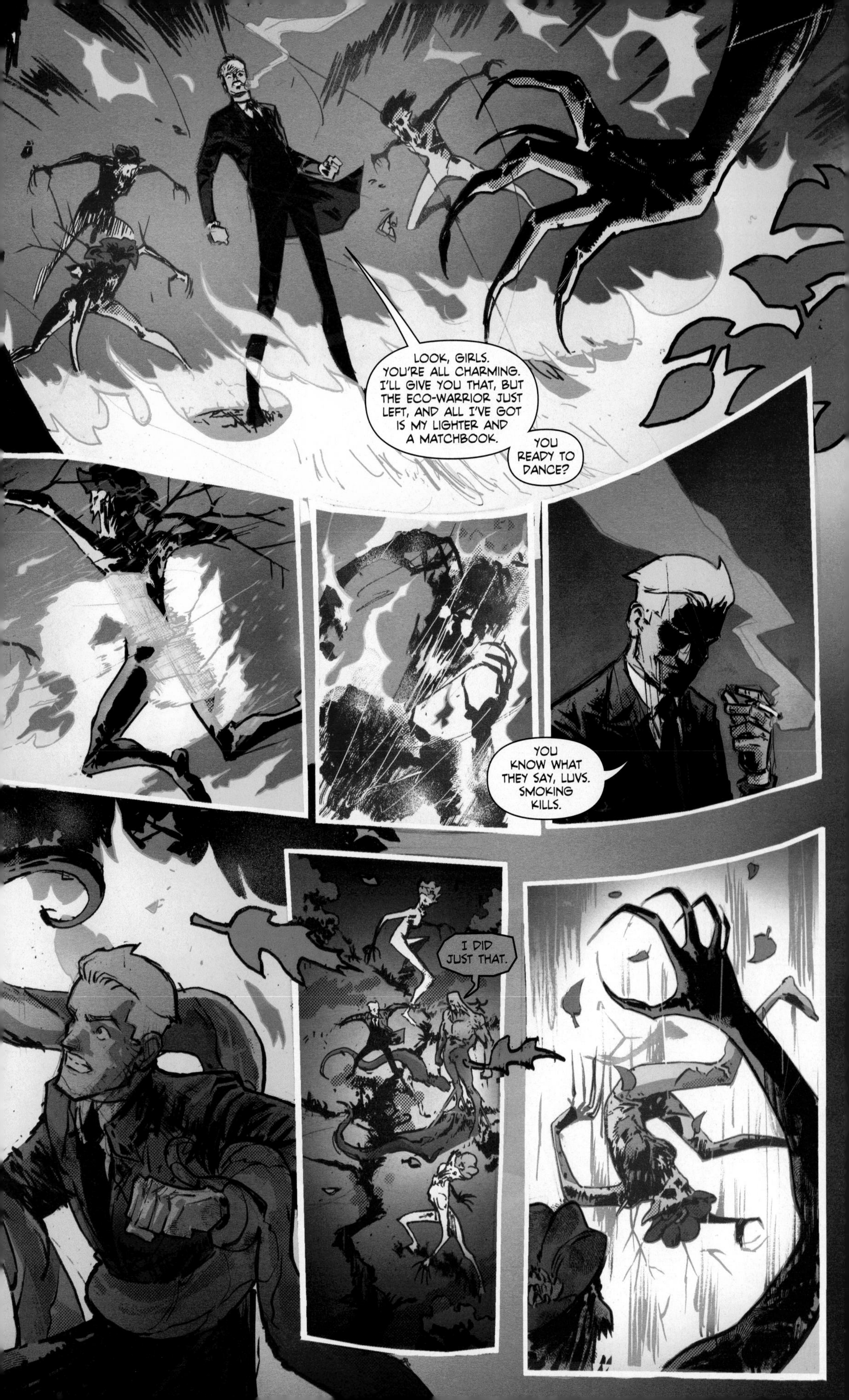
LOOK, GIRLS. YOU'RE ALL CHARMING. I'LL GIVE YOU THAT, BUT THE ECO-WARRIOR JUST LEFT, AND ALL I'VE GOT IS MY LIGHTER AND A MATCHBOOK.
YOU READY TO DANCE?
YOU KNOW WHAT THEY SAY, LUVS. SMOKING KILLS.
I DID JUST THAT.

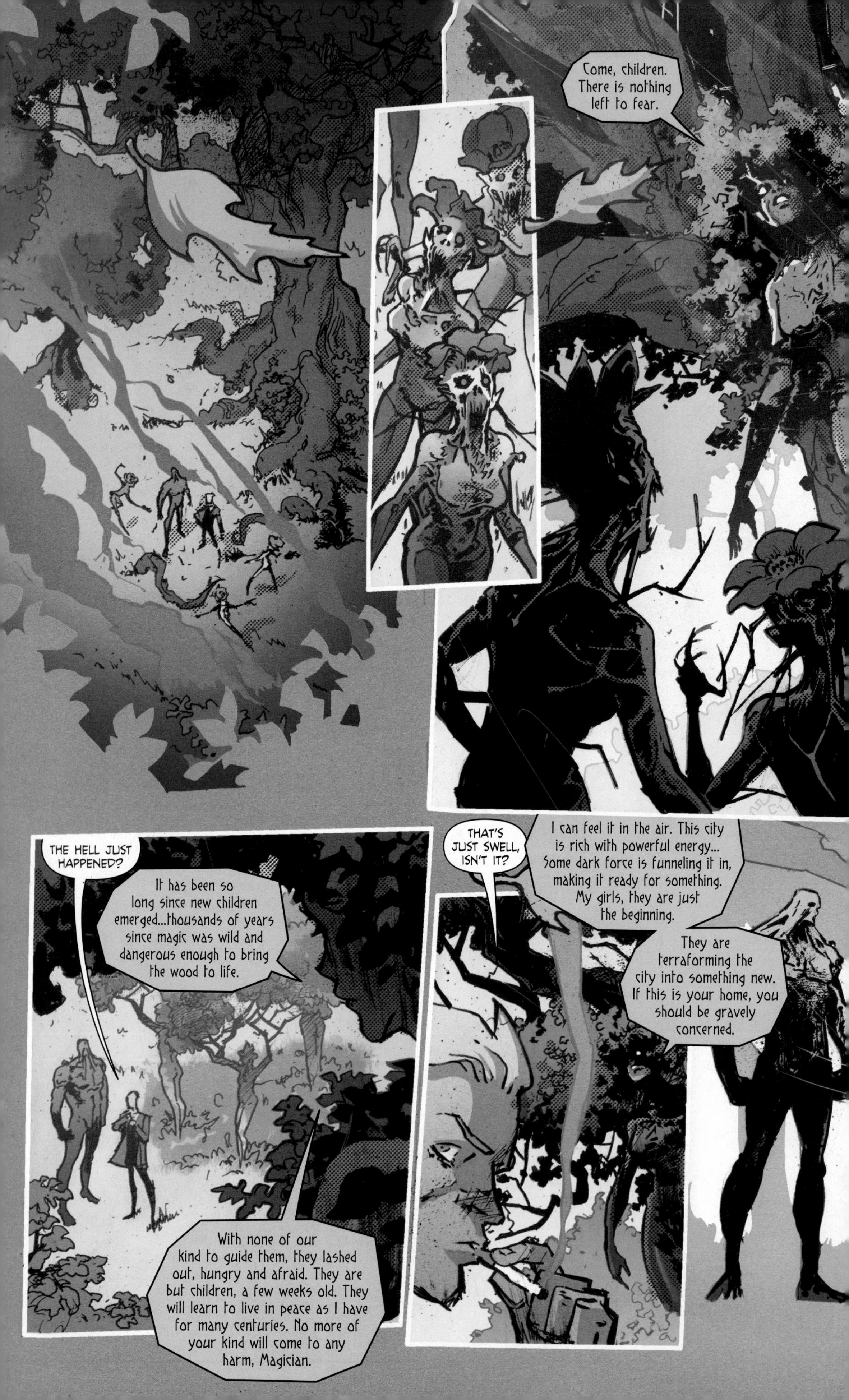
Come, children. There is nothing left to fear.
THE HELL JUST HAPPENED?
It has been so long since new children emerged...thousands of years since magic was wild and dangerous enough to bring the wood to life.
With none of our kind to guide them, they lashed out, hungry and afraid. They are but children, a few weeks old. They will learn to live in peace as I have for many centuries. No more of your kind will come to any harm, Magician.
THAT'S JUST SWELL, ISN'T IT?
I can feel it in the air. This city is rich with powerful energy... Some dark force is funneling it in, making it ready for something. My girls, they are just the beginning.
They are terraforming the city into something new. If this is your home, you should be gravely concerned.

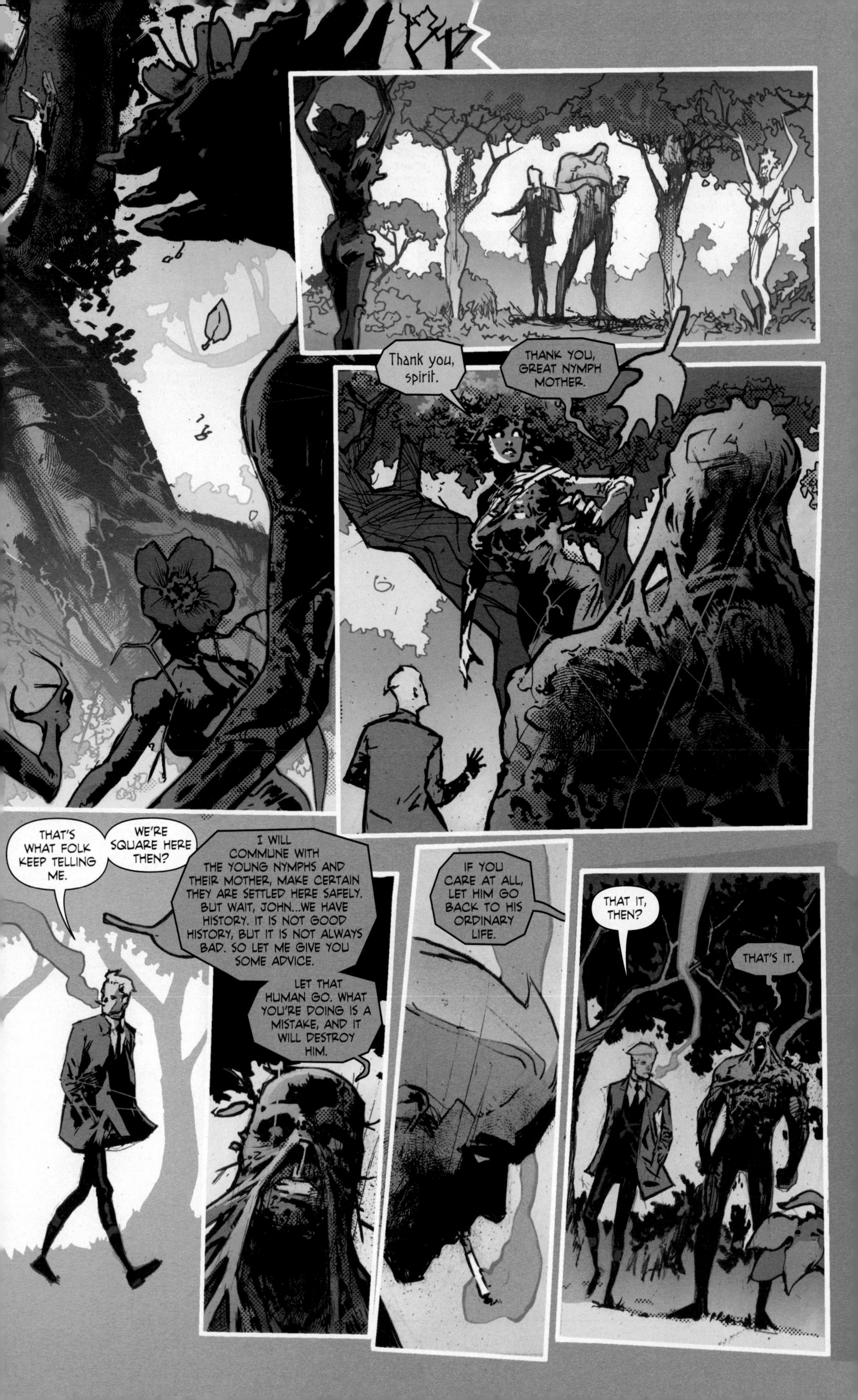
Thank you, spirit.
THANK YOU, GREAT NYMPH MOTHER.
THAT'S WHAT FOLK KEEP TELLING ME.
WE'RE SQUARE HERE THEN?
I WILL COMMUNE WITH THE YOUNG NYMPHS AND THEIR MOTHER, MAKE CERTAIN THEY ARE SETTLED HERE SAFELY. BUT WAIT, JOHN...WE HAVE HISTORY. IT IS NOT GOOD HISTORY, BUT IT IS NOT ALWAYS BAD. SO LET ME GIVE YOU SOME ADVICE.
LET THAT HUMAN GO. WHAT YOU'RE DOING IS A MISTAKE, AND IT WILL DESTROY HIM.
IF YOU CARE AT ALL, LET HIM GO BACK TO HIS ORDINARY LIFE.
THAT IT, THEN?
THAT'S IT.

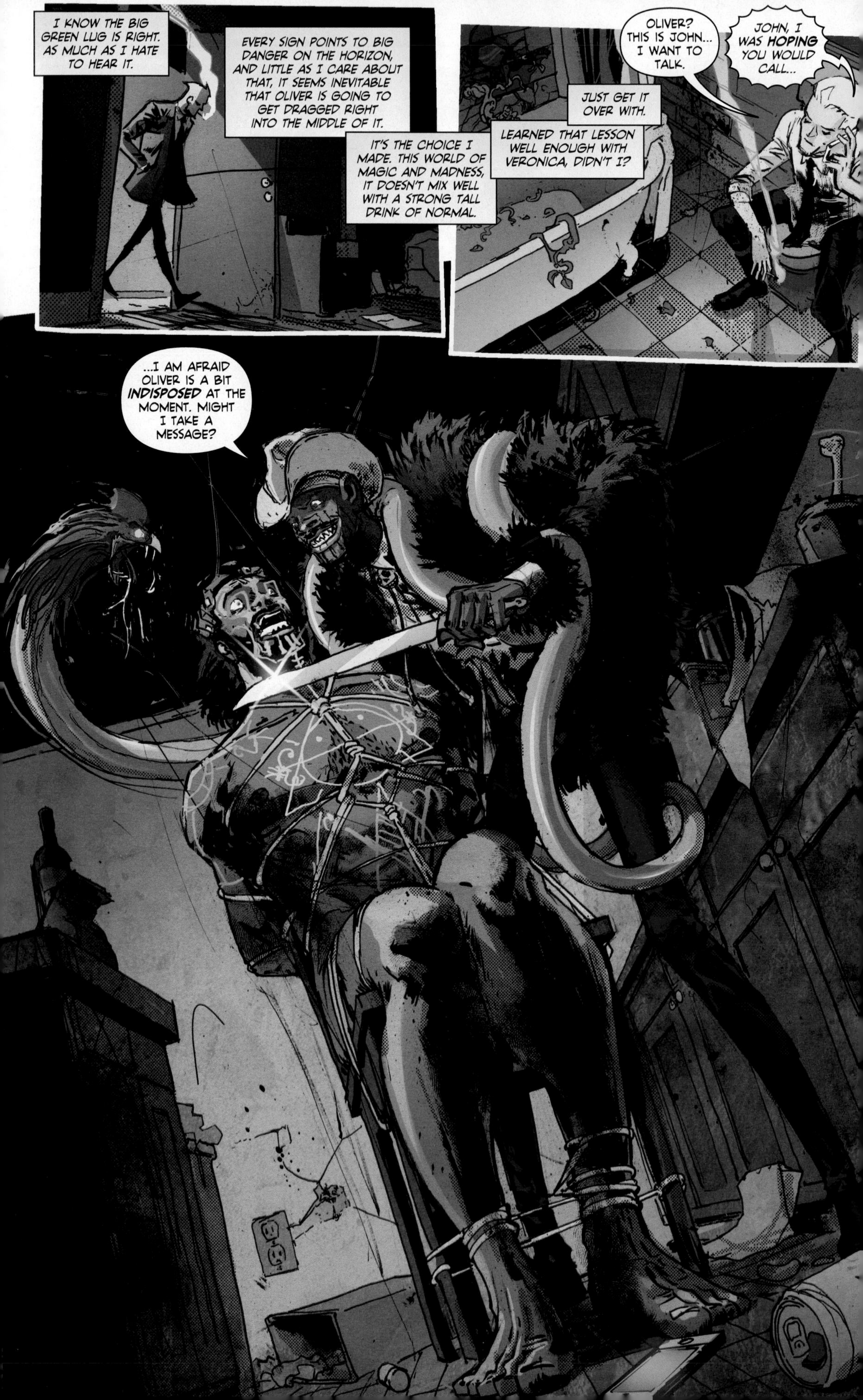
I KNOW THE BIG GREEN LUG IS RIGHT. AS MUCH AS I HATE TO HEAR IT.
EVERY SIGN POINTS TO BIG DANGER ON THE HORIZON, AND LITTLE AS I CARE ABOUT THAT, IT SEEMS INEVITABLE THAT OLIVER IS GOING TO GET DRAGGED RIGHT INTO THE MIDDLE OF IT.
IT'S THE CHOICE I MADE. THIS WORLD OF MAGIC AND MADNESS, IT DOESN'T MIX WELL WITH A STRONG TALL DRINK OF NORMAL.
LEARNED THAT LESSON WELL ENOUGH WITH VERONICA, DIDN'T I?
JUST GET IT OVER WITH.
OLIVER? THIS IS JOHN... I WANT TO TALK.
JOHN, I WAS **HOPING** YOU WOULD CALL...
...I AM AFRAID OLIVER IS A BIT **INDISPOSED** AT THE MOMENT. MIGHT I TAKE A MESSAGE?

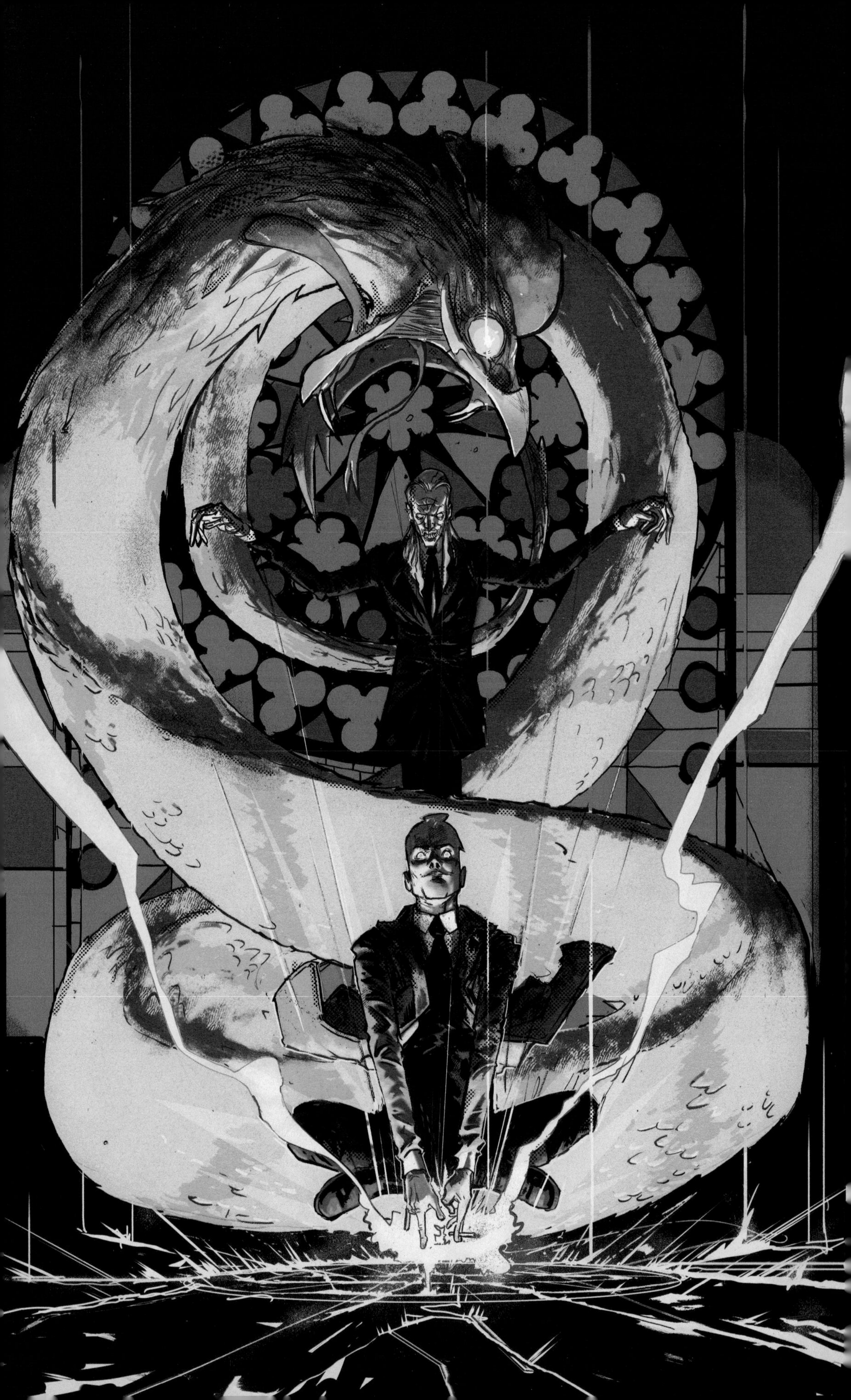

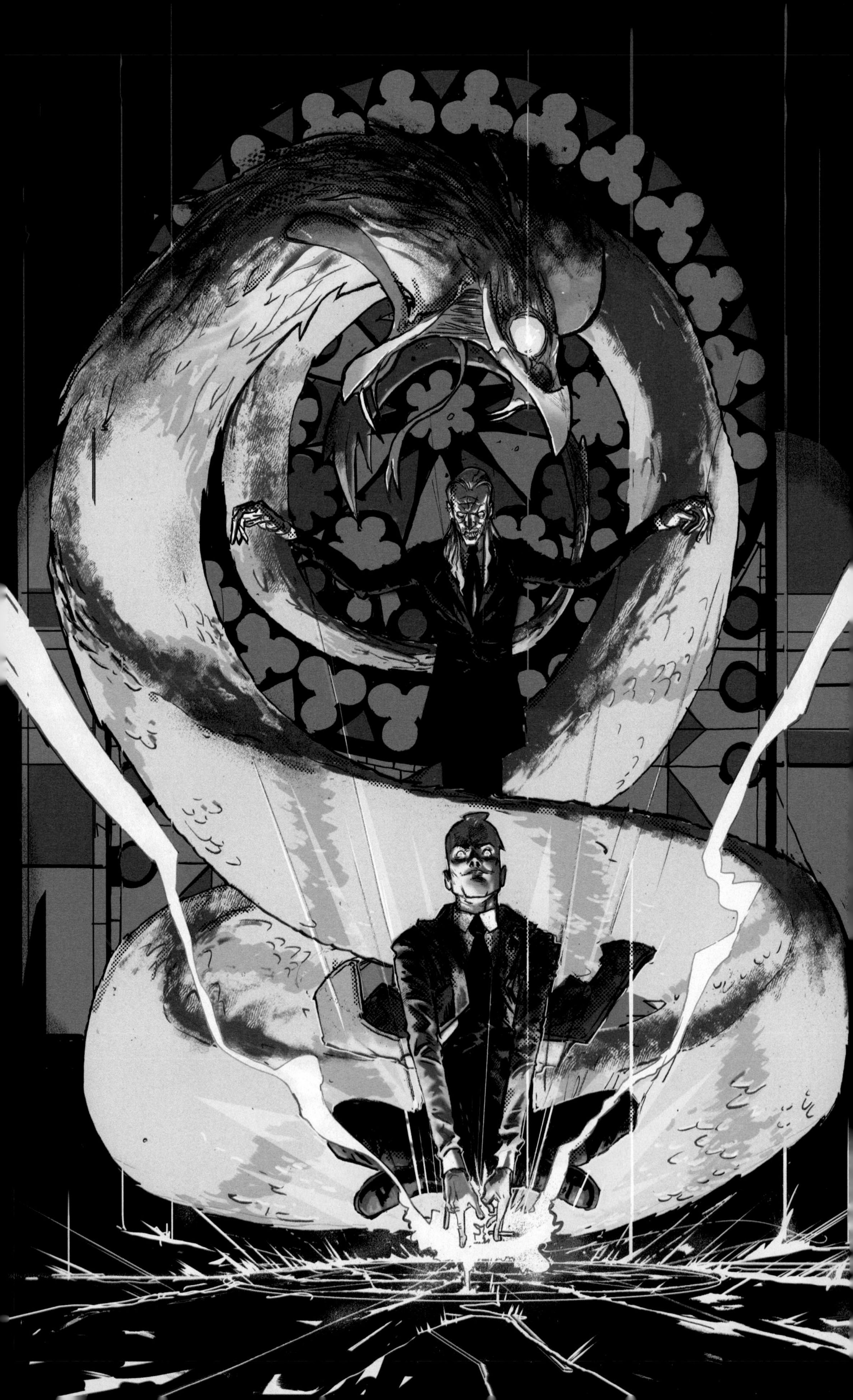

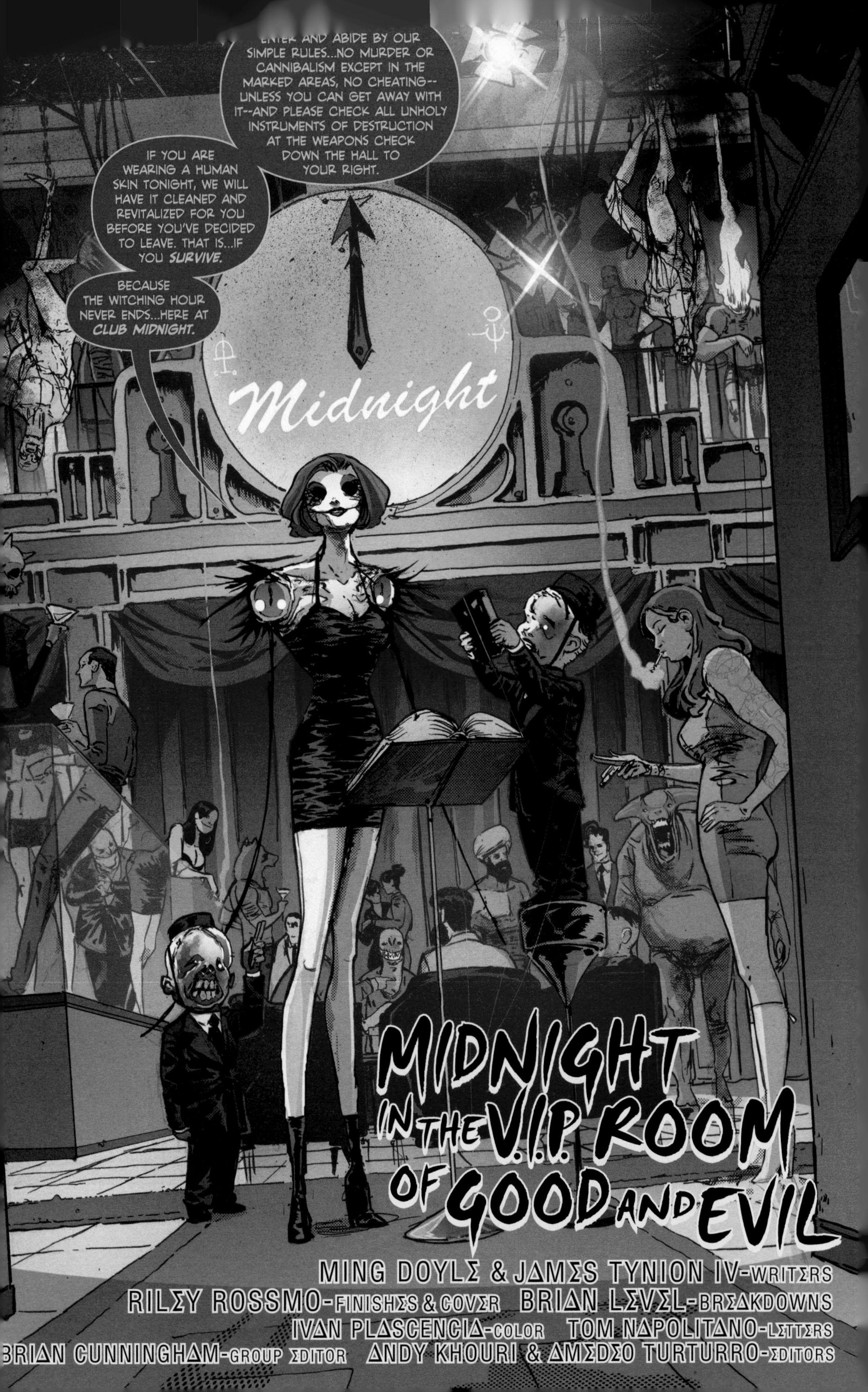
ENTER AND ABIDE BY OUR SIMPLE RULES...NO MURDER OR CANNIBALISM EXCEPT IN THE MARKED AREAS, NO CHEATING--UNLESS YOU CAN GET AWAY WITH IT--AND PLEASE CHECK ALL UNHOLY INSTRUMENTS OF DESTRUCTION AT THE WEAPONS CHECK DOWN THE HALL TO YOUR RIGHT.
IF YOU ARE WEARING A HUMAN SKIN TONIGHT, WE WILL HAVE IT CLEANED AND REVITALIZED FOR YOU BEFORE YOU'VE DECIDED TO LEAVE. THAT IS...IF YOU SURVIVE.
BECAUSE THE WITCHING HOUR NEVER ENDS...HERE AT CLUB MIDNIGHT.
Midnight
MIDNIGHT IN THE V.I.P. ROOM OF GOOD AND EVIL
MING DOYLE & JAMES TYNION IV-WRITERS
RILEY ROSSMO-FINISHES & COVER
BRIAN LEVEL-BREAKDOWNS
IVAN PLASCENCIA-COLOR
TOM NAPOLITANO-LETTERS
BRIAN CUNNINGHAM-GROUP EDITOR
ANDY KHOURI & AMEDEO TURTURRO-EDITORS

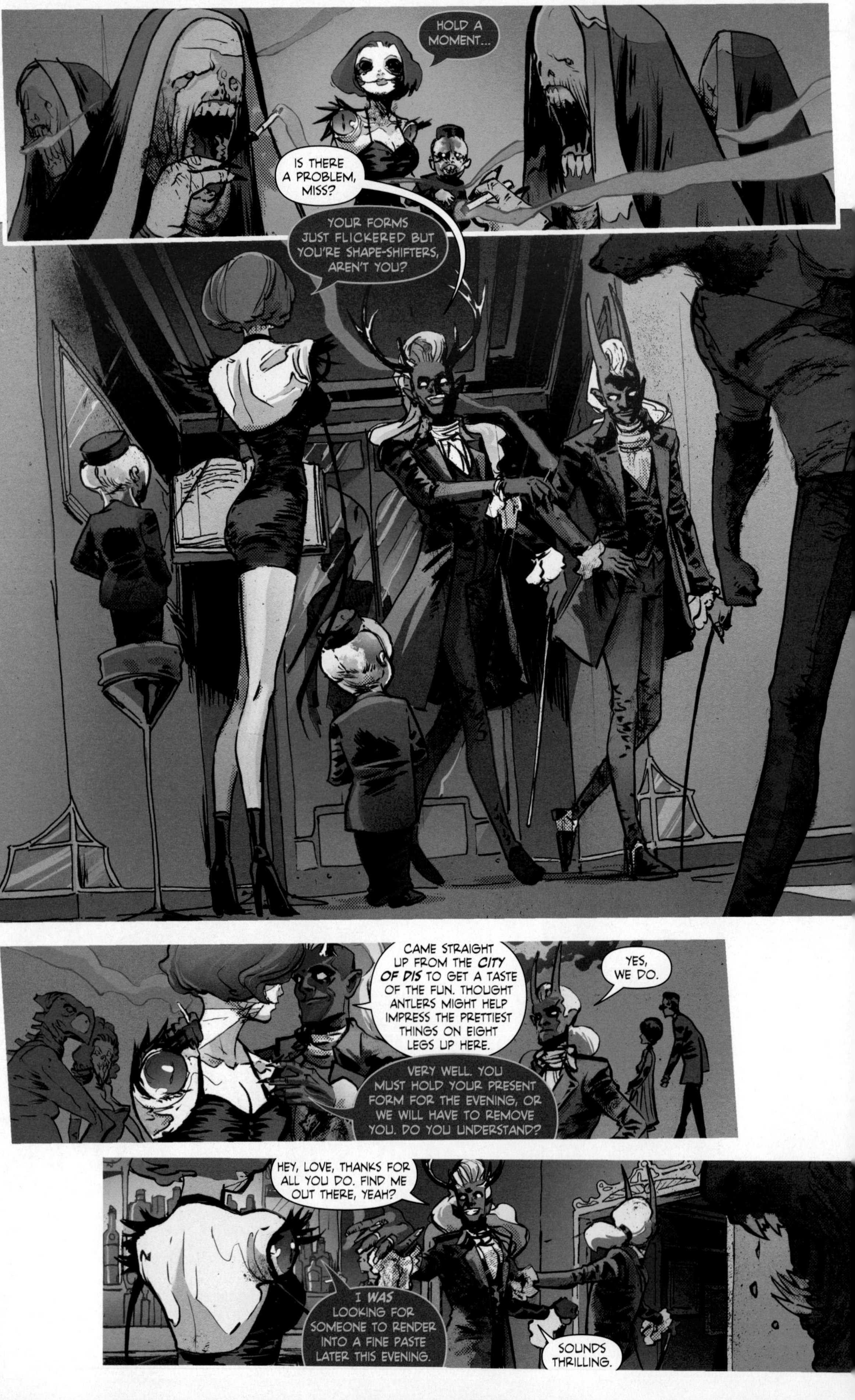
HOLD A MOMENT...
IS THERE A PROBLEM, MISS?
YOUR FORMS JUST FLICKERED BUT YOU'RE SHAPE-SHIFTERS, AREN'T YOU?
CAME STRAIGHT UP FROM THE *CITY OF DIS* TO GET A TASTE OF THE FUN. THOUGHT ANTLERS MIGHT HELP IMPRESS THE PRETTIEST THINGS ON EIGHT LEGS UP HERE.
YES, WE DO.
VERY WELL. YOU MUST HOLD YOUR PRESENT FORM FOR THE EVENING, OR WE WILL HAVE TO REMOVE YOU. DO YOU UNDERSTAND?
HEY, LOVE, THANKS FOR ALL YOU DO. FIND ME OUT THERE, YEAH?
I *WAS* LOOKING FOR SOMEONE TO RENDER INTO A FINE PASTE LATER THIS EVENING.
SOUNDS THRILLING.

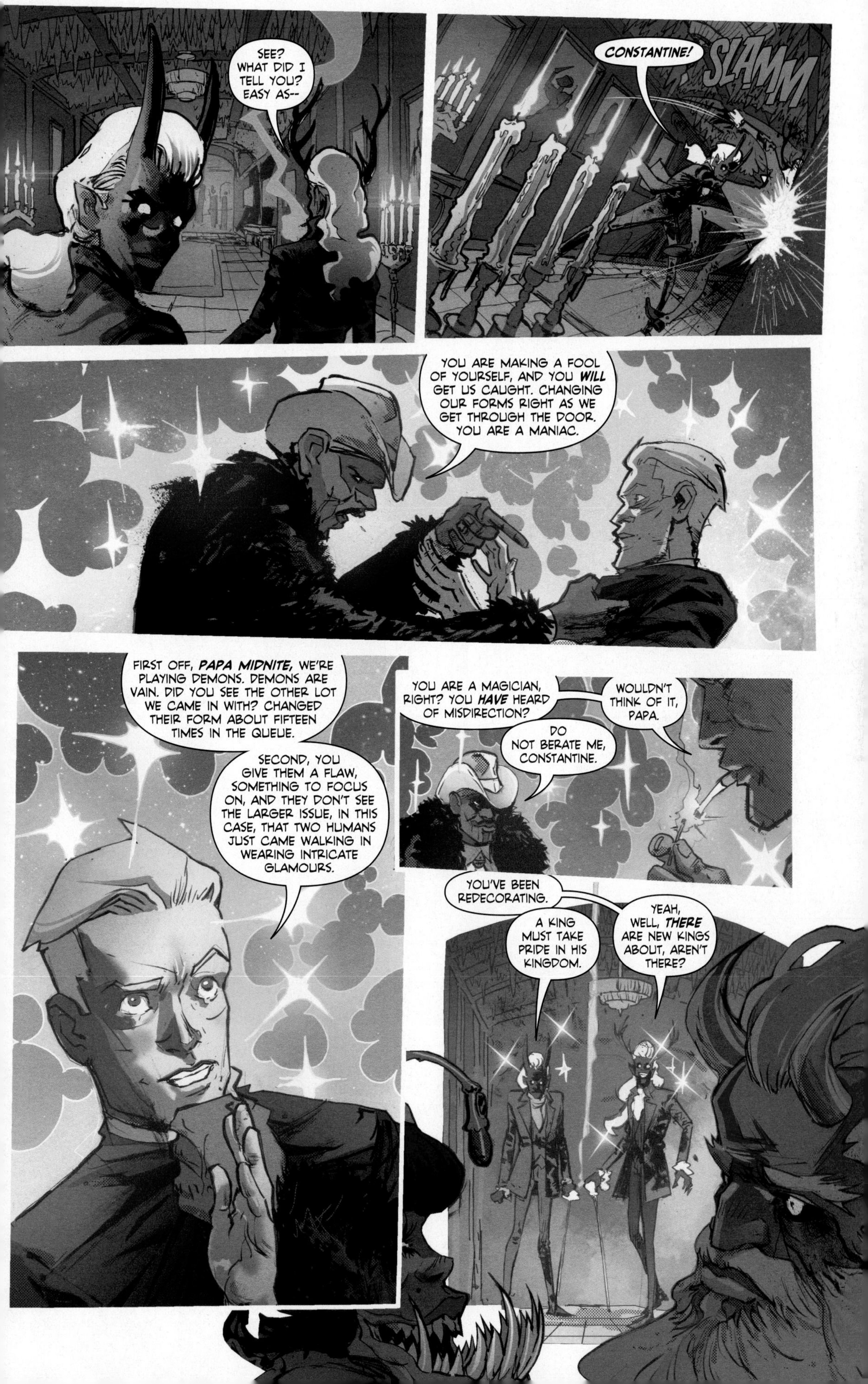
SEE? WHAT DID I TELL YOU? EASY AS--
CONSTANTINE!
SLAMM
YOU ARE MAKING A FOOL OF YOURSELF, AND YOU WILL GET US CAUGHT. CHANGING OUR FORMS RIGHT AS WE GET THROUGH THE DOOR. YOU ARE A MANIAC.
FIRST OFF, PAPA MIDNITE, WE'RE PLAYING DEMONS. DEMONS ARE VAIN. DID YOU SEE THE OTHER LOT WE CAME IN WITH? CHANGED THEIR FORM ABOUT FIFTEEN TIMES IN THE QUEUE.
SECOND, YOU GIVE THEM A FLAW, SOMETHING TO FOCUS ON, AND THEY DON'T SEE THE LARGER ISSUE, IN THIS CASE, THAT TWO HUMANS JUST CAME WALKING IN WEARING INTRICATE GLAMOURS.
YOU ARE A MAGICIAN, RIGHT? YOU HAVE HEARD OF MISDIRECTION?
WOULDN'T THINK OF IT, PAPA.
DO NOT BERATE ME, CONSTANTINE.
YOU'VE BEEN REDECORATING.
YEAH, WELL, THERE ARE NEW KINGS ABOUT, AREN'T THERE?
A KING MUST TAKE PRIDE IN HIS KINGDOM.

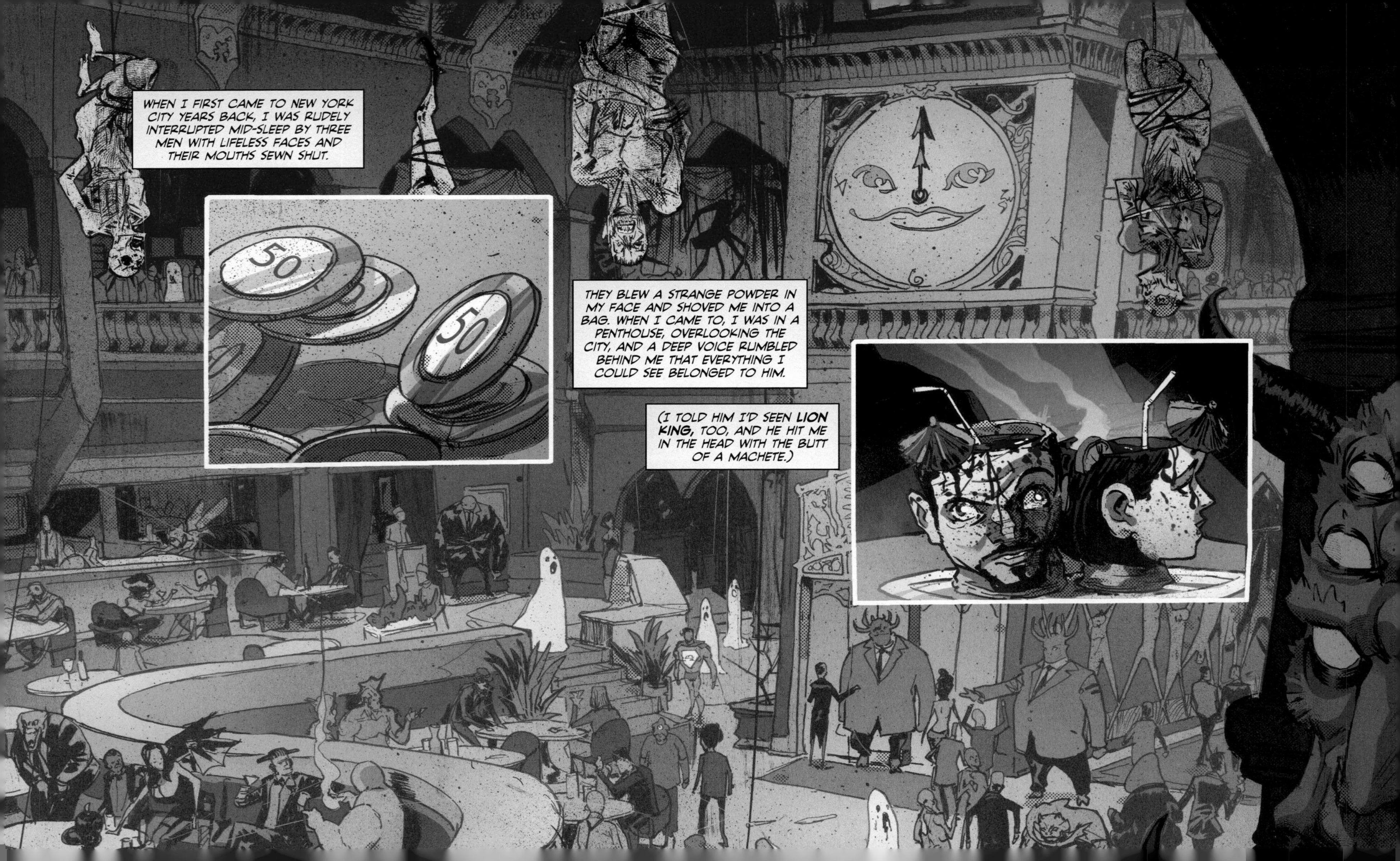
WHEN I FIRST CAME TO NEW YORK CITY YEARS BACK, I WAS RUDELY INTERRUPTED MID-SLEEP BY THREE MEN WITH LIFELESS FACES AND THEIR MOUTHS SEWN SHUT.
50
50
THEY BLEW A STRANGE POWDER IN MY FACE AND SHOVED ME INTO A BAG. WHEN I CAME TO, I WAS IN A PENTHOUSE, OVERLOOKING THE CITY, AND A DEEP VOICE RUMBLED BEHIND ME THAT EVERYTHING I COULD SEE BELONGED TO HIM.
(I TOLD HIM I'D SEEN **LION KING,** TOO, AND HE HIT ME IN THE HEAD WITH THE BUTT OF A MACHETE.)

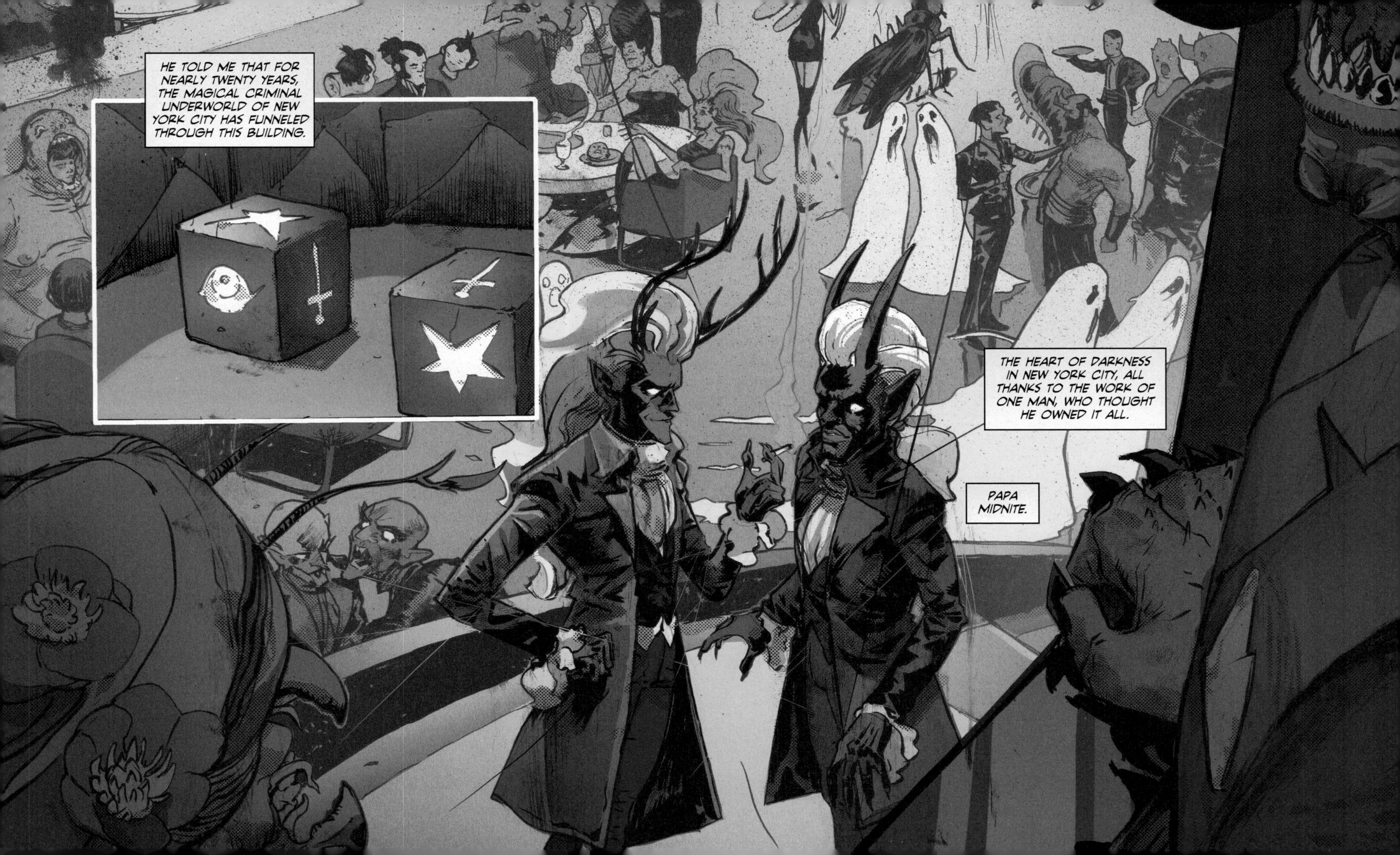
HE TOLD ME THAT FOR NEARLY TWENTY YEARS, THE MAGICAL CRIMINAL UNDERWORLD OF NEW YORK CITY HAS FUNNELED THROUGH THIS BUILDING.
THE HEART OF DARKNESS IN NEW YORK CITY, ALL THANKS TO THE WORK OF ONE MAN, WHO THOUGHT HE OWNED IT ALL.
PAPA MIDNITE.

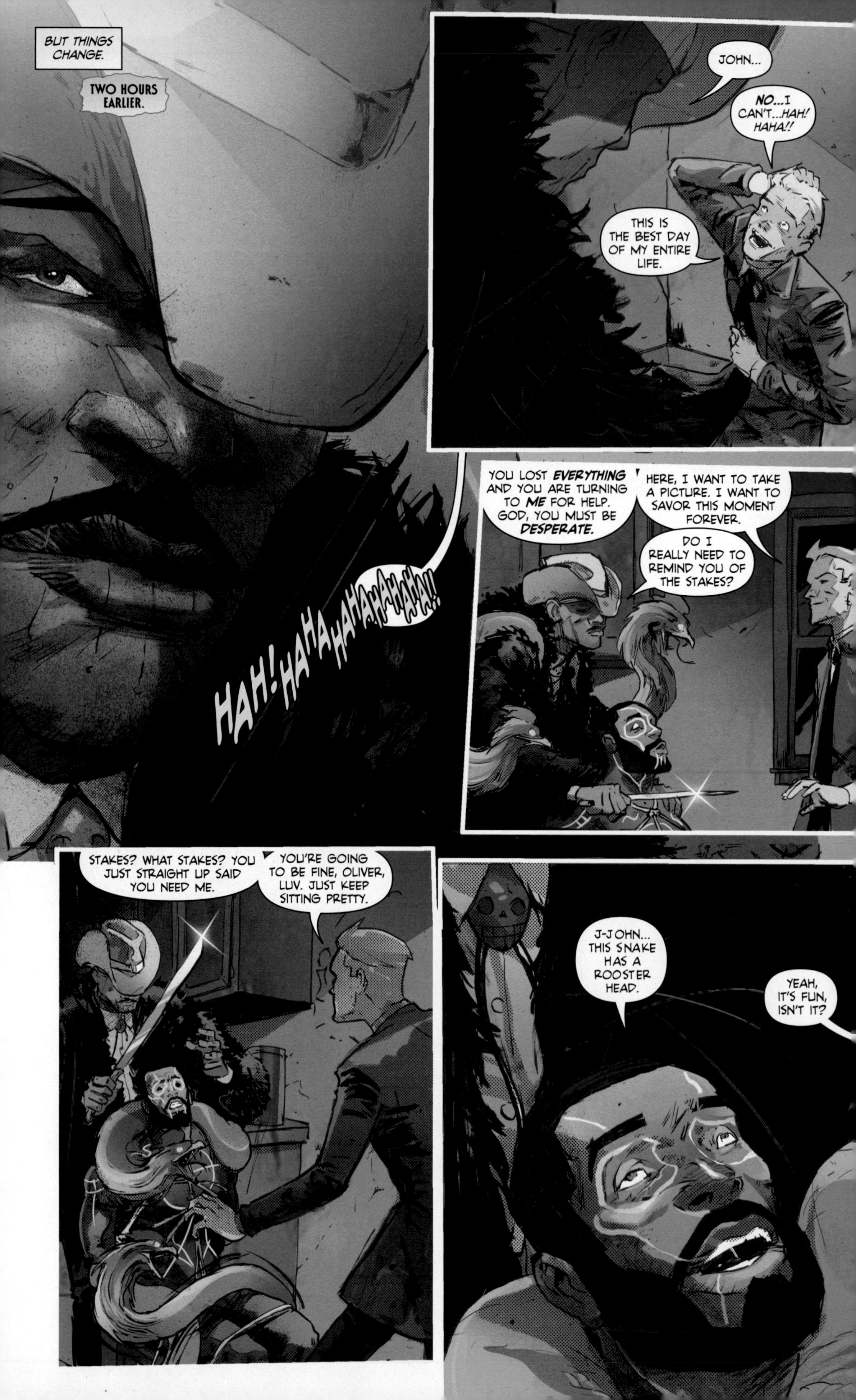
BUT THINGS CHANGE.
TWO HOURS EARLIER.
HAH! HAHAHAHAHAHAHAHA!!
JOHN...
NO...I CAN'T...HAH! HAHA!!
THIS IS THE BEST DAY OF MY ENTIRE LIFE.
YOU LOST EVERYTHING AND YOU ARE TURNING TO ME FOR HELP. GOD, YOU MUST BE DESPERATE.
HERE, I WANT TO TAKE A PICTURE. I WANT TO SAVOR THIS MOMENT FOREVER.
DO I REALLY NEED TO REMIND YOU OF THE STAKES?
STAKES? WHAT STAKES? YOU JUST STRAIGHT UP SAID YOU NEED ME.
YOU'RE GOING TO BE FINE, OLIVER, LUV. JUST KEEP SITTING PRETTY.
J-JOHN... THIS SNAKE HAS A ROOSTER HEAD.
YEAH, IT'S FUN, ISN'T IT?

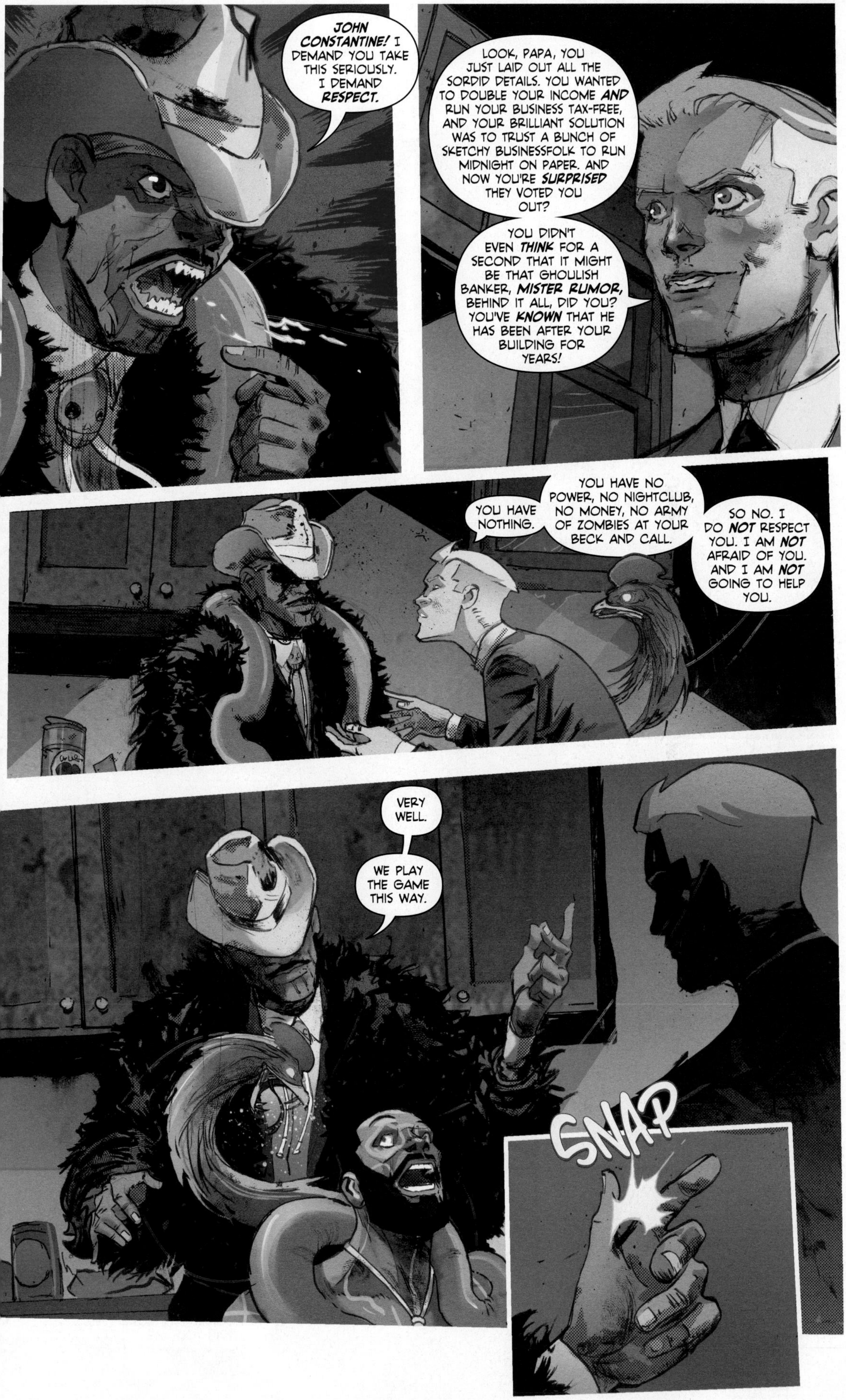

**JOHN CONSTANTINE!** I DEMAND YOU TAKE THIS SERIOUSLY. I DEMAND ***RESPECT.***
LOOK, PAPA, YOU JUST LAID OUT ALL THE SORDID DETAILS. YOU WANTED TO DOUBLE YOUR INCOME ***AND*** RUN YOUR BUSINESS TAX-FREE, AND YOUR BRILLIANT SOLUTION WAS TO TRUST A BUNCH OF SKETCHY BUSINESSFOLK TO RUN MIDNIGHT ON PAPER. AND NOW YOU'RE ***SURPRISED*** THEY VOTED YOU OUT?
YOU DIDN'T EVEN ***THINK*** FOR A SECOND THAT IT MIGHT BE THAT GHOULISH BANKER, ***MISTER RUMOR,*** BEHIND IT ALL, DID YOU? YOU'VE ***KNOWN*** THAT HE HAS BEEN AFTER YOUR BUILDING FOR YEARS!
YOU HAVE NOTHING.
YOU HAVE NO POWER, NO NIGHTCLUB, NO MONEY, NO ARMY OF ZOMBIES AT YOUR BECK AND CALL.
SO NO. I DO ***NOT*** RESPECT YOU. I AM ***NOT*** AFRAID OF YOU. AND I AM ***NOT*** GOING TO HELP YOU.
VERY WELL.
WE PLAY THE GAME THIS WAY.
SNAP

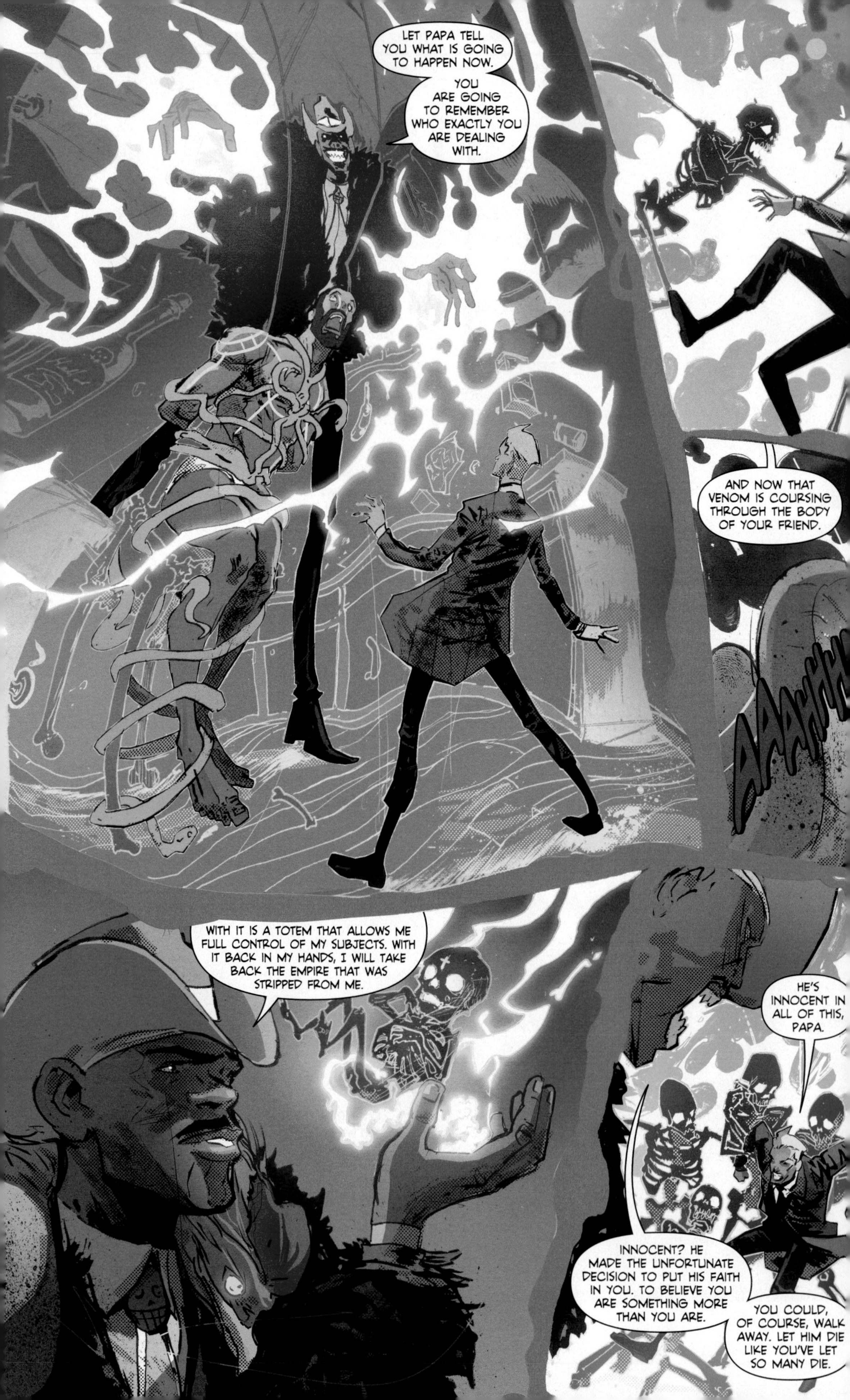
LET PAPA TELL YOU WHAT IS GOING TO HAPPEN NOW.
YOU ARE GOING TO REMEMBER WHO EXACTLY YOU ARE DEALING WITH.
AND NOW THAT VENOM IS COURSING THROUGH THE BODY OF YOUR FRIEND.
AAAHHHH
WITH IT IS A TOTEM THAT ALLOWS ME FULL CONTROL OF MY SUBJECTS. WITH IT BACK IN MY HANDS, I WILL TAKE BACK THE EMPIRE THAT WAS STRIPPED FROM ME.
HE'S INNOCENT IN ALL OF THIS, PAPA.
INNOCENT? HE MADE THE UNFORTUNATE DECISION TO PUT HIS FAITH IN YOU. TO BELIEVE YOU ARE SOMETHING MORE THAN YOU ARE.
YOU COULD, OF COURSE, WALK AWAY. LET HIM DIE LIKE YOU'VE LET SO MANY DIE.

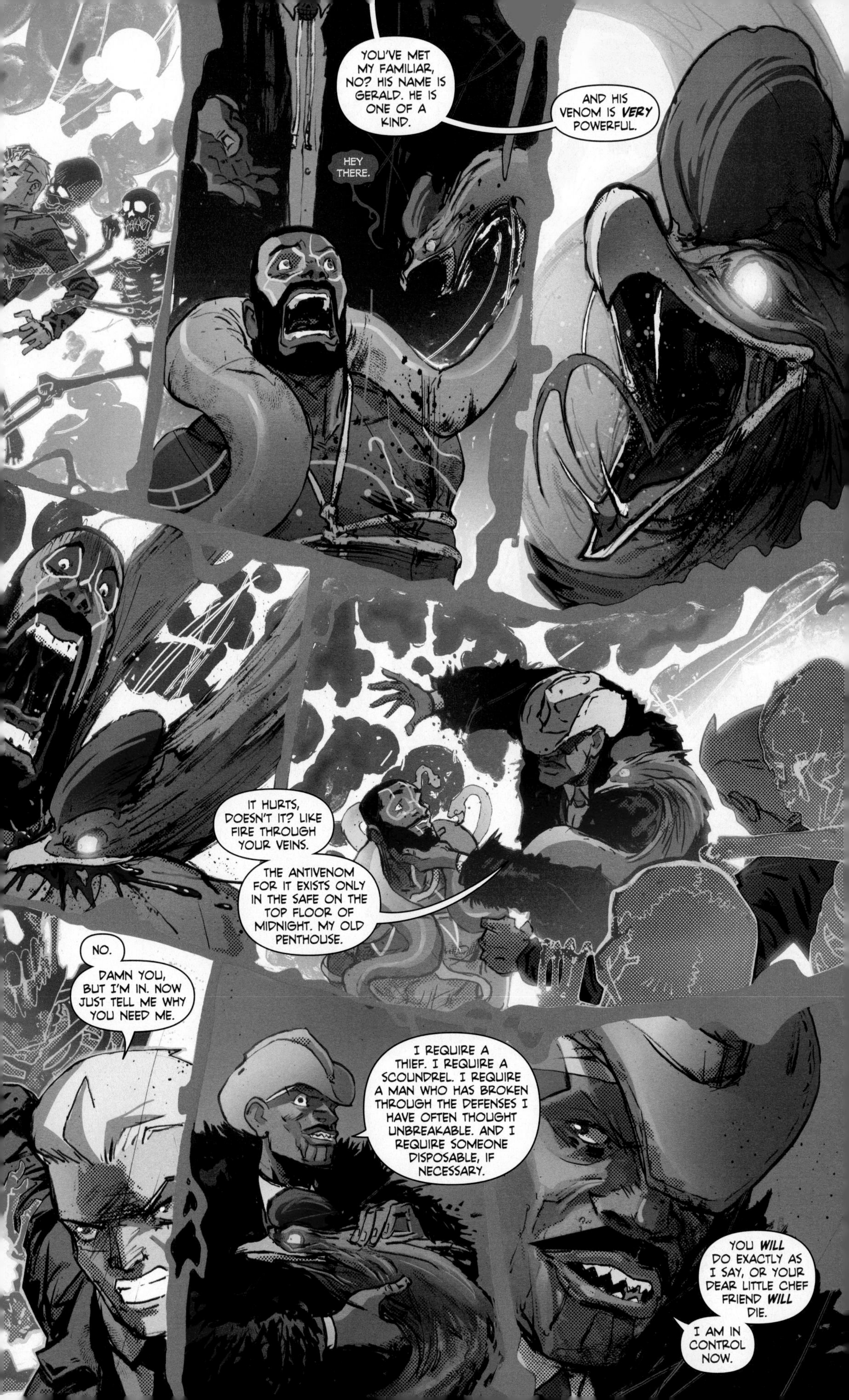
YOU'VE MET MY FAMILIAR, NO? HIS NAME IS GERALD. HE IS ONE OF A KIND.
AND HIS VENOM IS **VERY** POWERFUL.
HEY THERE.
IT HURTS, DOESN'T IT? LIKE FIRE THROUGH YOUR VEINS.
THE ANTIVENOM FOR IT EXISTS ONLY IN THE SAFE ON THE TOP FLOOR OF MIDNIGHT. MY OLD PENTHOUSE.
NO.
DAMN YOU, BUT I'M IN. NOW JUST TELL ME WHY YOU NEED ME.
I REQUIRE A THIEF. I REQUIRE A SCOUNDREL. I REQUIRE A MAN WHO HAS BROKEN THROUGH THE DEFENSES I HAVE OFTEN THOUGHT UNBREAKABLE. AND I REQUIRE SOMEONE DISPOSABLE, IF NECESSARY.
YOU **WILL** DO EXACTLY AS I SAY, OR YOUR DEAR LITTLE CHEF FRIEND **WILL** DIE.
I AM IN CONTROL NOW.

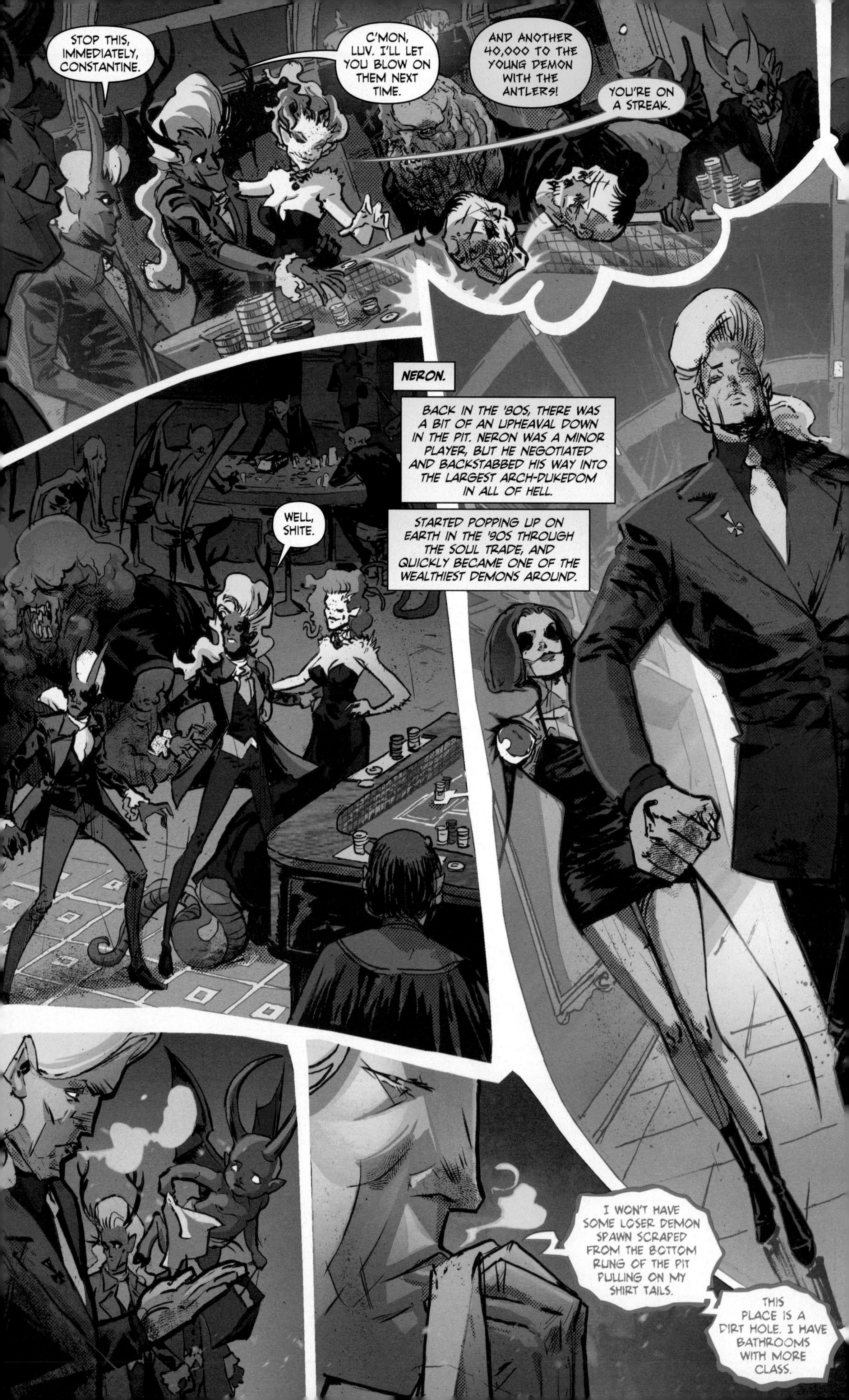
STOP THIS, IMMEDIATELY, CONSTANTINE.
C'MON, LUV. I'LL LET YOU BLOW ON THEM NEXT TIME.
AND ANOTHER 40,000 TO THE YOUNG DEMON WITH THE ANTLERS!
YOU'RE ON A STREAK.
NERON.
BACK IN THE '80S, THERE WAS A BIT OF AN UPHEAVAL DOWN IN THE PIT. NERON WAS A MINOR PLAYER, BUT HE NEGOTIATED AND BACKSTABBED HIS WAY INTO THE LARGEST ARCH-DUKEDOM IN ALL OF HELL.
STARTED POPPING UP ON EARTH IN THE '90S THROUGH THE SOUL TRADE, AND QUICKLY BECAME ONE OF THE WEALTHIEST DEMONS AROUND.
WELL, SHITE.
I WON'T HAVE SOME LOSER DEMON SPAWN SCRAPED FROM THE BOTTOM RUNG OF THE PIT PULLING ON MY SHIRT TAILS.
THIS PLACE IS A DIRT HOLE. I HAVE BATHROOMS WITH MORE CLASS.

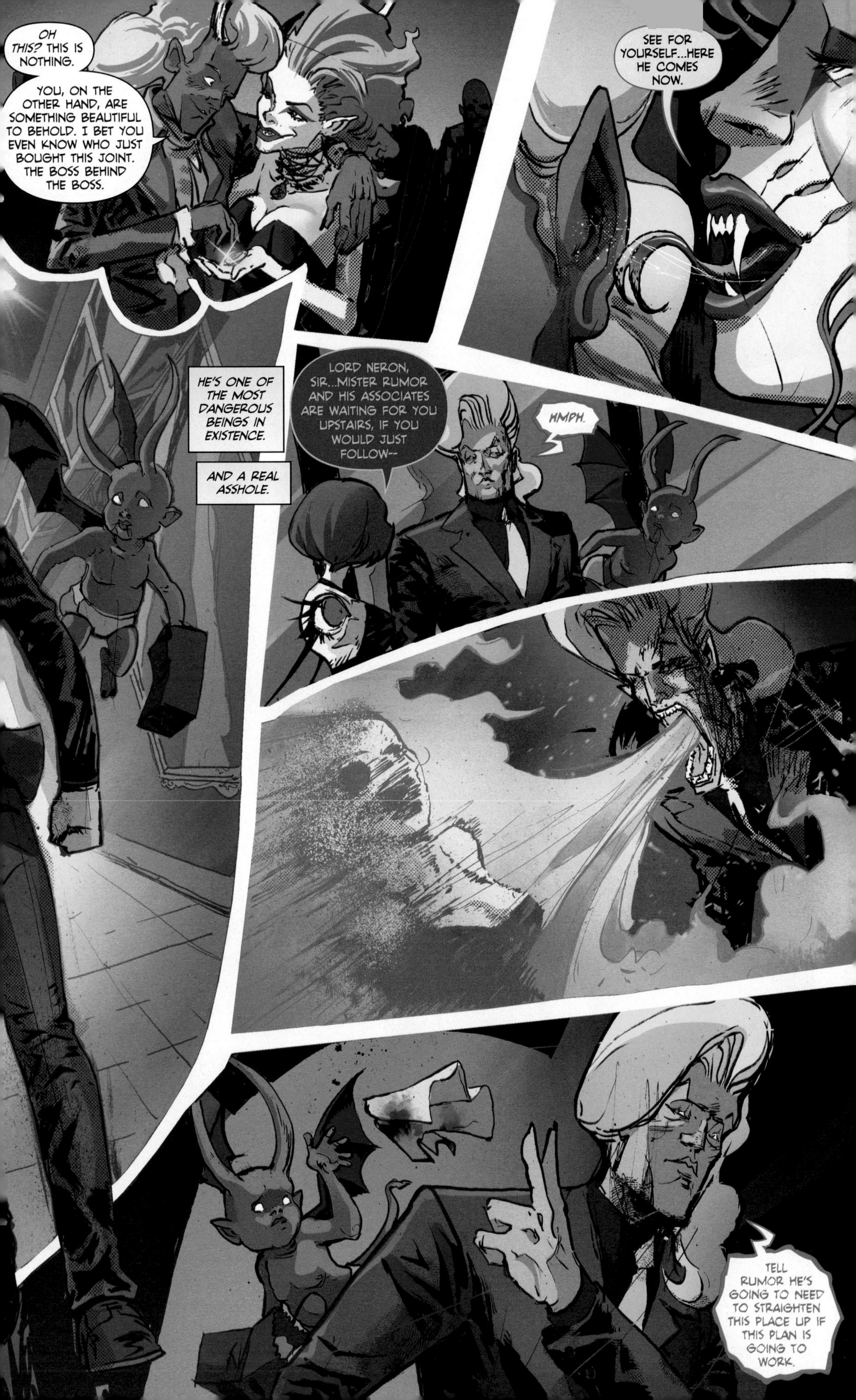
OH THIS? THIS IS NOTHING.
YOU, ON THE OTHER HAND, ARE SOMETHING BEAUTIFUL TO BEHOLD. I BET YOU EVEN KNOW WHO JUST BOUGHT THIS JOINT. THE BOSS BEHIND THE BOSS.
SEE FOR YOURSELF...HERE HE COMES NOW.
HE'S ONE OF THE MOST DANGEROUS BEINGS IN EXISTENCE.
AND A REAL ASSHOLE.
LORD NERON, SIR...MISTER RUMOR AND HIS ASSOCIATES ARE WAITING FOR YOU UPSTAIRS, IF YOU WOULD JUST FOLLOW--
HMPH.
TELL RUMOR HE'S GOING TO NEED TO STRAIGHTEN THIS PLACE UP IF THIS PLAN IS GOING TO WORK.

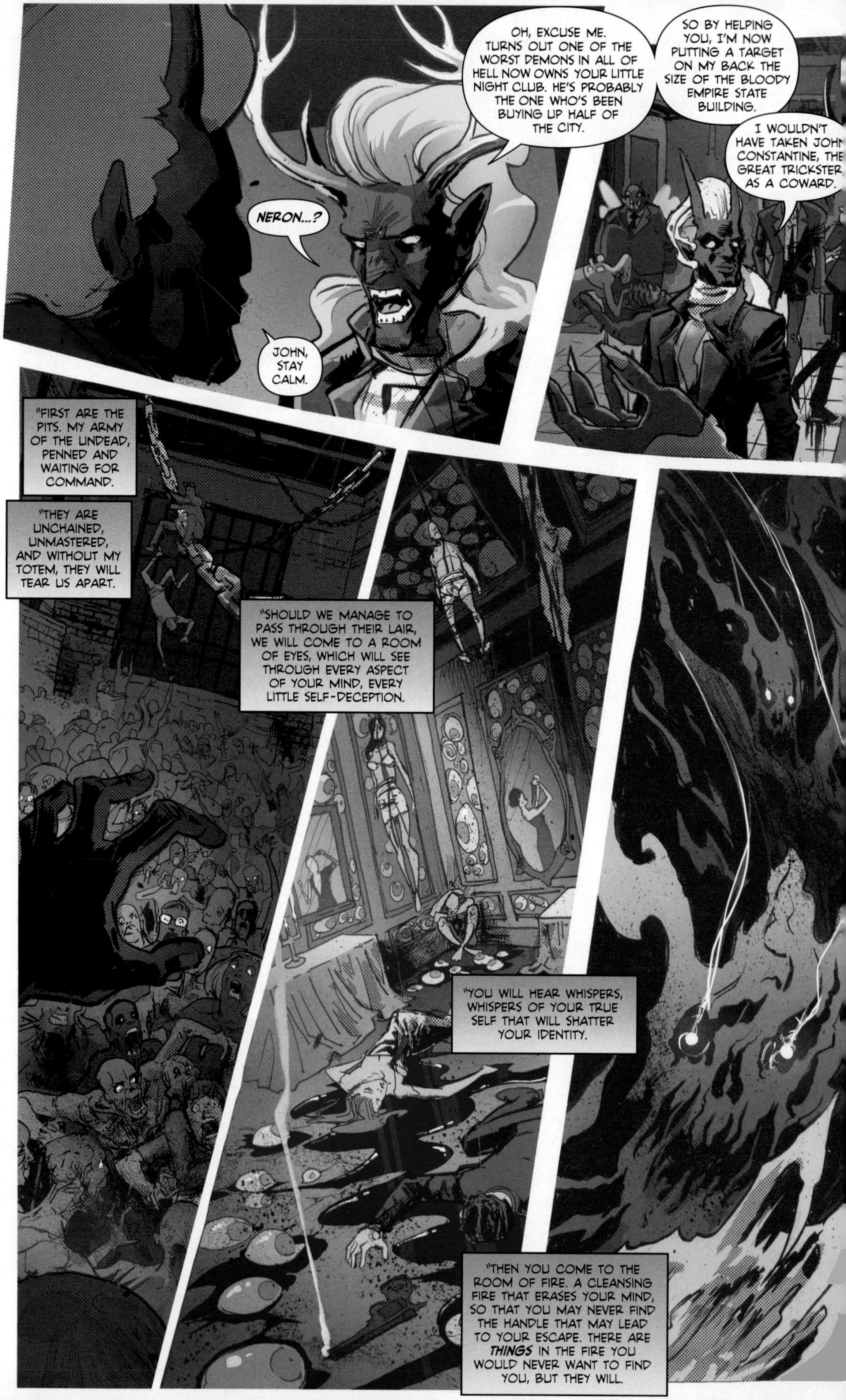
NERON...?
JOHN, STAY CALM.
OH, EXCUSE ME. TURNS OUT ONE OF THE WORST DEMONS IN ALL OF HELL NOW OWNS YOUR LITTLE NIGHT CLUB. HE'S PROBABLY THE ONE WHO'S BEEN BUYING UP HALF OF THE CITY.
SO BY HELPING YOU, I'M NOW PUTTING A TARGET ON MY BACK THE SIZE OF THE BLOODY EMPIRE STATE BUILDING.
I WOULDN'T HAVE TAKEN JOHN CONSTANTINE, THE GREAT TRICKSTER, AS A COWARD.
"FIRST ARE THE PITS. MY ARMY OF THE UNDEAD, PENNED AND WAITING FOR COMMAND.
"THEY ARE UNCHAINED, UNMASTERED, AND WITHOUT MY TOTEM, THEY WILL TEAR US APART.
"SHOULD WE MANAGE TO PASS THROUGH THEIR LAIR, WE WILL COME TO A ROOM OF EYES, WHICH WILL SEE THROUGH EVERY ASPECT OF YOUR MIND, EVERY LITTLE SELF-DECEPTION.
"YOU WILL HEAR WHISPERS, WHISPERS OF YOUR TRUE SELF THAT WILL SHATTER YOUR IDENTITY.
"THEN YOU COME TO THE ROOM OF FIRE. A CLEANSING FIRE THAT ERASES YOUR MIND, SO THAT YOU MAY NEVER FIND THE HANDLE THAT MAY LEAD TO YOUR ESCAPE. THERE ARE *THINGS* IN THE FIRE YOU WOULD NEVER WANT TO FIND YOU, BUT THEY WILL.

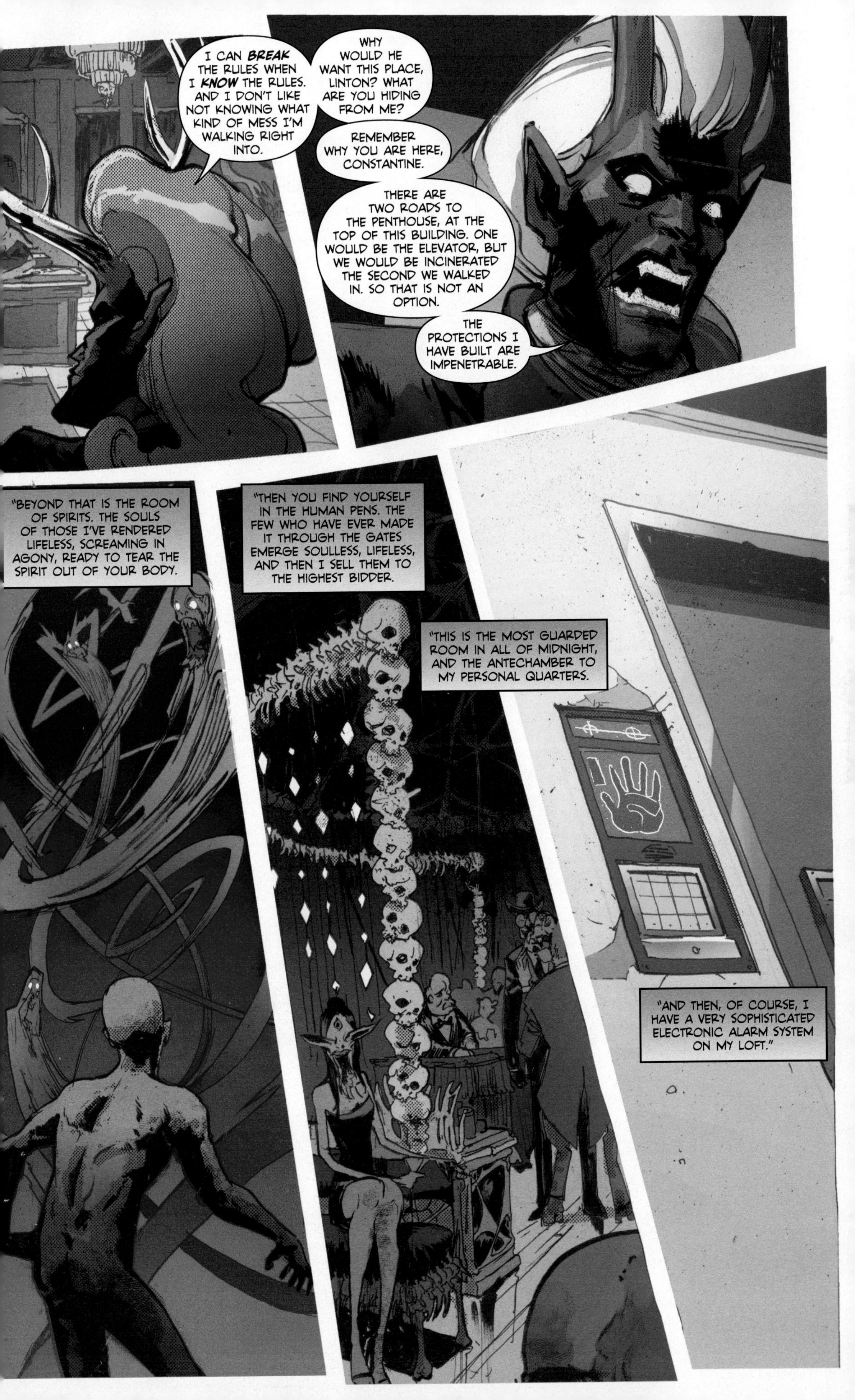
I CAN BREAK THE RULES WHEN I KNOW THE RULES. AND I DON'T LIKE NOT KNOWING WHAT KIND OF MESS I'M WALKING RIGHT INTO.
WHY WOULD HE WANT THIS PLACE, LINTON? WHAT ARE YOU HIDING FROM ME?
REMEMBER WHY YOU ARE HERE, CONSTANTINE.
THERE ARE TWO ROADS TO THE PENTHOUSE, AT THE TOP OF THIS BUILDING. ONE WOULD BE THE ELEVATOR, BUT WE WOULD BE INCINERATED THE SECOND WE WALKED IN. SO THAT IS NOT AN OPTION.
THE PROTECTIONS I HAVE BUILT ARE IMPENETRABLE.
"BEYOND THAT IS THE ROOM OF SPIRITS. THE SOULS OF THOSE I'VE RENDERED LIFELESS, SCREAMING IN AGONY, READY TO TEAR THE SPIRIT OUT OF YOUR BODY.
"THEN YOU FIND YOURSELF IN THE HUMAN PENS. THE FEW WHO HAVE EVER MADE IT THROUGH THE GATES EMERGE SOULLESS, LIFELESS, AND THEN I SELL THEM TO THE HIGHEST BIDDER.
"THIS IS THE MOST GUARDED ROOM IN ALL OF MIDNIGHT, AND THE ANTECHAMBER TO MY PERSONAL QUARTERS.
"AND THEN, OF COURSE, I HAVE A VERY SOPHISTICATED ELECTRONIC ALARM SYSTEM ON MY LOFT."

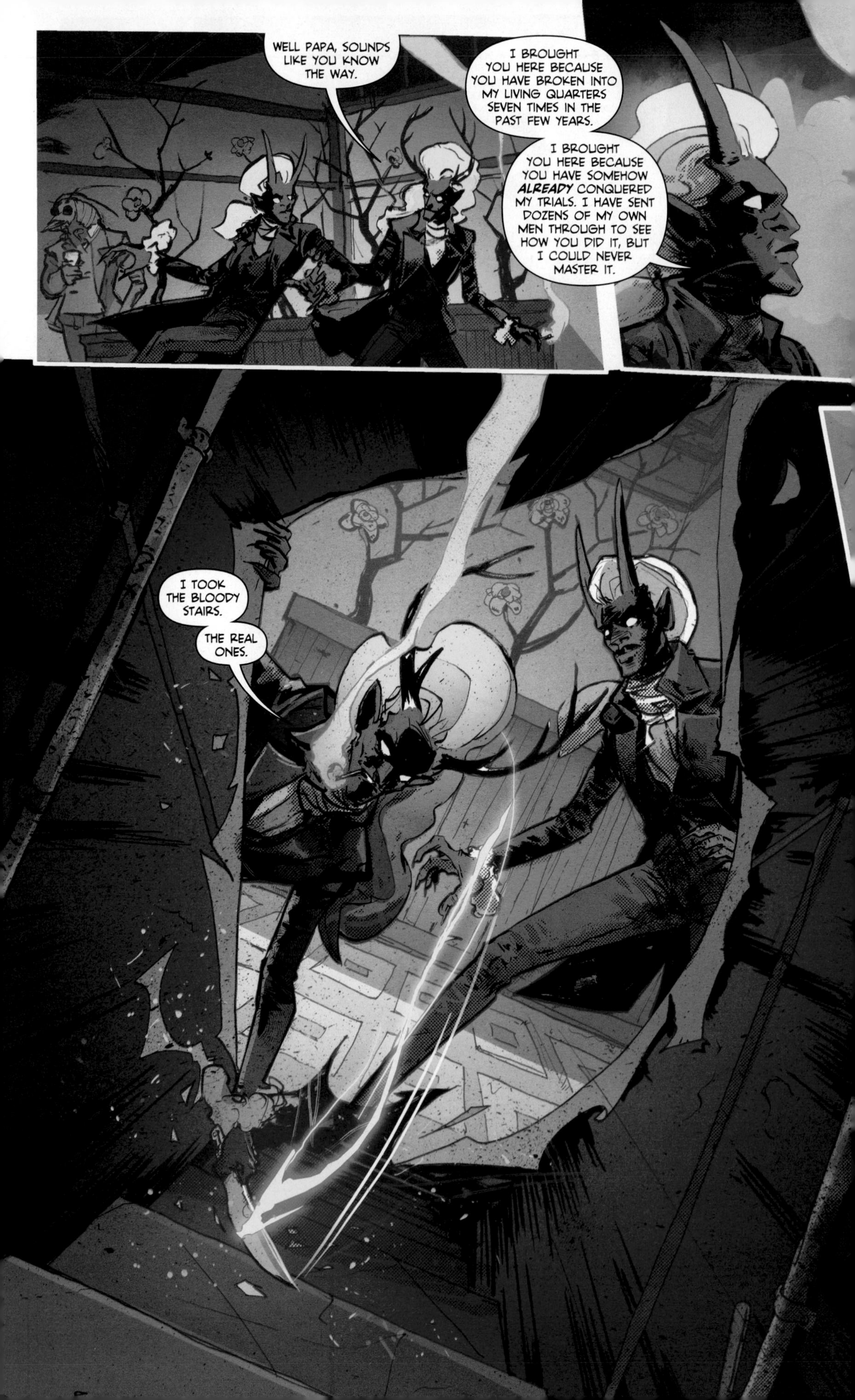
WELL PAPA, SOUNDS LIKE YOU KNOW THE WAY.
I BROUGHT YOU HERE BECAUSE YOU HAVE BROKEN INTO MY LIVING QUARTERS SEVEN TIMES IN THE PAST FEW YEARS.
I BROUGHT YOU HERE BECAUSE YOU HAVE SOMEHOW ALREADY CONQUERED MY TRIALS. I HAVE SENT DOZENS OF MY OWN MEN THROUGH TO SEE HOW YOU DID IT, BUT I COULD NEVER MASTER IT.
I TOOK THE BLOODY STAIRS.
THE REAL ONES.

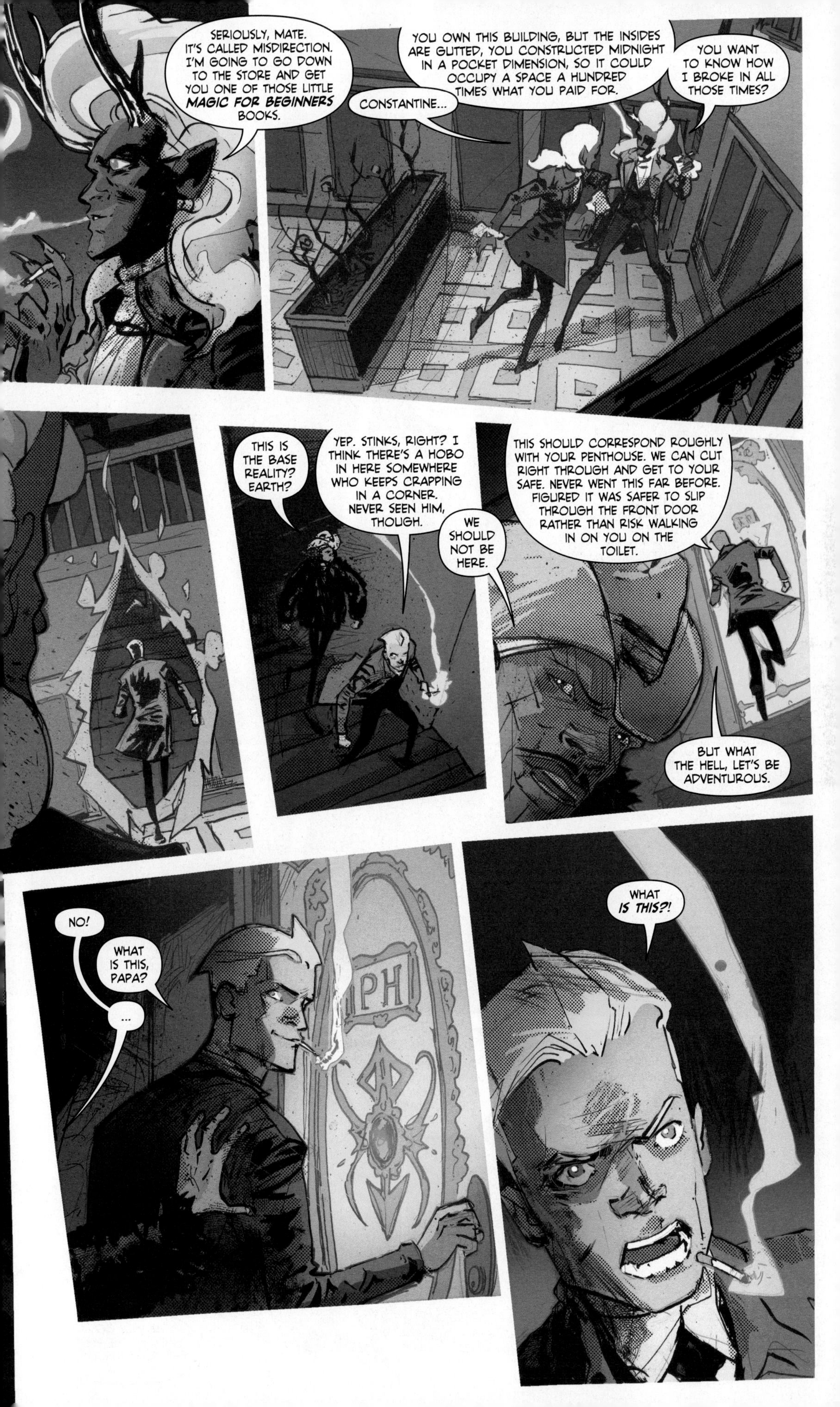
SERIOUSLY, MATE. IT'S CALLED MISDIRECTION. I'M GOING TO GO DOWN TO THE STORE AND GET YOU ONE OF THOSE LITTLE **MAGIC FOR BEGINNERS** BOOKS.
CONSTANTINE...
YOU OWN THIS BUILDING, BUT THE INSIDES ARE GUTTED, YOU CONSTRUCTED MIDNIGHT IN A POCKET DIMENSION, SO IT COULD OCCUPY A SPACE A HUNDRED TIMES WHAT YOU PAID FOR.
YOU WANT TO KNOW HOW I BROKE IN ALL THOSE TIMES?
THIS IS THE BASE REALITY? EARTH?
YEP. STINKS, RIGHT? I THINK THERE'S A HOBO IN HERE SOMEWHERE WHO KEEPS CRAPPING IN A CORNER. NEVER SEEN HIM, THOUGH.
WE SHOULD NOT BE HERE.
THIS SHOULD CORRESPOND ROUGHLY WITH YOUR PENTHOUSE. WE CAN CUT RIGHT THROUGH AND GET TO YOUR SAFE. NEVER WENT THIS FAR BEFORE. FIGURED IT WAS SAFER TO SLIP THROUGH THE FRONT DOOR RATHER THAN RISK WALKING IN ON YOU ON THE TOILET.
BUT WHAT THE HELL, LET'S BE ADVENTUROUS.
NO!
WHAT IS THIS, PAPA?
...
PH
WHAT *IS THIS?!*

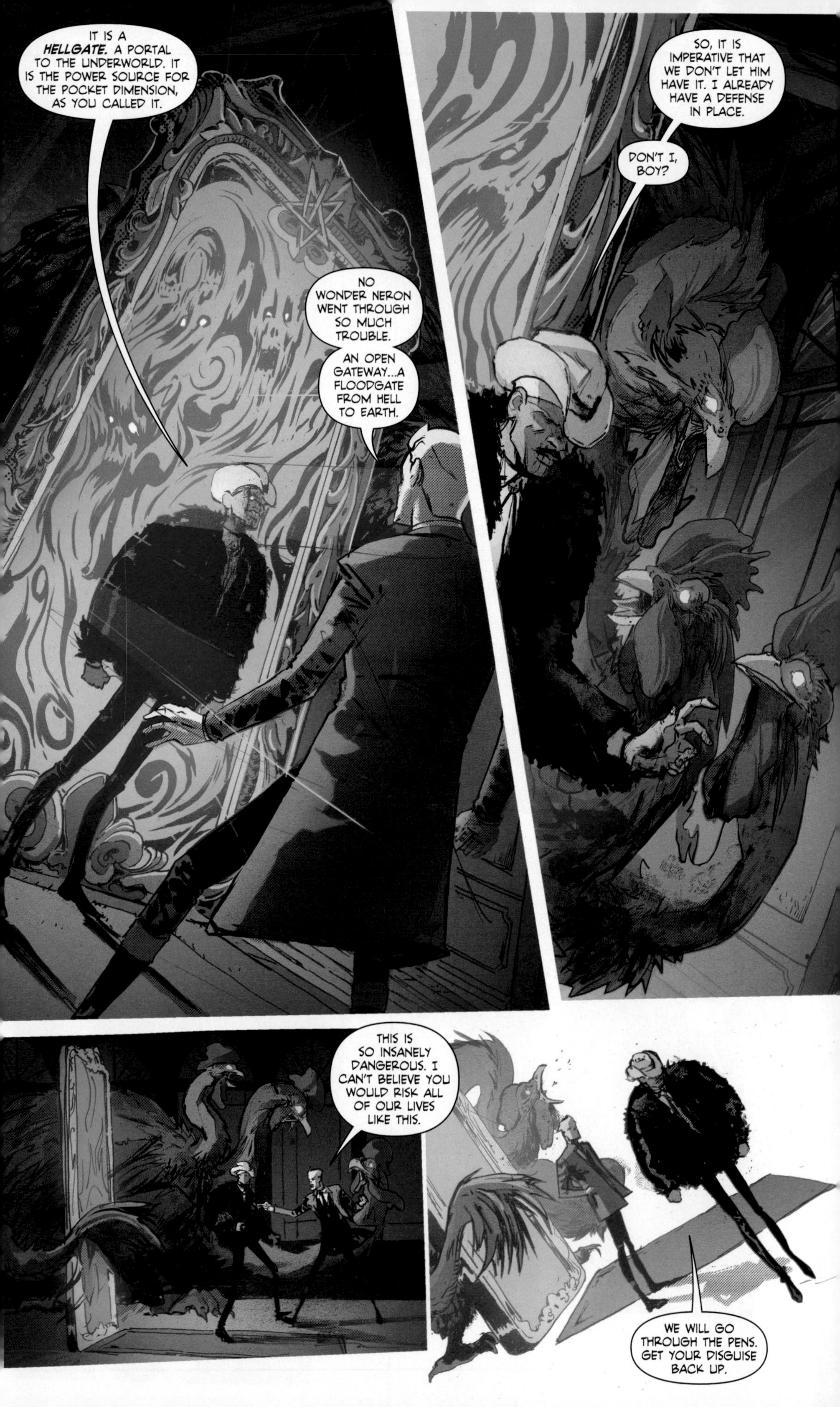
IT IS A *HELLGATE.* A PORTAL TO THE UNDERWORLD. IT IS THE POWER SOURCE FOR THE POCKET DIMENSION, AS YOU CALLED IT.
NO WONDER NERON WENT THROUGH SO MUCH TROUBLE.
AN OPEN GATEWAY...A FLOODGATE FROM HELL TO EARTH.
SO, IT IS IMPERATIVE THAT WE DON'T LET HIM HAVE IT. I ALREADY HAVE A DEFENSE IN PLACE.
DON'T I, BOY?
THIS IS SO INSANELY DANGEROUS. I CAN'T BELIEVE YOU WOULD RISK ALL OF OUR LIVES LIKE THIS.
WE WILL GO THROUGH THE PENS. GET YOUR DISGUISE BACK UP.

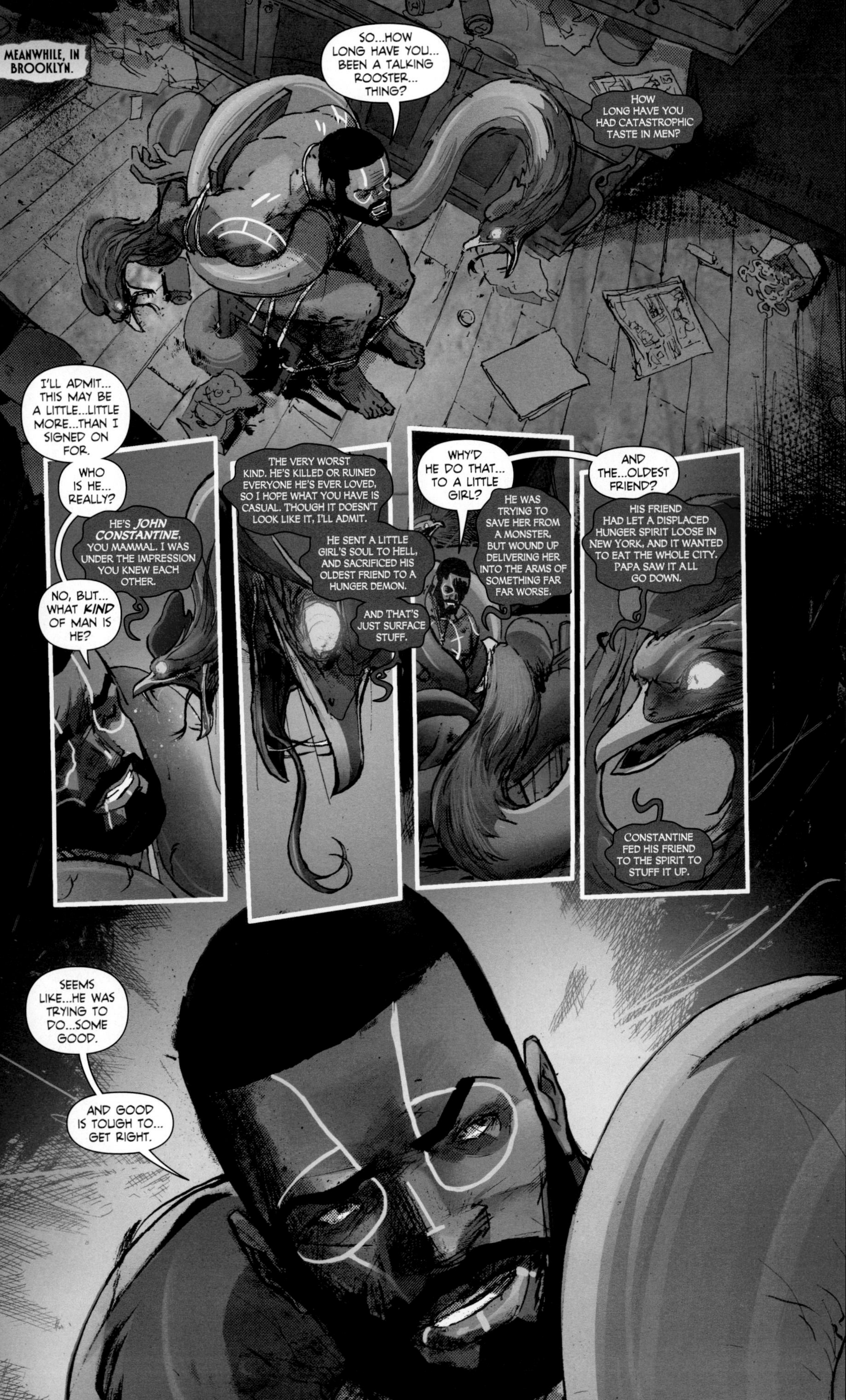

MEANWHILE, IN BROOKLYN.
SO...HOW LONG HAVE YOU... BEEN A TALKING ROOSTER... THING?
HOW LONG HAVE YOU HAD CATASTROPHIC TASTE IN MEN?
I'LL ADMIT... THIS MAY BE A LITTLE...LITTLE MORE...THAN I SIGNED ON FOR.
WHO IS HE... REALLY?
HE'S JOHN CONSTANTINE, YOU MAMMAL. I WAS UNDER THE IMPRESSION YOU KNEW EACH OTHER.
NO, BUT... WHAT KIND OF MAN IS HE?
THE VERY WORST KIND. HE'S KILLED OR RUINED EVERYONE HE'S EVER LOVED, SO I HOPE WHAT YOU HAVE IS CASUAL. THOUGH IT DOESN'T LOOK LIKE IT, I'LL ADMIT.
HE SENT A LITTLE GIRL'S SOUL TO HELL, AND SACRIFICED HIS OLDEST FRIEND TO A HUNGER DEMON.
AND THAT'S JUST SURFACE STUFF.
WHY'D HE DO THAT... TO A LITTLE GIRL?
HE WAS TRYING TO SAVE HER FROM A MONSTER, BUT WOUND UP DELIVERING HER INTO THE ARMS OF SOMETHING FAR FAR WORSE.
AND THE...OLDEST FRIEND?
HIS FRIEND HAD LET A DISPLACED HUNGER SPIRIT LOOSE IN NEW YORK, AND IT WANTED TO EAT THE WHOLE CITY. PAPA SAW IT ALL GO DOWN.
CONSTANTINE FED HIS FRIEND TO THE SPIRIT TO STUFF IT UP.
SEEMS LIKE...HE WAS TRYING TO DO...SOME GOOD.
AND GOOD IS TOUGH TO... GET RIGHT.

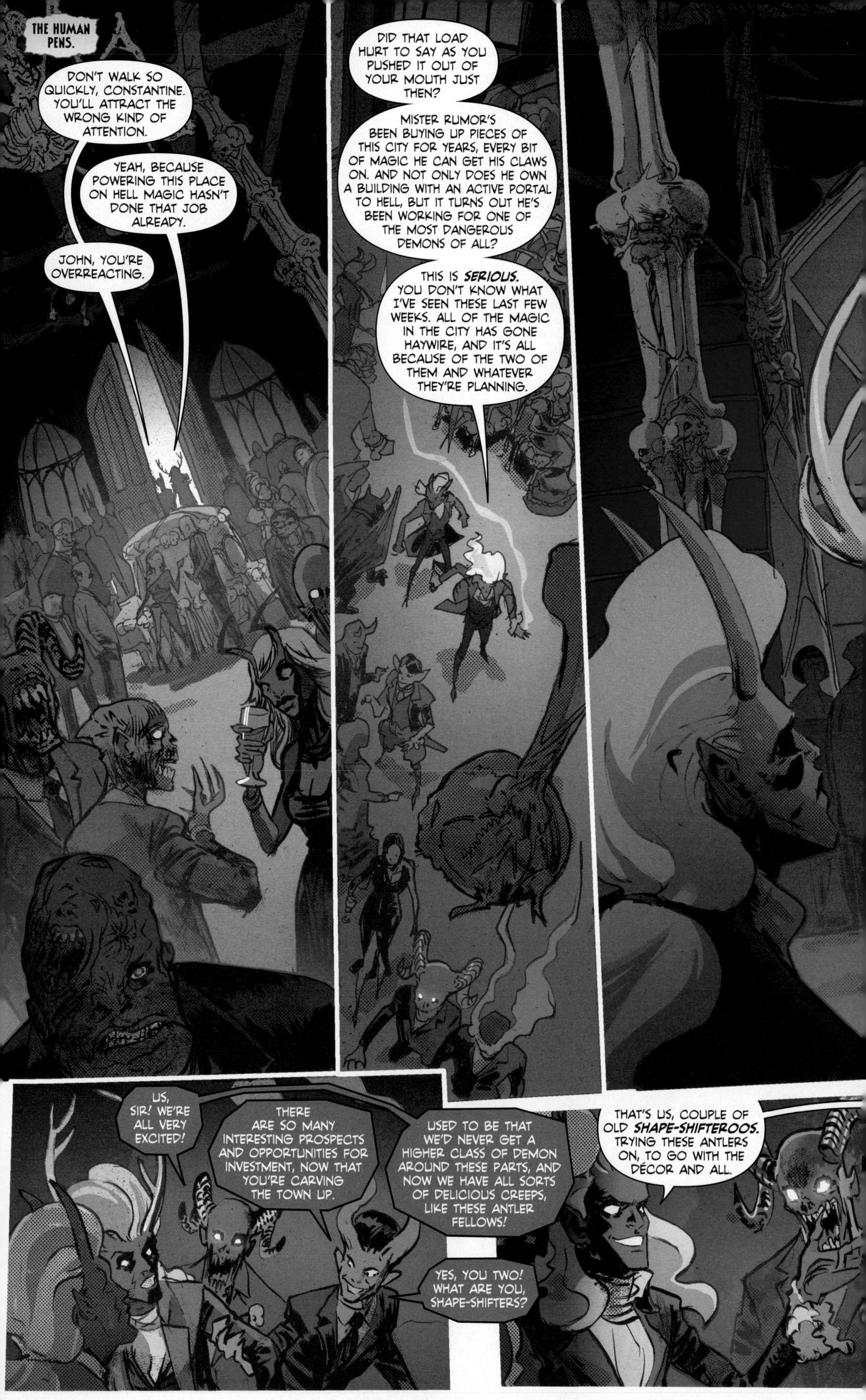
THE HUMAN PENS.
DON'T WALK SO QUICKLY, CONSTANTINE. YOU'LL ATTRACT THE WRONG KIND OF ATTENTION.
YEAH, BECAUSE POWERING THIS PLACE ON HELL MAGIC HASN'T DONE THAT JOB ALREADY.
JOHN, YOU'RE OVERREACTING.
DID THAT LOAD HURT TO SAY AS YOU PUSHED IT OUT OF YOUR MOUTH JUST THEN?
MISTER RUMOR'S BEEN BUYING UP PIECES OF THIS CITY FOR YEARS, EVERY BIT OF MAGIC HE CAN GET HIS CLAWS ON. AND NOT ONLY DOES HE OWN A BUILDING WITH AN ACTIVE PORTAL TO HELL, BUT IT TURNS OUT HE'S BEEN WORKING FOR ONE OF THE MOST DANGEROUS DEMONS OF ALL?
THIS IS ***SERIOUS.*** YOU DON'T KNOW WHAT I'VE SEEN THESE LAST FEW WEEKS. ALL OF THE MAGIC IN THE CITY HAS GONE HAYWIRE, AND IT'S ALL BECAUSE OF THE TWO OF THEM AND WHATEVER THEY'RE PLANNING.
US, SIR! WE'RE ALL VERY EXCITED!
THERE ARE SO MANY INTERESTING PROSPECTS AND OPPORTUNITIES FOR INVESTMENT, NOW THAT YOU'RE CARVING THE TOWN UP.
USED TO BE THAT WE'D NEVER GET A HIGHER CLASS OF DEMON AROUND THESE PARTS, AND NOW WE HAVE ALL SORTS OF DELICIOUS CREEPS, LIKE THESE ANTLER FELLOWS!
YES, YOU TWO! WHAT ARE YOU, SHAPE-SHIFTERS?
THAT'S US, COUPLE OF OLD ***SHAPE-SHIFTEROOS.*** TRYING THESE ANTLERS ON, TO GO WITH THE DÉCOR AND ALL.

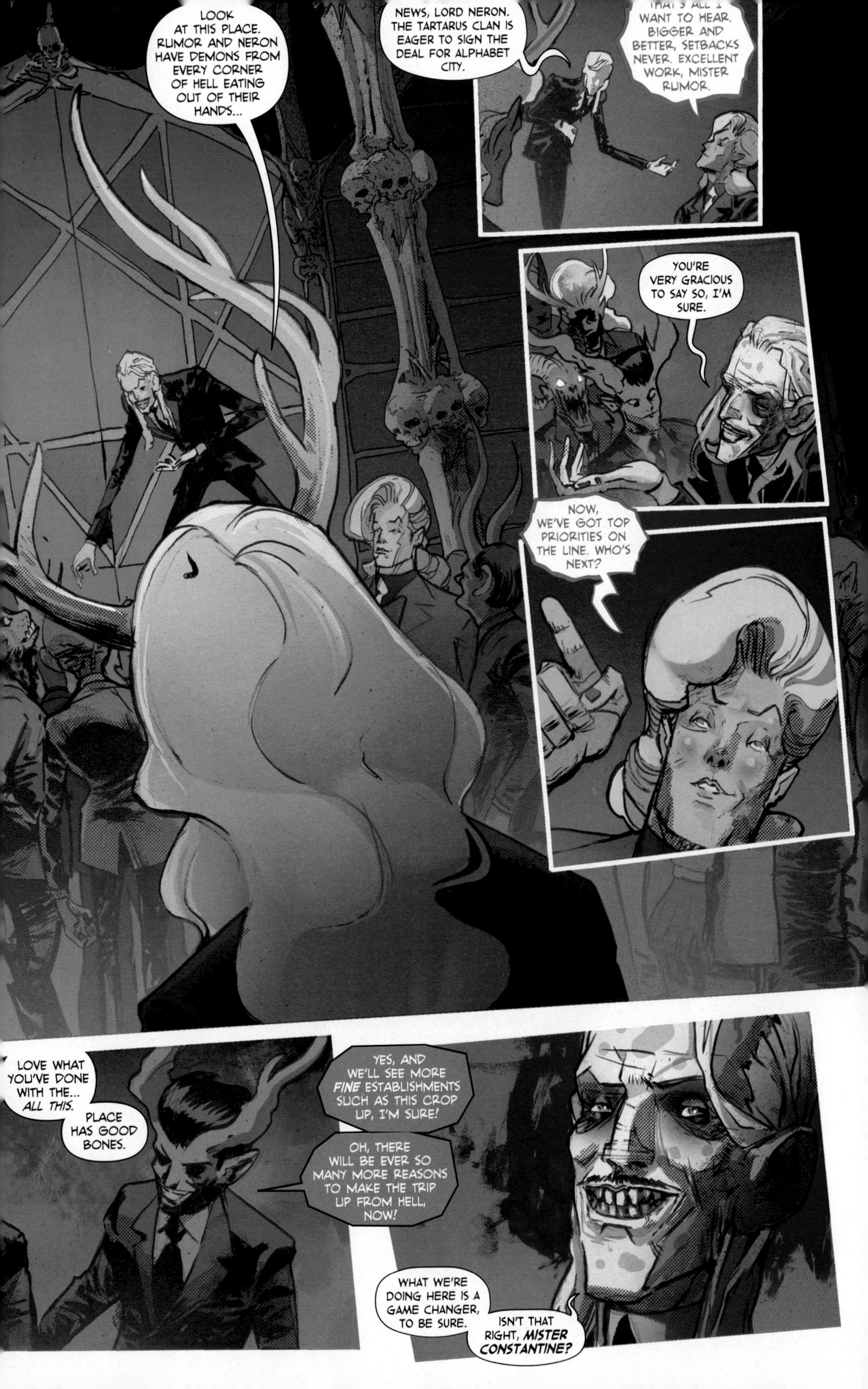
LOOK AT THIS PLACE. RUMOR AND NERON HAVE DEMONS FROM EVERY CORNER OF HELL EATING OUT OF THEIR HANDS...
NEWS, LORD NERON. THE TARTARUS CLAN IS EAGER TO SIGN THE DEAL FOR ALPHABET CITY.
THAT'S ALL I WANT TO HEAR. BIGGER AND BETTER, SETBACKS NEVER. EXCELLENT WORK, MISTER RUMOR.
YOU'RE VERY GRACIOUS TO SAY SO, I'M SURE.
NOW, WE'VE GOT TOP PRIORITIES ON THE LINE. WHO'S NEXT?
LOVE WHAT YOU'VE DONE WITH THE... *ALL THIS.*
PLACE HAS GOOD BONES.
YES, AND WE'LL SEE MORE *FINE* ESTABLISHMENTS SUCH AS THIS CROP UP, I'M SURE!
OH, THERE WILL BE EVER SO MANY MORE REASONS TO MAKE THE TRIP UP FROM HELL, NOW!
WHAT WE'RE DOING HERE IS A GAME CHANGER, TO BE SURE.
ISN'T THAT RIGHT, *MISTER CONSTANTINE?*

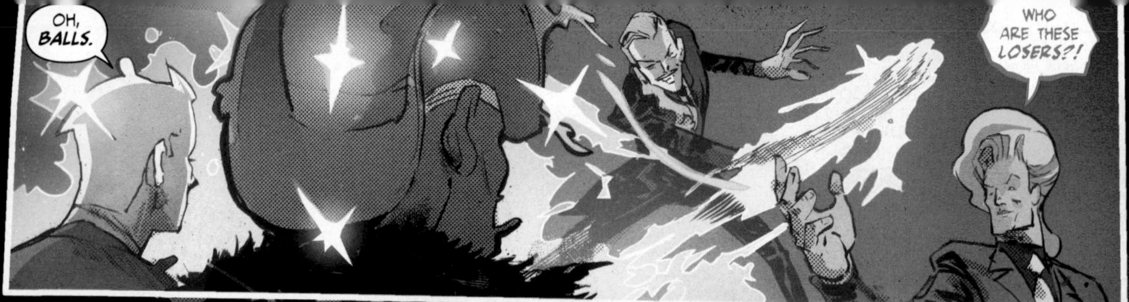
OH, BALLS.
WHO ARE THESE LOSERS?!

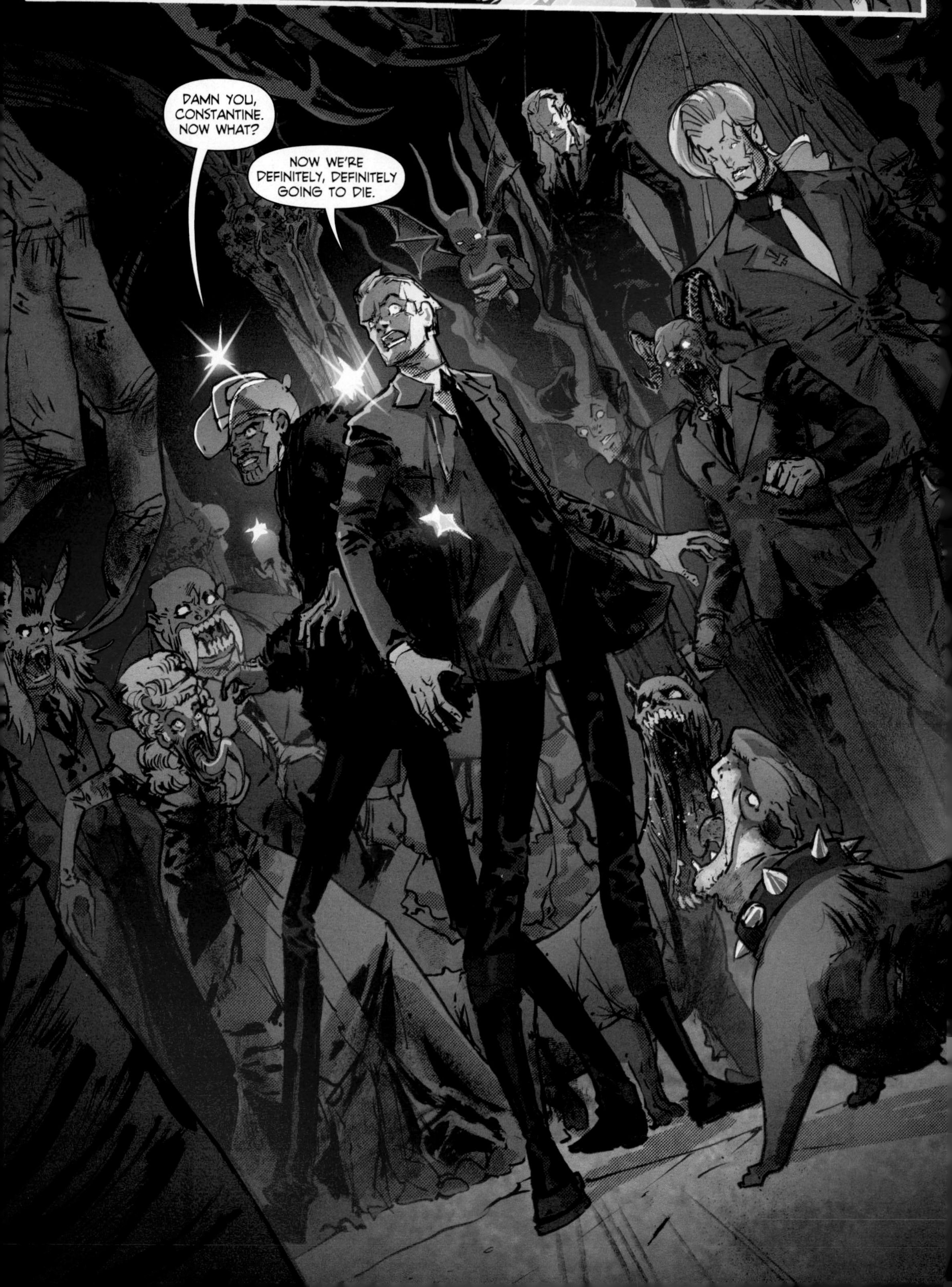
DAMN YOU, CONSTANTINE. NOW WHAT?
NOW WE'RE DEFINITELY, DEFINITELY GOING TO DIE.

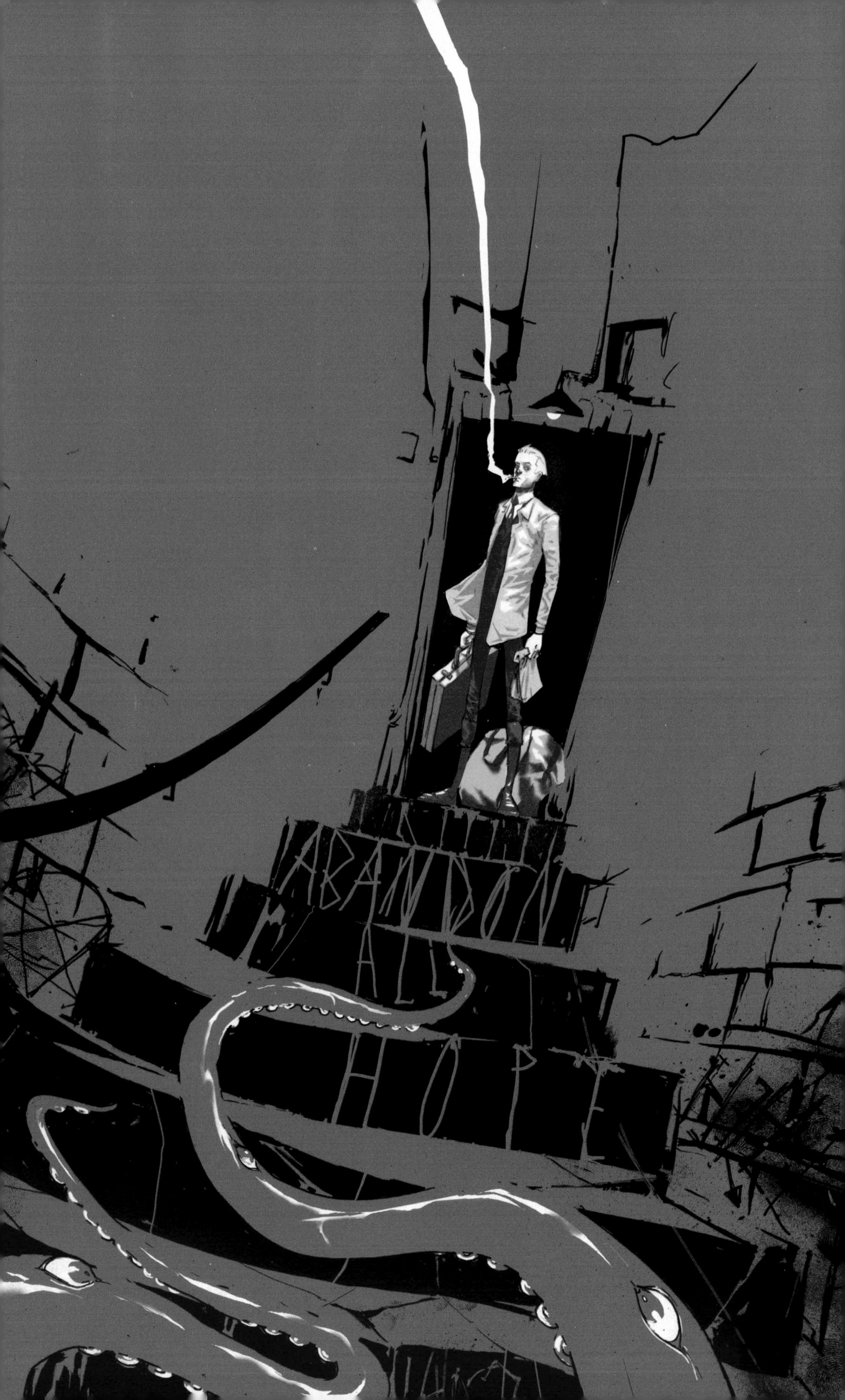
ABANDON ALL HOPE

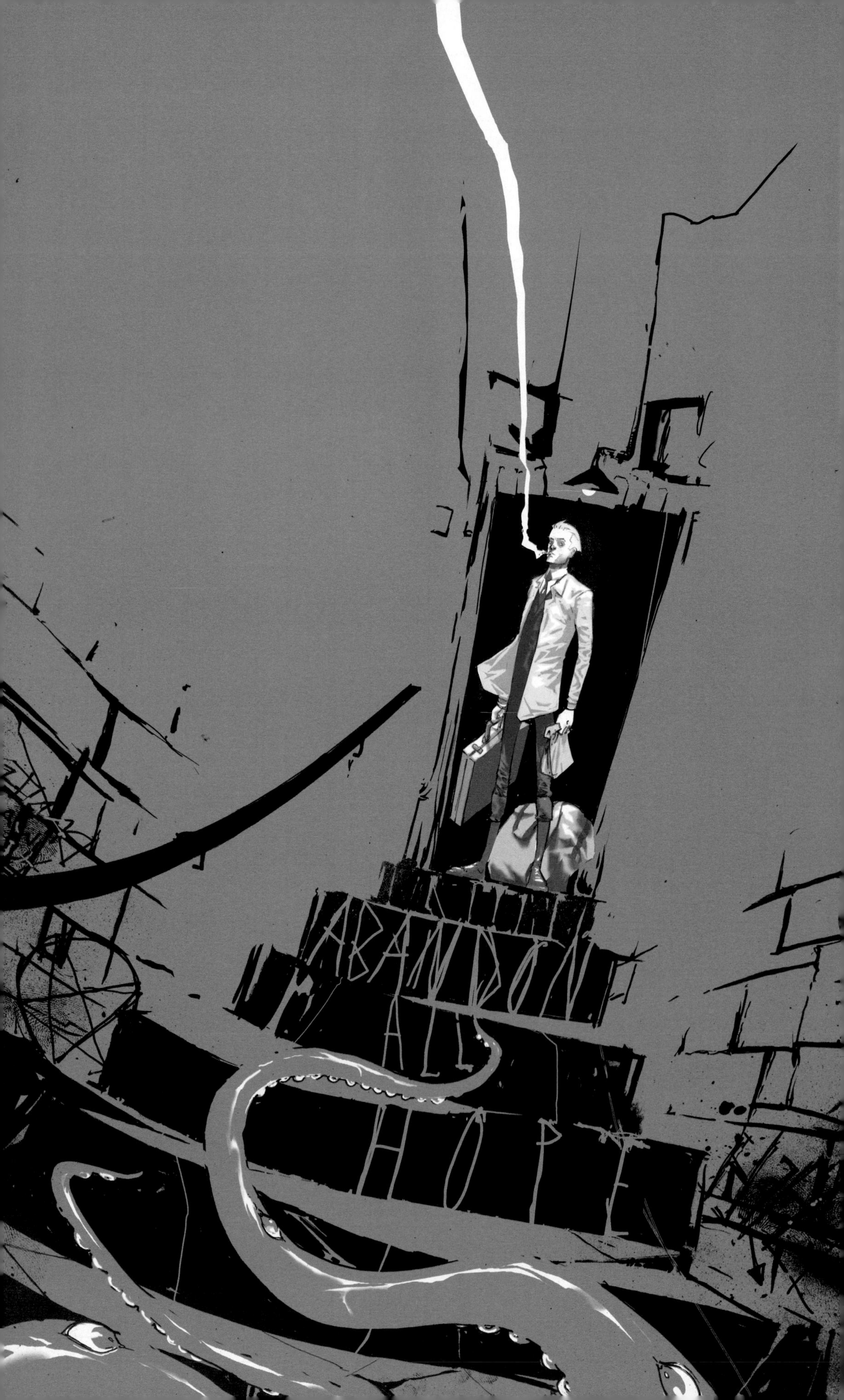
ABANDON
ALL
HOPE

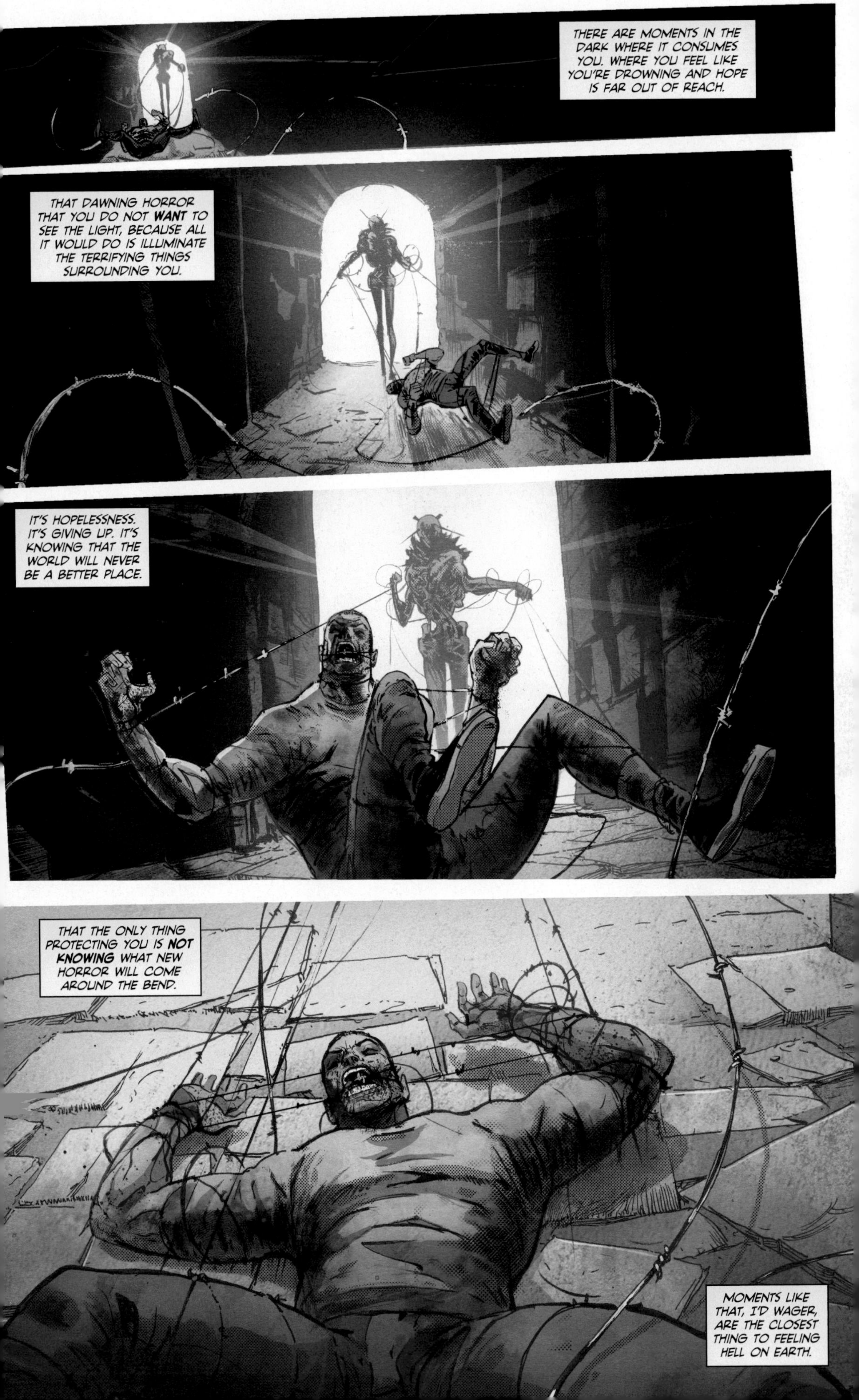
THERE ARE MOMENTS IN THE DARK WHERE IT CONSUMES YOU. WHERE YOU FEEL LIKE YOU'RE DROWNING AND HOPE IS FAR OUT OF REACH.
THAT DAWNING HORROR THAT YOU DO NOT **WANT** TO SEE THE LIGHT, BECAUSE ALL IT WOULD DO IS ILLUMINATE THE TERRIFYING THINGS SURROUNDING YOU.
IT'S HOPELESSNESS. IT'S GIVING UP. IT'S KNOWING THAT THE WORLD WILL NEVER BE A BETTER PLACE.
THAT THE ONLY THING PROTECTING YOU IS **NOT KNOWING** WHAT NEW HORROR WILL COME AROUND THE BEND.
MOMENTS LIKE THAT, I'D WAGER, ARE THE CLOSEST THING TO FEELING HELL ON EARTH.

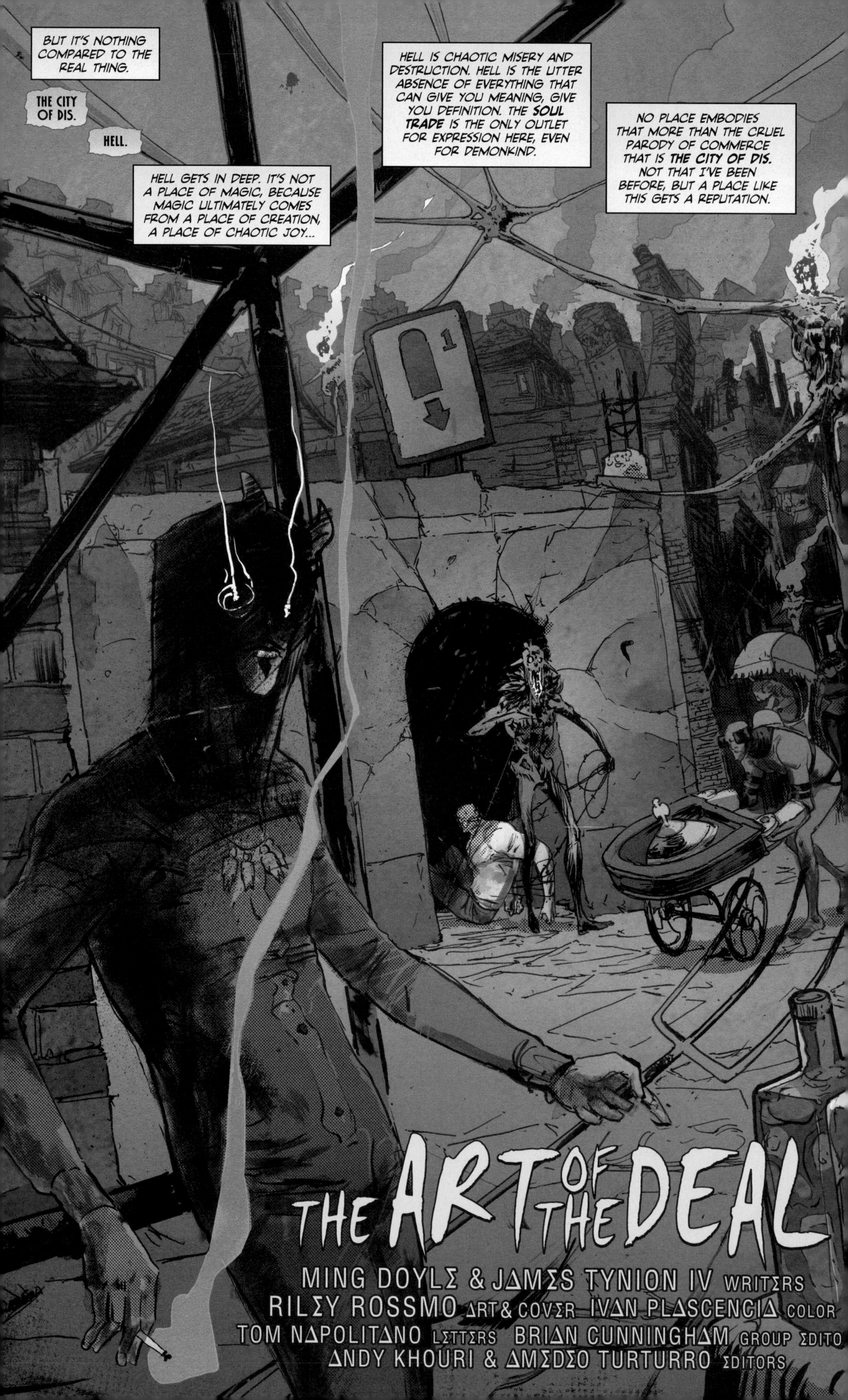
BUT IT'S NOTHING COMPARED TO THE REAL THING.
THE CITY OF DIS.
HELL.
HELL GETS IN DEEP. IT'S NOT A PLACE OF MAGIC, BECAUSE MAGIC ULTIMATELY COMES FROM A PLACE OF CREATION, A PLACE OF CHAOTIC JOY...
HELL IS CHAOTIC MISERY AND DESTRUCTION. HELL IS THE UTTER ABSENCE OF EVERYTHING THAT CAN GIVE YOU MEANING, GIVE YOU DEFINITION. THE SOUL TRADE IS THE ONLY OUTLET FOR EXPRESSION HERE, EVEN FOR DEMONKIND.
NO PLACE EMBODIES THAT MORE THAN THE CRUEL PARODY OF COMMERCE THAT IS THE CITY OF DIS. NOT THAT I'VE BEEN BEFORE, BUT A PLACE LIKE THIS GETS A REPUTATION.
1
THE ART OF THE DEAL
MING DOYLE & JAMES TYNION IV WRITERS
RILEY ROSSMO ART & COVER IVAN PLASCENCIA COLOR
TOM NAPOLITANO LETTERS BRIAN CUNNINGHAM GROUP EDITO
ANDY KHOURI & AMEDEO TURTURRO EDITORS

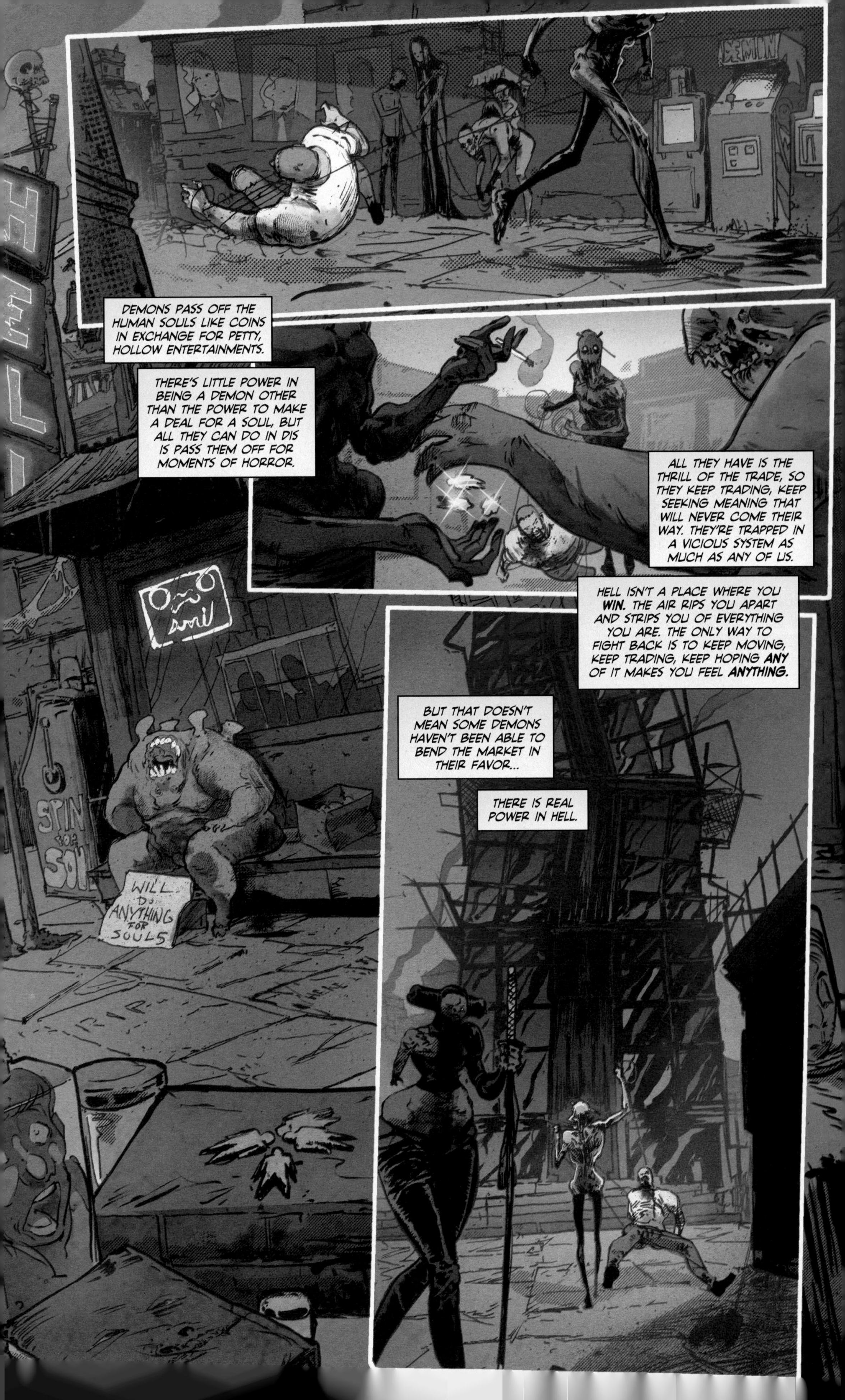
DEMONS PASS OFF THE HUMAN SOULS LIKE COINS IN EXCHANGE FOR PETTY, HOLLOW ENTERTAINMENTS.
THERE'S LITTLE POWER IN BEING A DEMON OTHER THAN THE POWER TO MAKE A DEAL FOR A SOUL, BUT ALL THEY CAN DO IN DIS IS PASS THEM OFF FOR MOMENTS OF HORROR.
ALL THEY HAVE IS THE THRILL OF THE TRADE, SO THEY KEEP TRADING, KEEP SEEKING MEANING THAT WILL NEVER COME THEIR WAY. THEY'RE TRAPPED IN A VICIOUS SYSTEM AS MUCH AS ANY OF US.
WILL DO ANYTHING FOR SOULS
HELL ISN'T A PLACE WHERE YOU **WIN.** THE AIR RIPS YOU APART AND STRIPS YOU OF EVERYTHING YOU ARE. THE ONLY WAY TO FIGHT BACK IS TO KEEP MOVING, KEEP TRADING, KEEP HOPING **ANY** OF IT MAKES YOU FEEL **ANYTHING.**
BUT THAT DOESN'T MEAN SOME DEMONS HAVEN'T BEEN ABLE TO BEND THE MARKET IN THEIR FAVOR...
THERE IS REAL POWER IN HELL.

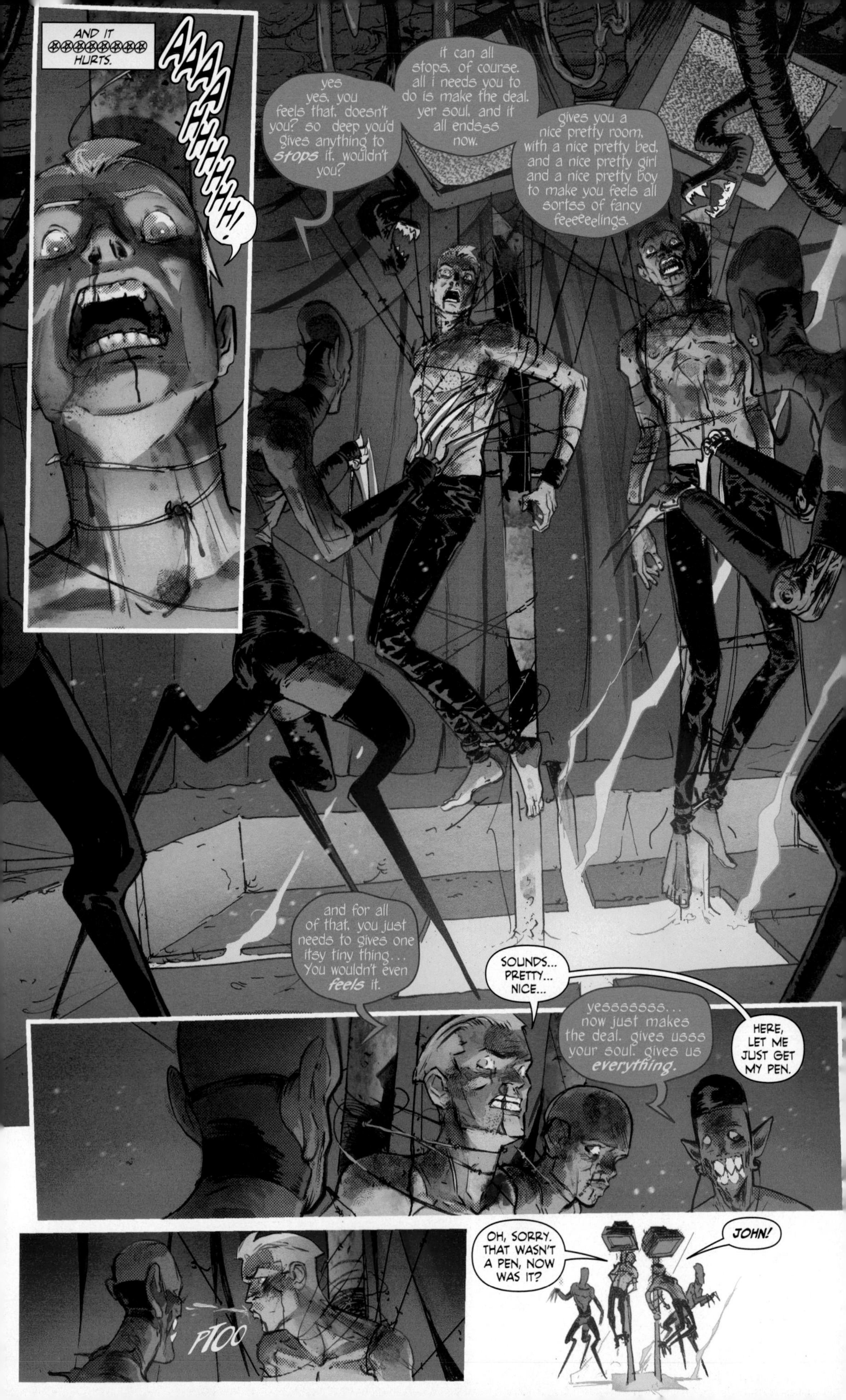
AND IT ✡✡✡✡✡✡✡✡ HURTS.
AAAAHHHHHH!
yes yes, you feels that, doesn't you? so deep you'd gives anything to stops it, wouldn't you?
it can all stops, of course. all i needs you to do is make the deal. yer soul, and it all endsss now.
gives you a nice pretty room, with a nice pretty bed, and a nice pretty girl and a nice pretty boy to make you feels all sortss of fancy feeeeeelings.
and for all of that, you just needs to gives one itsy tiny thing... You wouldn't even feels it.
SOUNDS... PRETTY... NICE...
yesssssss... now just makes the deal. gives usss your soul. gives us everything.
HERE, LET ME JUST GET MY PEN.
PTOO
OH, SORRY. THAT WASN'T A PEN, NOW WAS IT?
JOHN!

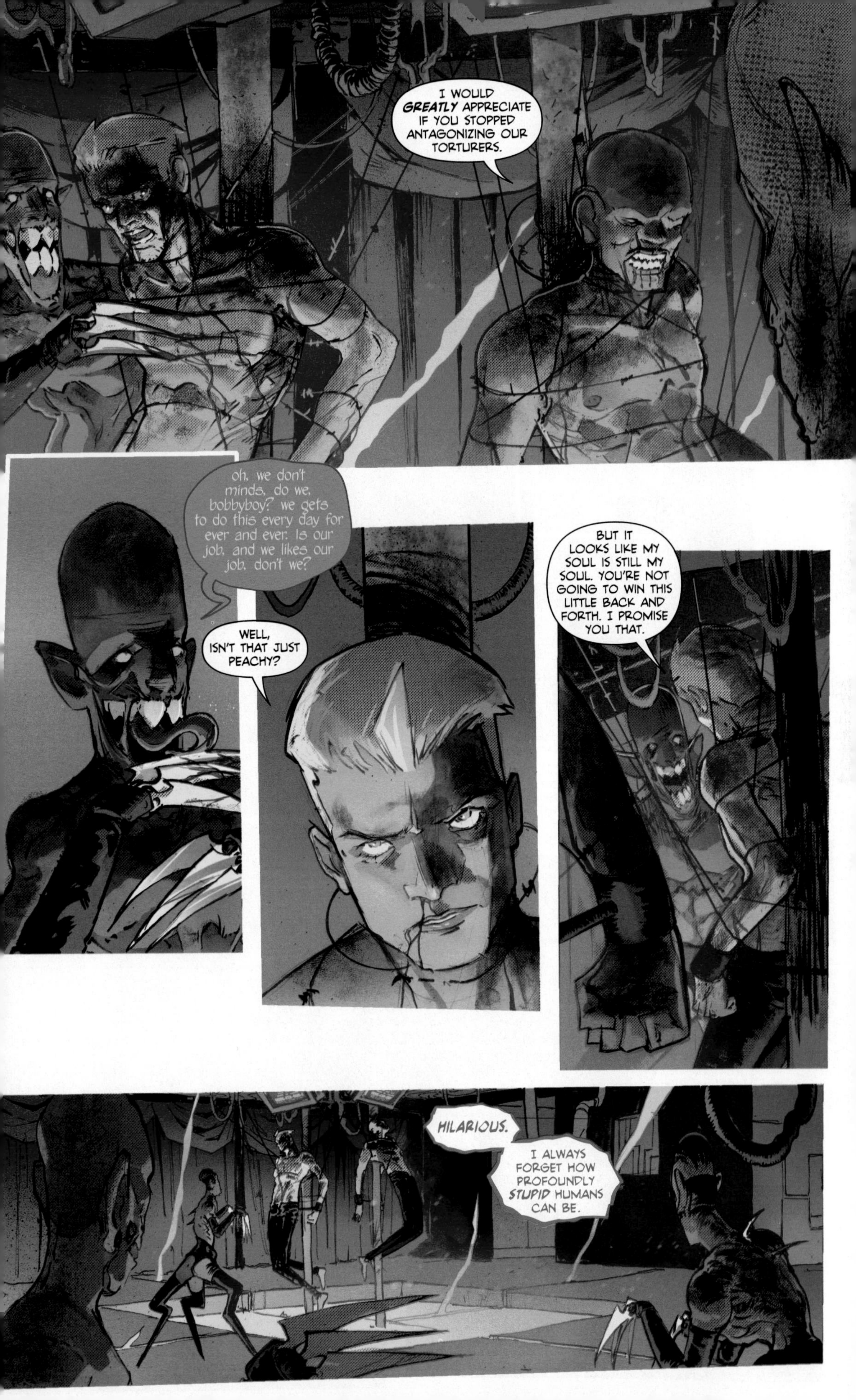
I WOULD GREATLY APPRECIATE IF YOU STOPPED ANTAGONIZING OUR TORTURERS.
oh, we don't minds, do we, bobbyboy? we gets to do this every day for ever and ever. Is our job, and we likes our job, don't we?
WELL, ISN'T THAT JUST PEACHY?
BUT IT LOOKS LIKE MY SOUL IS STILL MY SOUL. YOU'RE NOT GOING TO WIN THIS LITTLE BACK AND FORTH. I PROMISE YOU THAT.
HILARIOUS.
I ALWAYS FORGET HOW PROFOUNDLY STUPID HUMANS CAN BE.

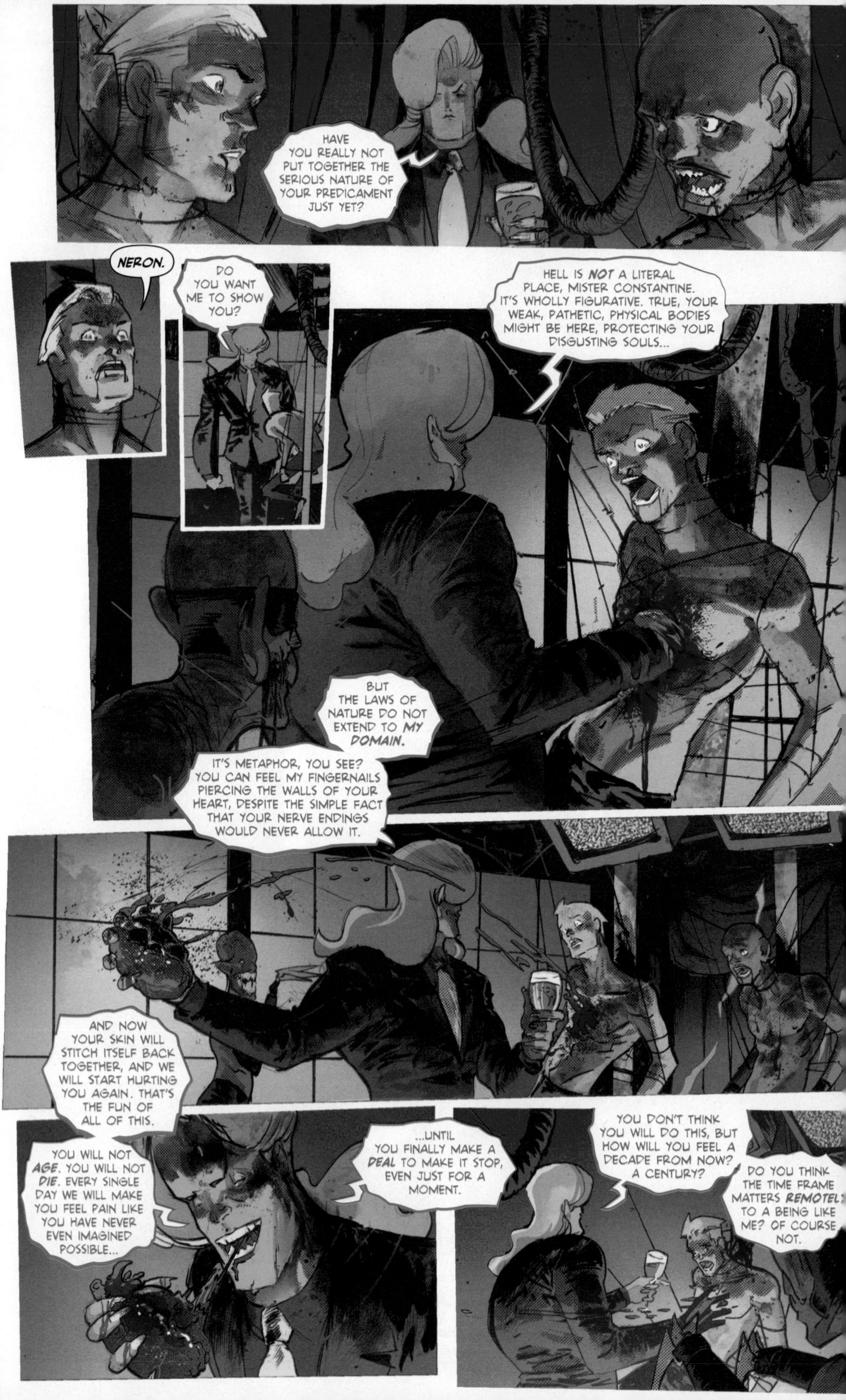
HAVE YOU REALLY NOT PUT TOGETHER THE SERIOUS NATURE OF YOUR PREDICAMENT JUST YET?
NERON.
DO YOU WANT ME TO SHOW YOU?
HELL IS NOT A LITERAL PLACE, MISTER CONSTANTINE. IT'S WHOLLY FIGURATIVE. TRUE, YOUR WEAK, PATHETIC, PHYSICAL BODIES MIGHT BE HERE, PROTECTING YOUR DISGUSTING SOULS...
BUT THE LAWS OF NATURE DO NOT EXTEND TO MY DOMAIN.
IT'S METAPHOR, YOU SEE? YOU CAN FEEL MY FINGERNAILS PIERCING THE WALLS OF YOUR HEART, DESPITE THE SIMPLE FACT THAT YOUR NERVE ENDINGS WOULD NEVER ALLOW IT.
AND NOW YOUR SKIN WILL STITCH ITSELF BACK TOGETHER, AND WE WILL START HURTING YOU AGAIN. THAT'S THE FUN OF ALL OF THIS.
YOU WILL NOT AGE. YOU WILL NOT DIE. EVERY SINGLE DAY WE WILL MAKE YOU FEEL PAIN LIKE YOU HAVE NEVER EVEN IMAGINED POSSIBLE...
...UNTIL YOU FINALLY MAKE A DEAL TO MAKE IT STOP, EVEN JUST FOR A MOMENT.
YOU DON'T THINK YOU WILL DO THIS, BUT HOW WILL YOU FEEL A DECADE FROM NOW? A CENTURY?
DO YOU THINK THE TIME FRAME MATTERS REMOTELY TO A BEING LIKE ME? OF COURSE NOT.

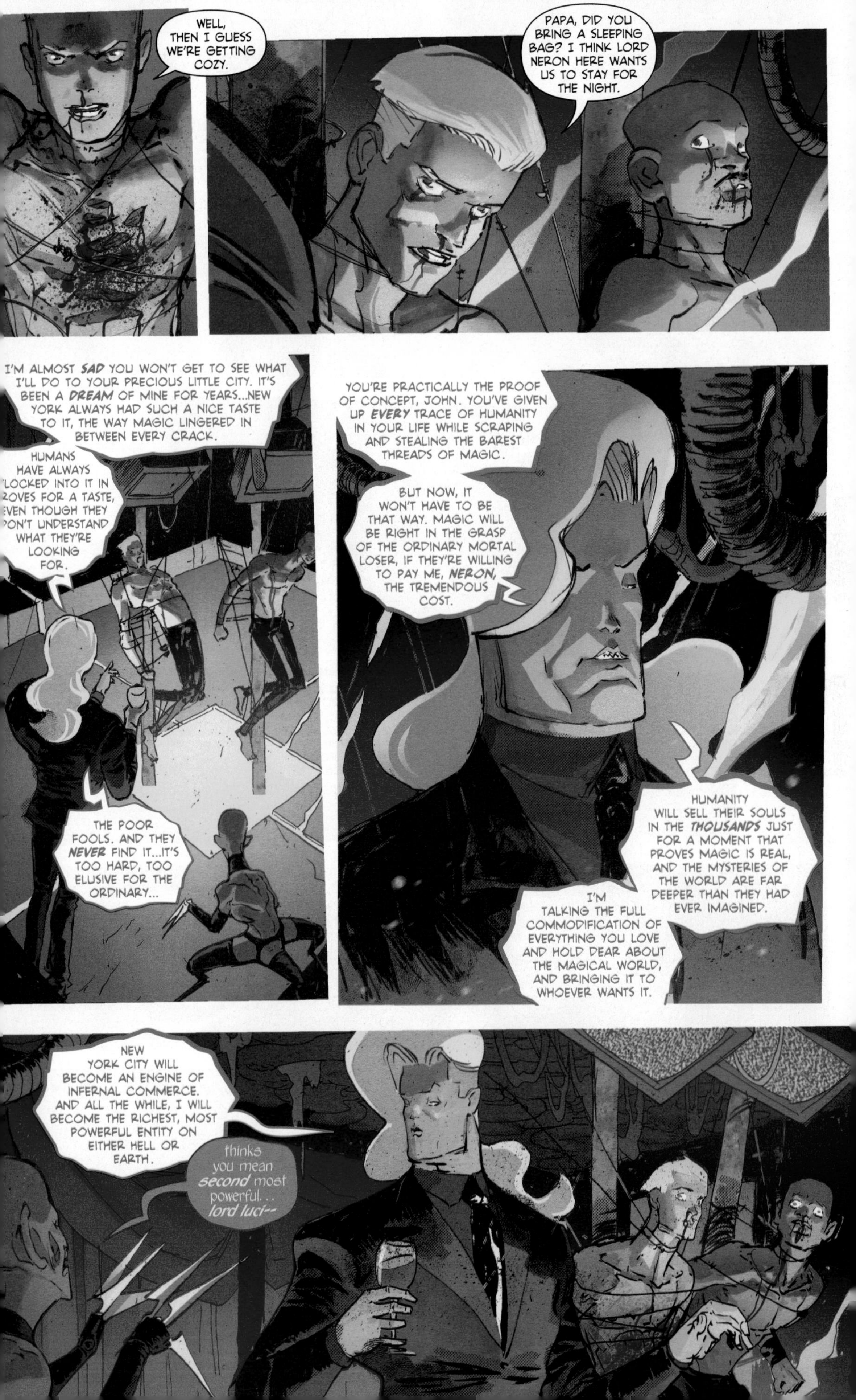

WELL, THEN I GUESS WE'RE GETTING COZY.
PAPA, DID YOU BRING A SLEEPING BAG? I THINK LORD NERON HERE WANTS US TO STAY FOR THE NIGHT.
I'M ALMOST SAD YOU WON'T GET TO SEE WHAT I'LL DO TO YOUR PRECIOUS LITTLE CITY. IT'S BEEN A DREAM OF MINE FOR YEARS...NEW YORK ALWAYS HAD SUCH A NICE TASTE TO IT, THE WAY MAGIC LINGERED IN BETWEEN EVERY CRACK.
HUMANS HAVE ALWAYS FLOCKED INTO IT IN DROVES FOR A TASTE, EVEN THOUGH THEY DON'T UNDERSTAND WHAT THEY'RE LOOKING FOR.
THE POOR FOOLS. AND THEY NEVER FIND IT...IT'S TOO HARD, TOO ELUSIVE FOR THE ORDINARY...
YOU'RE PRACTICALLY THE PROOF OF CONCEPT, JOHN. YOU'VE GIVEN UP EVERY TRACE OF HUMANITY IN YOUR LIFE WHILE SCRAPING AND STEALING THE BAREST THREADS OF MAGIC.
BUT NOW, IT WON'T HAVE TO BE THAT WAY. MAGIC WILL BE RIGHT IN THE GRASP OF THE ORDINARY MORTAL LOSER, IF THEY'RE WILLING TO PAY ME, NERON, THE TREMENDOUS COST.
HUMANITY WILL SELL THEIR SOULS IN THE THOUSANDS JUST FOR A MOMENT THAT PROVES MAGIC IS REAL, AND THE MYSTERIES OF THE WORLD ARE FAR DEEPER THAN THEY HAD EVER IMAGINED.
I'M TALKING THE FULL COMMODIFICATION OF EVERYTHING YOU LOVE AND HOLD DEAR ABOUT THE MAGICAL WORLD, AND BRINGING IT TO WHOEVER WANTS IT.
NEW YORK CITY WILL BECOME AN ENGINE OF INFERNAL COMMERCE. AND ALL THE WHILE, I WILL BECOME THE RICHEST, MOST POWERFUL ENTITY ON EITHER HELL OR EARTH.
thinks you mean second most powerful... lord luci--

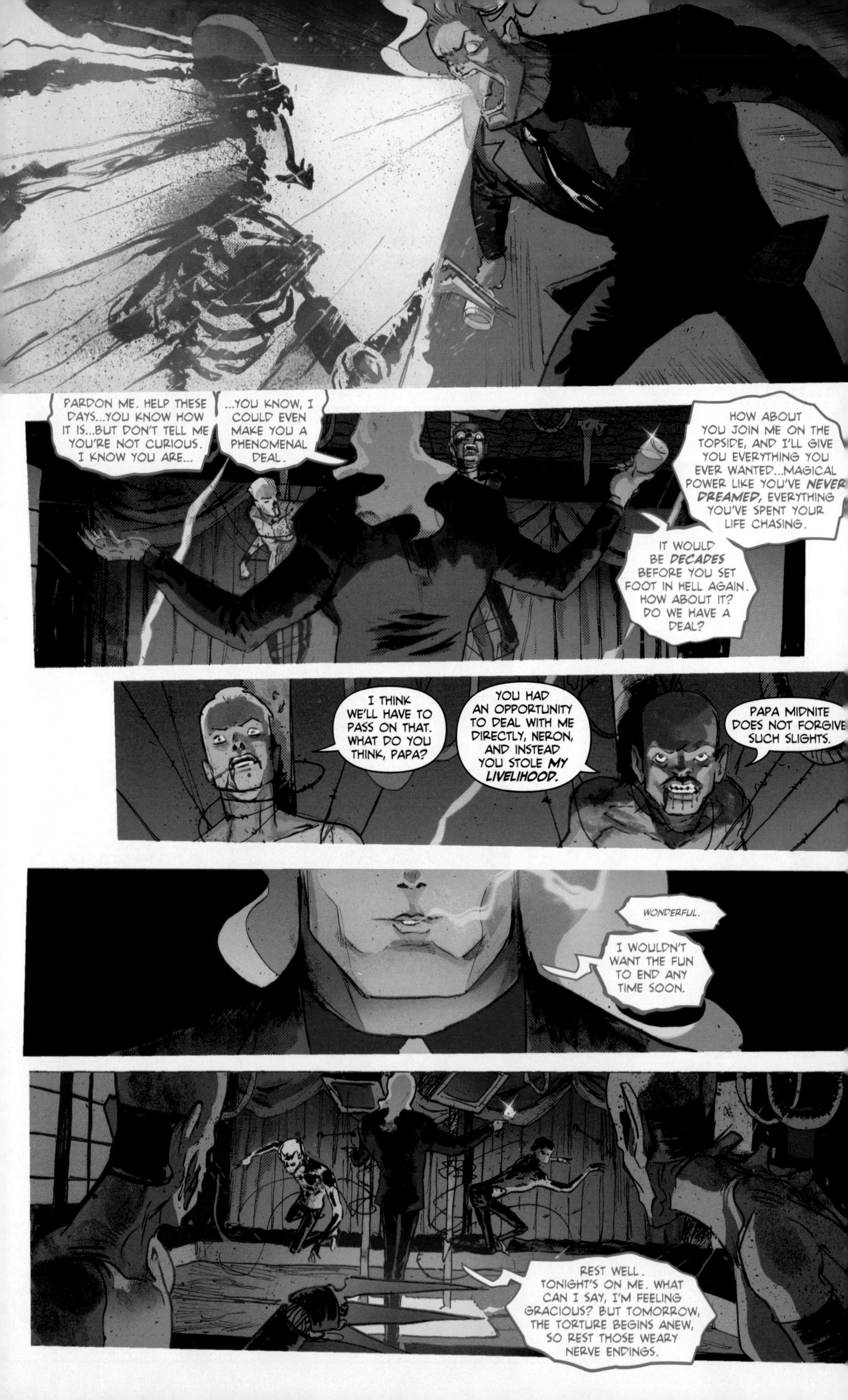
PARDON ME. HELP THESE DAYS...YOU KNOW HOW IT IS...BUT DON'T TELL ME YOU'RE NOT CURIOUS. I KNOW YOU ARE...
...YOU KNOW, I COULD EVEN MAKE YOU A PHENOMENAL DEAL.
HOW ABOUT YOU JOIN ME ON THE TOPSIDE, AND I'LL GIVE YOU EVERYTHING YOU EVER WANTED...MAGICAL POWER LIKE YOU'VE NEVER DREAMED, EVERYTHING YOU'VE SPENT YOUR LIFE CHASING.
IT WOULD BE DECADES BEFORE YOU SET FOOT IN HELL AGAIN. HOW ABOUT IT? DO WE HAVE A DEAL?
I THINK WE'LL HAVE TO PASS ON THAT. WHAT DO YOU THINK, PAPA?
YOU HAD AN OPPORTUNITY TO DEAL WITH ME DIRECTLY, NERON, AND INSTEAD YOU STOLE MY LIVELIHOOD.
PAPA MIDNITE DOES NOT FORGIVE SUCH SLIGHTS.
WONDERFUL.
I WOULDN'T WANT THE FUN TO END ANY TIME SOON.
REST WELL. TONIGHT'S ON ME. WHAT CAN I SAY, I'M FEELING GRACIOUS? BUT TOMORROW, THE TORTURE BEGINS ANEW, SO REST THOSE WEARY NERVE ENDINGS.

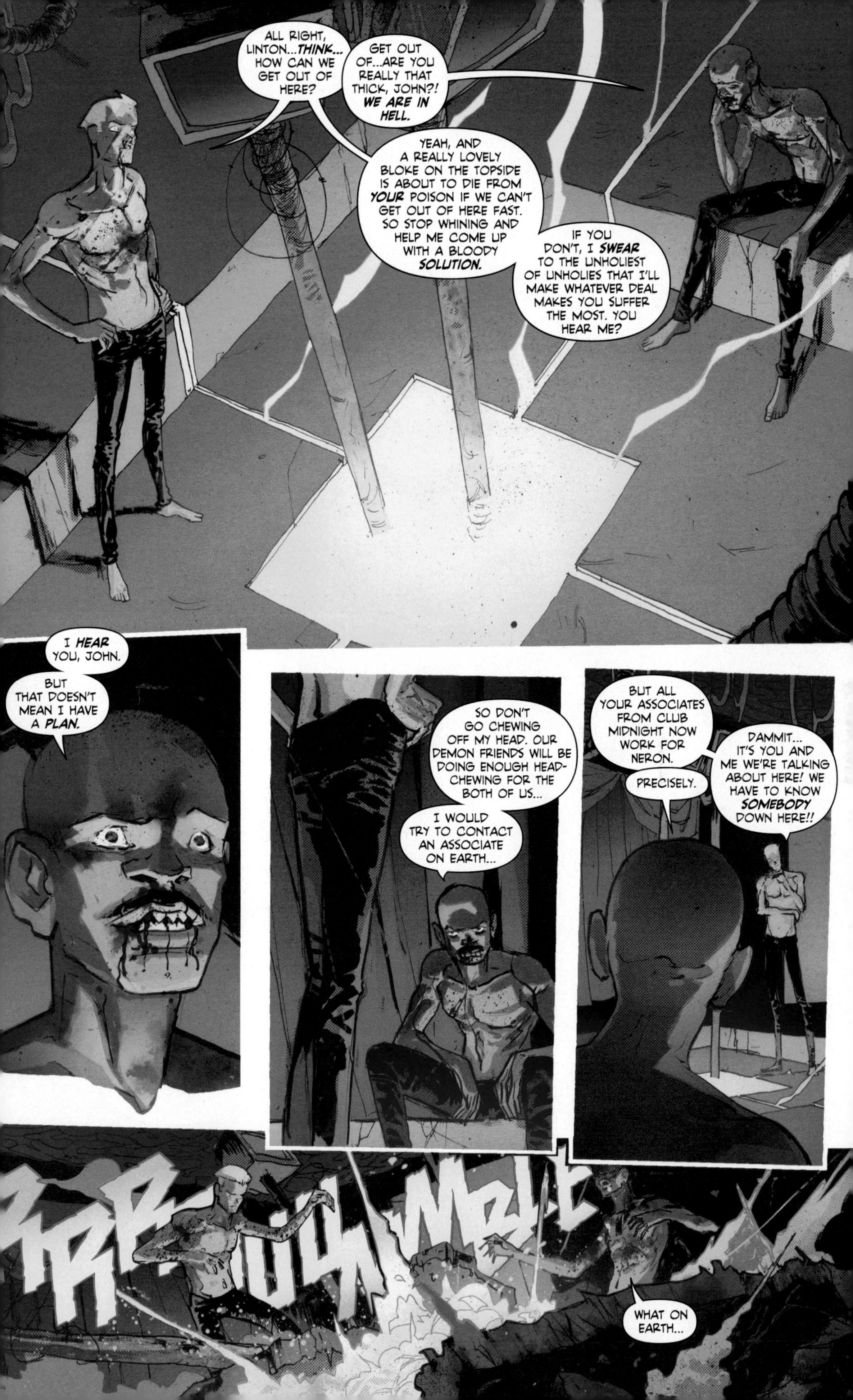
ALL RIGHT, LINTON...THINK... HOW CAN WE GET OUT OF HERE?
GET OUT OF...ARE YOU REALLY THAT THICK, JOHN?! WE ARE IN HELL.
YEAH, AND A REALLY LOVELY BLOKE ON THE TOPSIDE IS ABOUT TO DIE FROM YOUR POISON IF WE CAN'T GET OUT OF HERE FAST. SO STOP WHINING AND HELP ME COME UP WITH A BLOODY SOLUTION.
IF YOU DON'T, I SWEAR TO THE UNHOLIEST OF UNHOLIES THAT I'LL MAKE WHATEVER DEAL MAKES YOU SUFFER THE MOST. YOU HEAR ME?
I HEAR YOU, JOHN.
BUT THAT DOESN'T MEAN I HAVE A PLAN.
SO DON'T GO CHEWING OFF MY HEAD. OUR DEMON FRIENDS WILL BE DOING ENOUGH HEAD-CHEWING FOR THE BOTH OF US...
I WOULD TRY TO CONTACT AN ASSOCIATE ON EARTH...
BUT ALL YOUR ASSOCIATES FROM CLUB MIDNIGHT NOW WORK FOR NERON.
PRECISELY.
DAMMIT... IT'S YOU AND ME WE'RE TALKING ABOUT HERE! WE HAVE TO KNOW SOMEBODY DOWN HERE!!
WHAT ON EARTH...

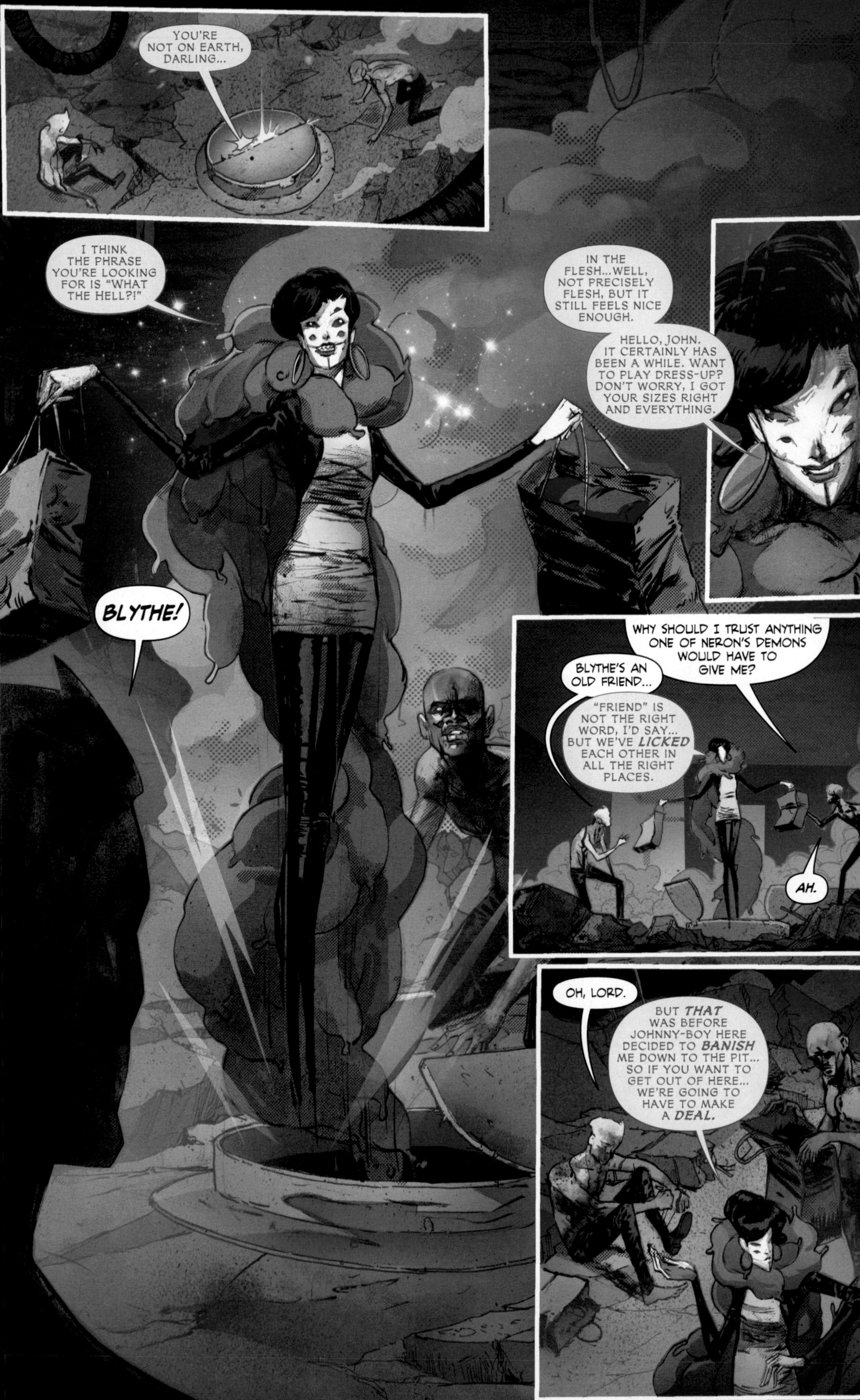

YOU'RE NOT ON EARTH, DARLING...
I THINK THE PHRASE YOU'RE LOOKING FOR IS "WHAT THE HELL?!"
BLYTHE!
IN THE FLESH...WELL, NOT PRECISELY FLESH, BUT IT STILL FEELS NICE ENOUGH.
HELLO, JOHN. IT CERTAINLY HAS BEEN A WHILE. WANT TO PLAY DRESS-UP? DON'T WORRY, I GOT YOUR SIZES RIGHT AND EVERYTHING.
WHY SHOULD I TRUST ANYTHING ONE OF NERON'S DEMONS WOULD HAVE TO GIVE ME?
BLYTHE'S AN OLD FRIEND...
"FRIEND" IS NOT THE RIGHT WORD, I'D SAY... BUT WE'VE LICKED EACH OTHER IN ALL THE RIGHT PLACES.
AH.
OH, LORD.
BUT THAT WAS BEFORE JOHNNY-BOY HERE DECIDED TO BANISH ME DOWN TO THE PIT... SO IF YOU WANT TO GET OUT OF HERE... WE'RE GOING TO HAVE TO MAKE A DEAL.

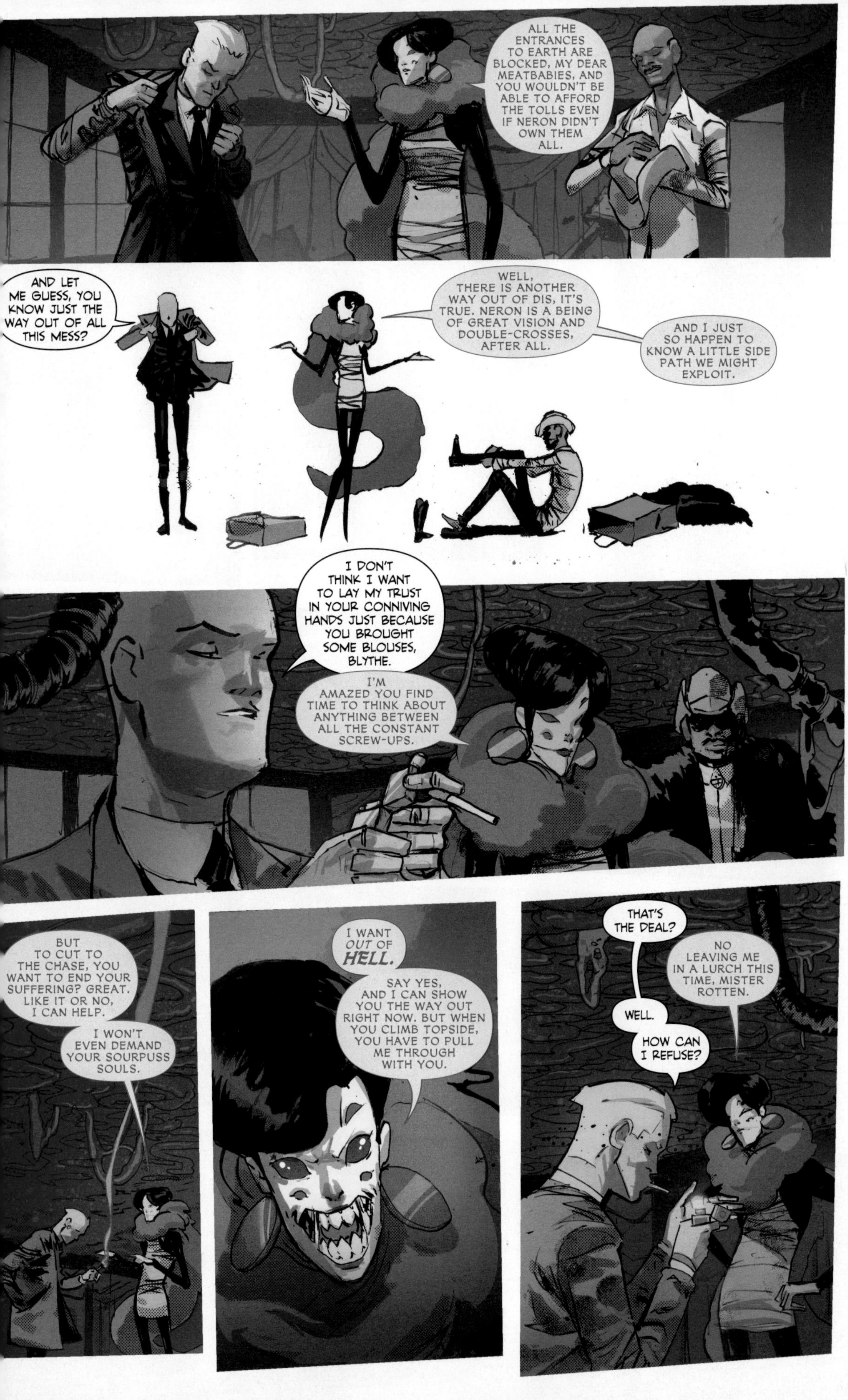
ALL THE ENTRANCES TO EARTH ARE BLOCKED, MY DEAR MEATBABIES, AND YOU WOULDN'T BE ABLE TO AFFORD THE TOLLS EVEN IF NERON DIDN'T OWN THEM ALL.
AND LET ME GUESS, YOU KNOW JUST THE WAY OUT OF ALL THIS MESS?
WELL, THERE IS ANOTHER WAY OUT OF DIS, IT'S TRUE. NERON IS A BEING OF GREAT VISION AND DOUBLE-CROSSES, AFTER ALL.
AND I JUST SO HAPPEN TO KNOW A LITTLE SIDE PATH WE MIGHT EXPLOIT.
I DON'T THINK I WANT TO LAY MY TRUST IN YOUR CONNIVING HANDS JUST BECAUSE YOU BROUGHT SOME BLOUSES, BLYTHE.
I'M AMAZED YOU FIND TIME TO THINK ABOUT ANYTHING BETWEEN ALL THE CONSTANT SCREW-UPS.
BUT TO CUT TO THE CHASE, YOU WANT TO END YOUR SUFFERING? GREAT. LIKE IT OR NO, I CAN HELP.
I WON'T EVEN DEMAND YOUR SOURPUSS SOULS.
I WANT *OUT* OF **HELL.**
SAY YES, AND I CAN SHOW YOU THE WAY OUT RIGHT NOW. BUT WHEN YOU CLIMB TOPSIDE, YOU HAVE TO PULL ME THROUGH WITH YOU.
THAT'S THE DEAL?
NO LEAVING ME IN A LURCH THIS TIME, MISTER ROTTEN.
WELL.
HOW CAN I REFUSE?

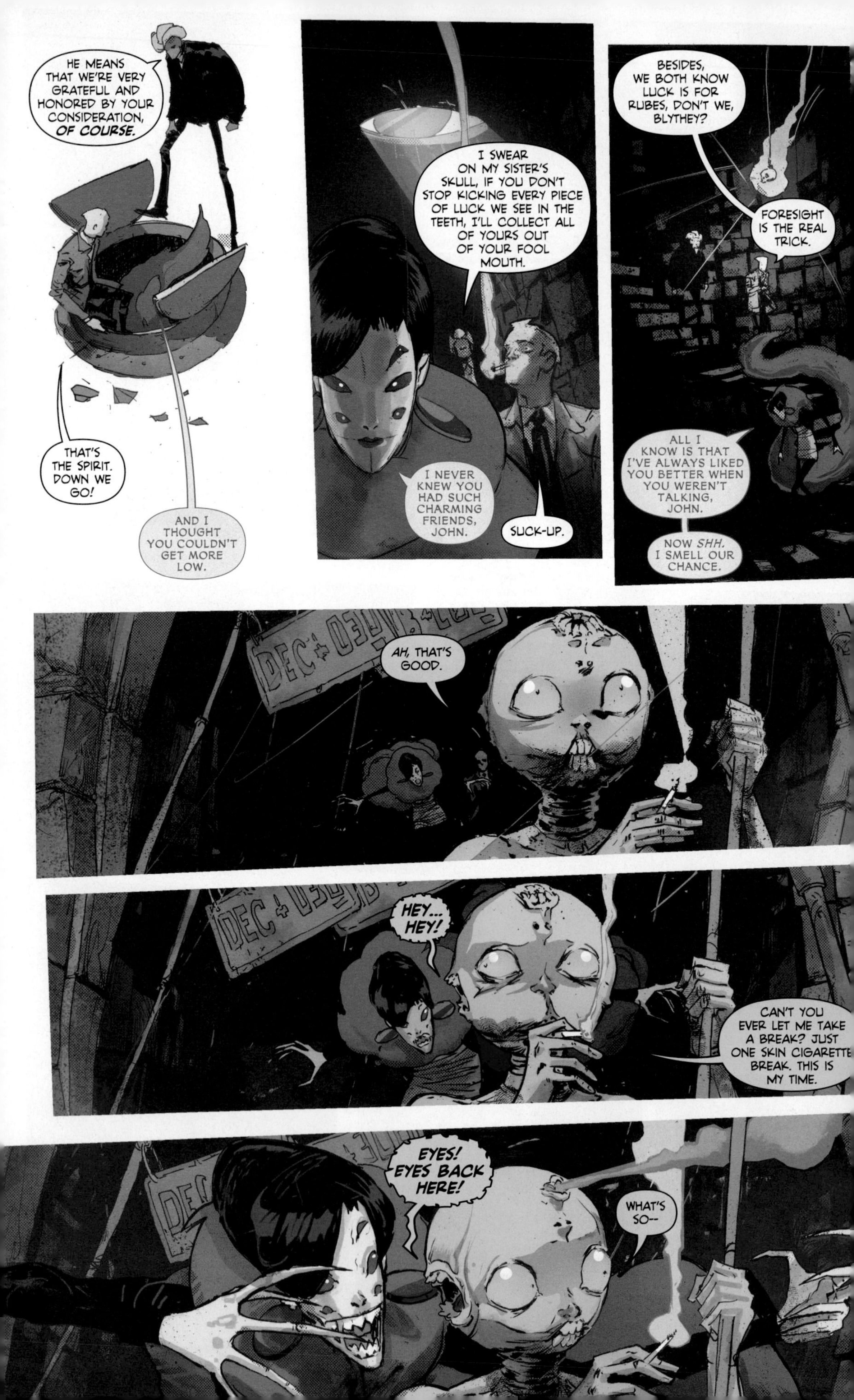
HE MEANS THAT WE'RE VERY GRATEFUL AND HONORED BY YOUR CONSIDERATION, OF COURSE.
THAT'S THE SPIRIT. DOWN WE GO!
AND I THOUGHT YOU COULDN'T GET MORE LOW.
I SWEAR ON MY SISTER'S SKULL, IF YOU DON'T STOP KICKING EVERY PIECE OF LUCK WE SEE IN THE TEETH, I'LL COLLECT ALL OF YOURS OUT OF YOUR FOOL MOUTH.
I NEVER KNEW YOU HAD SUCH CHARMING FRIENDS, JOHN.
SUCK-UP.
BESIDES, WE BOTH KNOW LUCK IS FOR RUBES, DON'T WE, BLYTHEY?
FORESIGHT IS THE REAL TRICK.
ALL I KNOW IS THAT I'VE ALWAYS LIKED YOU BETTER WHEN YOU WEREN'T TALKING, JOHN.
NOW SHH. I SMELL OUR CHANCE.
AH, THAT'S GOOD.
HEY... HEY!
CAN'T YOU EVER LET ME TAKE A BREAK? JUST ONE SKIN CIGARETTE BREAK. THIS IS MY TIME.
EYES! EYES BACK HERE!
WHAT'S SO--

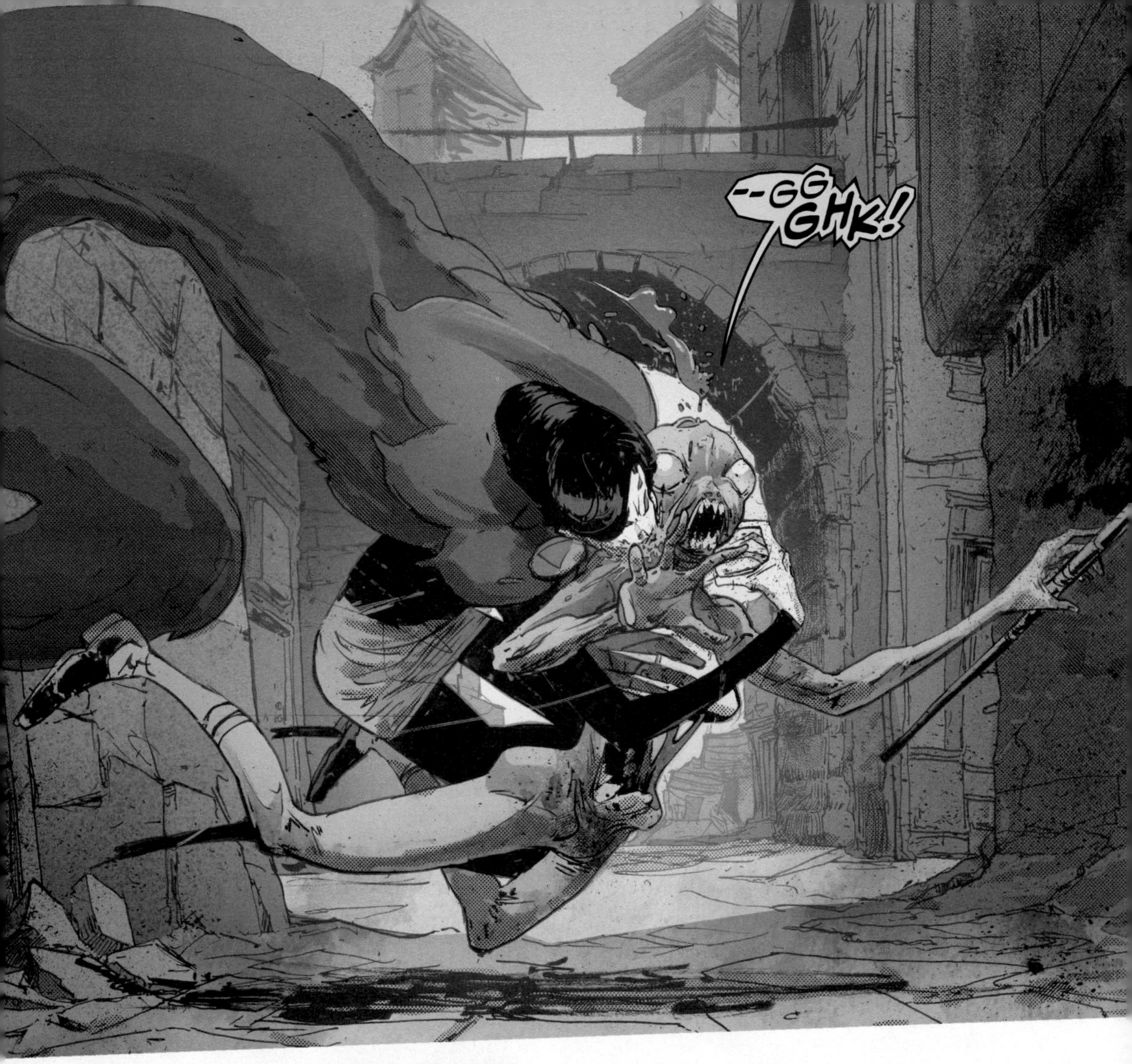
--GG GHK!

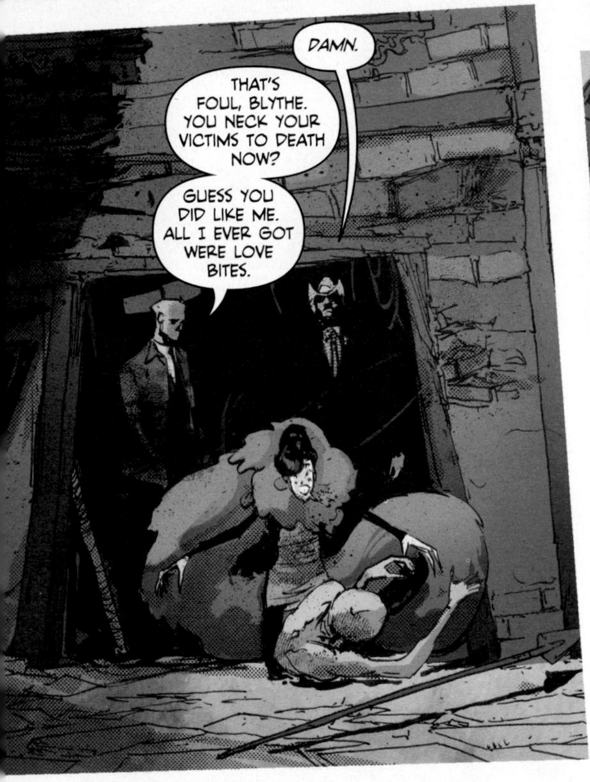
THAT'S FOUL, BLYTHE. YOU NECK YOUR VICTIMS TO DEATH NOW?
GUESS YOU DID LIKE ME. ALL I EVER GOT WERE LOVE BITES.
DAMN.

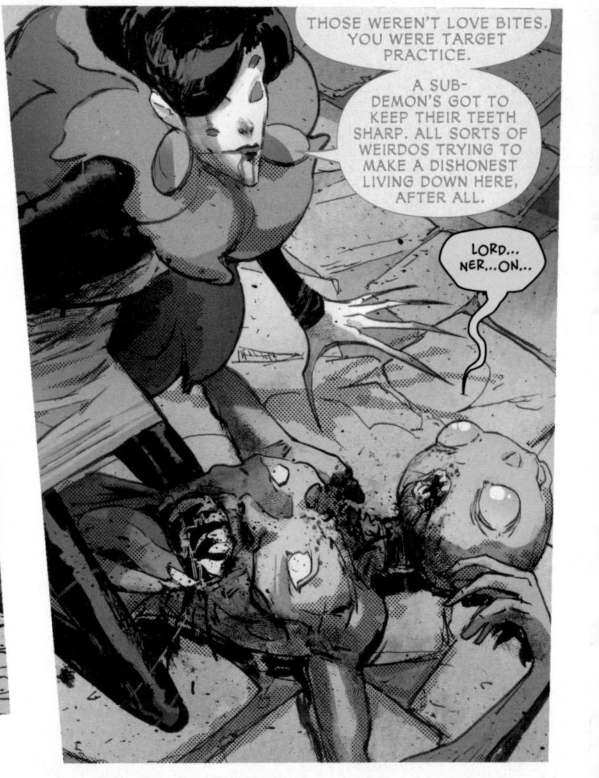
THOSE WEREN'T LOVE BITES. YOU WERE TARGET PRACTICE.
A SUB-DEMON'S GOT TO KEEP THEIR TEETH SHARP. ALL SORTS OF WEIRDOS TRYING TO MAKE A DISHONEST LIVING DOWN HERE, AFTER ALL.
LORD... NER...ON...

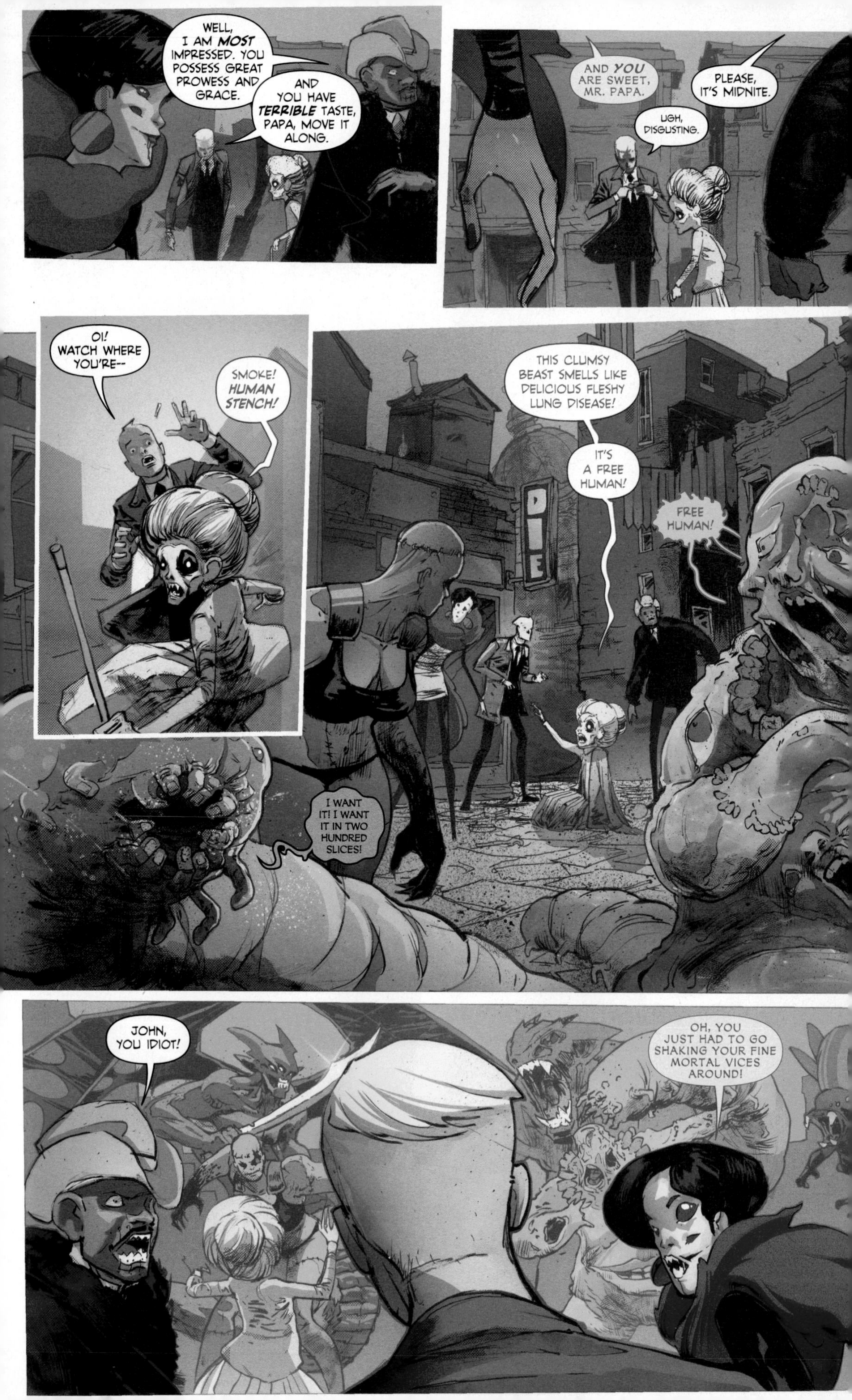
WELL, I AM MOST IMPRESSED. YOU POSSESS GREAT PROWESS AND GRACE.
AND YOU HAVE TERRIBLE TASTE, PAPA, MOVE IT ALONG.
AND YOU ARE SWEET, MR. PAPA.
PLEASE, IT'S MIDNITE.
UGH, DISGUSTING.
OI! WATCH WHERE YOU'RE--
SMOKE! HUMAN STENCH!
THIS CLUMSY BEAST SMELLS LIKE DELICIOUS FLESHY LUNG DISEASE!
IT'S A FREE HUMAN!
FREE HUMAN!
DIE
I WANT IT! I WANT IT IN TWO HUNDRED SLICES!
JOHN, YOU IDIOT!
OH, YOU JUST HAD TO GO SHAKING YOUR FINE MORTAL VICES AROUND!

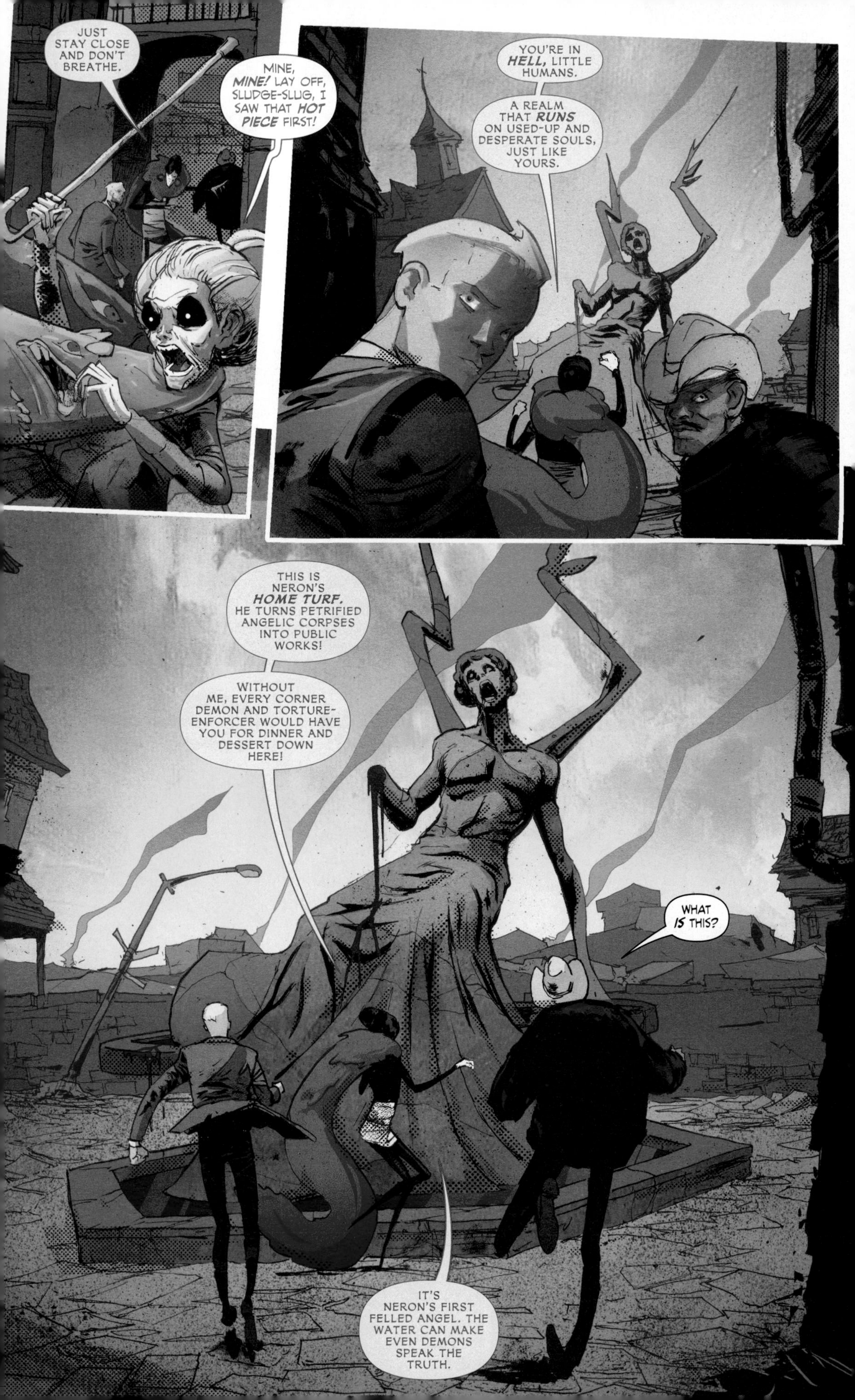
JUST STAY CLOSE AND DON'T BREATHE.
MINE, MINE! LAY OFF, SLUDGE-SLUG, I SAW THAT HOT PIECE FIRST!
YOU'RE IN HELL, LITTLE HUMANS.
A REALM THAT RUNS ON USED-UP AND DESPERATE SOULS, JUST LIKE YOURS.
THIS IS NERON'S HOME TURF. HE TURNS PETRIFIED ANGELIC CORPSES INTO PUBLIC WORKS!
WITHOUT ME, EVERY CORNER DEMON AND TORTURE-ENFORCER WOULD HAVE YOU FOR DINNER AND DESSERT DOWN HERE!
WHAT IS THIS?
IT'S NERON'S FIRST FELLED ANGEL. THE WATER CAN MAKE EVEN DEMONS SPEAK THE TRUTH.

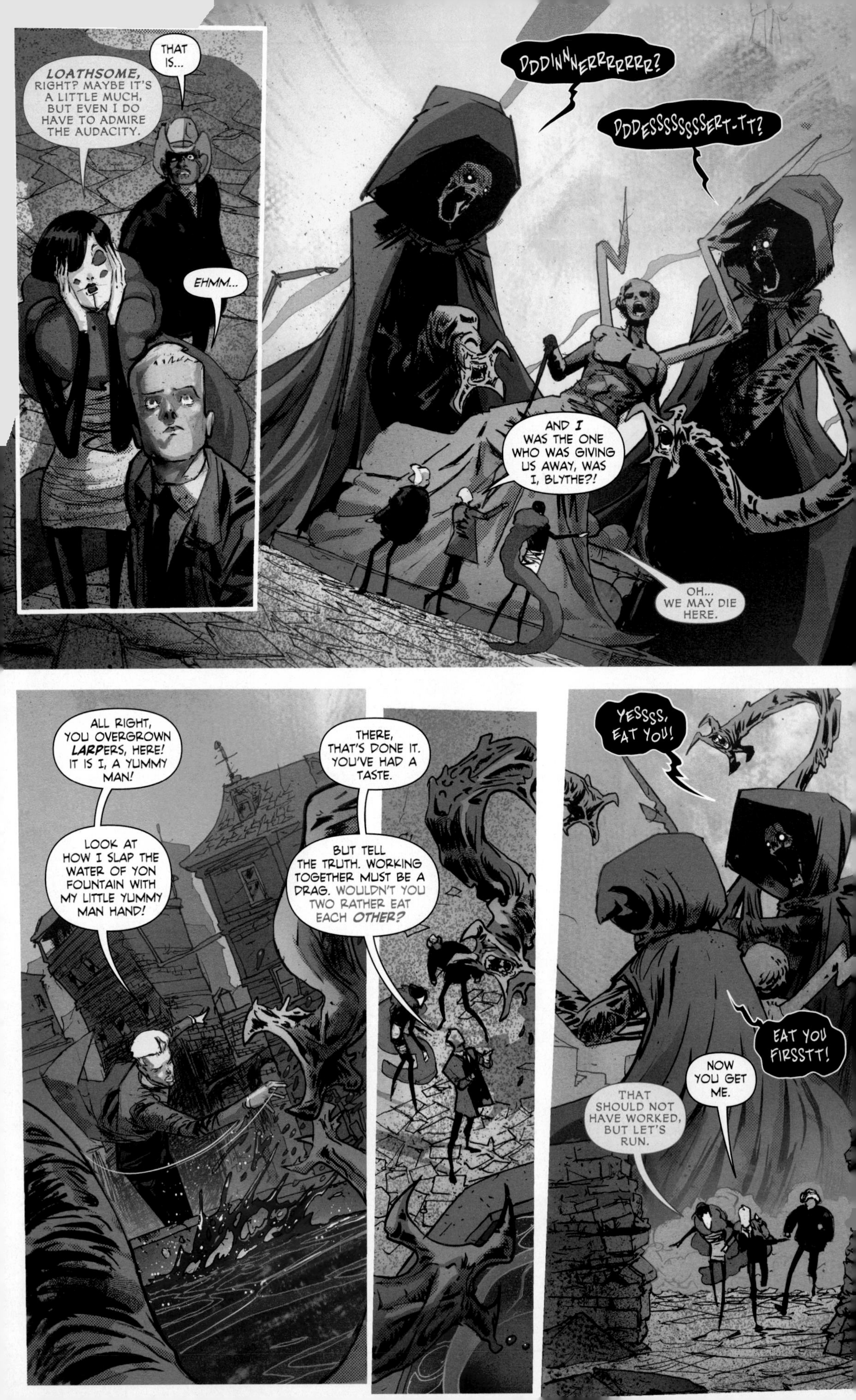
THAT IS...
LOATHSOME, RIGHT? MAYBE IT'S A LITTLE MUCH, BUT EVEN I DO HAVE TO ADMIRE THE AUDACITY.
EHMM...
DDDINNNERRRRRRR?
DDDESSSSSSSSERT-TT?
AND I WAS THE ONE WHO WAS GIVING US AWAY, WAS I, BLYTHE?!
OH... WE MAY DIE HERE.
ALL RIGHT, YOU OVERGROWN LARPERS, HERE! IT IS I, A YUMMY MAN!
LOOK AT HOW I SLAP THE WATER OF YON FOUNTAIN WITH MY LITTLE YUMMY MAN HAND!
THERE, THAT'S DONE IT. YOU'VE HAD A TASTE.
BUT TELL THE TRUTH. WORKING TOGETHER MUST BE A DRAG. WOULDN'T YOU TWO RATHER EAT EACH OTHER?
YESSSS, EAT YOU!
EAT YOU FIRSSTT!
NOW YOU GET ME.
THAT SHOULD NOT HAVE WORKED, BUT LET'S RUN.

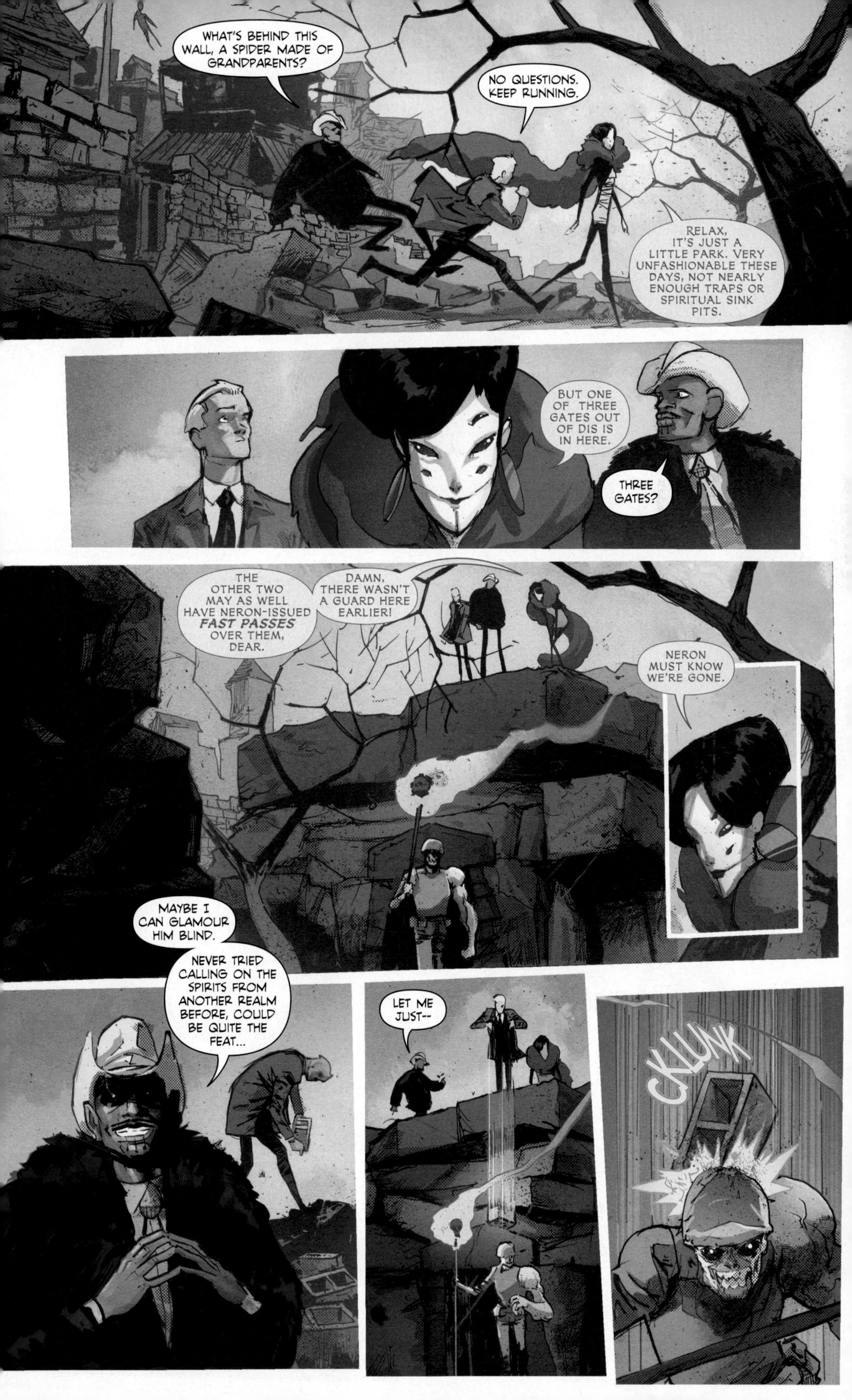
WHAT'S BEHIND THIS WALL, A SPIDER MADE OF GRANDPARENTS?
NO QUESTIONS. KEEP RUNNING.
RELAX, IT'S JUST A LITTLE PARK. VERY UNFASHIONABLE THESE DAYS, NOT NEARLY ENOUGH TRAPS OR SPIRITUAL SINK PITS.
BUT ONE OF THREE GATES OUT OF DIS IS IN HERE.
THREE GATES?
THE OTHER TWO MAY AS WELL HAVE NERON-ISSUED FAST PASSES OVER THEM, DEAR.
DAMN, THERE WASN'T A GUARD HERE EARLIER!
NERON MUST KNOW WE'RE GONE.
MAYBE I CAN GLAMOUR HIM BLIND.
NEVER TRIED CALLING ON THE SPIRITS FROM ANOTHER REALM BEFORE, COULD BE QUITE THE FEAT...
LET ME JUST--
CKLUNK

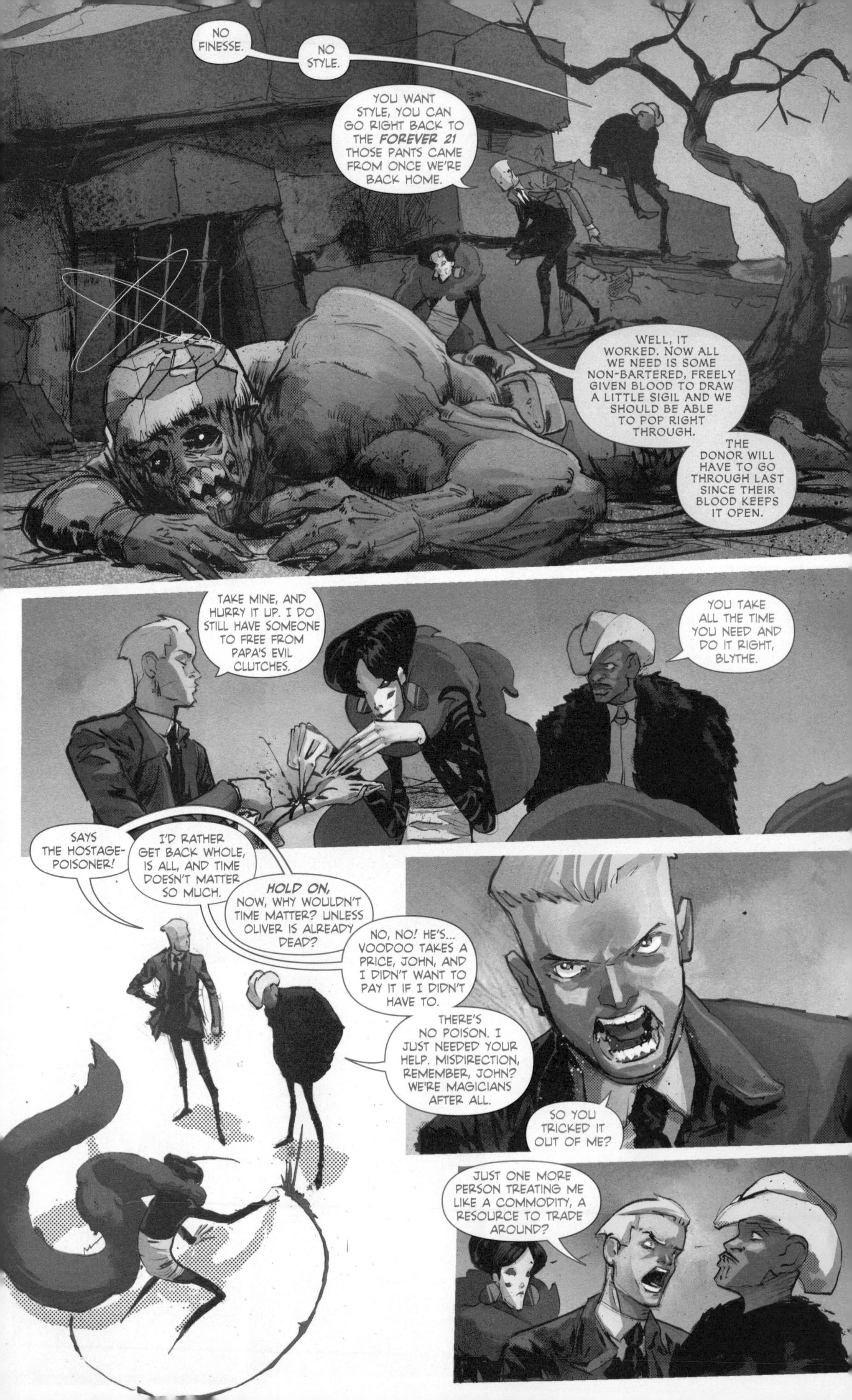
NO FINESSE.
NO STYLE.
YOU WANT STYLE, YOU CAN GO RIGHT BACK TO THE ***FOREVER 21*** THOSE PANTS CAME FROM ONCE WE'RE BACK HOME.
WELL, IT WORKED. NOW ALL WE NEED IS SOME NON-BARTERED, FREELY GIVEN BLOOD TO DRAW A LITTLE SIGIL AND WE SHOULD BE ABLE TO POP RIGHT THROUGH.
THE DONOR WILL HAVE TO GO THROUGH LAST SINCE THEIR BLOOD KEEPS IT OPEN.
TAKE MINE, AND HURRY IT UP. I DO STILL HAVE SOMEONE TO FREE FROM PAPA'S EVIL CLUTCHES.
YOU TAKE ALL THE TIME YOU NEED AND DO IT RIGHT, BLYTHE.
SAYS THE HOSTAGE-POISONER!
I'D RATHER GET BACK WHOLE, IS ALL, AND TIME DOESN'T MATTER SO MUCH.
***HOLD ON,*** NOW, WHY WOULDN'T TIME MATTER? UNLESS OLIVER IS ALREADY DEAD?
NO, NO! HE'S... VOODOO TAKES A PRICE, JOHN, AND I DIDN'T WANT TO PAY IT IF I DIDN'T HAVE TO.
THERE'S NO POISON. I JUST NEEDED YOUR HELP. MISDIRECTION, REMEMBER, JOHN? WE'RE MAGICIANS AFTER ALL.
SO YOU TRICKED IT OUT OF ME?
JUST ONE MORE PERSON TREATING ME LIKE A COMMODITY, A RESOURCE TO TRADE AROUND?

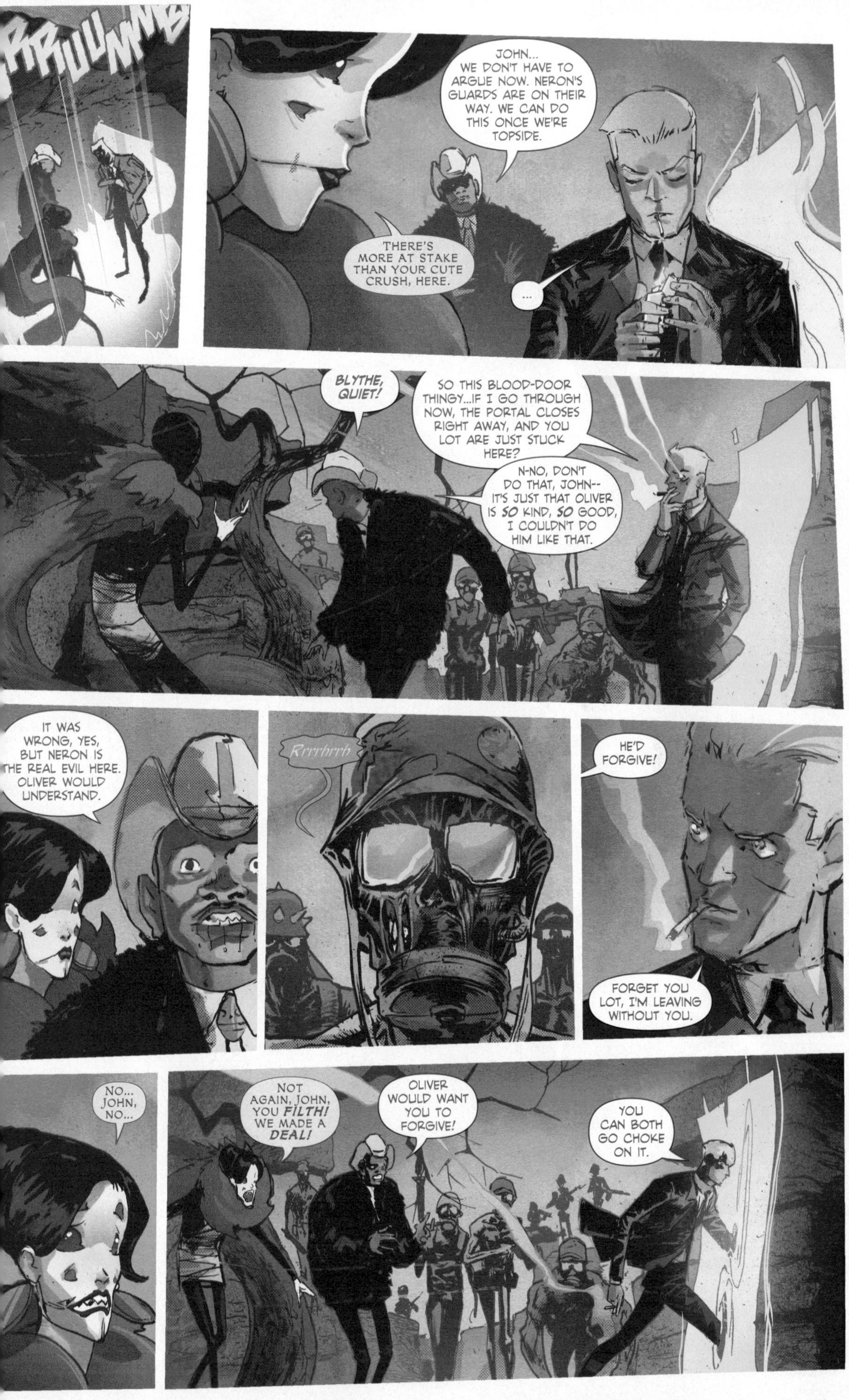
RRUUMMB
JOHN... WE DON'T HAVE TO ARGUE NOW. NERON'S GUARDS ARE ON THEIR WAY. WE CAN DO THIS ONCE WE'RE TOPSIDE.
THERE'S MORE AT STAKE THAN YOUR CUTE CRUSH, HERE.
...
BLYTHE, QUIET!
SO THIS BLOOD-DOOR THINGY...IF I GO THROUGH NOW, THE PORTAL CLOSES RIGHT AWAY, AND YOU LOT ARE JUST STUCK HERE?
N-NO, DON'T DO THAT, JOHN-- IT'S JUST THAT OLIVER IS SO KIND, SO GOOD, I COULDN'T DO HIM LIKE THAT.
IT WAS WRONG, YES, BUT NERON IS THE REAL EVIL HERE. OLIVER WOULD UNDERSTAND.
Rrrrhrrh
HE'D FORGIVE!
FORGET YOU LOT, I'M LEAVING WITHOUT YOU.
NO... JOHN, NO...
NOT AGAIN, JOHN, YOU FILTH! WE MADE A DEAL!
OLIVER WOULD WANT YOU TO FORGIVE!
YOU CAN BOTH GO CHOKE ON IT.

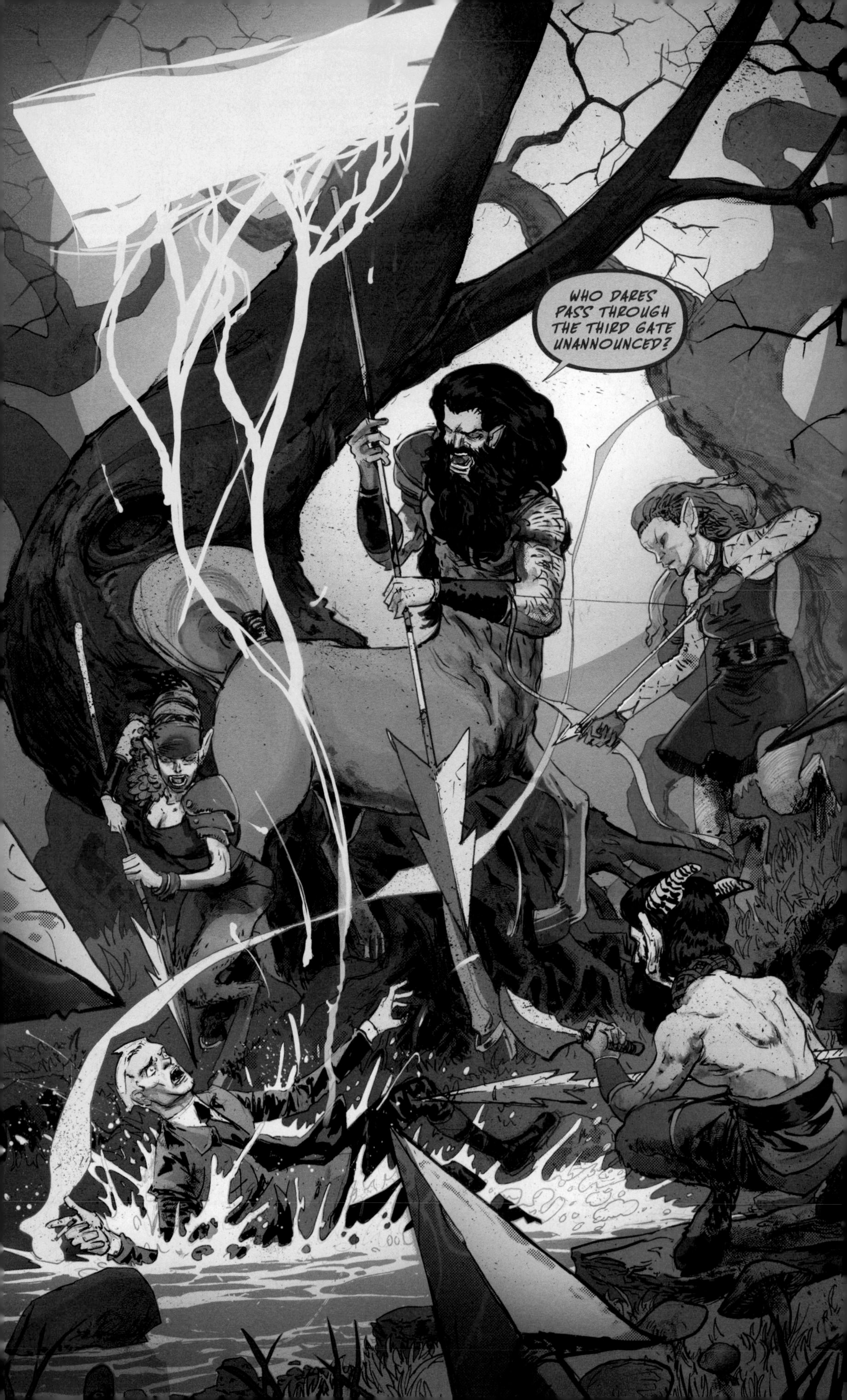
WHO DARES PASS THROUGH THE THIRD GATE UNANNOUNCED?

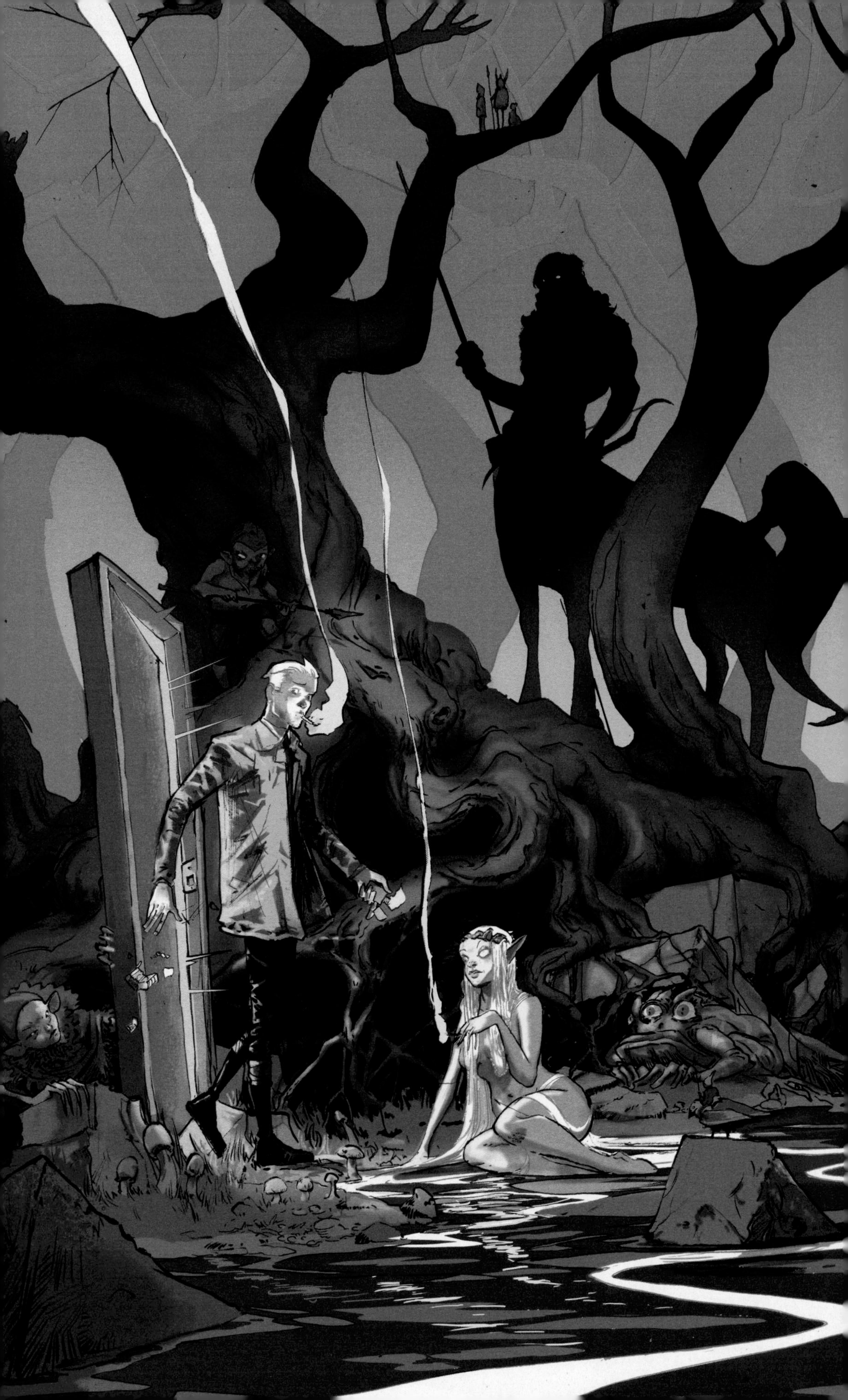

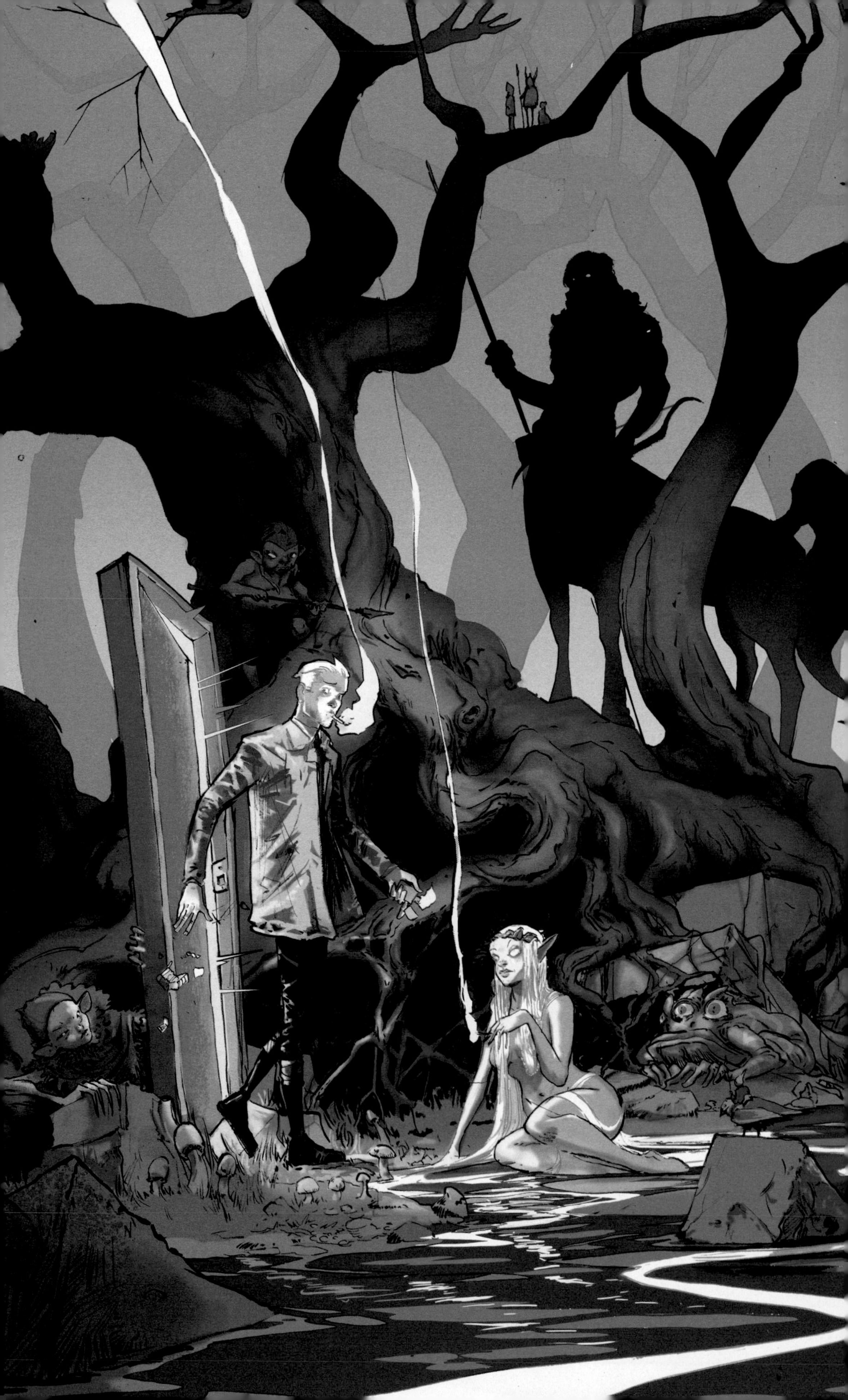

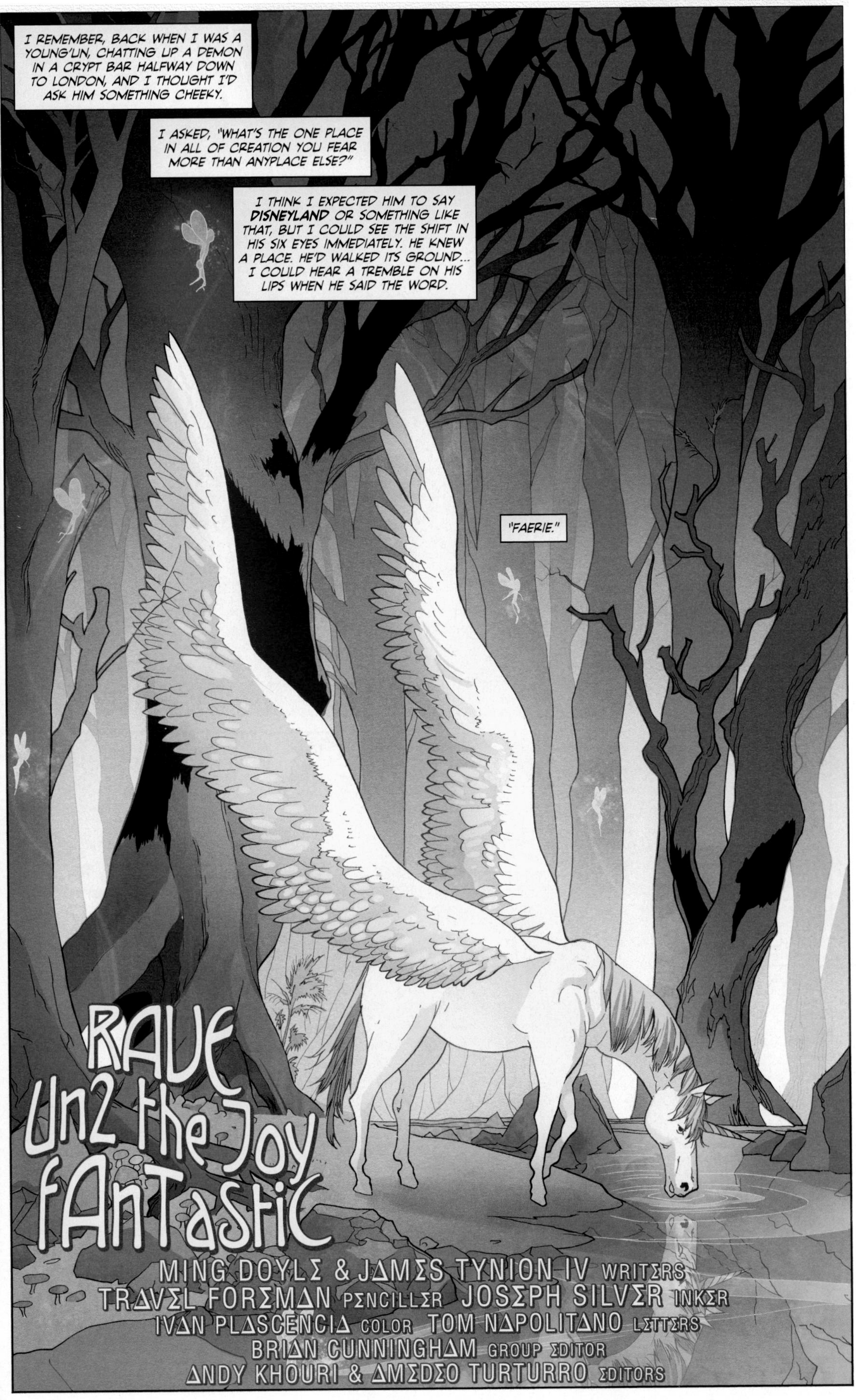
I REMEMBER, BACK WHEN I WAS A YOUNG'UN, CHATTING UP A DEMON IN A CRYPT BAR HALFWAY DOWN TO LONDON, AND I THOUGHT I'D ASK HIM SOMETHING CHEEKY.
I ASKED, "WHAT'S THE ONE PLACE IN ALL OF CREATION YOU FEAR MORE THAN ANYPLACE ELSE?"
I THINK I EXPECTED HIM TO SAY DISNEYLAND OR SOMETHING LIKE THAT, BUT I COULD SEE THE SHIFT IN HIS SIX EYES IMMEDIATELY. HE KNEW A PLACE. HE'D WALKED ITS GROUND... I COULD HEAR A TREMBLE ON HIS LIPS WHEN HE SAID THE WORD.
"FAERIE."
RAVE Un2 the Joy fAnTastiC
MING DOYLE & JAMES TYNION IV WRITERS
TRAVEL FOREMAN PENCILLER JOSEPH SILVER INKER
IVAN PLASCENCIA COLOR TOM NAPOLITANO LETTERS
BRIAN CUNNINGHAM GROUP EDITOR
ANDY KHOURI & AMEDEO TURTURRO EDITORS

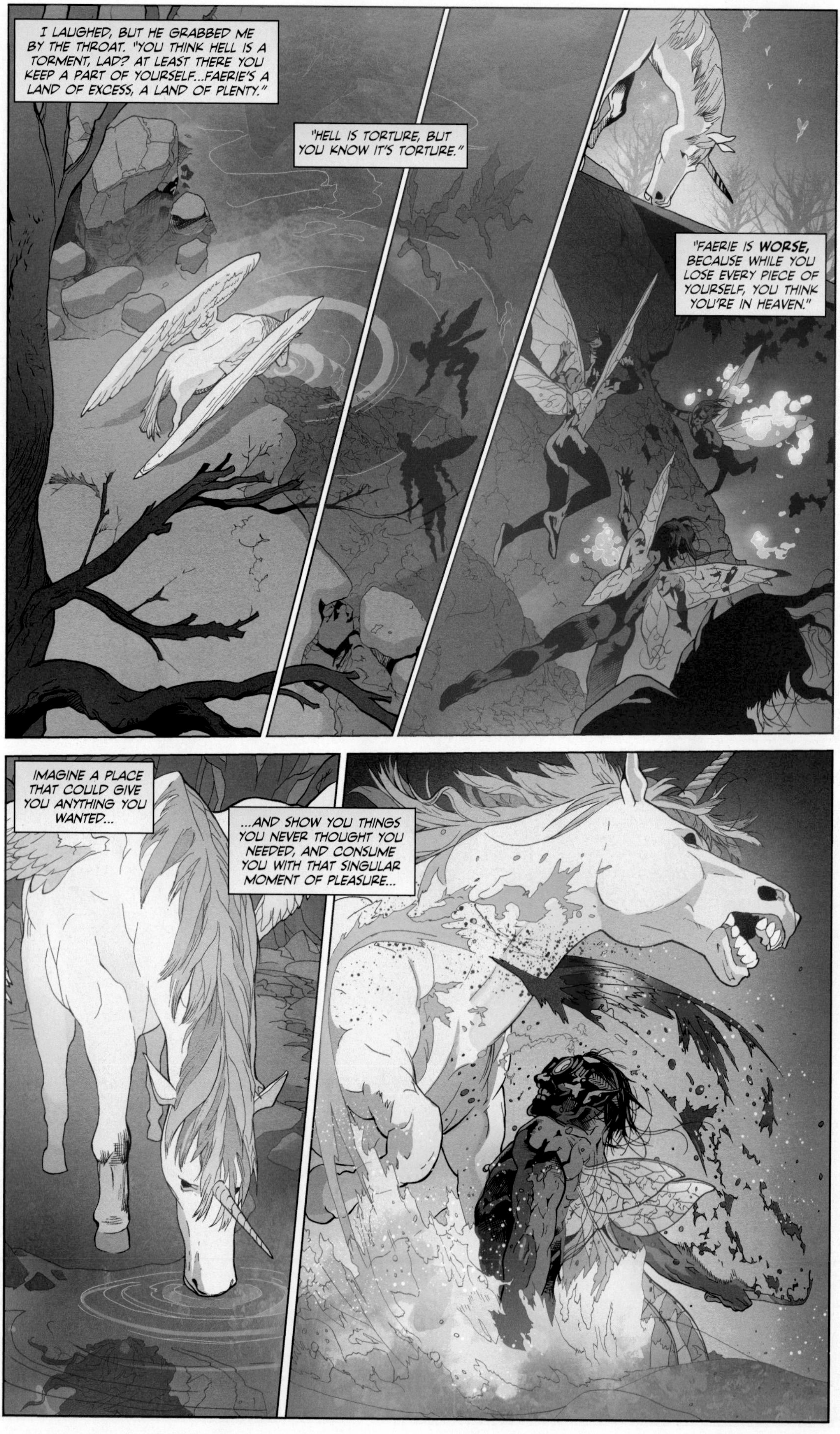
I LAUGHED, BUT HE GRABBED ME BY THE THROAT. "YOU THINK HELL IS A TORMENT, LAD? AT LEAST THERE YOU KEEP A PART OF YOURSELF...FAERIE'S A LAND OF EXCESS, A LAND OF PLENTY."
"HELL IS TORTURE, BUT YOU KNOW IT'S TORTURE."
"FAERIE IS **WORSE,** BECAUSE WHILE YOU LOSE EVERY PIECE OF YOURSELF, YOU THINK YOU'RE IN HEAVEN."
IMAGINE A PLACE THAT COULD GIVE YOU ANYTHING YOU WANTED...
...AND SHOW YOU THINGS YOU NEVER THOUGHT YOU NEEDED, AND CONSUME YOU WITH THAT SINGULAR MOMENT OF PLEASURE...

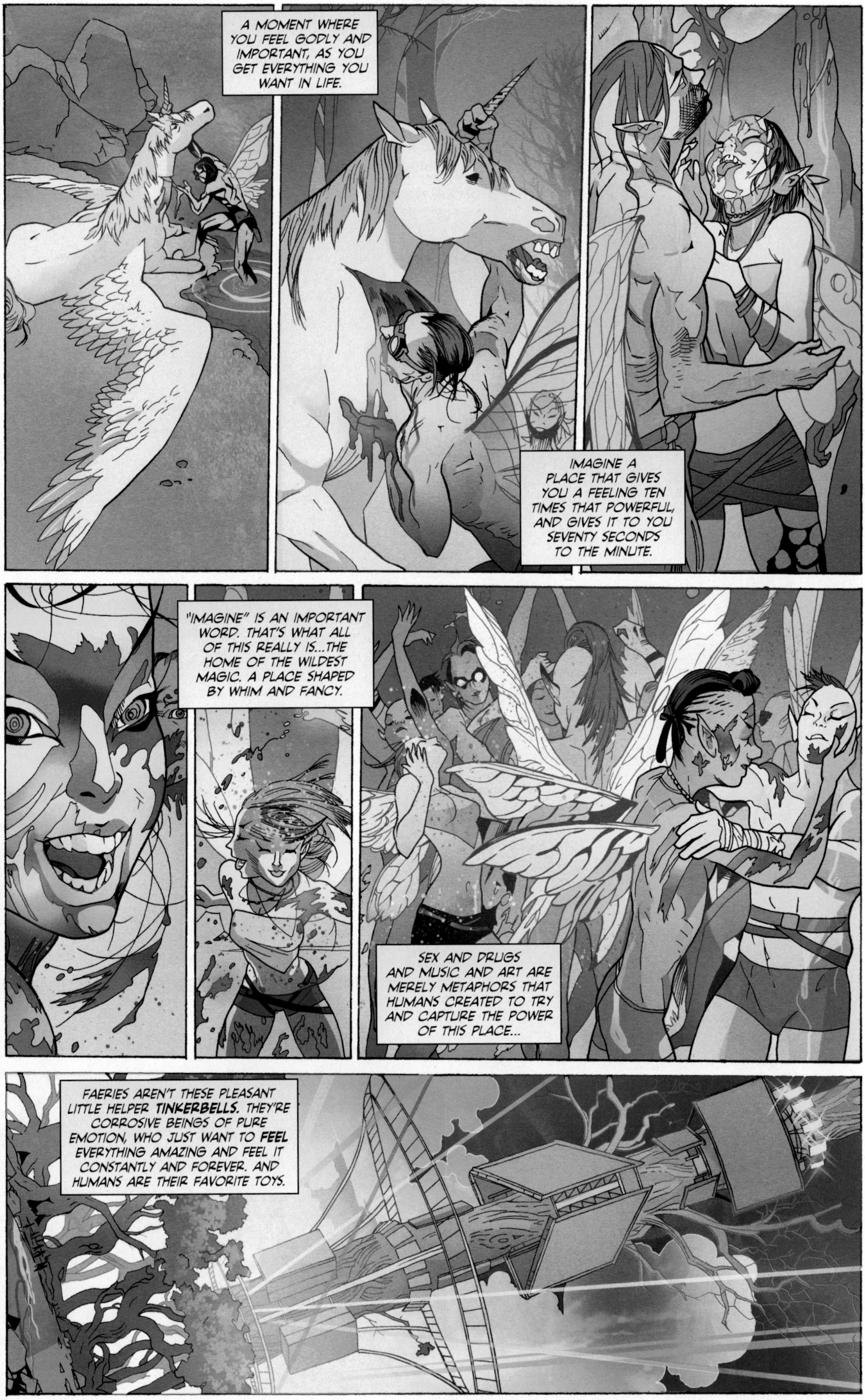
A MOMENT WHERE YOU FEEL GODLY AND IMPORTANT, AS YOU GET EVERYTHING YOU WANT IN LIFE.
IMAGINE A PLACE THAT GIVES YOU A FEELING TEN TIMES THAT POWERFUL, AND GIVES IT TO YOU SEVENTY SECONDS TO THE MINUTE.
"IMAGINE" IS AN IMPORTANT WORD. THAT'S WHAT ALL OF THIS REALLY IS...THE HOME OF THE WILDEST MAGIC. A PLACE SHAPED BY WHIM AND FANCY.
SEX AND DRUGS AND MUSIC AND ART ARE MERELY METAPHORS THAT HUMANS CREATED TO TRY AND CAPTURE THE POWER OF THIS PLACE...
FAERIES AREN'T THESE PLEASANT LITTLE HELPER TINKERBELLS. THEY'RE CORROSIVE BEINGS OF PURE EMOTION, WHO JUST WANT TO FEEL EVERYTHING AMAZING AND FEEL IT CONSTANTLY AND FOREVER. AND HUMANS ARE THEIR FAVORITE TOYS.

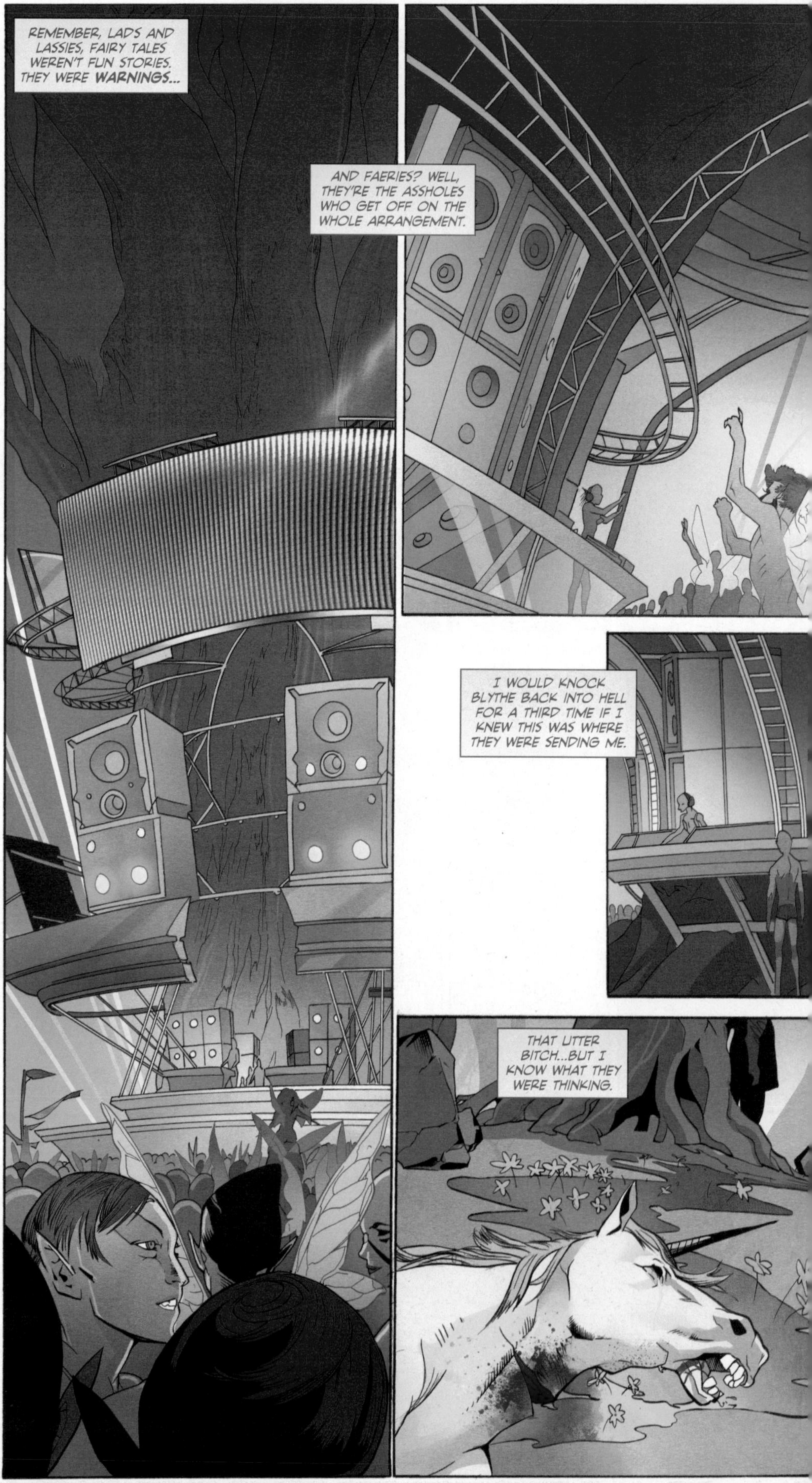
REMEMBER, LADS AND LASSIES, FAIRY TALES WEREN'T FUN STORIES. THEY WERE **WARNINGS...**
AND FAERIES? WELL, THEY'RE THE ASSHOLES WHO GET OFF ON THE WHOLE ARRANGEMENT.
I WOULD KNOCK BLYTHE BACK INTO HELL FOR A THIRD TIME IF I KNEW THIS WAS WHERE THEY WERE SENDING ME.
THAT UTTER BITCH...BUT I KNOW WHAT THEY WERE THINKING.

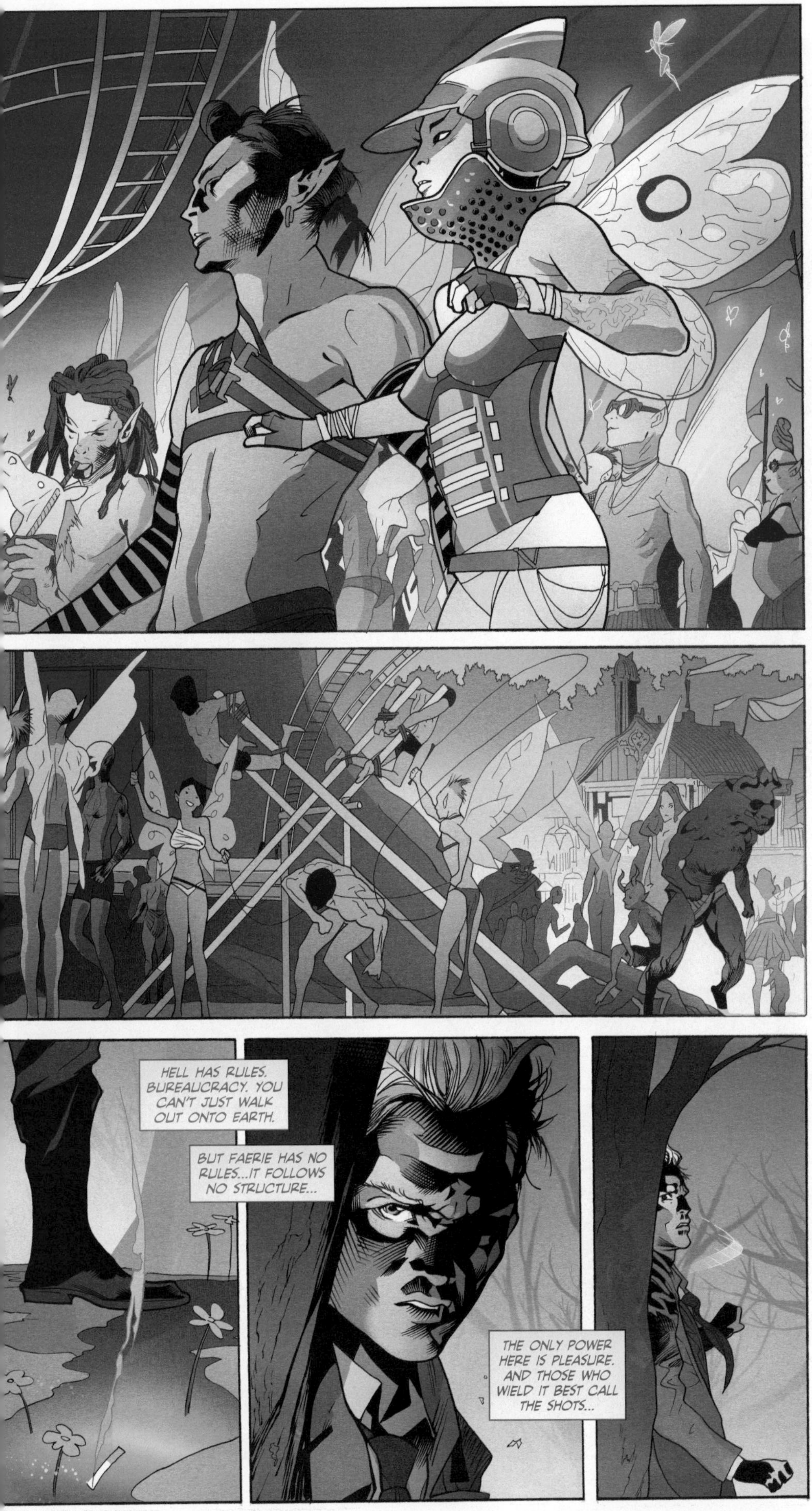
HELL HAS RULES. BUREAUCRACY. YOU CAN'T JUST WALK OUT ONTO EARTH.
BUT FAERIE HAS NO RULES...IT FOLLOWS NO STRUCTURE...
THE ONLY POWER HERE IS PLEASURE. AND THOSE WHO WIELD IT BEST CALL THE SHOTS...

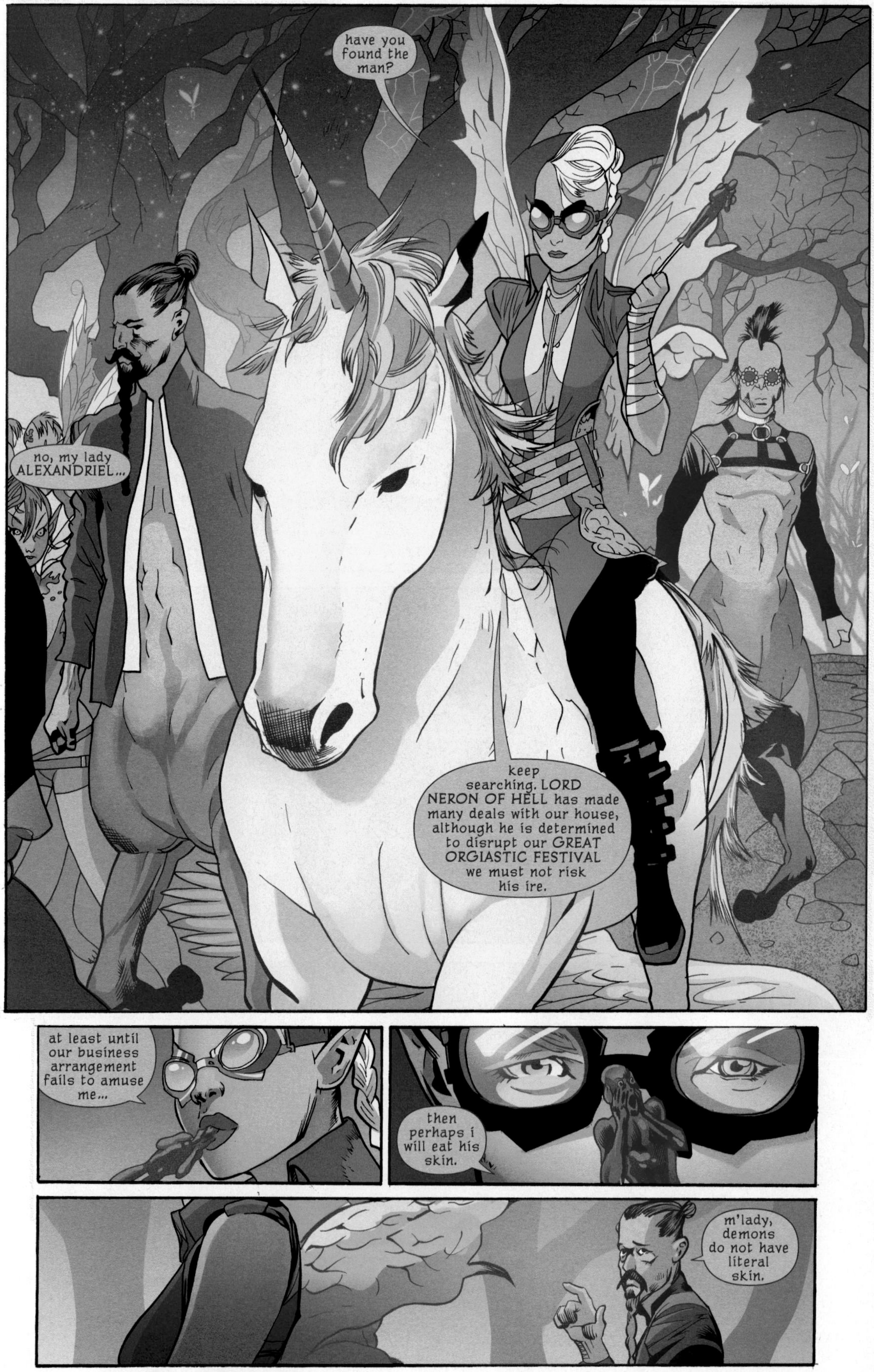
have you found the man?
no, my lady ALEXANDRIEL...
keep searching. LORD NERON OF HELL has made many deals with our house, although he is determined to disrupt our GREAT ORGIASTIC FESTIVAL we must not risk his ire.
at least until our business arrangement fails to amuse me...
then perhaps i will eat his skin.
m'lady, demons do not have literal skin.

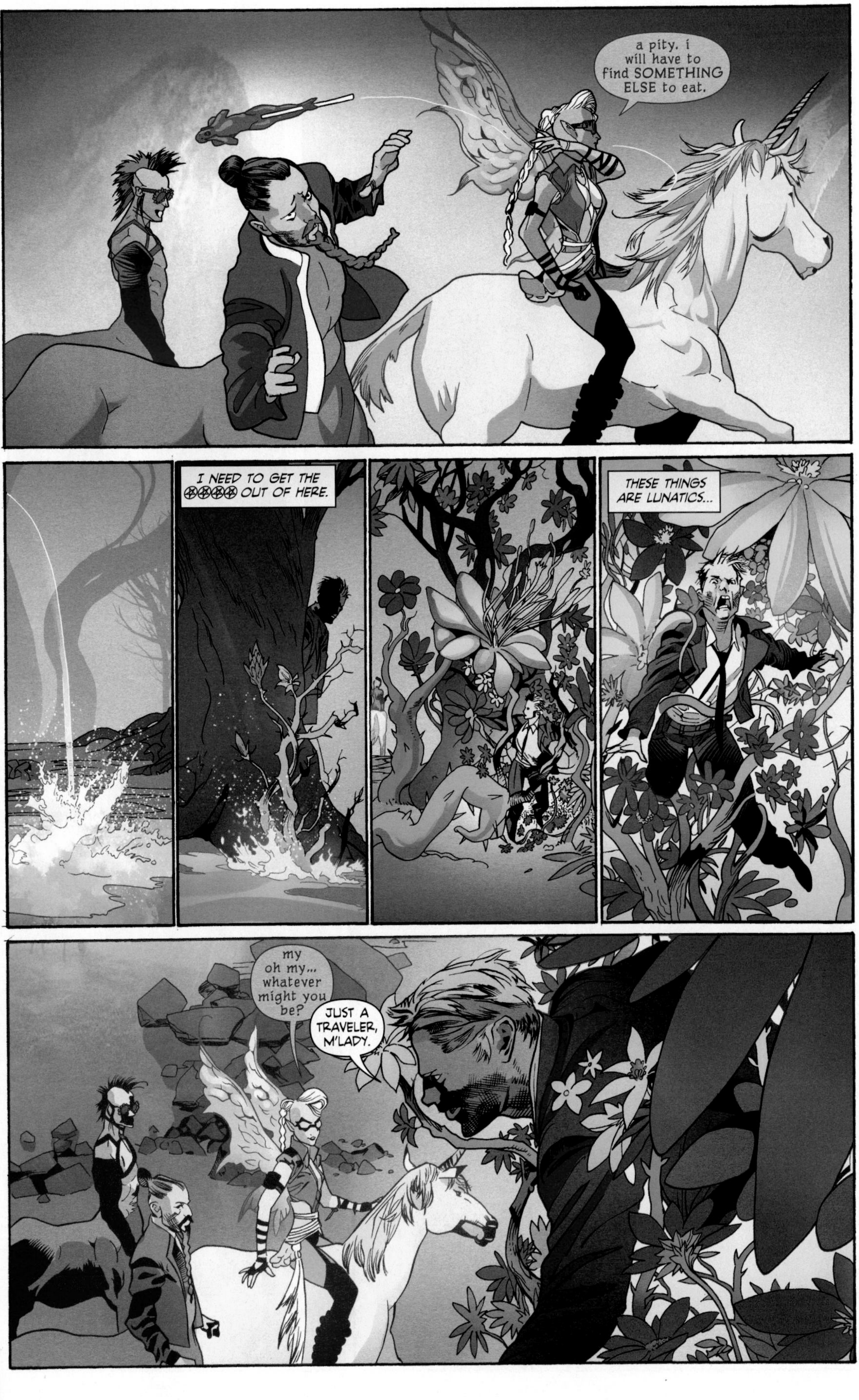

a pity. i will have to find SOMETHING ELSE to eat.
I NEED TO GET THE ⊗⊗⊗⊗ OUT OF HERE.
THESE THINGS ARE LUNATICS...
my oh my... whatever might you be?
JUST A TRAVELER, M'LADY.

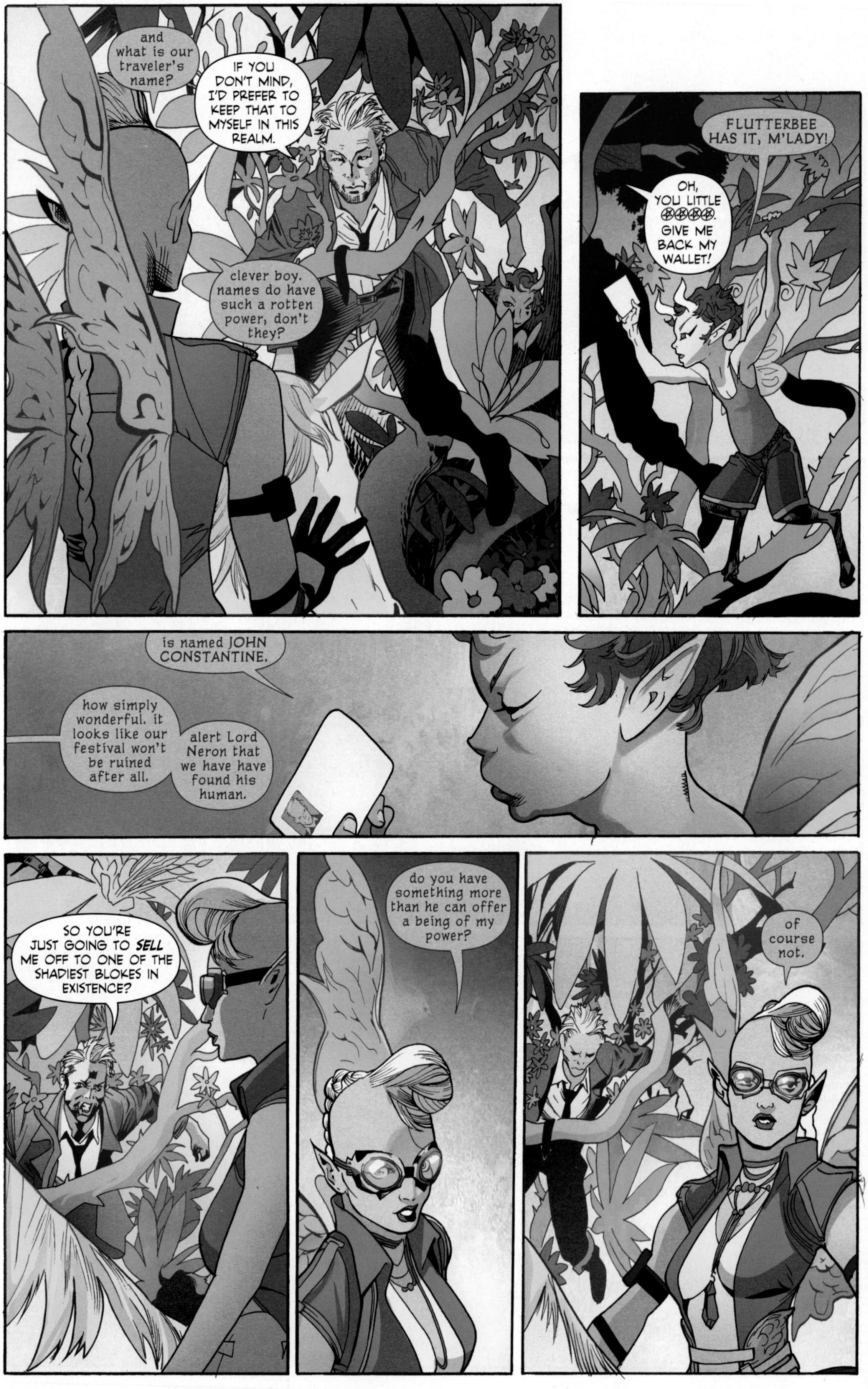
and what is our traveler's name?
IF YOU DON'T MIND, I'D PREFER TO KEEP THAT TO MYSELF IN THIS REALM.
clever boy. names do have such a rotten power, don't they?
FLUTTERBEE HAS IT, M'LADY!
OH, YOU LITTLE ⊗⊗⊗⊗. GIVE ME BACK MY WALLET!
is named JOHN CONSTANTINE.
how simply wonderful. it looks like our festival won't be ruined after all.
alert Lord Neron that we have have found his human.
SO YOU'RE JUST GOING TO *SELL* ME OFF TO ONE OF THE SHADIEST BLOKES IN EXISTENCE?
do you have something more than he can offer a being of my power?
of course not.

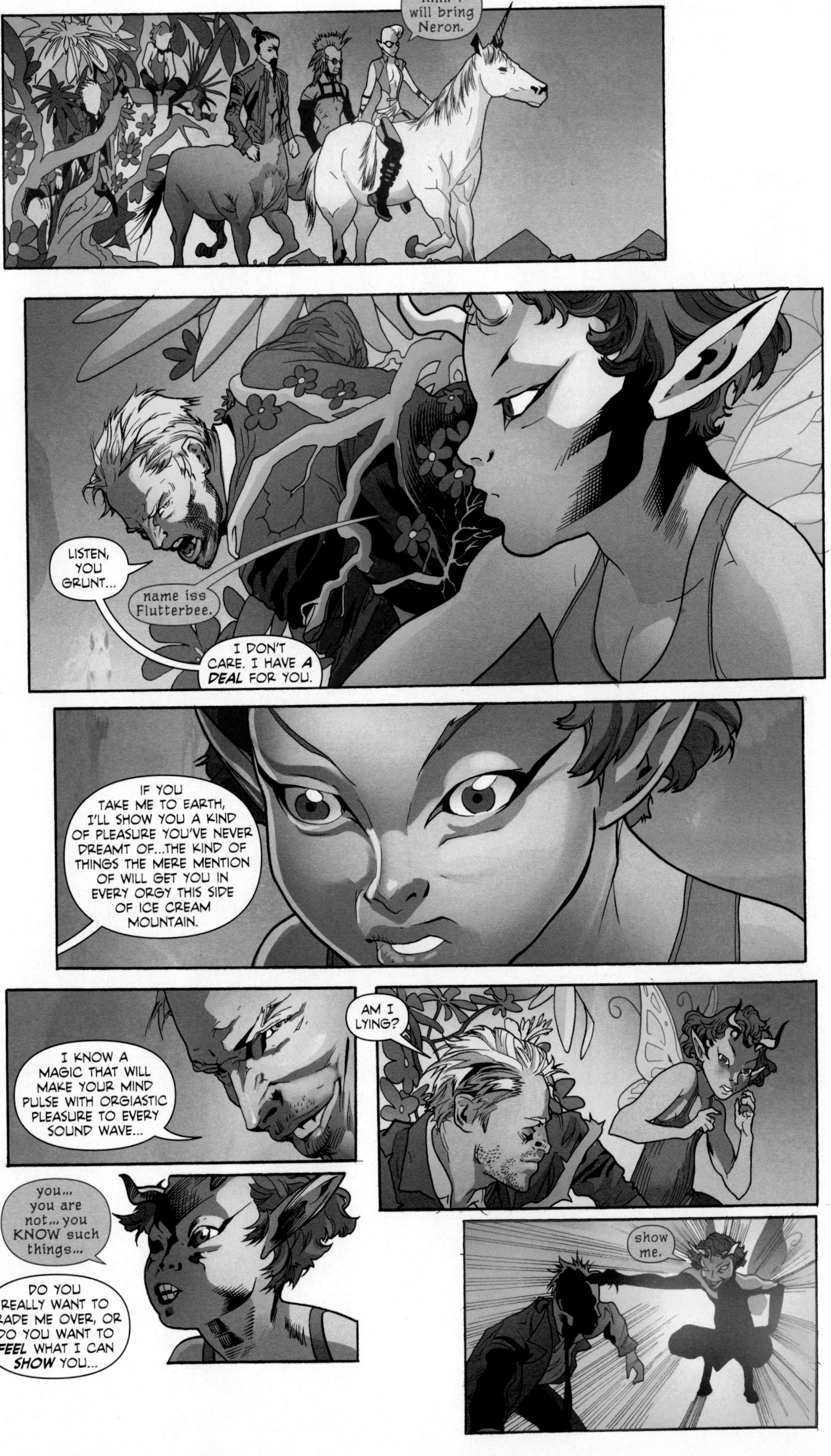
hold him. i will bring Neron.
LISTEN, YOU GRUNT...
name iss Flutterbee.
I DON'T CARE. I HAVE A DEAL FOR YOU.
IF YOU TAKE ME TO EARTH, I'LL SHOW YOU A KIND OF PLEASURE YOU'VE NEVER DREAMT OF...THE KIND OF THINGS THE MERE MENTION OF WILL GET YOU IN EVERY ORGY THIS SIDE OF ICE CREAM MOUNTAIN.
I KNOW A MAGIC THAT WILL MAKE YOUR MIND PULSE WITH ORGIASTIC PLEASURE TO EVERY SOUND WAVE...
AM I LYING?
you... you are not... you KNOW such things...
DO YOU REALLY WANT TO TRADE ME OVER, OR DO YOU WANT TO FEEL WHAT I CAN SHOW YOU...
show me.

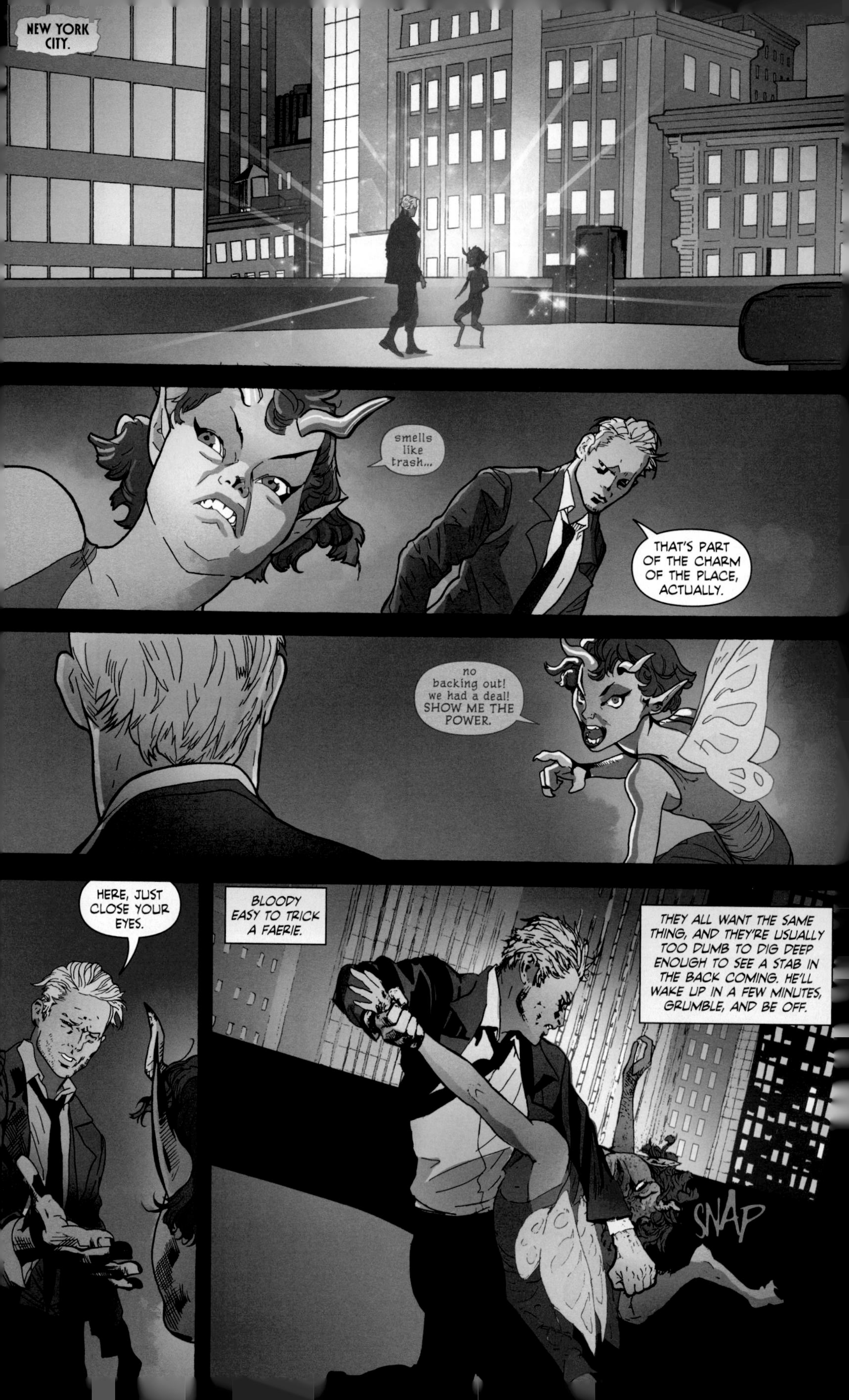
NEW YORK CITY.
smells like trash...
THAT'S PART OF THE CHARM OF THE PLACE, ACTUALLY.
no backing out! we had a deal! SHOW ME THE POWER.
HERE, JUST CLOSE YOUR EYES.
BLOODY EASY TO TRICK A FAERIE.
THEY ALL WANT THE SAME THING, AND THEY'RE USUALLY TOO DUMB TO DIG DEEP ENOUGH TO SEE A STAB IN THE BACK COMING. HE'LL WAKE UP IN A FEW MINUTES, GRUMBLE, AND BE OFF.
SNAP

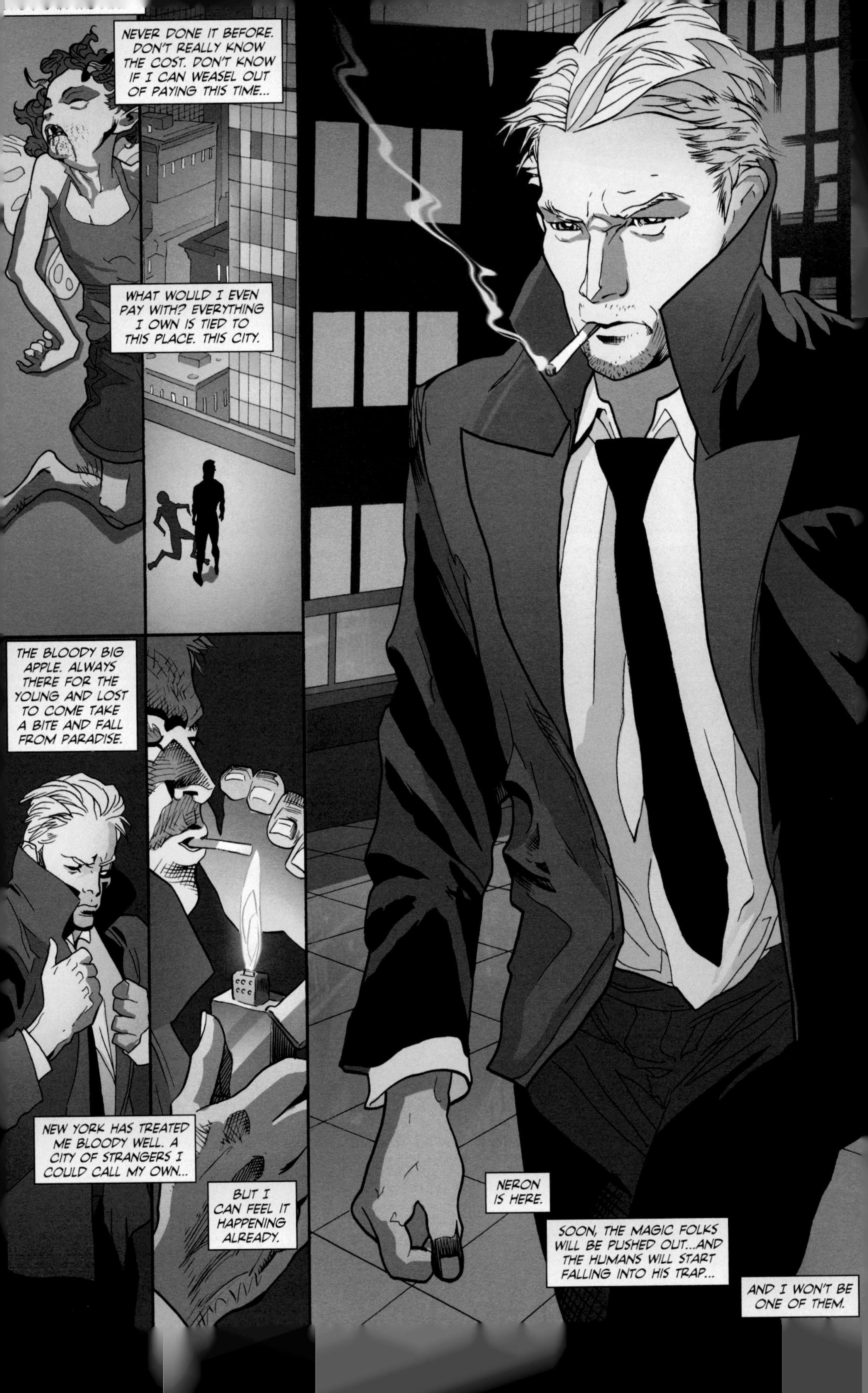
NEVER DONE IT BEFORE. DON'T REALLY KNOW THE COST. DON'T KNOW IF I CAN WEASEL OUT OF PAYING THIS TIME...
WHAT WOULD I EVEN PAY WITH? EVERYTHING I OWN IS TIED TO THIS PLACE. THIS CITY.
THE BLOODY BIG APPLE. ALWAYS THERE FOR THE YOUNG AND LOST TO COME TAKE A BITE AND FALL FROM PARADISE.
NEW YORK HAS TREATED ME BLOODY WELL. A CITY OF STRANGERS I COULD CALL MY OWN...
BUT I CAN FEEL IT HAPPENING ALREADY.
NERON IS HERE.
SOON, THE MAGIC FOLKS WILL BE PUSHED OUT...AND THE HUMANS WILL START FALLING INTO HIS TRAP...
AND I WON'T BE ONE OF THEM.

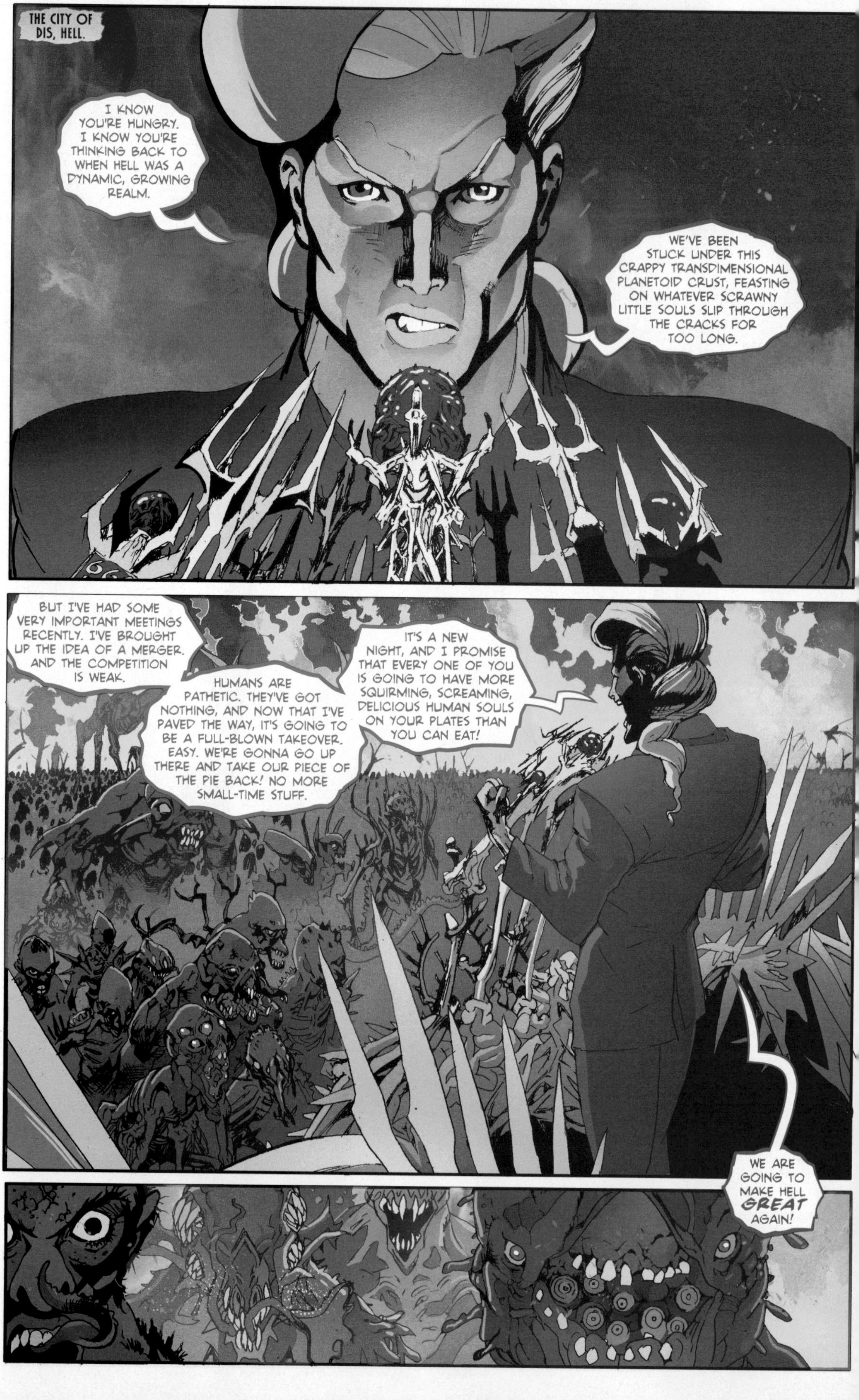
THE CITY OF DIS, HELL.
I KNOW YOU'RE HUNGRY. I KNOW YOU'RE THINKING BACK TO WHEN HELL WAS A DYNAMIC, GROWING REALM.
WE'VE BEEN STUCK UNDER THIS CRAPPY TRANSDIMENSIONAL PLANETOID CRUST, FEASTING ON WHATEVER SCRAWNY LITTLE SOULS SLIP THROUGH THE CRACKS FOR TOO LONG.
BUT I'VE HAD SOME VERY IMPORTANT MEETINGS RECENTLY. I'VE BROUGHT UP THE IDEA OF A MERGER. AND THE COMPETITION IS WEAK.
HUMANS ARE PATHETIC. THEY'VE GOT NOTHING, AND NOW THAT I'VE PAVED THE WAY, IT'S GOING TO BE A FULL-BLOWN TAKEOVER. EASY. WE'RE GONNA GO UP THERE AND TAKE OUR PIECE OF THE PIE BACK! NO MORE SMALL-TIME STUFF.
IT'S A NEW NIGHT, AND I PROMISE THAT EVERY ONE OF YOU IS GOING TO HAVE MORE SQUIRMING, SCREAMING, DELICIOUS HUMAN SOULS ON YOUR PLATES THAN YOU CAN EAT!
WE ARE GOING TO MAKE HELL GREAT AGAIN!

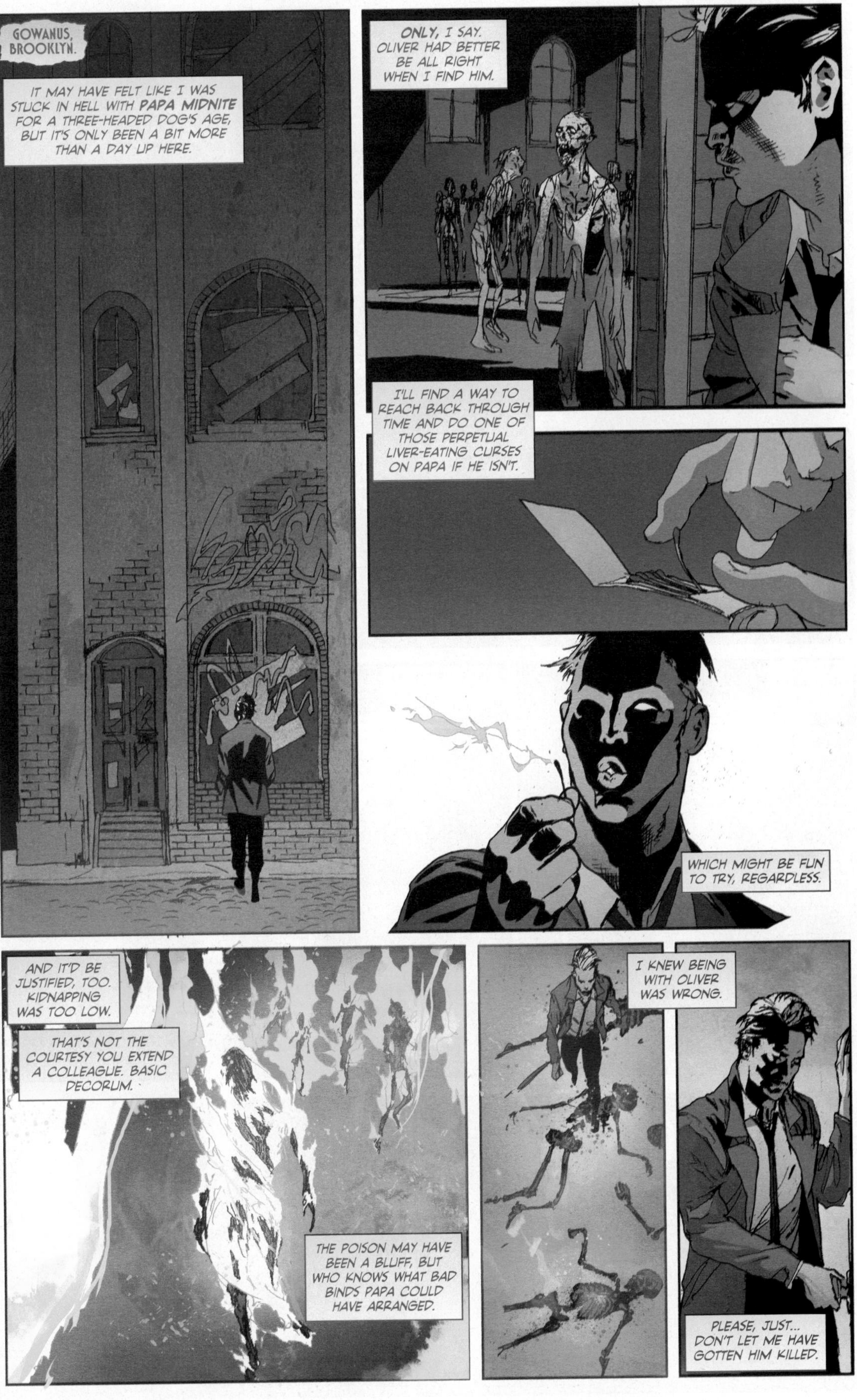
GOWANUS, BROOKLYN.
IT MAY HAVE FELT LIKE I WAS STUCK IN HELL WITH PAPA MIDNITE FOR A THREE-HEADED DOG'S AGE, BUT IT'S ONLY BEEN A BIT MORE THAN A DAY UP HERE.
ONLY, I SAY. OLIVER HAD BETTER BE ALL RIGHT WHEN I FIND HIM.
I'LL FIND A WAY TO REACH BACK THROUGH TIME AND DO ONE OF THOSE PERPETUAL LIVER-EATING CURSES ON PAPA IF HE ISN'T.
WHICH MIGHT BE FUN TO TRY, REGARDLESS.
AND IT'D BE JUSTIFIED, TOO. KIDNAPPING WAS TOO LOW.
THAT'S NOT THE COURTESY YOU EXTEND A COLLEAGUE. BASIC DECORUM.
THE POISON MAY HAVE BEEN A BLUFF, BUT WHO KNOWS WHAT BAD BINDS PAPA COULD HAVE ARRANGED.
I KNEW BEING WITH OLIVER WAS WRONG.
PLEASE, JUST... DON'T LET ME HAVE GOTTEN HIM KILLED.

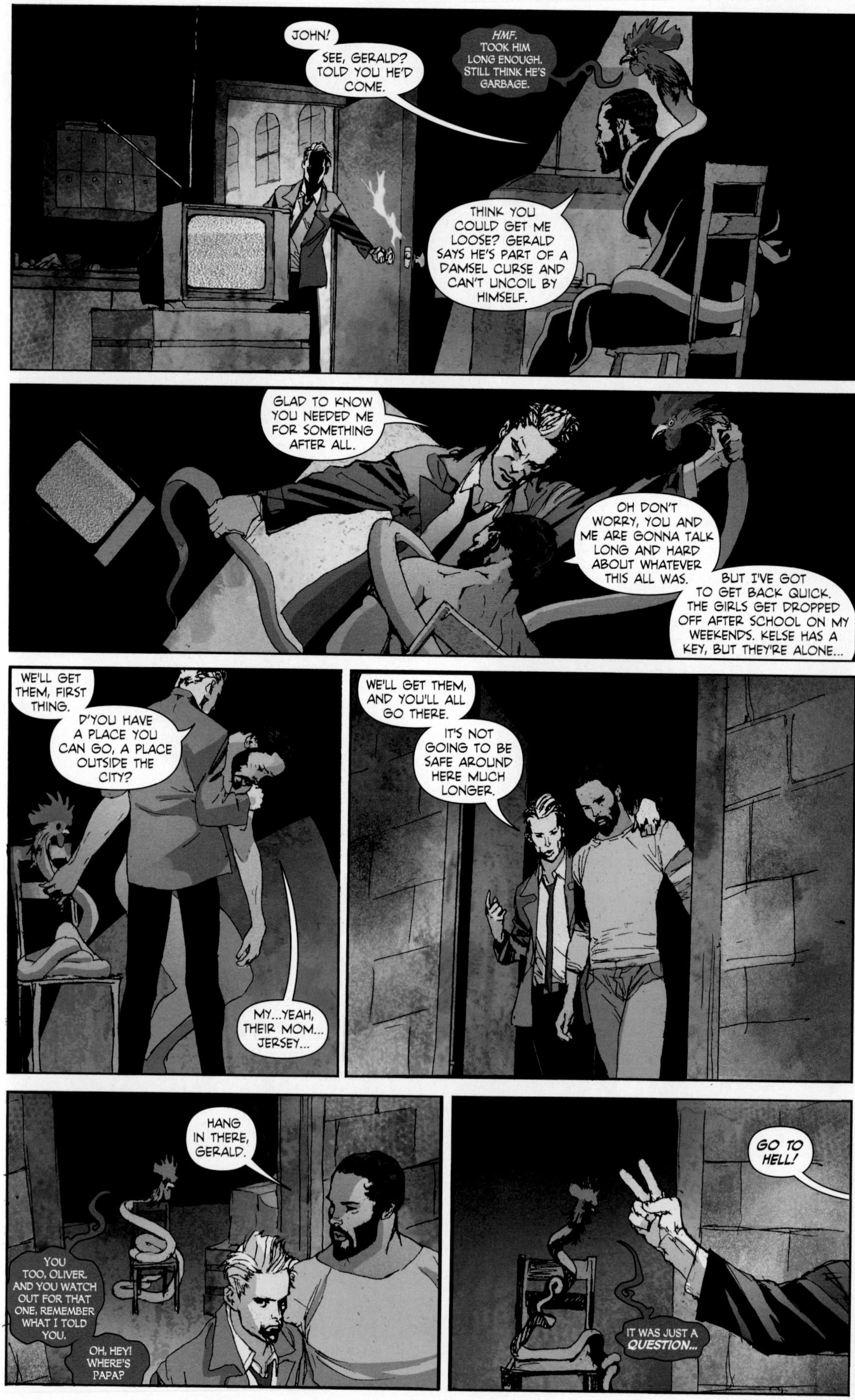
JOHN!
SEE, GERALD? TOLD YOU HE'D COME.
HMF. TOOK HIM LONG ENOUGH. STILL THINK HE'S GARBAGE.
THINK YOU COULD GET ME LOOSE? GERALD SAYS HE'S PART OF A DAMSEL CURSE AND CAN'T UNCOIL BY HIMSELF.
GLAD TO KNOW YOU NEEDED ME FOR SOMETHING AFTER ALL.
OH DON'T WORRY, YOU AND ME ARE GONNA TALK LONG AND HARD ABOUT WHATEVER THIS ALL WAS.
BUT I'VE GOT TO GET BACK QUICK. THE GIRLS GET DROPPED OFF AFTER SCHOOL ON MY WEEKENDS. KELSE HAS A KEY, BUT THEY'RE ALONE...
WE'LL GET THEM, FIRST THING.
D'YOU HAVE A PLACE YOU CAN GO, A PLACE OUTSIDE THE CITY?
MY...YEAH, THEIR MOM... JERSEY...
WE'LL GET THEM, AND YOU'LL ALL GO THERE.
IT'S NOT GOING TO BE SAFE AROUND HERE MUCH LONGER.
HANG IN THERE, GERALD.
YOU TOO, OLIVER. AND YOU WATCH OUT FOR THAT ONE, REMEMBER WHAT I TOLD YOU.
OH, HEY! WHERE'S PAPA?
GO TO HELL!
IT WAS JUST A QUESTION...

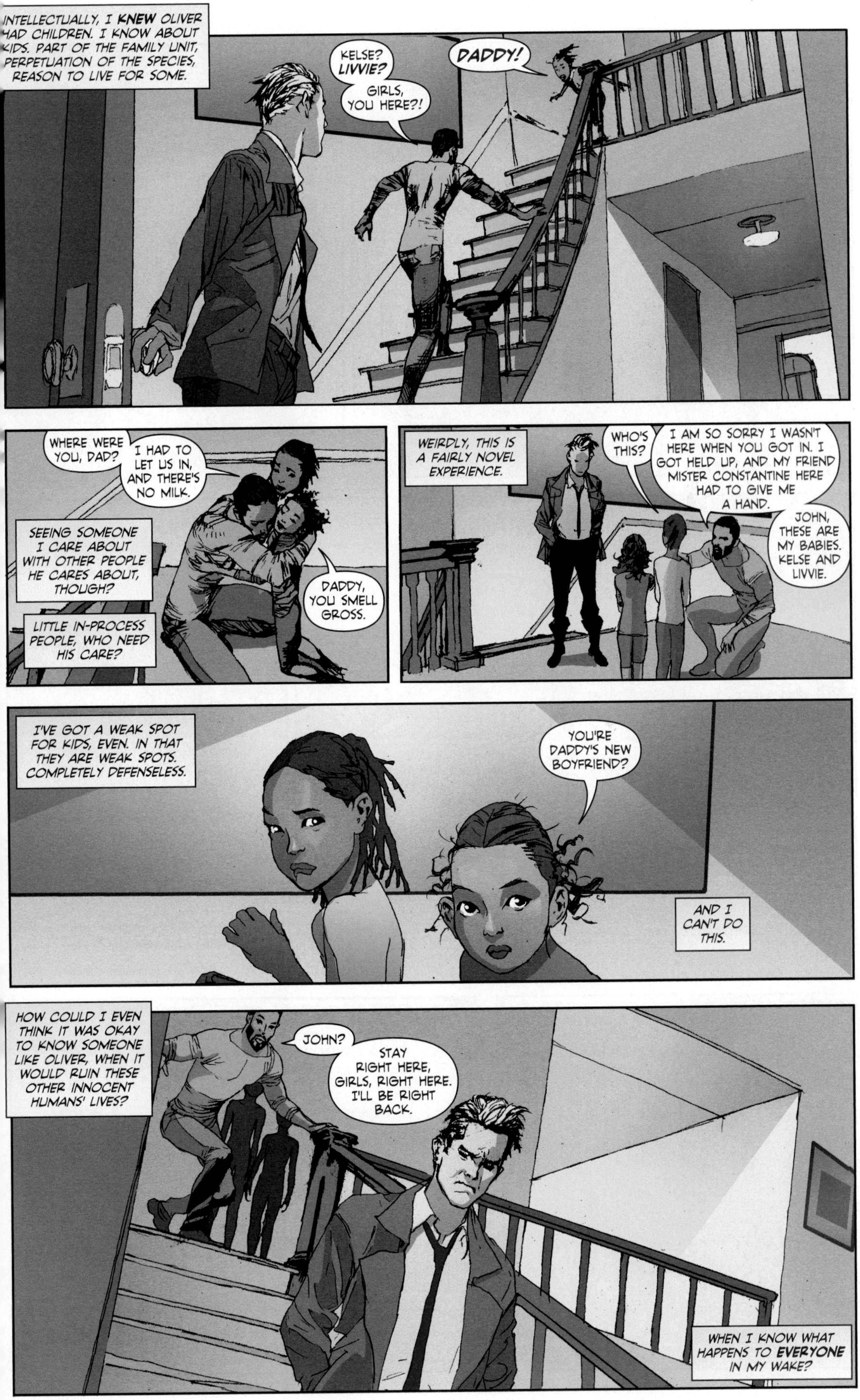
INTELLECTUALLY, I KNEW OLIVER HAD CHILDREN. I KNOW ABOUT KIDS. PART OF THE FAMILY UNIT, PERPETUATION OF THE SPECIES, REASON TO LIVE FOR SOME.
KELSE? LIVVIE?
GIRLS, YOU HERE?!
DADDY!
WHERE WERE YOU, DAD?
I HAD TO LET US IN, AND THERE'S NO MILK.
SEEING SOMEONE I CARE ABOUT WITH OTHER PEOPLE HE CARES ABOUT, THOUGH?
DADDY, YOU SMELL GROSS.
LITTLE IN-PROCESS PEOPLE, WHO NEED HIS CARE?
WEIRDLY, THIS IS A FAIRLY NOVEL EXPERIENCE.
WHO'S THIS?
I AM SO SORRY I WASN'T HERE WHEN YOU GOT IN. I GOT HELD UP, AND MY FRIEND MISTER CONSTANTINE HERE HAD TO GIVE ME A HAND.
JOHN, THESE ARE MY BABIES. KELSE AND LIVVIE.
I'VE GOT A WEAK SPOT FOR KIDS, EVEN. IN THAT THEY ARE WEAK SPOTS. COMPLETELY DEFENSELESS.
YOU'RE DADDY'S NEW BOYFRIEND?
AND I CAN'T DO THIS.
HOW COULD I EVEN THINK IT WAS OKAY TO KNOW SOMEONE LIKE OLIVER, WHEN IT WOULD RUIN THESE OTHER INNOCENT HUMANS' LIVES?
JOHN?
STAY RIGHT HERE, GIRLS, RIGHT HERE. I'LL BE RIGHT BACK.
WHEN I KNOW WHAT HAPPENS TO EVERYONE IN MY WAKE?

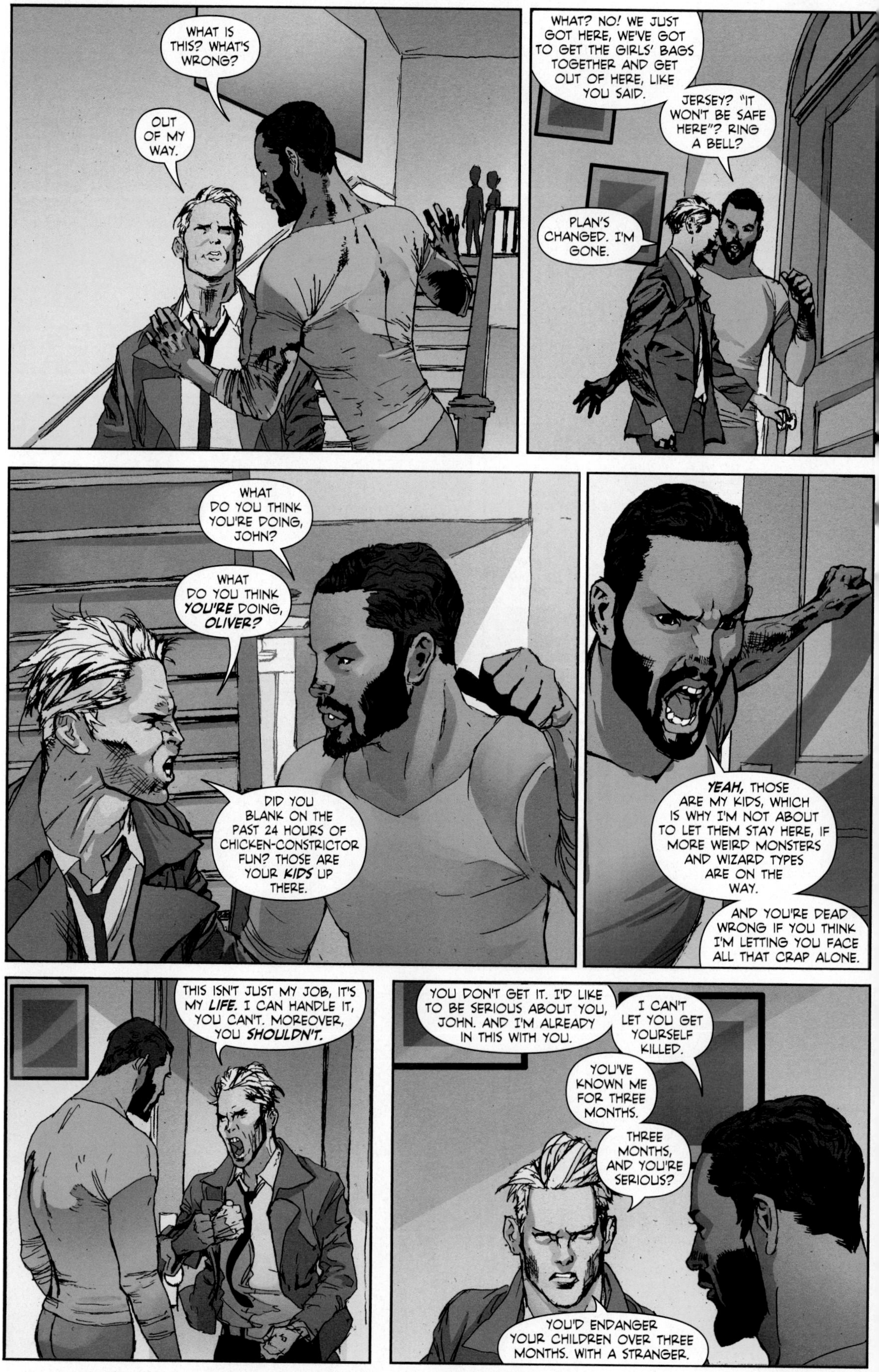
WHAT IS THIS? WHAT'S WRONG?
OUT OF MY WAY.
WHAT? NO! WE JUST GOT HERE, WE'VE GOT TO GET THE GIRLS' BAGS TOGETHER AND GET OUT OF HERE, LIKE YOU SAID.
JERSEY? "IT WON'T BE SAFE HERE"? RING A BELL?
PLAN'S CHANGED. I'M GONE.
WHAT DO YOU THINK YOU'RE DOING, JOHN?
WHAT DO YOU THINK *YOU'RE* DOING, *OLIVER?*
DID YOU BLANK ON THE PAST 24 HOURS OF CHICKEN-CONSTRICTOR FUN? THOSE ARE YOUR *KIDS* UP THERE.
*YEAH,* THOSE ARE MY KIDS, WHICH IS WHY I'M NOT ABOUT TO LET THEM STAY HERE, IF MORE WEIRD MONSTERS AND WIZARD TYPES ARE ON THE WAY.
AND YOU'RE DEAD WRONG IF YOU THINK I'M LETTING YOU FACE ALL THAT CRAP ALONE.
THIS ISN'T JUST MY JOB, IT'S MY *LIFE.* I CAN HANDLE IT, YOU CAN'T. MOREOVER, YOU *SHOULDN'T.*
YOU DON'T GET IT. I'D LIKE TO BE SERIOUS ABOUT YOU, JOHN. AND I'M ALREADY IN THIS WITH YOU.
I CAN'T LET YOU GET YOURSELF KILLED.
YOU'VE KNOWN ME FOR THREE MONTHS.
THREE MONTHS, AND YOU'RE SERIOUS?
YOU'D ENDANGER YOUR CHILDREN OVER THREE MONTHS. WITH A STRANGER.

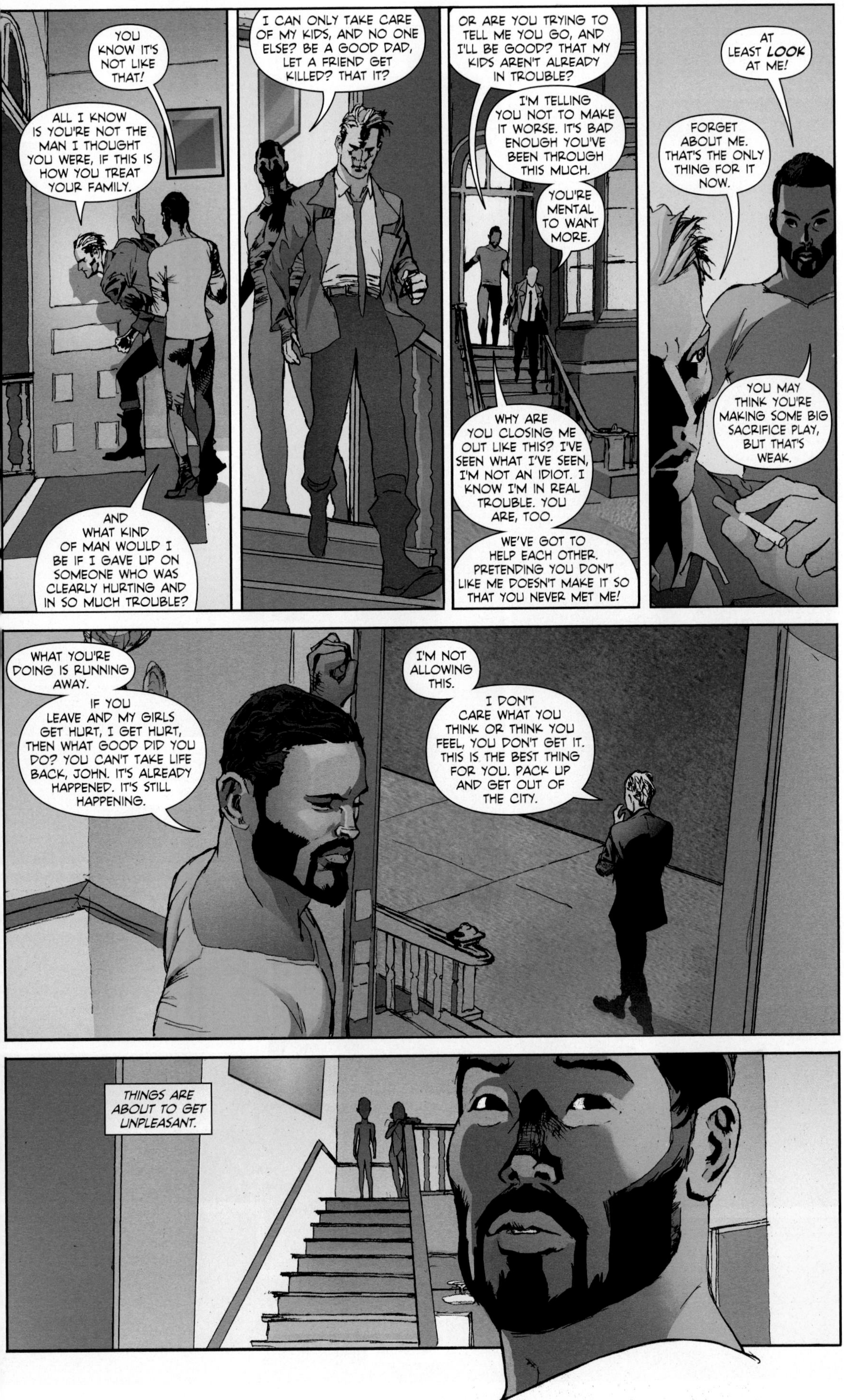
YOU KNOW IT'S NOT LIKE THAT!
ALL I KNOW IS YOU'RE NOT THE MAN I THOUGHT YOU WERE, IF THIS IS HOW YOU TREAT YOUR FAMILY.
AND WHAT KIND OF MAN WOULD I BE IF I GAVE UP ON SOMEONE WHO WAS CLEARLY HURTING AND IN SO MUCH TROUBLE?
I CAN ONLY TAKE CARE OF MY KIDS, AND NO ONE ELSE? BE A GOOD DAD, LET A FRIEND GET KILLED? THAT IT?
OR ARE YOU TRYING TO TELL ME YOU GO, AND I'LL BE GOOD? THAT MY KIDS AREN'T ALREADY IN TROUBLE?
I'M TELLING YOU NOT TO MAKE IT WORSE. IT'S BAD ENOUGH YOU'VE BEEN THROUGH THIS MUCH.
YOU'RE MENTAL TO WANT MORE.
WHY ARE YOU CLOSING ME OUT LIKE THIS? I'VE SEEN WHAT I'VE SEEN, I'M NOT AN IDIOT. I KNOW I'M IN REAL TROUBLE. YOU ARE, TOO.
WE'VE GOT TO HELP EACH OTHER. PRETENDING YOU DON'T LIKE ME DOESN'T MAKE IT SO THAT YOU NEVER MET ME!
AT LEAST LOOK AT ME!
FORGET ABOUT ME. THAT'S THE ONLY THING FOR IT NOW.
YOU MAY THINK YOU'RE MAKING SOME BIG SACRIFICE PLAY, BUT THAT'S WEAK.
WHAT YOU'RE DOING IS RUNNING AWAY.
IF YOU LEAVE AND MY GIRLS GET HURT, I GET HURT, THEN WHAT GOOD DID YOU DO? YOU CAN'T TAKE LIFE BACK, JOHN. IT'S ALREADY HAPPENED. IT'S STILL HAPPENING.
I'M NOT ALLOWING THIS.
I DON'T CARE WHAT YOU THINK OR THINK YOU FEEL, YOU DON'T GET IT. THIS IS THE BEST THING FOR YOU. PACK UP AND GET OUT OF THE CITY.
THINGS ARE ABOUT TO GET UNPLEASANT.

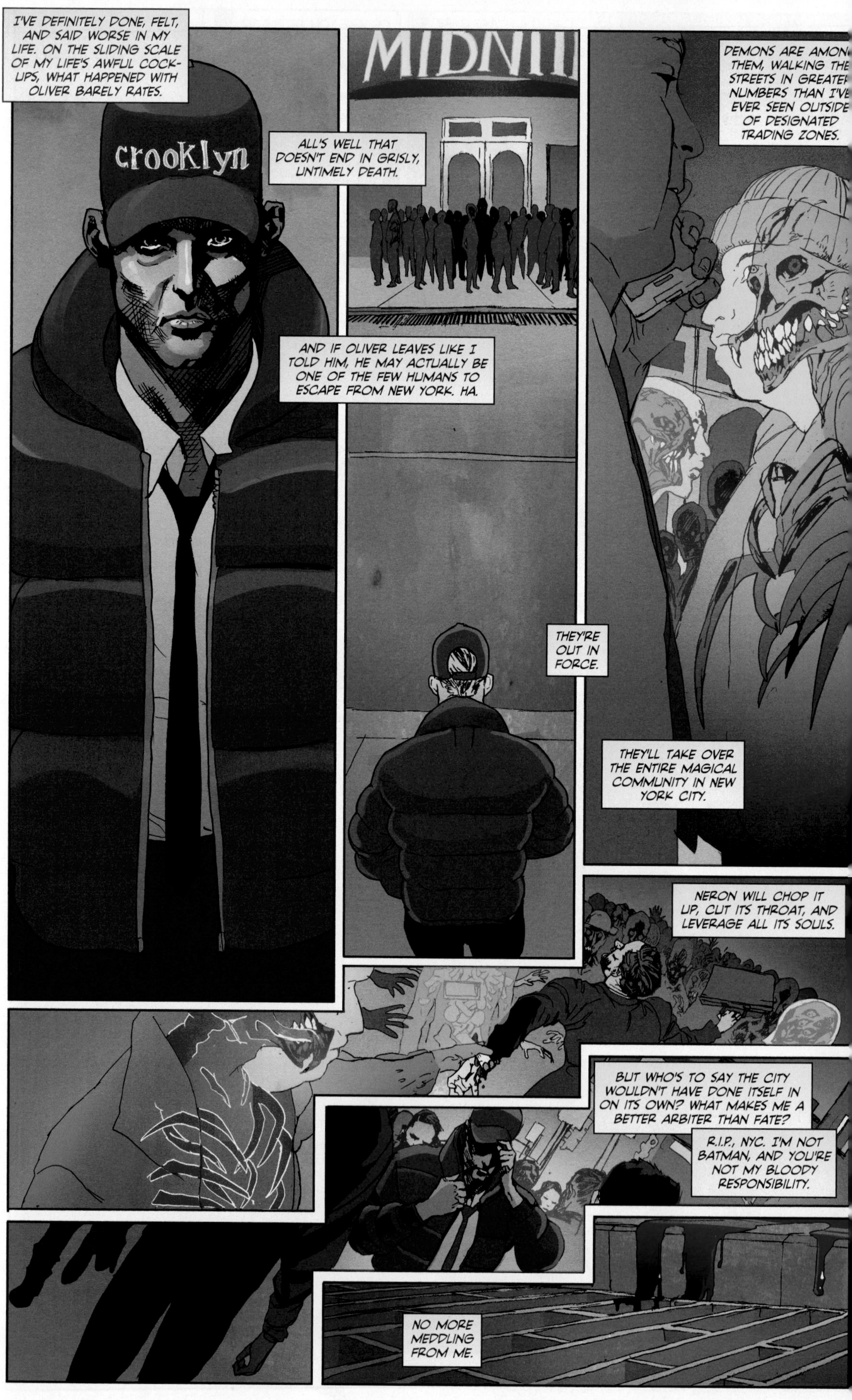
I'VE DEFINITELY DONE, FELT, AND SAID WORSE IN MY LIFE. ON THE SLIDING SCALE OF MY LIFE'S AWFUL COCK-UPS, WHAT HAPPENED WITH OLIVER BARELY RATES.
crooKlyn
MIDNI
ALL'S WELL THAT DOESN'T END IN GRISLY, UNTIMELY DEATH.
AND IF OLIVER LEAVES LIKE I TOLD HIM, HE MAY ACTUALLY BE ONE OF THE FEW HUMANS TO ESCAPE FROM NEW YORK. HA.
THEY'RE OUT IN FORCE.
DEMONS ARE AMON THEM, WALKING THE STREETS IN GREATE NUMBERS THAN I'VE EVER SEEN OUTSIDE OF DESIGNATED TRADING ZONES.
THEY'LL TAKE OVER THE ENTIRE MAGICAL COMMUNITY IN NEW YORK CITY.
NERON WILL CHOP IT UP, CUT ITS THROAT, AND LEVERAGE ALL ITS SOULS.
BUT WHO'S TO SAY THE CITY WOULDN'T HAVE DONE ITSELF IN ON ITS OWN? WHAT MAKES ME A BETTER ARBITER THAN FATE?
R.I.P., NYC. I'M NOT BATMAN, AND YOU'RE NOT MY BLOODY RESPONSIBILITY.
NO MORE MEDDLING FROM ME.

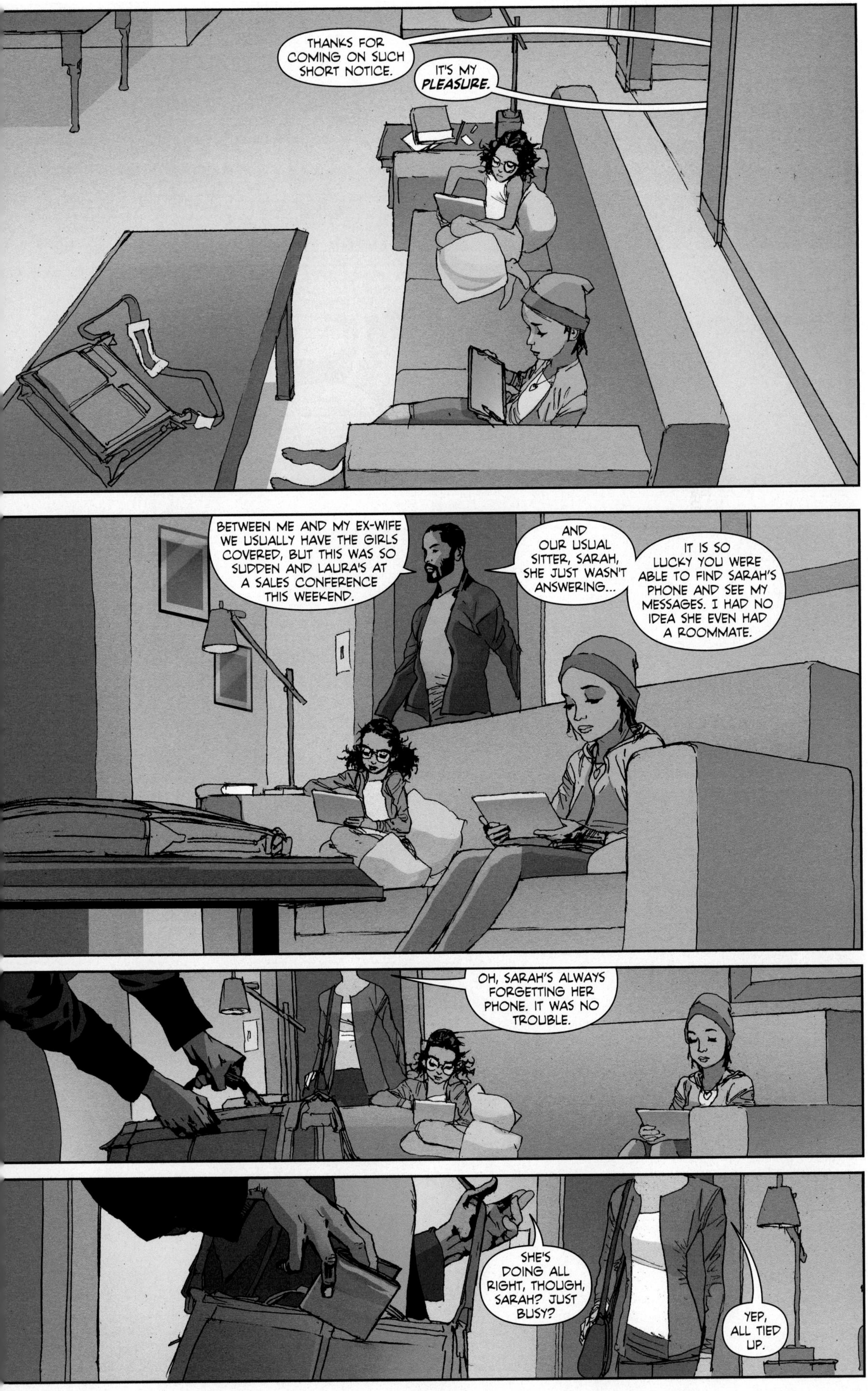
THANKS FOR COMING ON SUCH SHORT NOTICE.
IT'S MY *PLEASURE.*
BETWEEN ME AND MY EX-WIFE WE USUALLY HAVE THE GIRLS COVERED, BUT THIS WAS SO SUDDEN AND LAURA'S AT A SALES CONFERENCE THIS WEEKEND.
AND OUR USUAL SITTER, SARAH, SHE JUST WASN'T ANSWERING...
IT IS SO LUCKY YOU WERE ABLE TO FIND SARAH'S PHONE AND SEE MY MESSAGES. I HAD NO IDEA SHE EVEN HAD A ROOMMATE.
OH, SARAH'S ALWAYS FORGETTING HER PHONE. IT WAS NO TROUBLE.
SHE'S DOING ALL RIGHT, THOUGH, SARAH? JUST BUSY?
YEP, ALL TIED UP.

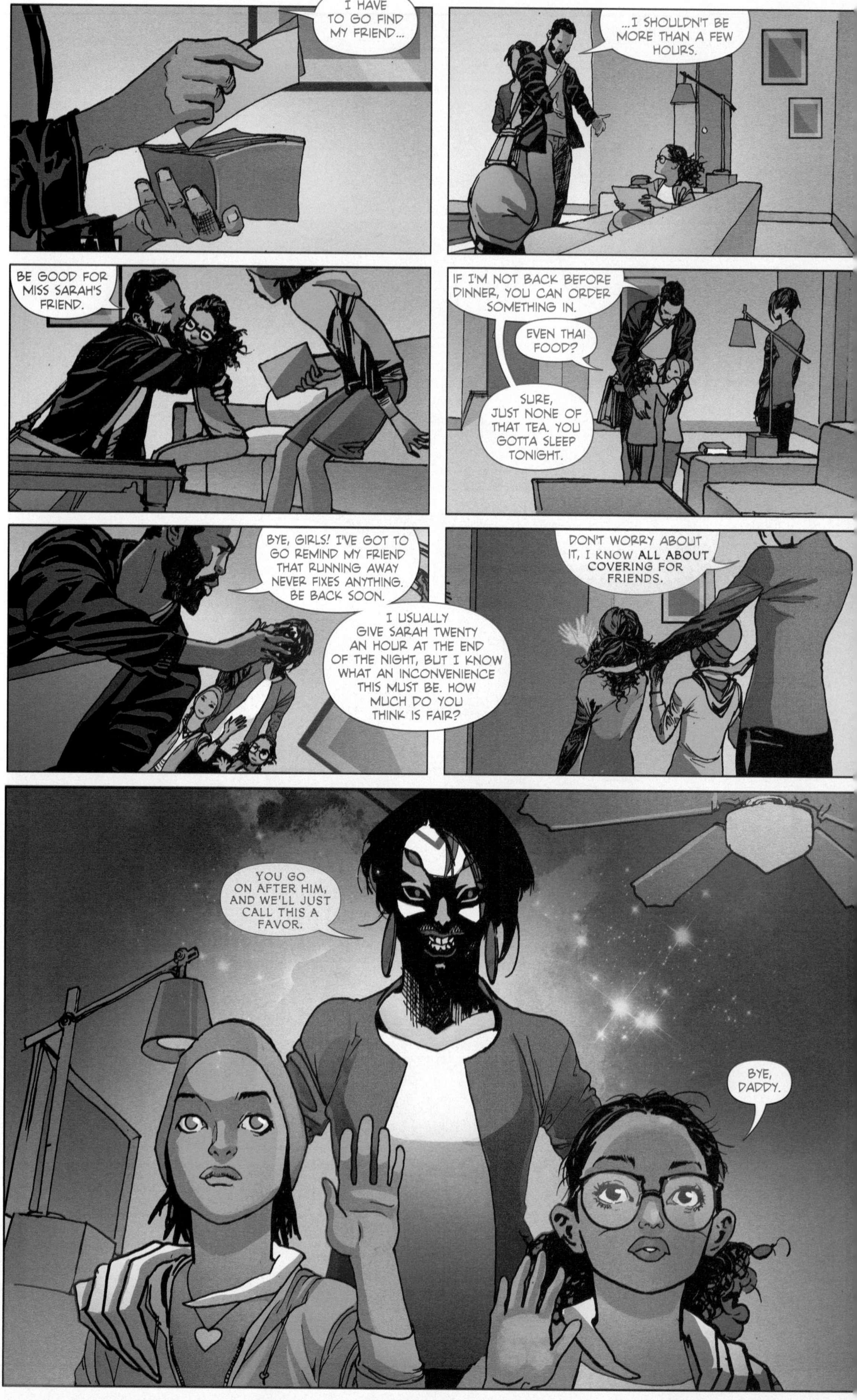
I HAVE TO GO FIND MY FRIEND...
...I SHOULDN'T BE MORE THAN A FEW HOURS.
BE GOOD FOR MISS SARAH'S FRIEND.
IF I'M NOT BACK BEFORE DINNER, YOU CAN ORDER SOMETHING IN.
EVEN THAI FOOD?
SURE, JUST NONE OF THAT TEA. YOU GOTTA SLEEP TONIGHT.
BYE, GIRLS! I'VE GOT TO GO REMIND MY FRIEND THAT RUNNING AWAY NEVER FIXES ANYTHING. BE BACK SOON.
I USUALLY GIVE SARAH TWENTY AN HOUR AT THE END OF THE NIGHT, BUT I KNOW WHAT AN INCONVENIENCE THIS MUST BE. HOW MUCH DO YOU THINK IS FAIR?
DON'T WORRY ABOUT IT, I KNOW ALL ABOUT COVERING FOR FRIENDS.
YOU GO ON AFTER HIM, AND WE'LL JUST CALL THIS A FAVOR.
BYE, DADDY.

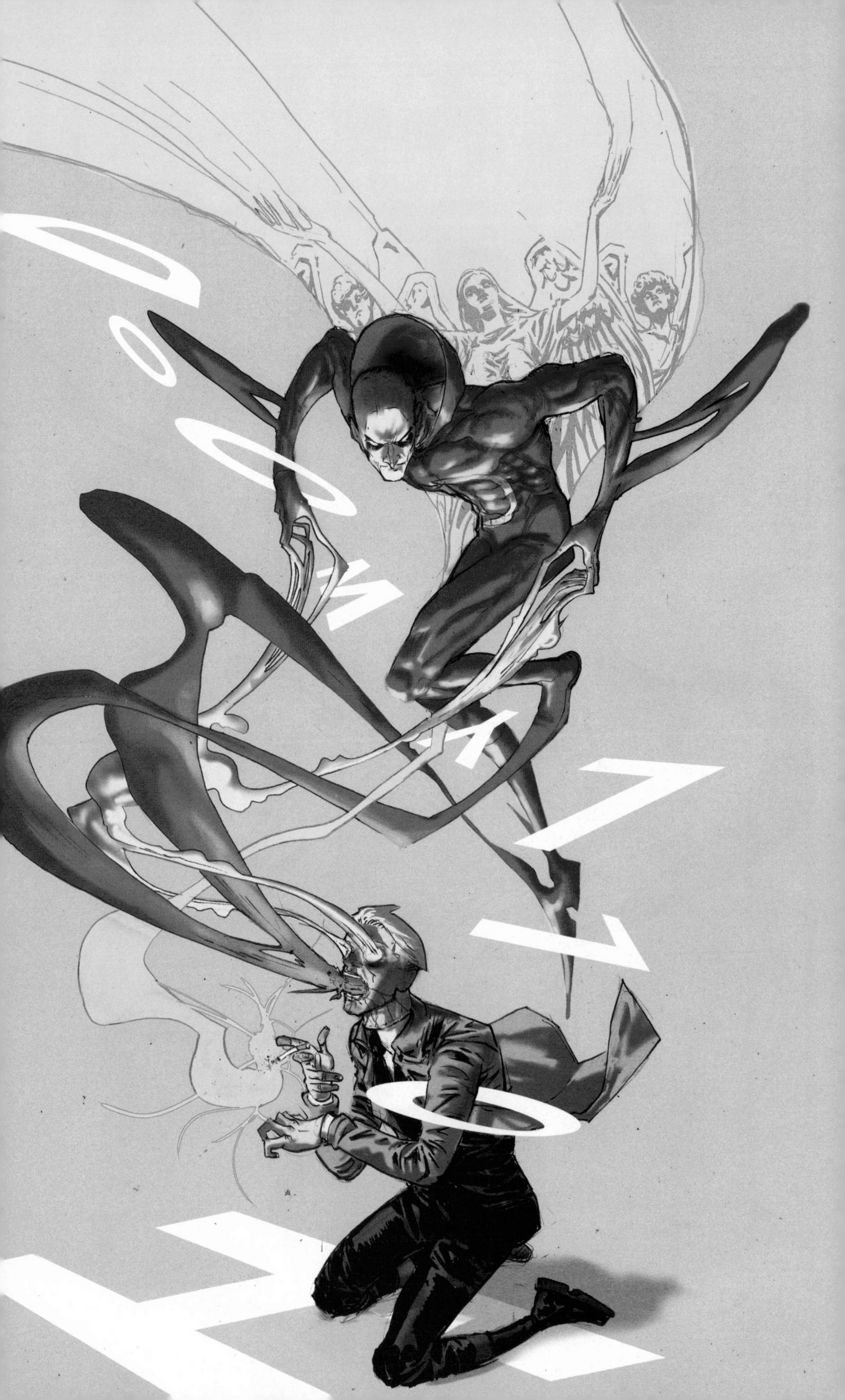

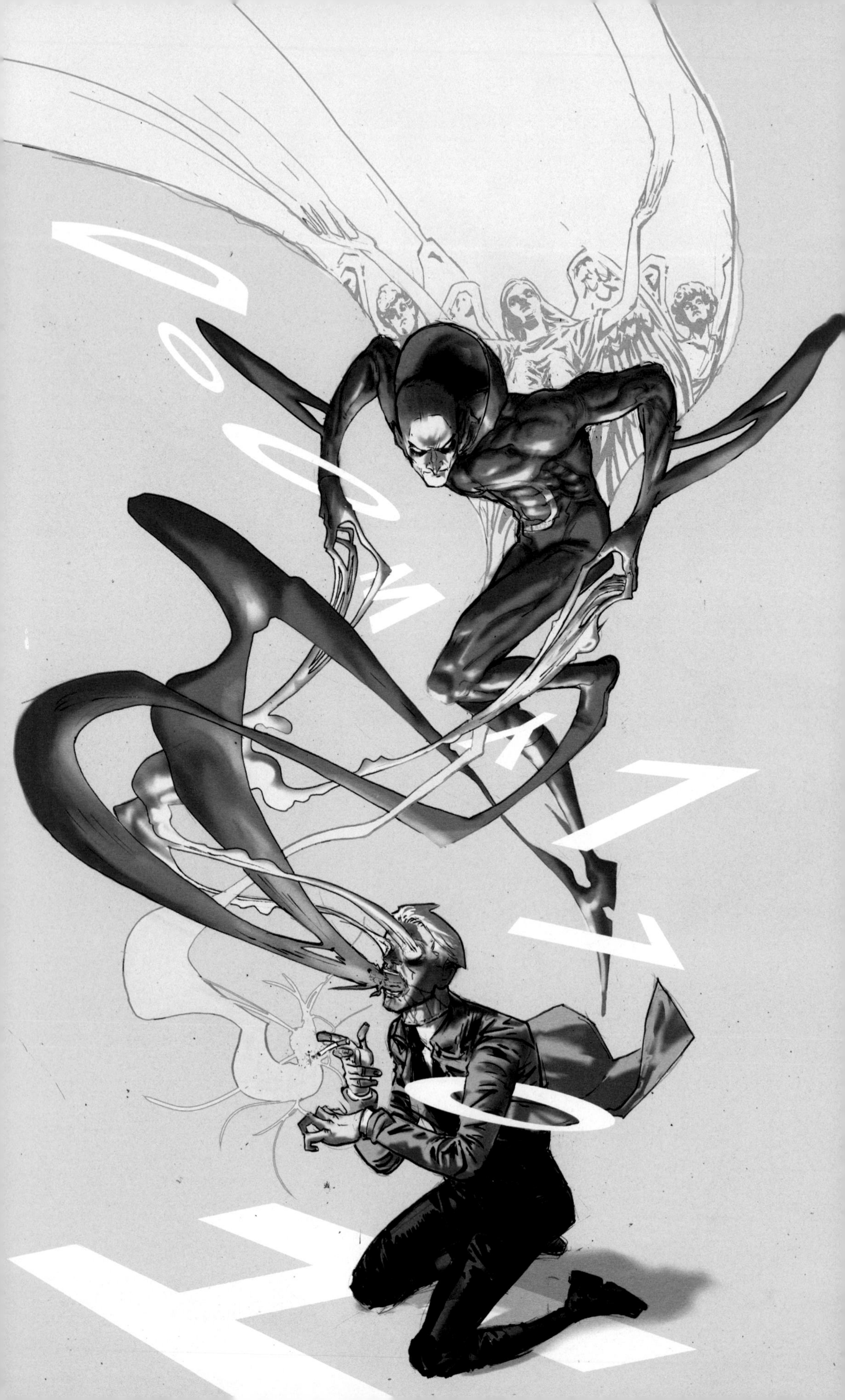

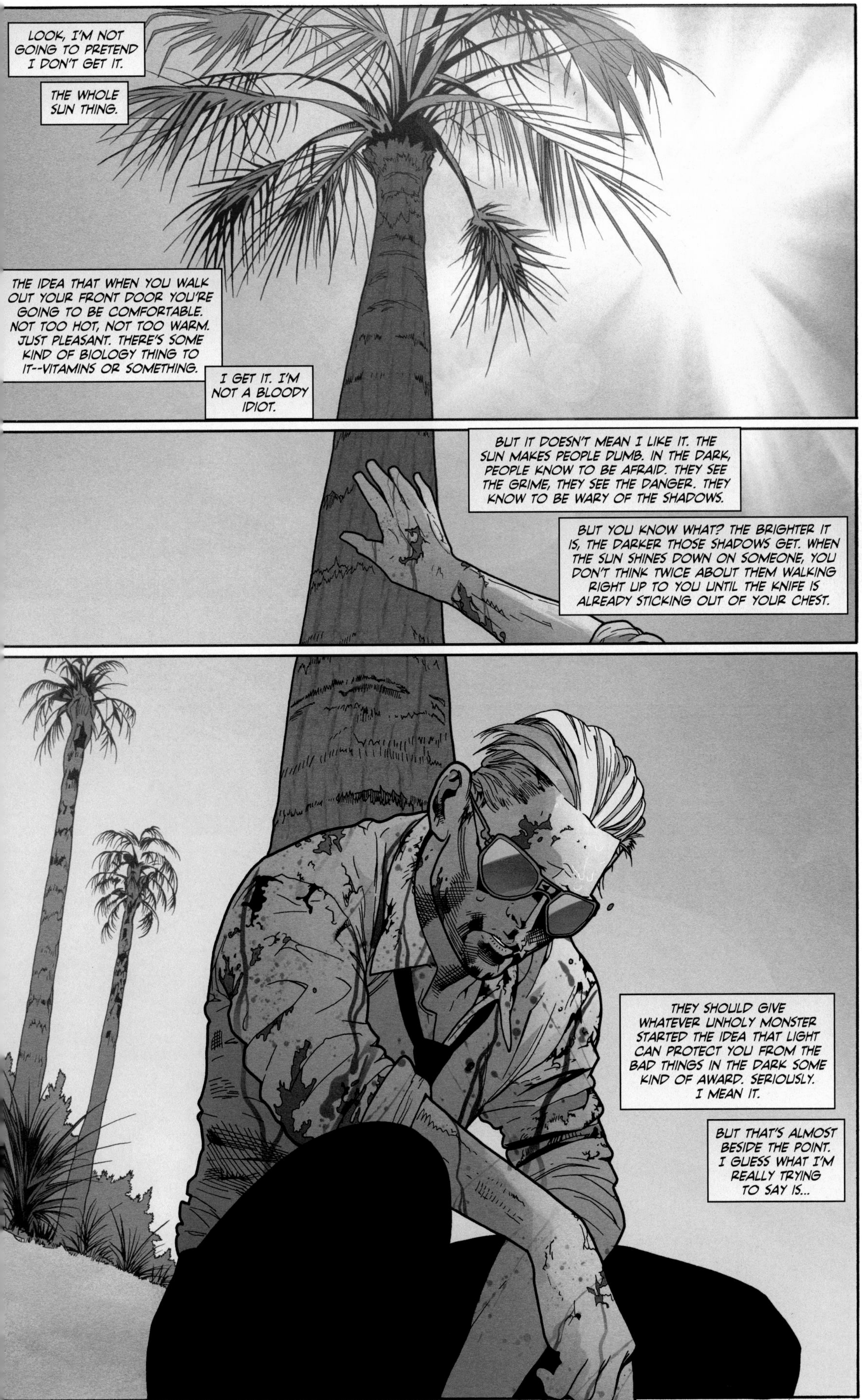
LOOK, I'M NOT GOING TO PRETEND I DON'T GET IT.
THE WHOLE SUN THING.
THE IDEA THAT WHEN YOU WALK OUT YOUR FRONT DOOR YOU'RE GOING TO BE COMFORTABLE. NOT TOO HOT, NOT TOO WARM. JUST PLEASANT. THERE'S SOME KIND OF BIOLOGY THING TO IT--VITAMINS OR SOMETHING.
I GET IT. I'M NOT A BLOODY IDIOT.
BUT IT DOESN'T MEAN I LIKE IT. THE SUN MAKES PEOPLE DUMB. IN THE DARK, PEOPLE KNOW TO BE AFRAID. THEY SEE THE GRIME, THEY SEE THE DANGER. THEY KNOW TO BE WARY OF THE SHADOWS.
BUT YOU KNOW WHAT? THE BRIGHTER IT IS, THE DARKER THOSE SHADOWS GET. WHEN THE SUN SHINES DOWN ON SOMEONE, YOU DON'T THINK TWICE ABOUT THEM WALKING RIGHT UP TO YOU UNTIL THE KNIFE IS ALREADY STICKING OUT OF YOUR CHEST.
THEY SHOULD GIVE WHATEVER UNHOLY MONSTER STARTED THE IDEA THAT LIGHT CAN PROTECT YOU FROM THE BAD THINGS IN THE DARK SOME KIND OF AWARD. SERIOUSLY. I MEAN IT.
BUT THAT'S ALMOST BESIDE THE POINT. I GUESS WHAT I'M REALLY TRYING TO SAY IS...

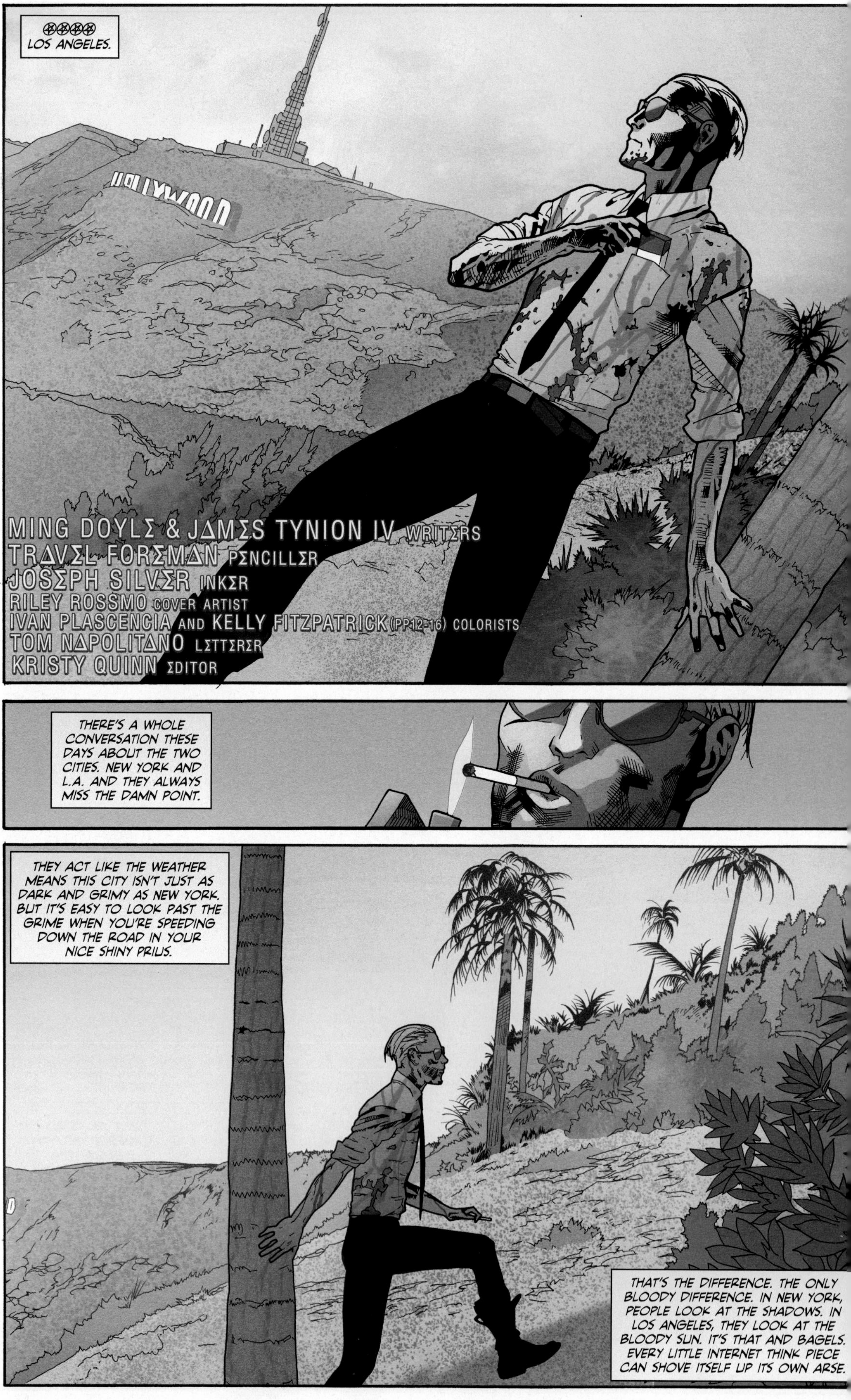
LOS ANGELES.
MING DOYLE & JAMES TYNION IV WRITERS
TRAVEL FOREMAN PENCILLER
JOSEPH SILVER INKER
RILEY ROSSMO COVER ARTIST
IVAN PLASCENCIA AND KELLY FITZPATRICK (PP12-16) COLORISTS
TOM NAPOLITANO LETTERER
KRISTY QUINN EDITOR
THERE'S A WHOLE CONVERSATION THESE DAYS ABOUT THE TWO CITIES. NEW YORK AND L.A. AND THEY ALWAYS MISS THE DAMN POINT.
THEY ACT LIKE THE WEATHER MEANS THIS CITY ISN'T JUST AS DARK AND GRIMY AS NEW YORK. BUT IT'S EASY TO LOOK PAST THE GRIME WHEN YOU'RE SPEEDING DOWN THE ROAD IN YOUR NICE SHINY PRIUS.
THAT'S THE DIFFERENCE. THE ONLY BLOODY DIFFERENCE. IN NEW YORK, PEOPLE LOOK AT THE SHADOWS. IN LOS ANGELES, THEY LOOK AT THE BLOODY SUN. IT'S THAT AND BAGELS. EVERY LITTLE INTERNET THINK PIECE CAN SHOVE ITSELF UP ITS OWN ARSE.

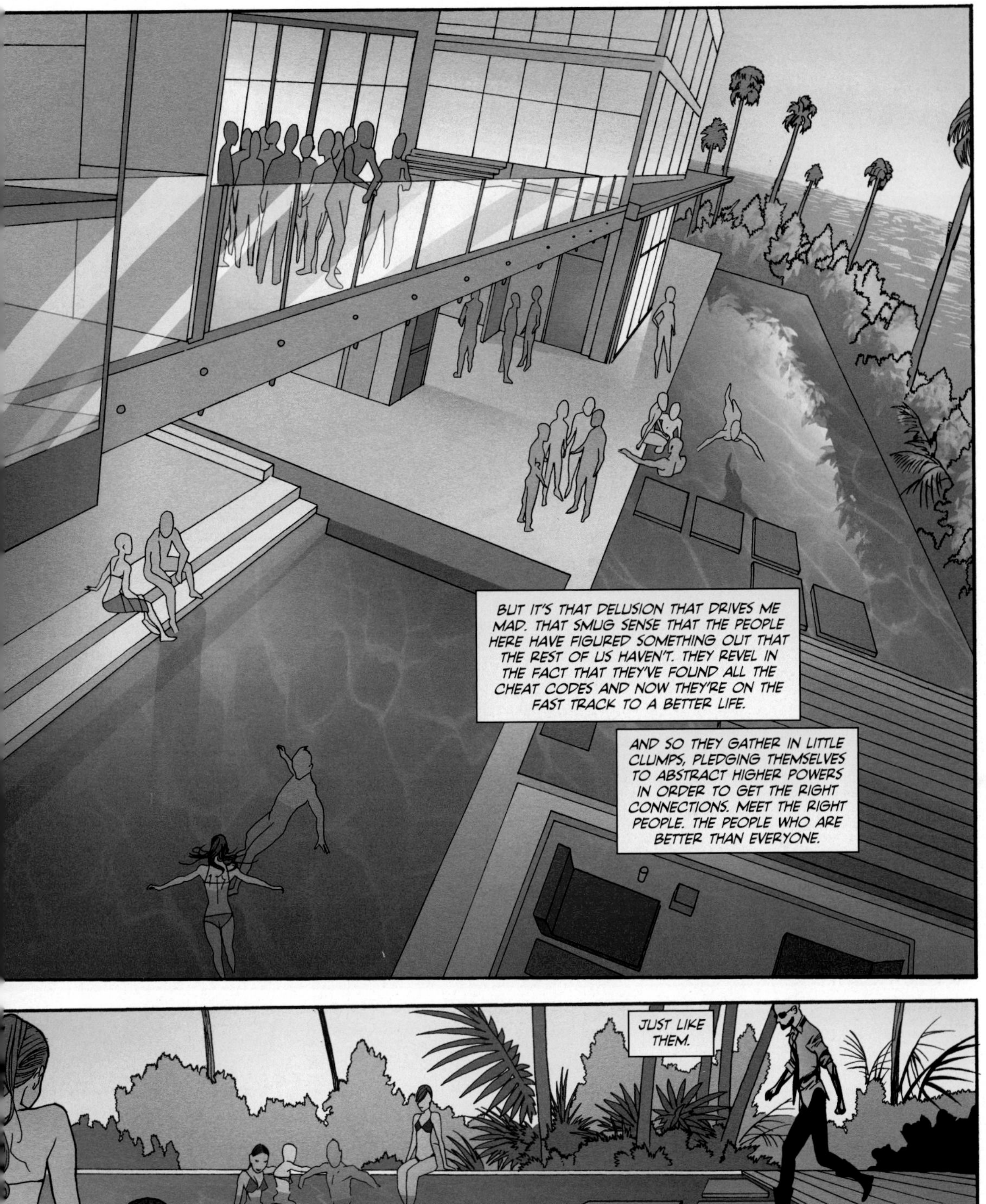
BUT IT'S THAT DELUSION THAT DRIVES ME MAD. THAT SMUG SENSE THAT THE PEOPLE HERE HAVE FIGURED SOMETHING OUT THAT THE REST OF US HAVEN'T. THEY REVEL IN THE FACT THAT THEY'VE FOUND ALL THE CHEAT CODES AND NOW THEY'RE ON THE FAST TRACK TO A BETTER LIFE.
AND SO THEY GATHER IN LITTLE CLUMPS, PLEDGING THEMSELVES TO ABSTRACT HIGHER POWERS IN ORDER TO GET THE RIGHT CONNECTIONS. MEET THE RIGHT PEOPLE. THE PEOPLE WHO ARE BETTER THAN EVERYONE.

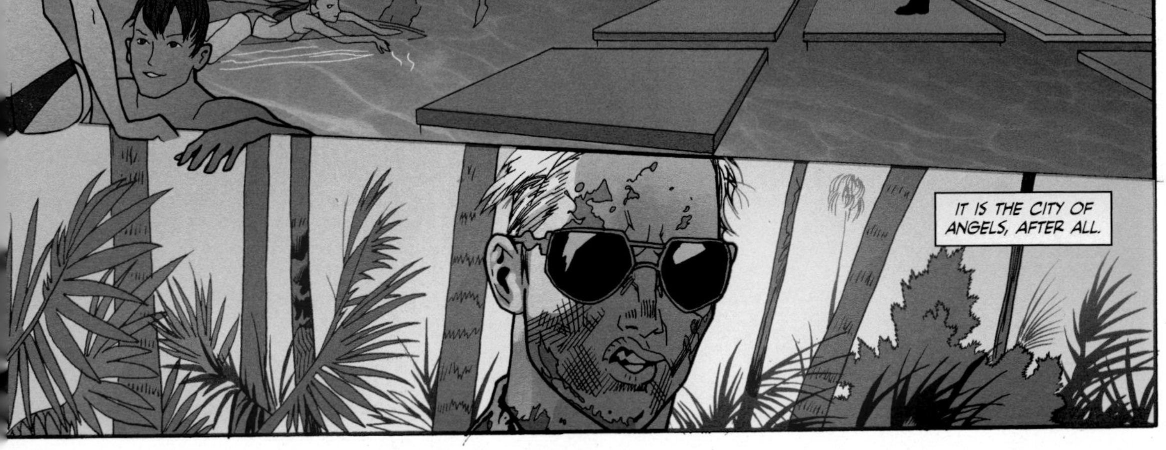
JUST LIKE THEM.
IT IS THE CITY OF ANGELS, AFTER ALL.

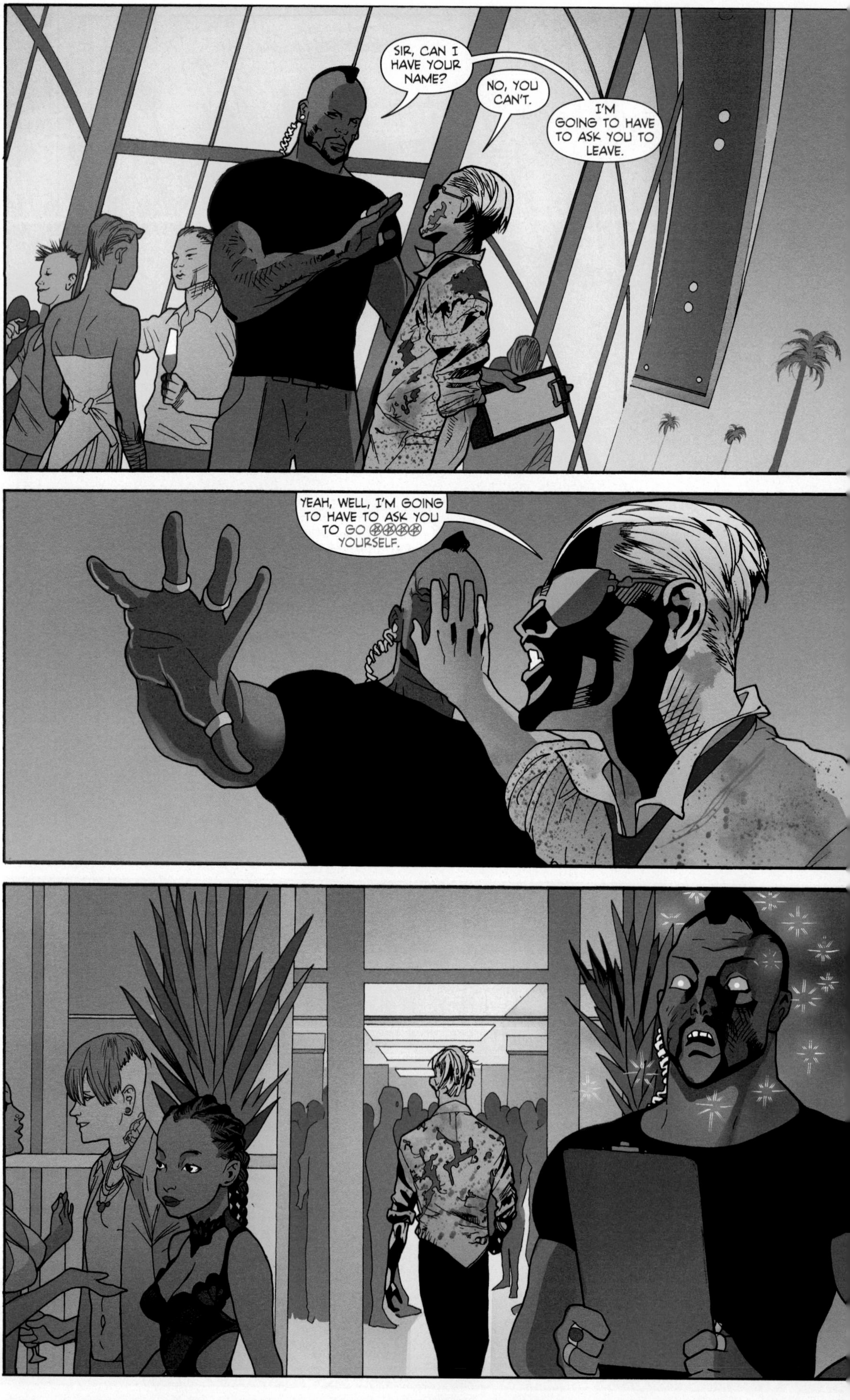

SIR, CAN I HAVE YOUR NAME?
NO, YOU CAN'T.
I'M GOING TO HAVE TO ASK YOU TO LEAVE.
YEAH, WELL, I'M GOING TO HAVE TO ASK YOU TO GO ⊛⊛⊛⊛ YOURSELF.

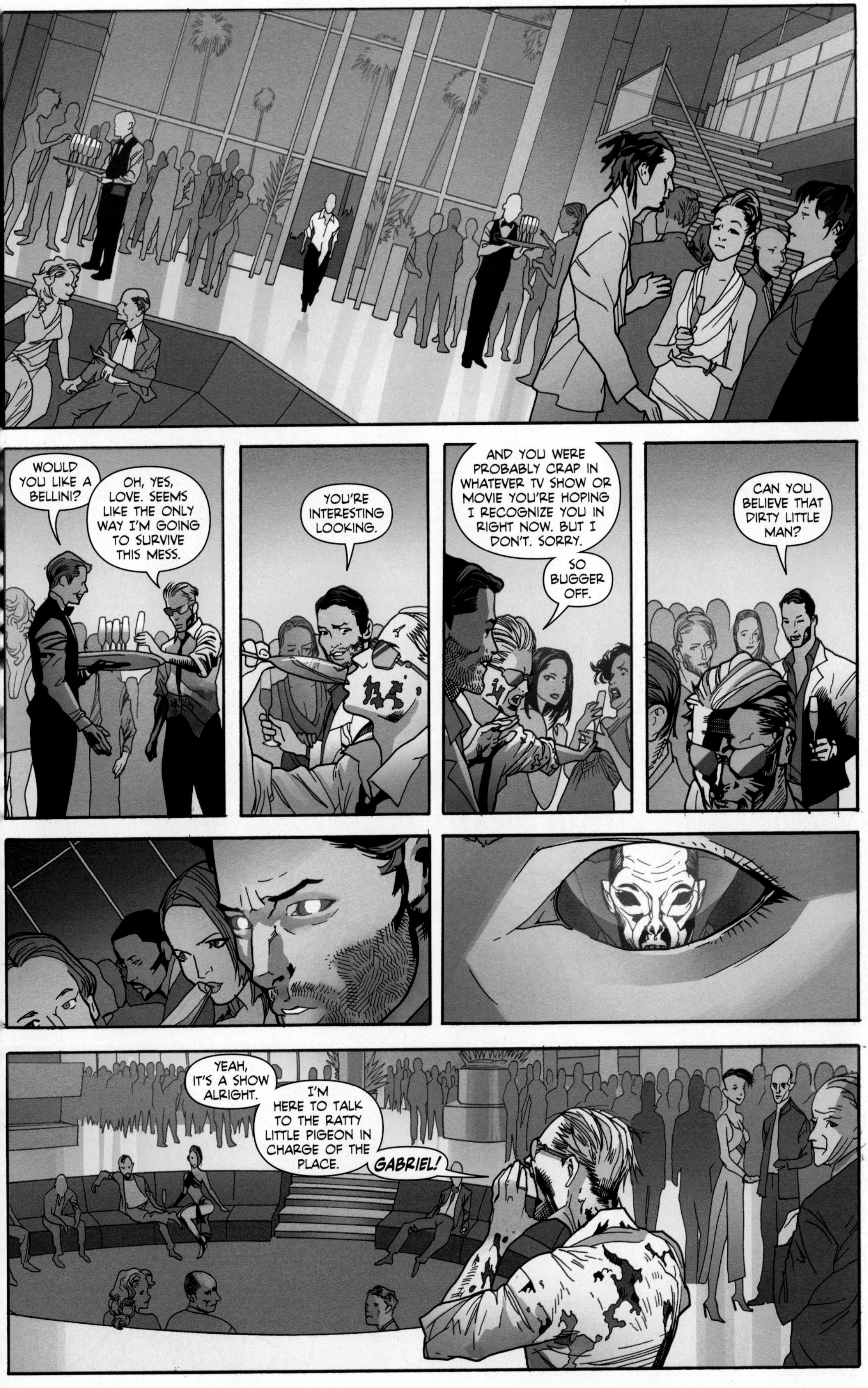

WOULD YOU LIKE A BELLINI?
OH, YES, LOVE. SEEMS LIKE THE ONLY WAY I'M GOING TO SURVIVE THIS MESS.
YOU'RE INTERESTING LOOKING.
AND YOU WERE PROBABLY CRAP IN WHATEVER TV SHOW OR MOVIE YOU'RE HOPING I RECOGNIZE YOU IN RIGHT NOW. BUT I DON'T. SORRY.
SO BUGGER OFF.
CAN YOU BELIEVE THAT DIRTY LITTLE MAN?
YEAH, IT'S A SHOW ALRIGHT.
I'M HERE TO TALK TO THE RATTY LITTLE PIGEON IN CHARGE OF THE PLACE.
GABRIEL!

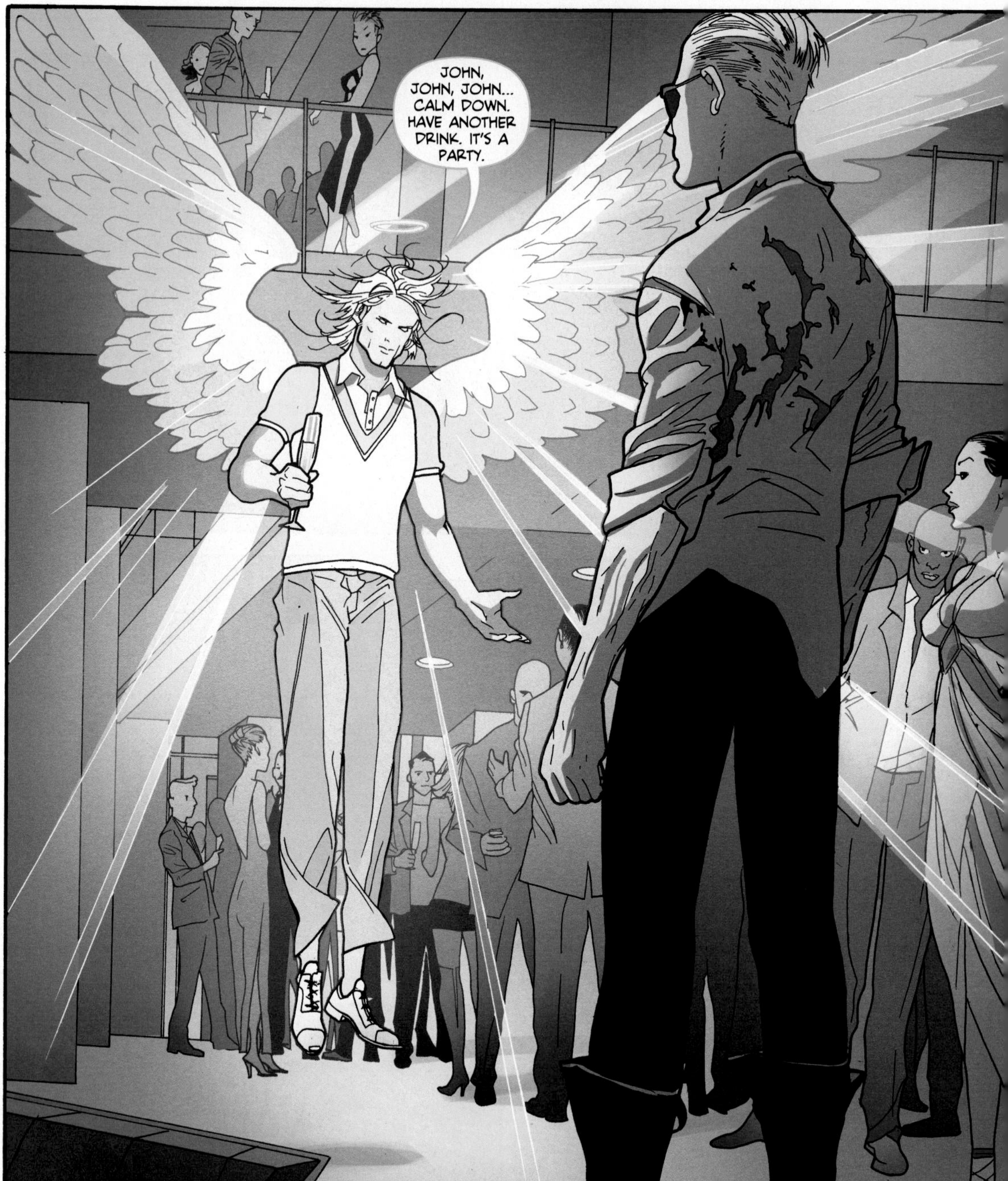
JOHN, JOHN, JOHN... CALM DOWN. HAVE ANOTHER DRINK. IT'S A PARTY.

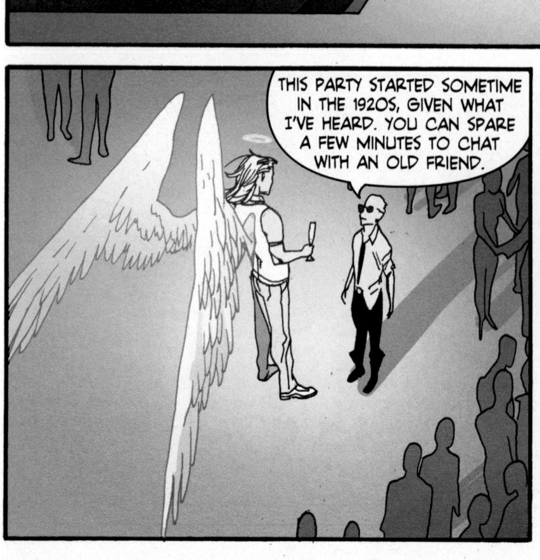
THIS PARTY STARTED SOMETIME IN THE 1920S, GIVEN WHAT I'VE HEARD. YOU CAN SPARE A FEW MINUTES TO CHAT WITH AN OLD FRIEND.

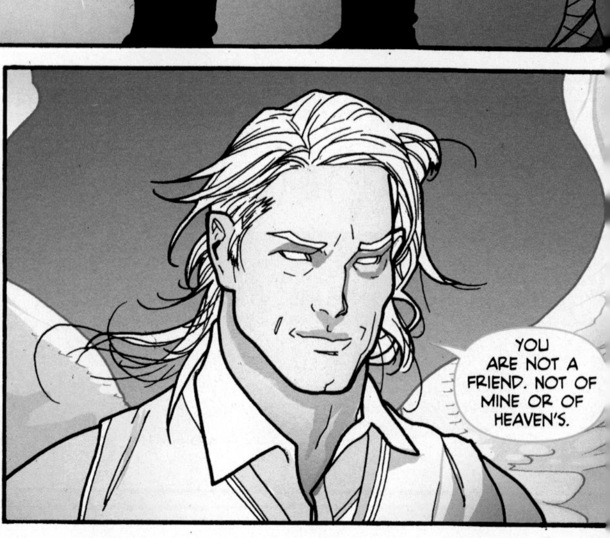
YOU ARE NOT A FRIEND. NOT OF MINE OR OF HEAVEN'S.

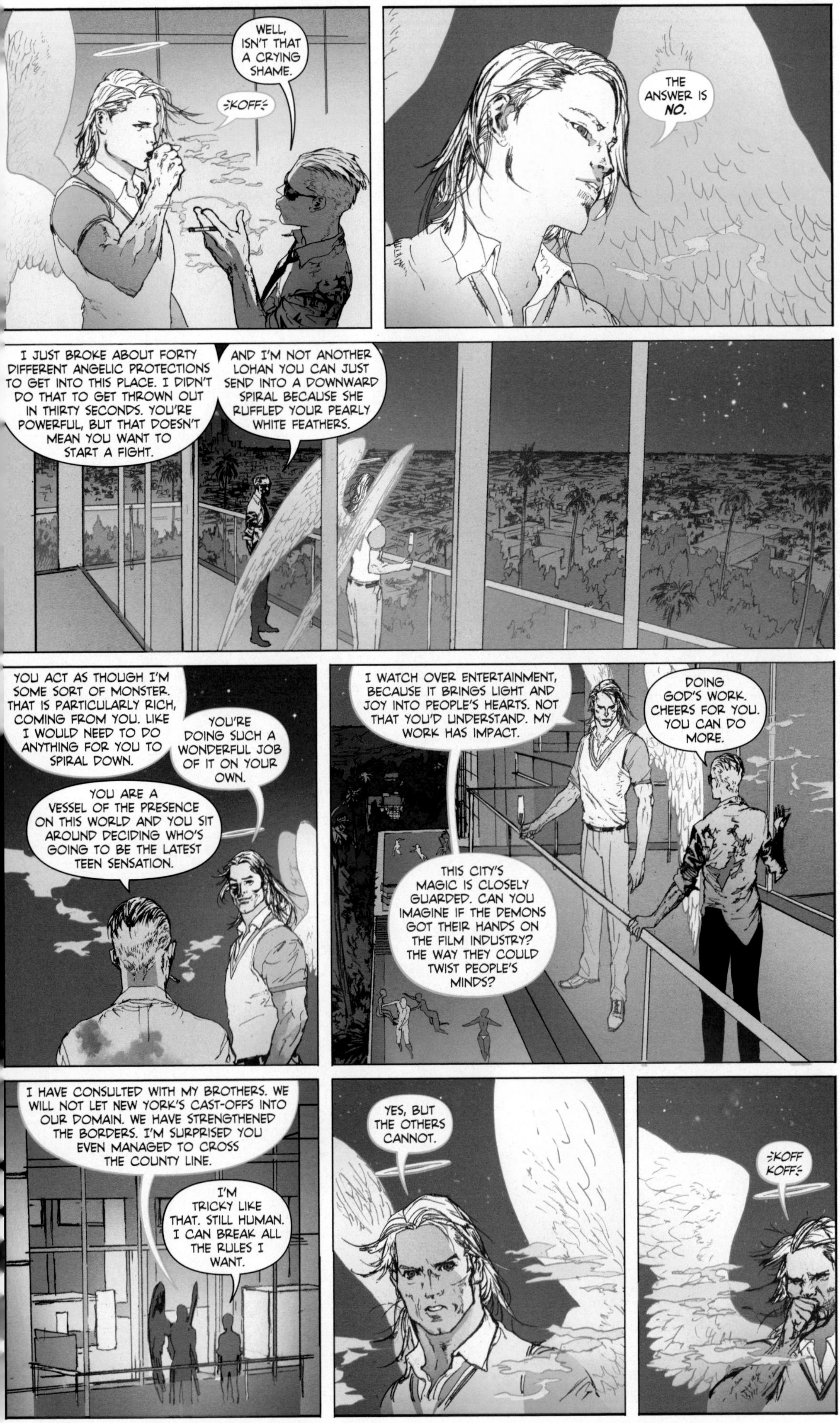
WELL, ISN'T THAT A CRYING SHAME.
KOFF
THE ANSWER IS NO.
I JUST BROKE ABOUT FORTY DIFFERENT ANGELIC PROTECTIONS TO GET INTO THIS PLACE. I DIDN'T DO THAT TO GET THROWN OUT IN THIRTY SECONDS. YOU'RE POWERFUL, BUT THAT DOESN'T MEAN YOU WANT TO START A FIGHT.
AND I'M NOT ANOTHER LOHAN YOU CAN JUST SEND INTO A DOWNWARD SPIRAL BECAUSE SHE RUFFLED YOUR PEARLY WHITE FEATHERS.
YOU ACT AS THOUGH I'M SOME SORT OF MONSTER. THAT IS PARTICULARLY RICH, COMING FROM YOU. LIKE I WOULD NEED TO DO ANYTHING FOR YOU TO SPIRAL DOWN.
YOU'RE DOING SUCH A WONDERFUL JOB OF IT ON YOUR OWN.
YOU ARE A VESSEL OF THE PRESENCE ON THIS WORLD AND YOU SIT AROUND DECIDING WHO'S GOING TO BE THE LATEST TEEN SENSATION.
I WATCH OVER ENTERTAINMENT, BECAUSE IT BRINGS LIGHT AND JOY INTO PEOPLE'S HEARTS. NOT THAT YOU'D UNDERSTAND. MY WORK HAS IMPACT.
DOING GOD'S WORK. CHEERS FOR YOU. YOU CAN DO MORE.
THIS CITY'S MAGIC IS CLOSELY GUARDED. CAN YOU IMAGINE IF THE DEMONS GOT THEIR HANDS ON THE FILM INDUSTRY? THE WAY THEY COULD TWIST PEOPLE'S MINDS?
I HAVE CONSULTED WITH MY BROTHERS. WE WILL NOT LET NEW YORK'S CAST-OFFS INTO OUR DOMAIN. WE HAVE STRENGTHENED THE BORDERS. I'M SURPRISED YOU EVEN MANAGED TO CROSS THE COUNTY LINE.
I'M TRICKY LIKE THAT. STILL HUMAN. I CAN BREAK ALL THE RULES I WANT.
YES, BUT THE OTHERS CANNOT.
KOFF KOFF

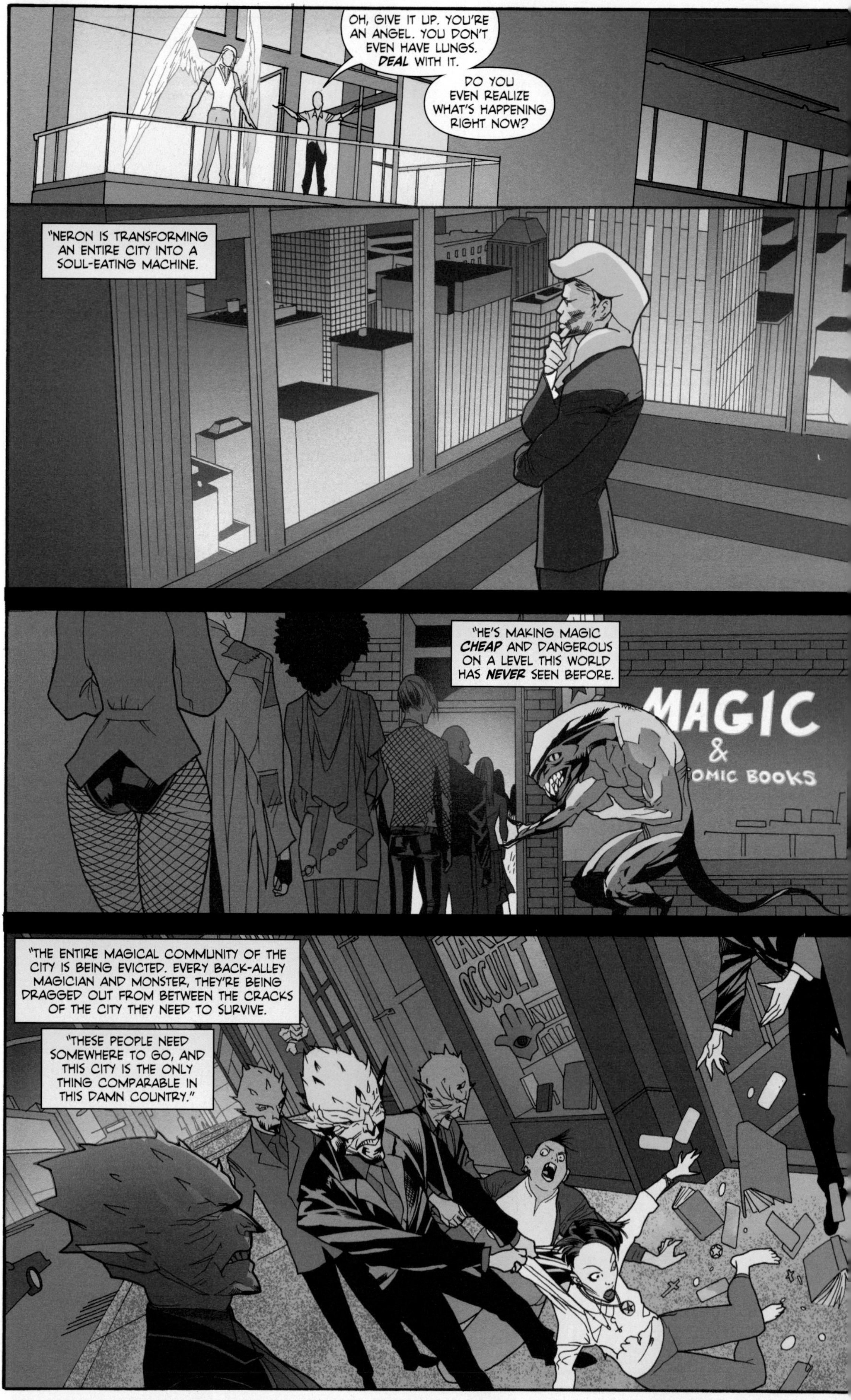

OH, GIVE IT UP. YOU'RE AN ANGEL. YOU DON'T EVEN HAVE LUNGS. **DEAL** WITH IT.
DO YOU EVEN REALIZE WHAT'S HAPPENING RIGHT NOW?
"NERON IS TRANSFORMING AN ENTIRE CITY INTO A SOUL-EATING MACHINE.
"HE'S MAKING MAGIC **CHEAP** AND DANGEROUS ON A LEVEL THIS WORLD HAS **NEVER** SEEN BEFORE.
MAGIC
&
OMIC BOOKS
"THE ENTIRE MAGICAL COMMUNITY OF THE CITY IS BEING EVICTED. EVERY BACK-ALLEY MAGICIAN AND MONSTER, THEY'RE BEING DRAGGED OUT FROM BETWEEN THE CRACKS OF THE CITY THEY NEED TO SURVIVE.
OCCULT
"THESE PEOPLE NEED SOMEWHERE TO GO, AND THIS CITY IS THE ONLY THING COMPARABLE IN THIS DAMN COUNTRY."

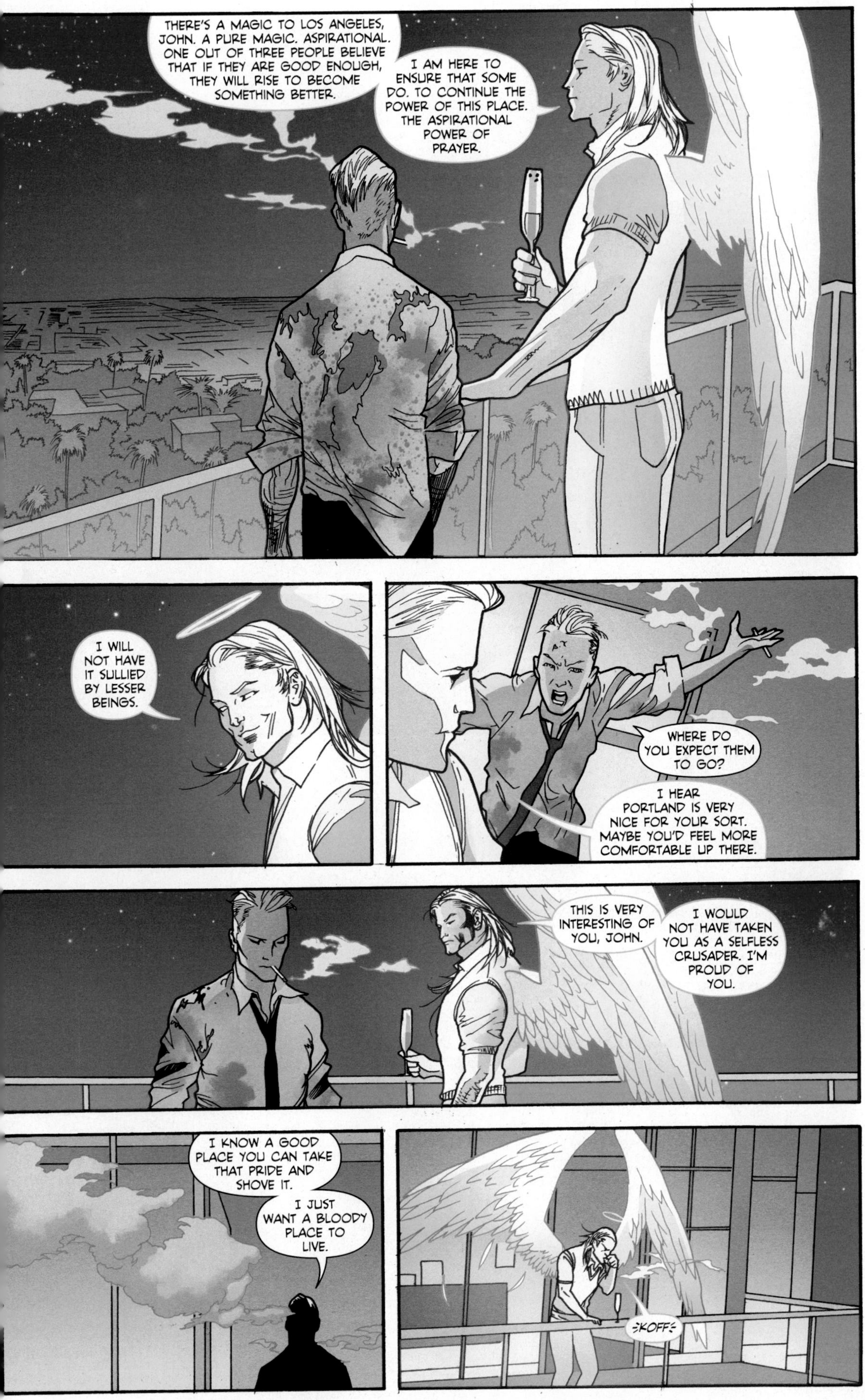
THERE'S A MAGIC TO LOS ANGELES, JOHN. A PURE MAGIC. ASPIRATIONAL. ONE OUT OF THREE PEOPLE BELIEVE THAT IF THEY ARE GOOD ENOUGH, THEY WILL RISE TO BECOME SOMETHING BETTER.
I AM HERE TO ENSURE THAT SOME DO. TO CONTINUE THE POWER OF THIS PLACE. THE ASPIRATIONAL POWER OF PRAYER.
I WILL NOT HAVE IT SULLIED BY LESSER BEINGS.
WHERE DO YOU EXPECT THEM TO GO?
I HEAR PORTLAND IS VERY NICE FOR YOUR SORT. MAYBE YOU'D FEEL MORE COMFORTABLE UP THERE.
THIS IS VERY INTERESTING OF YOU, JOHN.
I WOULD NOT HAVE TAKEN YOU AS A SELFLESS CRUSADER. I'M PROUD OF YOU.
I KNOW A GOOD PLACE YOU CAN TAKE THAT PRIDE AND SHOVE IT.
I JUST WANT A BLOODY PLACE TO LIVE.
KOFF

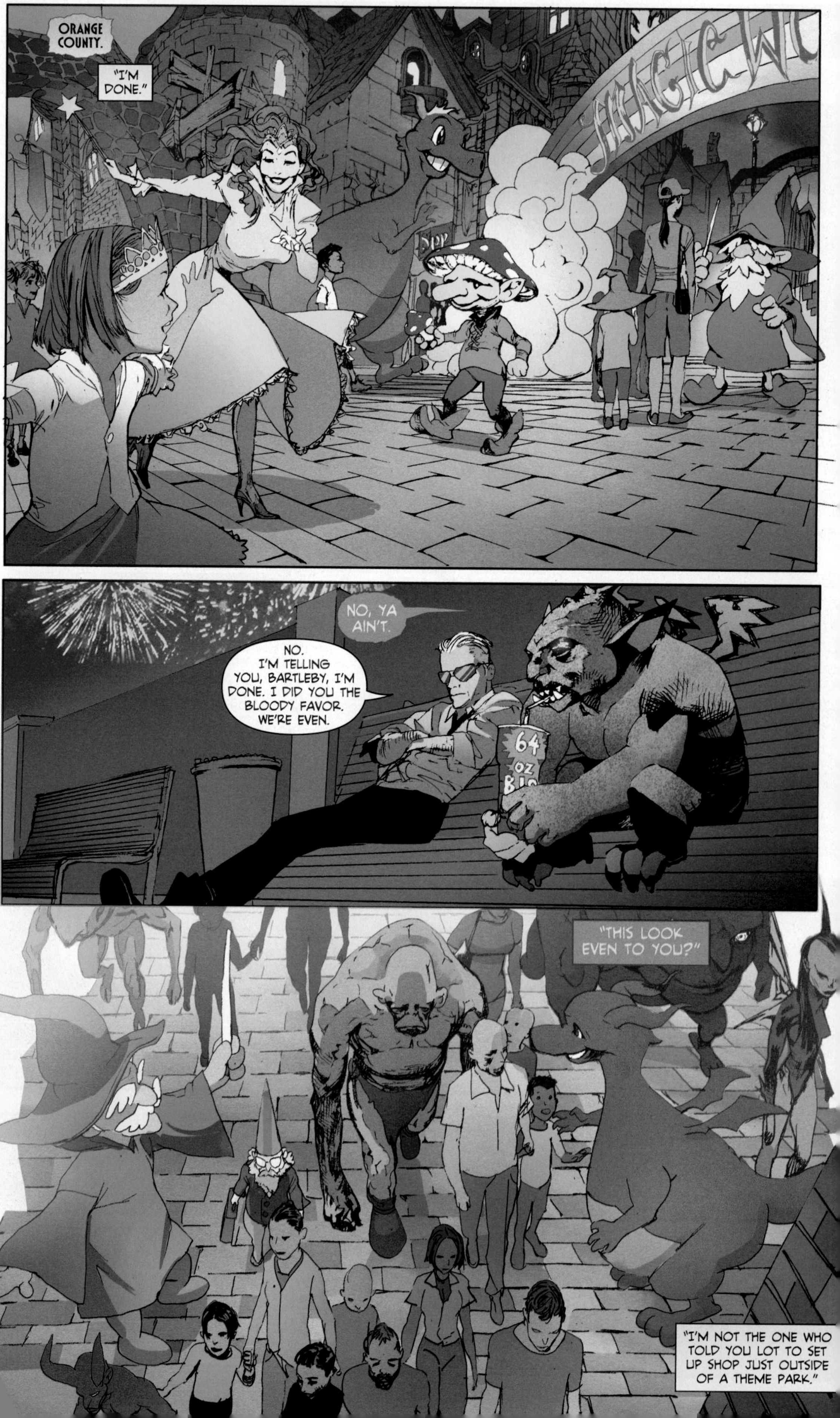
ORANGE COUNTY.
"I'M DONE."
NO, YA AIN'T.
NO. I'M TELLING YOU, BARTLEBY, I'M DONE. I DID YOU THE BLOODY FAVOR. WE'RE EVEN.
64 OZ
"THIS LOOK EVEN TO YOU?"
"I'M NOT THE ONE WHO TOLD YOU LOT TO SET UP SHOP JUST OUTSIDE OF A THEME PARK."

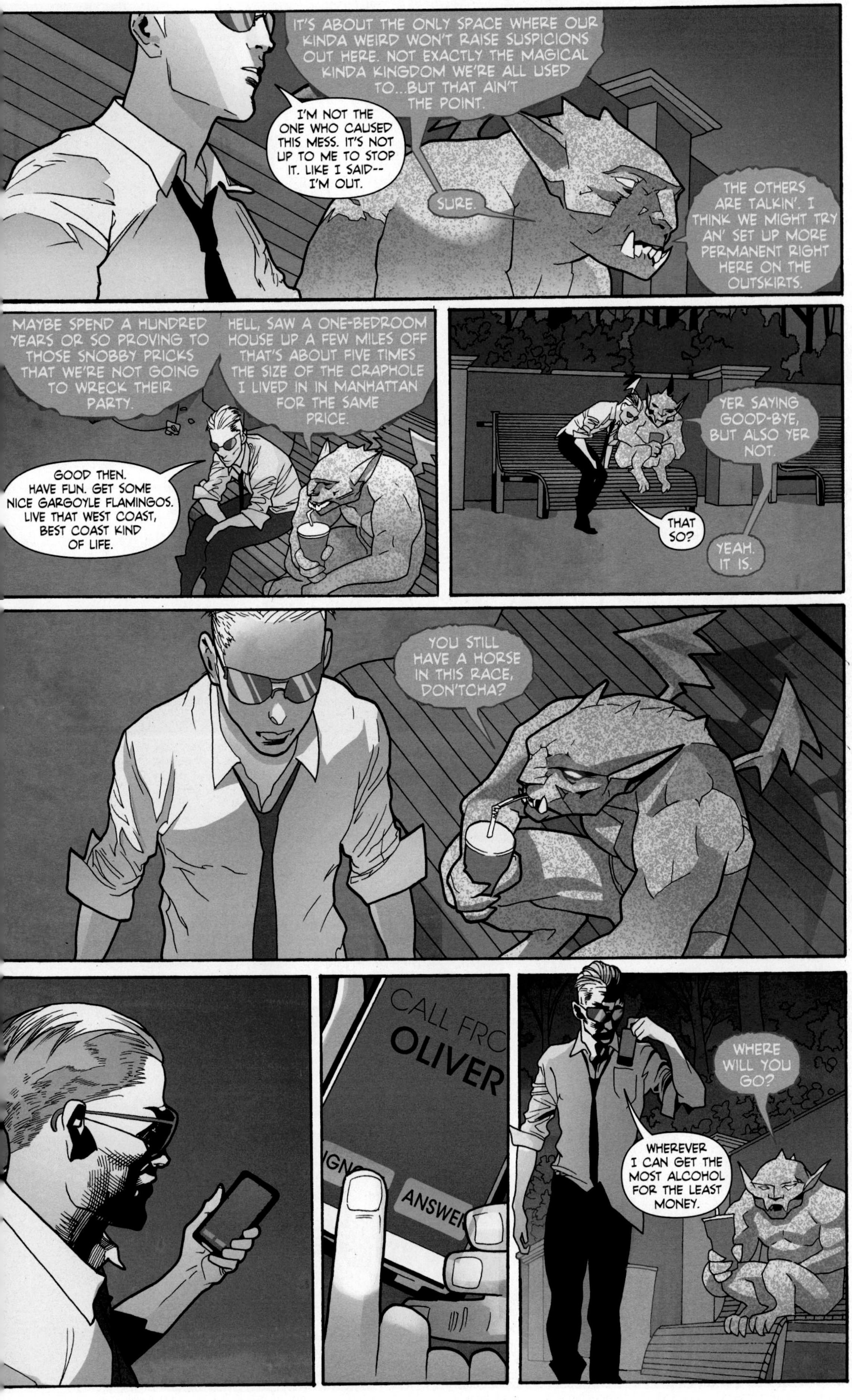
IT'S ABOUT THE ONLY SPACE WHERE OUR KINDA WEIRD WON'T RAISE SUSPICIONS OUT HERE. NOT EXACTLY THE MAGICAL KINDA KINGDOM WE'RE ALL USED TO...BUT THAT AIN'T THE POINT.
I'M NOT THE ONE WHO CAUSED THIS MESS. IT'S NOT UP TO ME TO STOP IT. LIKE I SAID-- I'M OUT.
SURE.
THE OTHERS ARE TALKIN'. I THINK WE MIGHT TRY AN' SET UP MORE PERMANENT RIGHT HERE ON THE OUTSKIRTS.
MAYBE SPEND A HUNDRED YEARS OR SO PROVING TO THOSE SNOBBY PRICKS THAT WE'RE NOT GOING TO WRECK THEIR PARTY.
HELL, SAW A ONE-BEDROOM HOUSE UP A FEW MILES OFF THAT'S ABOUT FIVE TIMES THE SIZE OF THE CRAPHOLE I LIVED IN IN MANHATTAN FOR THE SAME PRICE.
GOOD THEN. HAVE FUN. GET SOME NICE GARGOYLE FLAMINGOS. LIVE THAT WEST COAST, BEST COAST KIND OF LIFE.
YER SAYING GOOD-BYE, BUT ALSO YER NOT.
THAT SO?
YEAH. IT IS.
YOU STILL HAVE A HORSE IN THIS RACE, DON'TCHA?
CALL FRO
OLIVER
ANSWER
WHERE WILL YOU GO?
WHEREVER I CAN GET THE MOST ALCOHOL FOR THE LEAST MONEY.

AND UNFORTUNATELY, THIS IS WHAT PASSES FOR A DIVE IN ANAHEIM. EVEN THIS HOLE ADVERTISES LOCAL CRAFT BREWS AND AN "ARTISANAL MAI TAI" HAPPY HOUR.

HOW'S A BLOKE SUPPOSED TO FIND OBLIVION WITH A STOMACH FULL OF CORIANDER-INFUSED SMALL-BATCH *SWILL?*

STILL, THE LOCALS ARE CHARMING.

HULLO, LOVE. BUY YOU A DRINK?

WHATCHU CAN BUY ME IS A ONE-WAY TICKET FER YERSELF BACK TO NEW YORK, PAL, BEFORE I GOTTA SMACK SOME SENSE INTA YA DIRECT-LIKE.

MAN *ALIVE!*

YES 'N' NO. C'MON, JOHN-O, IT'S ME. BOSTON. DEADMAN. OOGA BOOGA?

JEEZ, THE SUN REALLY MUST BE GETTING TO YA.

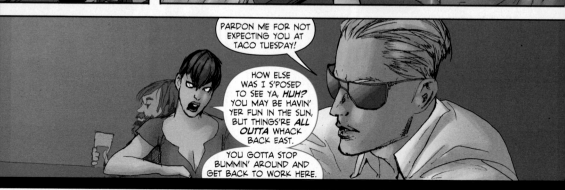

PARDON ME FOR NOT EXPECTING YOU AT TACO TUESDAY!

HOW ELSE WAS I S'POSED TO SEE YA, *HUH?* YOU MAY BE HAVIN' YER FUN IN THE SUN, BUT THINGS'RE *ALL OUTTA* WHACK BACK EAST.

YOU GOTTA STOP BUMMIN' AROUND AND GET BACK TO WORK HERE.

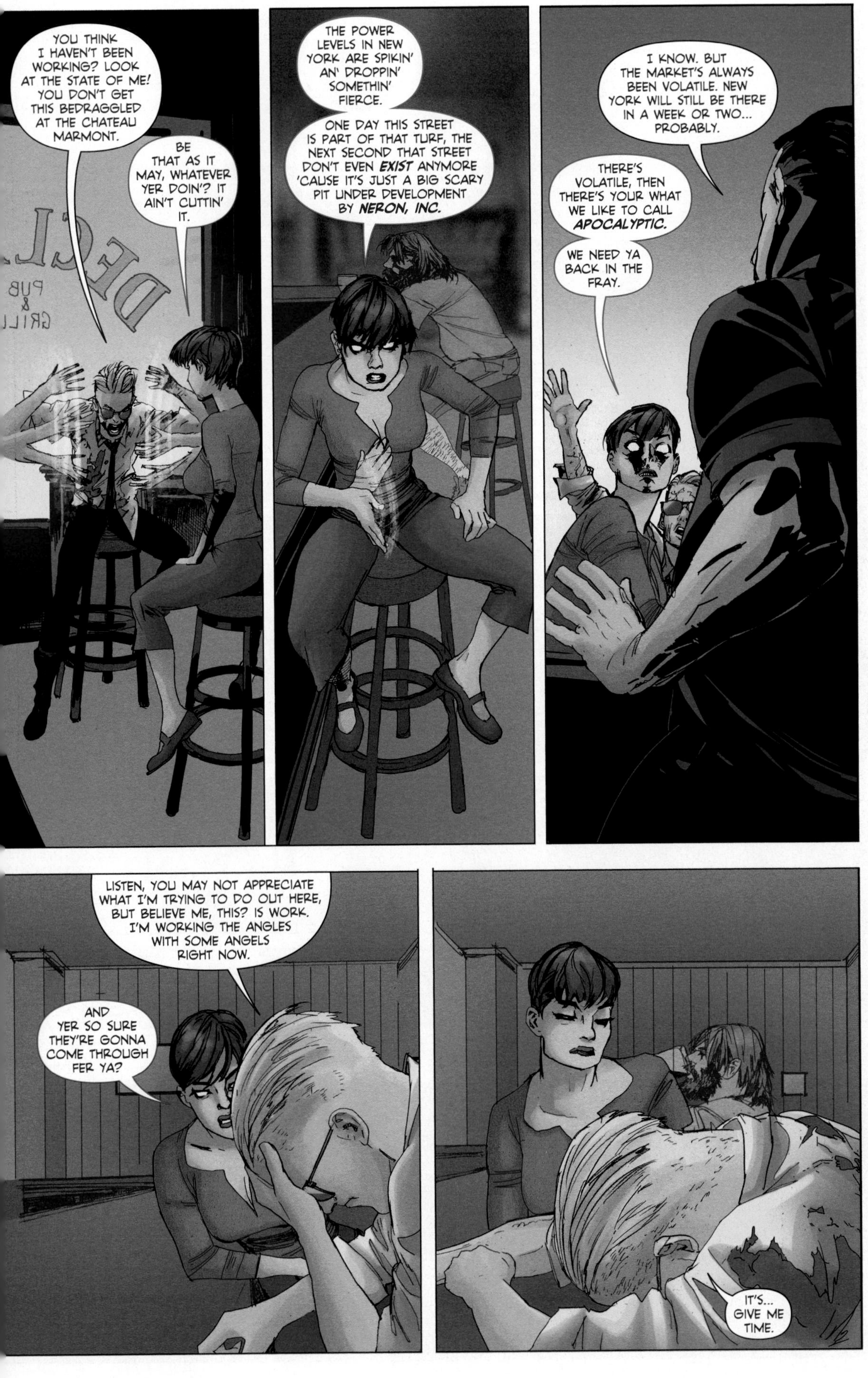
YOU THINK I HAVEN'T BEEN WORKING? LOOK AT THE STATE OF ME! YOU DON'T GET THIS BEDRAGGLED AT THE CHATEAU MARMONT.
BE THAT AS IT MAY, WHATEVER YER DOIN'? IT AIN'T CUTTIN' IT.
DECL...
PUB & GRILL
THE POWER LEVELS IN NEW YORK ARE SPIKIN' AN' DROPPIN' SOMETHIN' FIERCE.
ONE DAY THIS STREET IS PART OF THAT TURF, THE NEXT SECOND THAT STREET DON'T EVEN EXIST ANYMORE 'CAUSE IT'S JUST A BIG SCARY PIT UNDER DEVELOPMENT BY NERON, INC.
I KNOW. BUT THE MARKET'S ALWAYS BEEN VOLATILE. NEW YORK WILL STILL BE THERE IN A WEEK OR TWO... PROBABLY.
THERE'S VOLATILE, THEN THERE'S YOUR WHAT WE LIKE TO CALL APOCALYPTIC.
WE NEED YA BACK IN THE FRAY.
LISTEN, YOU MAY NOT APPRECIATE WHAT I'M TRYING TO DO OUT HERE, BUT BELIEVE ME, THIS? IS WORK. I'M WORKING THE ANGLES WITH SOME ANGELS RIGHT NOW.
AND YER SO SURE THEY'RE GONNA COME THROUGH FER YA?
IT'S... GIVE ME TIME.

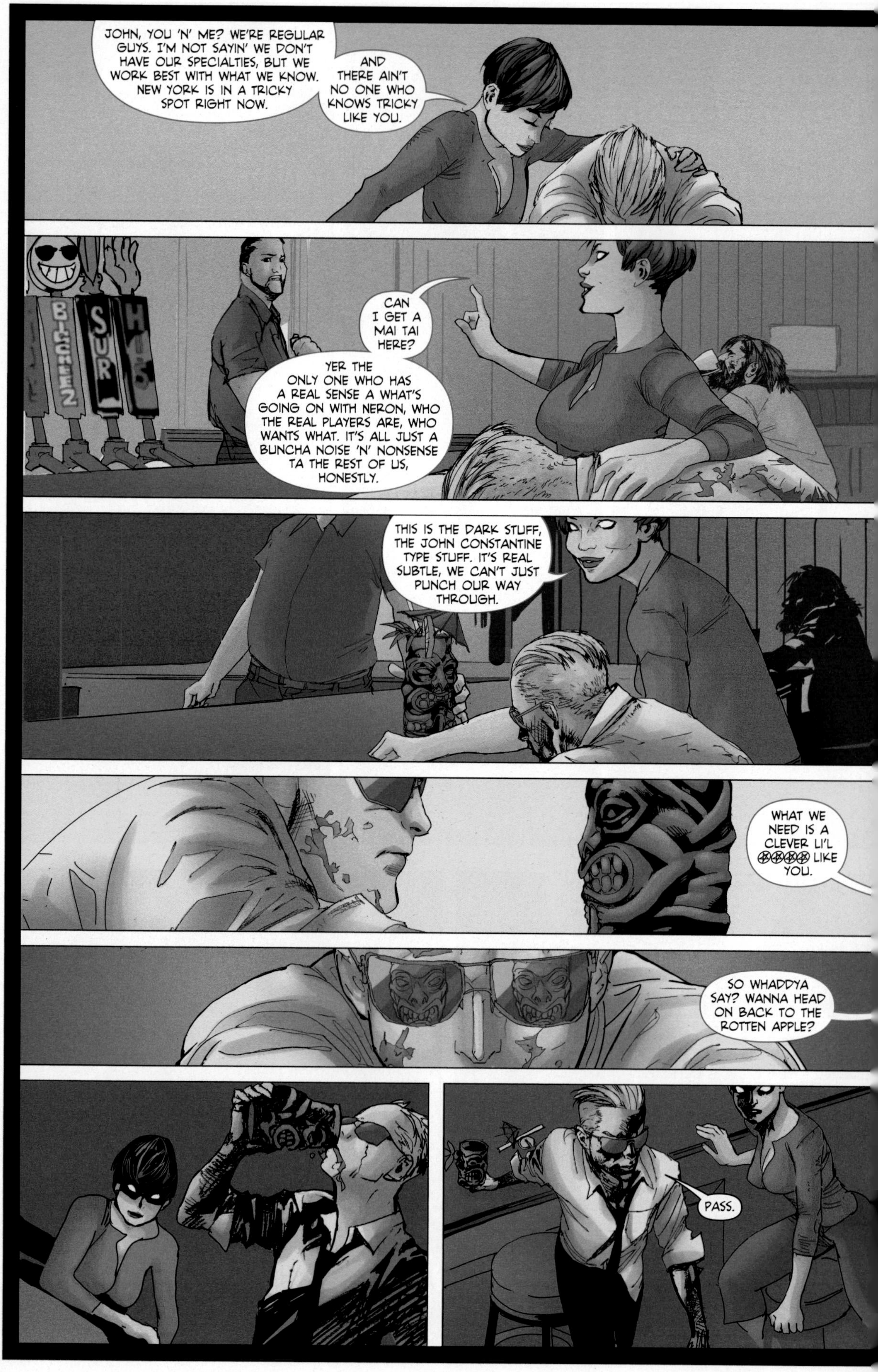
JOHN, YOU 'N' ME? WE'RE REGULAR GUYS. I'M NOT SAYIN' WE DON'T HAVE OUR SPECIALTIES, BUT WE WORK BEST WITH WHAT WE KNOW. NEW YORK IS IN A TRICKY SPOT RIGHT NOW.
AND THERE AIN'T NO ONE WHO KNOWS TRICKY LIKE YOU.
BICHEZ
SUR
H
CAN I GET A MAI TAI HERE?
YER THE ONLY ONE WHO HAS A REAL SENSE A WHAT'S GOING ON WITH NERON, WHO THE REAL PLAYERS ARE, WHO WANTS WHAT. IT'S ALL JUST A BUNCHA NOISE 'N' NONSENSE TA THE REST OF US, HONESTLY.
THIS IS THE DARK STUFF, THE JOHN CONSTANTINE TYPE STUFF. IT'S REAL SUBTLE, WE CAN'T JUST PUNCH OUR WAY THROUGH.
WHAT WE NEED IS A CLEVER LI'L ⊗⊗⊗⊗ LIKE YOU.
SO WHADDYA SAY? WANNA HEAD ON BACK TO THE ROTTEN APPLE?
PASS.

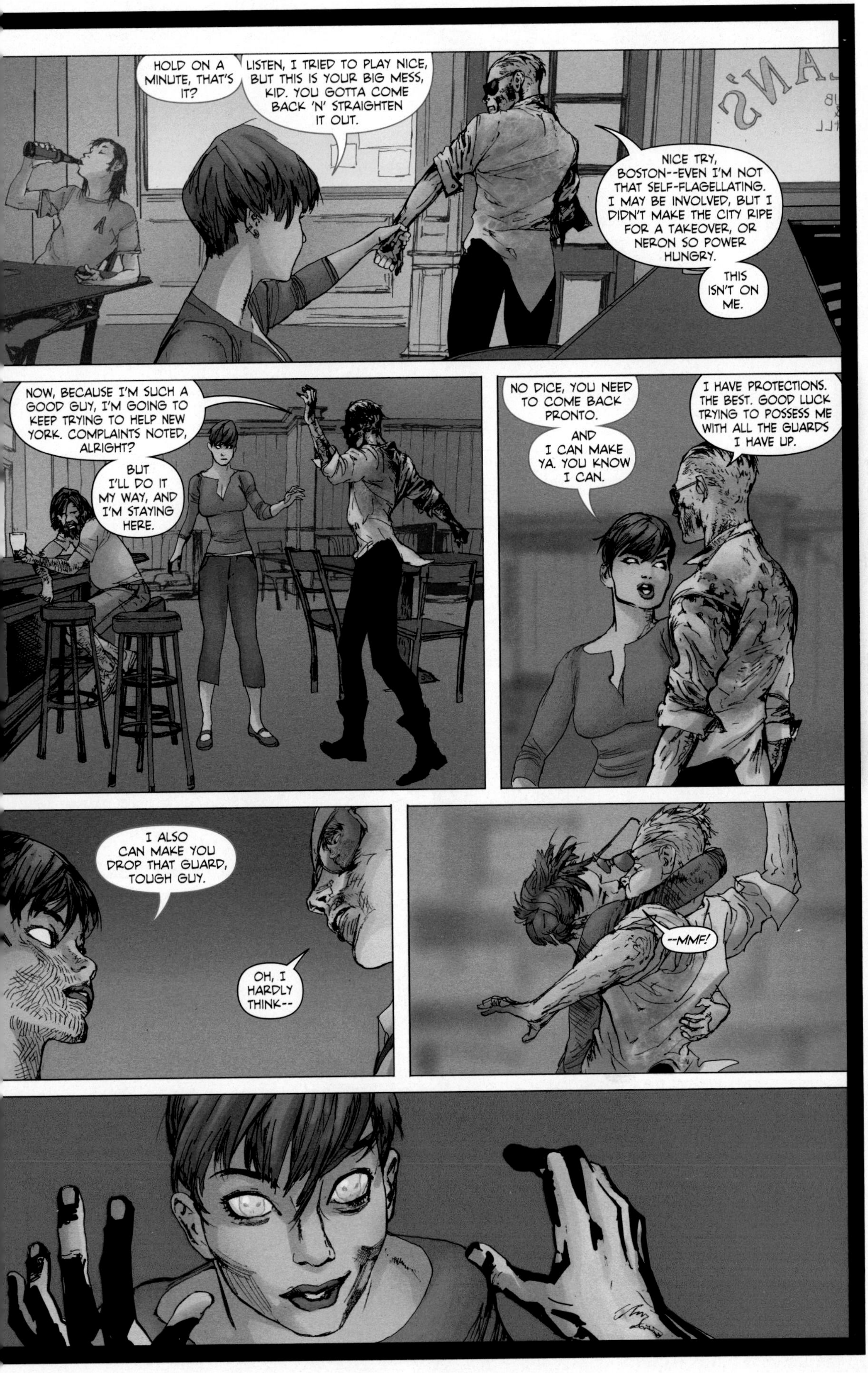
HOLD ON A MINUTE, THAT'S IT?
LISTEN, I TRIED TO PLAY NICE, BUT THIS IS YOUR BIG MESS, KID. YOU GOTTA COME BACK 'N' STRAIGHTEN IT OUT.
NICE TRY, BOSTON--EVEN I'M NOT THAT SELF-FLAGELLATING. I MAY BE INVOLVED, BUT I DIDN'T MAKE THE CITY RIPE FOR A TAKEOVER, OR NERON SO POWER HUNGRY.
THIS ISN'T ON ME.
NOW, BECAUSE I'M SUCH A GOOD GUY, I'M GOING TO KEEP TRYING TO HELP NEW YORK. COMPLAINTS NOTED, ALRIGHT?
BUT I'LL DO IT MY WAY, AND I'M STAYING HERE.
NO DICE, YOU NEED TO COME BACK PRONTO.
AND I CAN MAKE YA. YOU KNOW I CAN.
I HAVE PROTECTIONS. THE BEST. GOOD LUCK TRYING TO POSSESS ME WITH ALL THE GUARDS I HAVE UP.
I ALSO CAN MAKE YOU DROP THAT GUARD, TOUGH GUY.
OH, I HARDLY THINK--
--MMF!

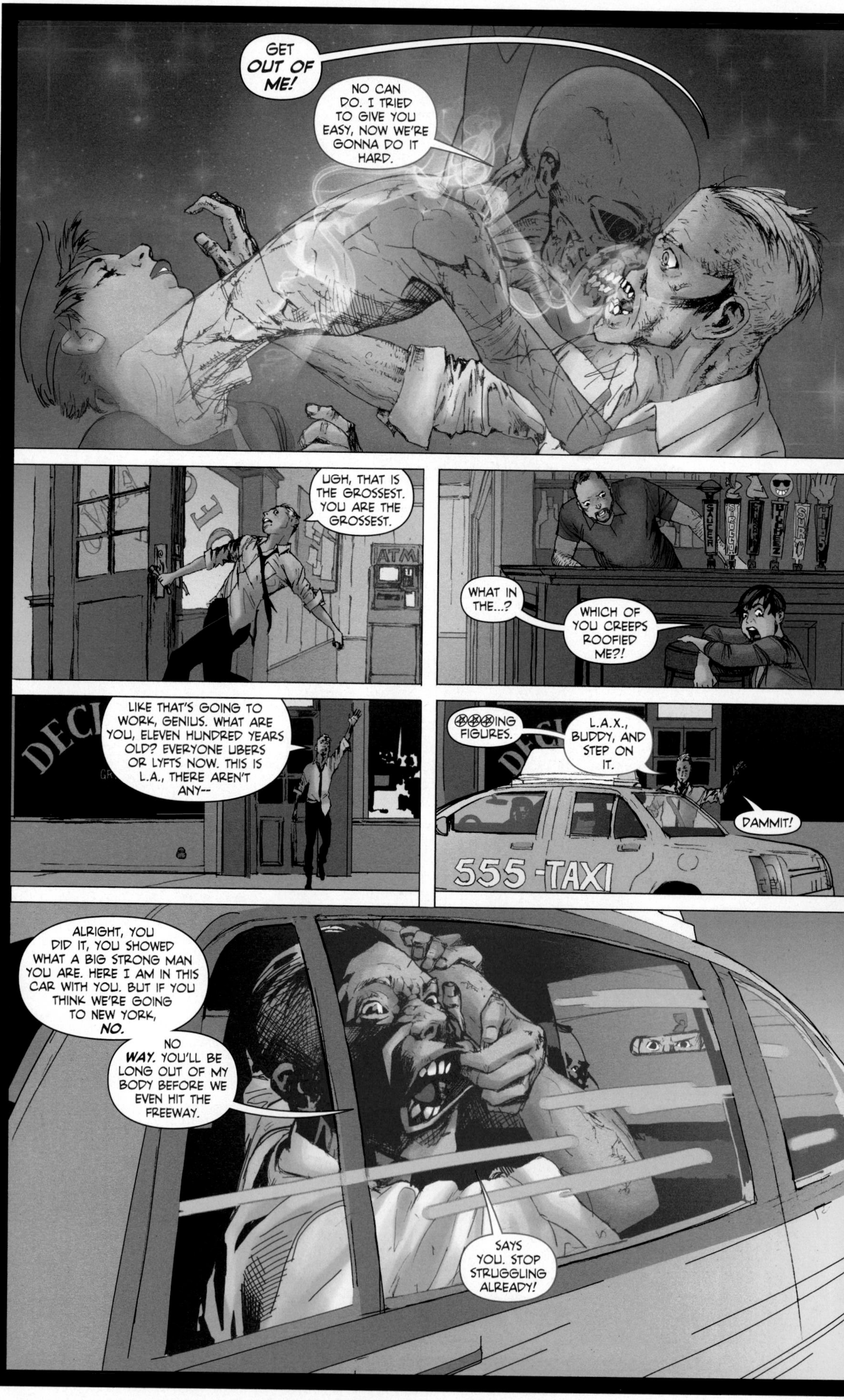
GET OUT OF ME!
NO CAN DO. I TRIED TO GIVE YOU EASY, NOW WE'RE GONNA DO IT HARD.
UGH, THAT IS THE GROSSEST. YOU ARE THE GROSSEST.
ATM
WHAT IN THE...?
WHICH OF YOU CREEPS ROOFIED ME?!
LIKE THAT'S GOING TO WORK, GENIUS. WHAT ARE YOU, ELEVEN HUNDRED YEARS OLD? EVERYONE UBERS OR LYFTS NOW. THIS IS L.A., THERE AREN'T ANY--
⊗⊗⊗ING FIGURES.
L.A.X., BUDDY, AND STEP ON IT.
DAMMIT!
555-TAXI
ALRIGHT, YOU DID IT, YOU SHOWED WHAT A BIG STRONG MAN YOU ARE. HERE I AM IN THIS CAR WITH YOU. BUT IF YOU THINK WE'RE GOING TO NEW YORK, NO.
NO WAY. YOU'LL BE LONG OUT OF MY BODY BEFORE WE EVEN HIT THE FREEWAY.
SAYS YOU. STOP STRUGGLING ALREADY!

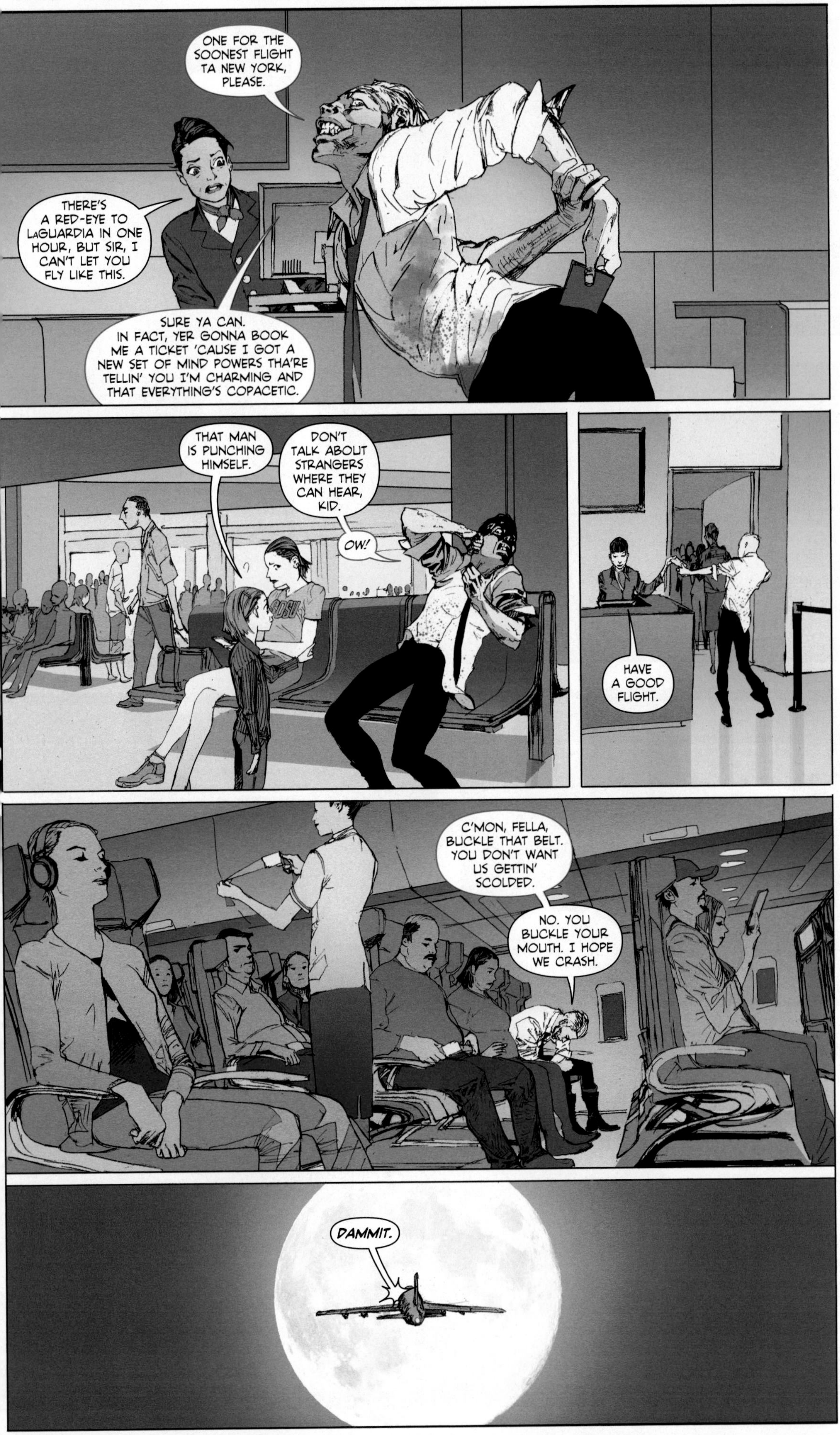
ONE FOR THE SOONEST FLIGHT TA NEW YORK, PLEASE.
THERE'S A RED-EYE TO LaGUARDIA IN ONE HOUR, BUT SIR, I CAN'T LET YOU FLY LIKE THIS.
SURE YA CAN. IN FACT, YER GONNA BOOK ME A TICKET 'CAUSE I GOT A NEW SET OF MIND POWERS THA'RE TELLIN' YOU I'M CHARMING AND THAT EVERYTHING'S COPACETIC.
THAT MAN IS PUNCHING HIMSELF.
DON'T TALK ABOUT STRANGERS WHERE THEY CAN HEAR, KID.
OW!
HAVE A GOOD FLIGHT.
C'MON, FELLA, BUCKLE THAT BELT. YOU DON'T WANT US GETTIN' SCOLDED.
NO. YOU BUCKLE YOUR MOUTH. I HOPE WE CRASH.
DAMMIT.

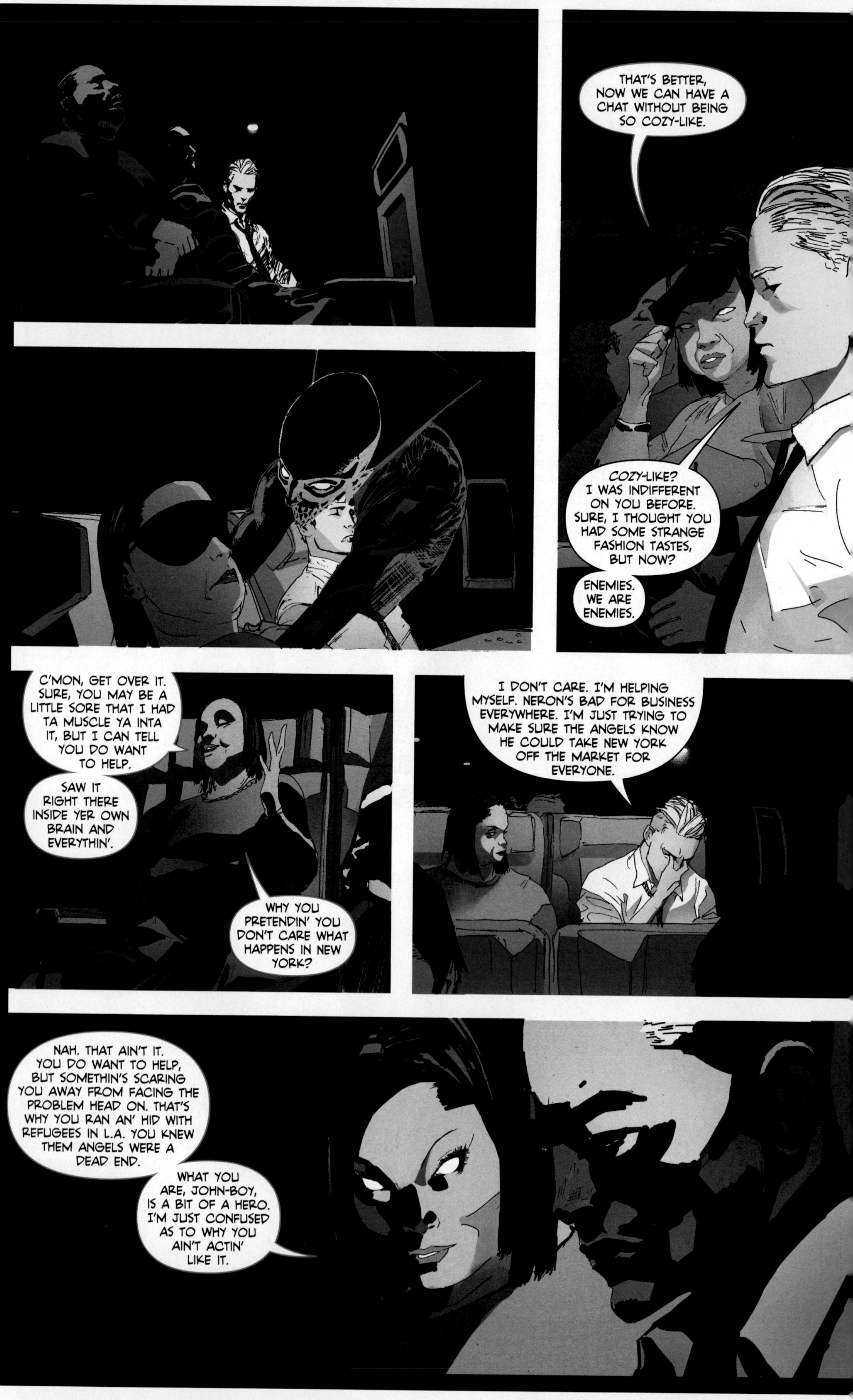
THAT'S BETTER, NOW WE CAN HAVE A CHAT WITHOUT BEING SO COZY-LIKE.
COZY-LIKE? I WAS INDIFFERENT ON YOU BEFORE. SURE, I THOUGHT YOU HAD SOME STRANGE FASHION TASTES, BUT NOW?
ENEMIES. WE ARE ENEMIES.
C'MON, GET OVER IT. SURE, YOU MAY BE A LITTLE SORE THAT I HAD TA MUSCLE YA INTA IT, BUT I CAN TELL YOU DO WANT TO HELP.
SAW IT RIGHT THERE INSIDE YER OWN BRAIN AND EVERYTHIN'.
WHY YOU PRETENDIN' YOU DON'T CARE WHAT HAPPENS IN NEW YORK?
I DON'T CARE. I'M HELPING MYSELF. NERON'S BAD FOR BUSINESS EVERYWHERE. I'M JUST TRYING TO MAKE SURE THE ANGELS KNOW HE COULD TAKE NEW YORK OFF THE MARKET FOR EVERYONE.
NAH. THAT AIN'T IT. YOU DO WANT TO HELP, BUT SOMETHIN'S SCARING YOU AWAY FROM FACING THE PROBLEM HEAD ON. THAT'S WHY YOU RAN AN' HID WITH REFUGEES IN L.A. YOU KNEW THEM ANGELS WERE A DEAD END.
WHAT YOU ARE, JOHN-BOY, IS A BIT OF A HERO. I'M JUST CONFUSED AS TO WHY YOU AIN'T ACTIN' LIKE IT.

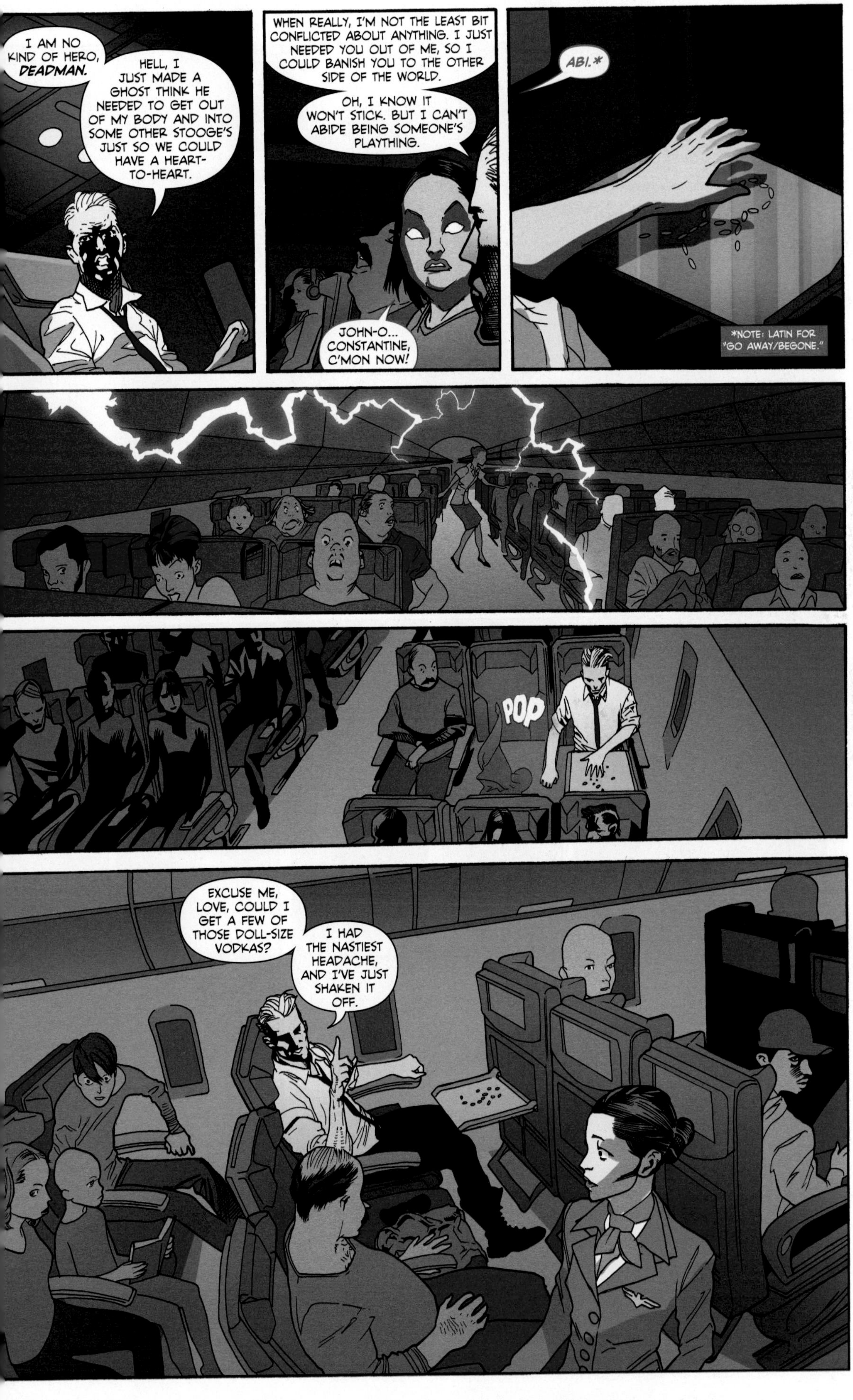
I AM NO KIND OF HERO, DEADMAN.
HELL, I JUST MADE A GHOST THINK HE NEEDED TO GET OUT OF MY BODY AND INTO SOME OTHER STOOGE'S JUST SO WE COULD HAVE A HEART-TO-HEART.
WHEN REALLY, I'M NOT THE LEAST BIT CONFLICTED ABOUT ANYTHING. I JUST NEEDED YOU OUT OF ME, SO I COULD BANISH YOU TO THE OTHER SIDE OF THE WORLD.
OH, I KNOW IT WON'T STICK. BUT I CAN'T ABIDE BEING SOMEONE'S PLAYTHING.
JOHN-O... CONSTANTINE, C'MON NOW!
ABI.*
*NOTE: LATIN FOR "GO AWAY/BEGONE."
POP
EXCUSE ME, LOVE, COULD I GET A FEW OF THOSE DOLL-SIZE VODKAS?
I HAD THE NASTIEST HEADACHE, AND I'VE JUST SHAKEN IT OFF.

ALL THAT, AND THERE WEREN'T ANY FLIGHTS BACK TO L.A. UNTIL TOMORROW.

I COULD'VE KIPPED RIGHT THERE ON THE AIRPORT FLOOR, BUT IT'S BEEN A WEEK. I DESERVE A NICE SLEEP IN MY OWN BED, WITH MY OWN ALCOHOL WHICH COMES IN MAN-SIZE BOTTLES.

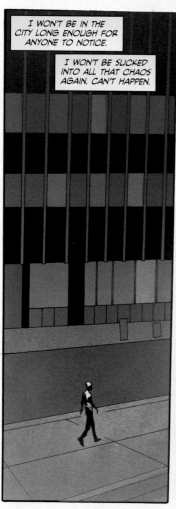

I WON'T BE IN THE CITY LONG ENOUGH FOR ANYONE TO NOTICE.

I WON'T BE SUCKED INTO ALL THAT CHAOS AGAIN. CAN'T HAPPEN.

JUST, FINALLY. ONE MOMENT OF REST.

JOHN, WHERE HAVE YOU BEEN? I'VE BEEN CALLING AND CALLING...

THEY TOOK THEM, JOHN, MY LITTLE GIRLS. THEY TOOK THEM TO HELL...AND YOU'RE THE ONLY ONE WHO CAN GET THEM BACK.

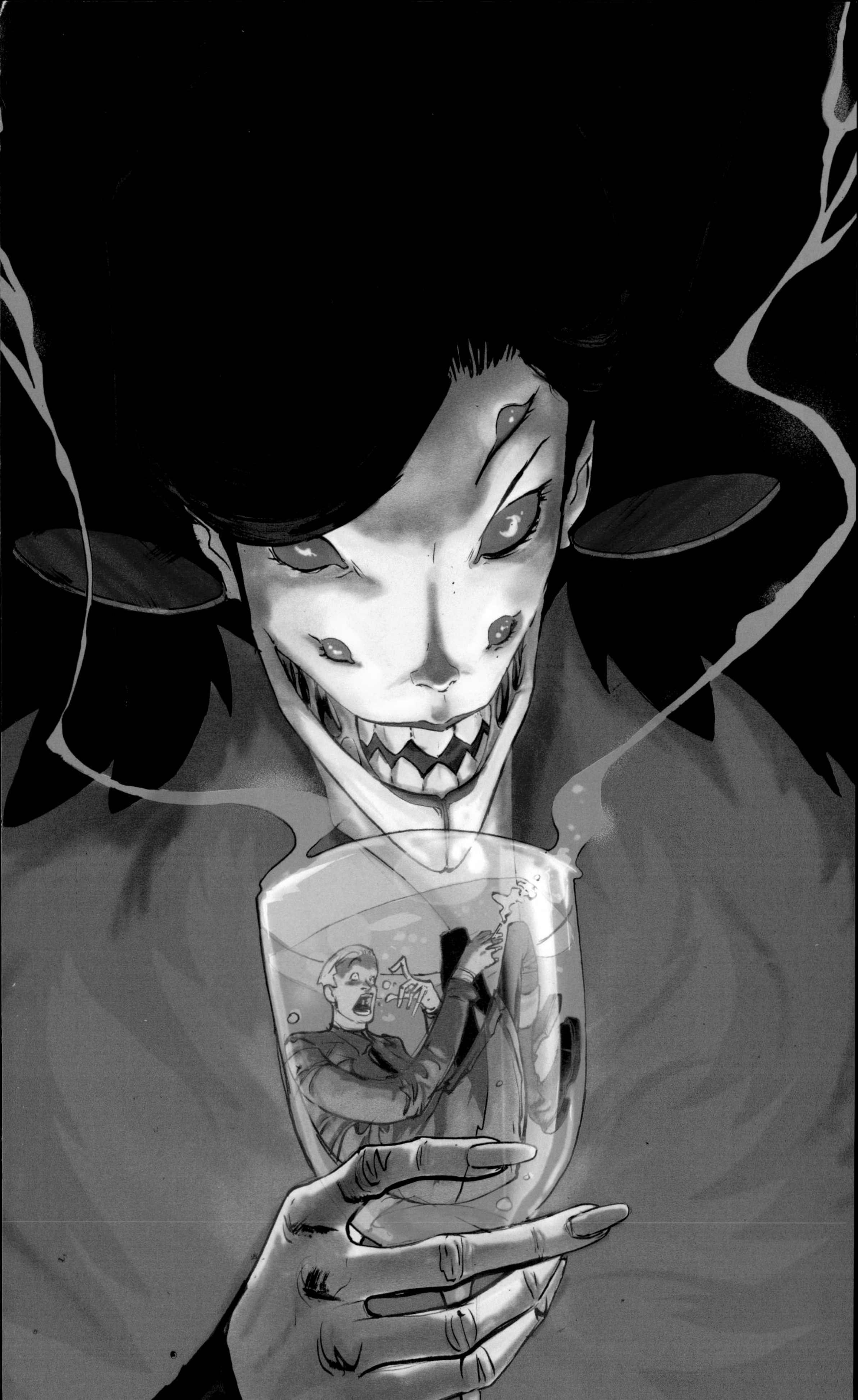

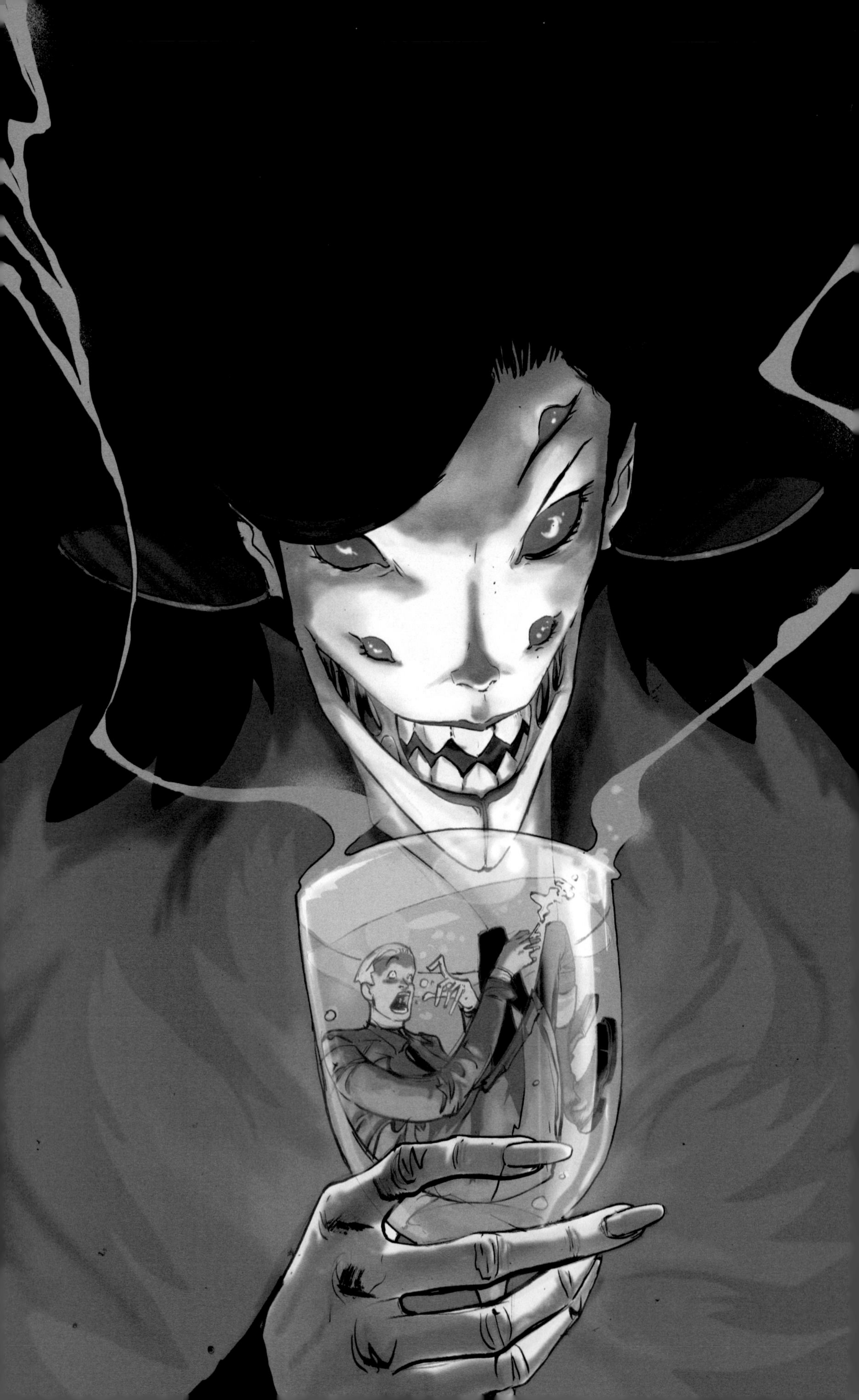

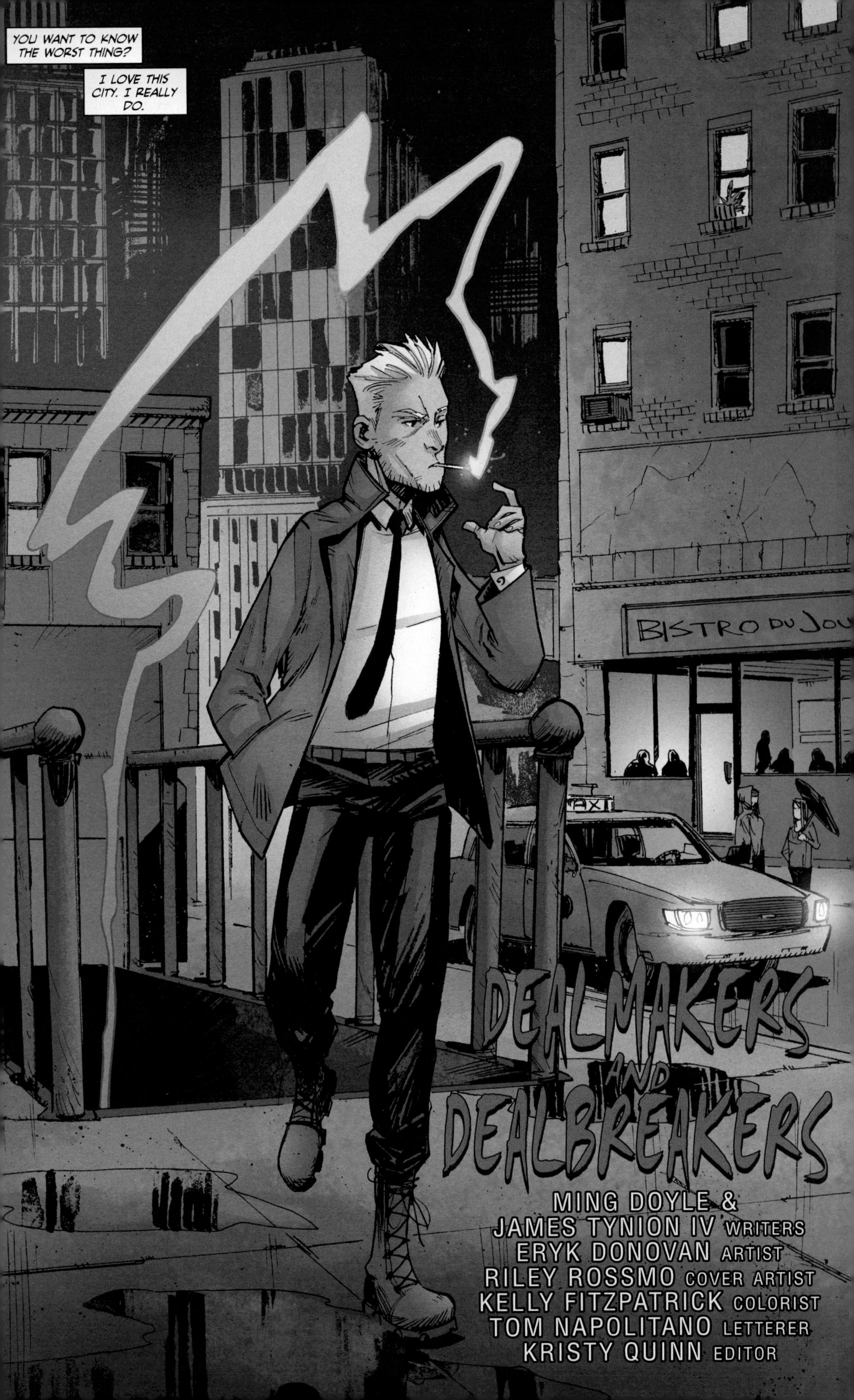

YOU WANT TO KNOW THE WORST THING?
I LOVE THIS CITY. I REALLY DO.
BISTRO DU JOU
TAXI
DEALMAKERS AND DEALBREAKERS
MING DOYLE & JAMES TYNION IV WRITERS
ERYK DONOVAN ARTIST
RILEY ROSSMO COVER ARTIST
KELLY FITZPATRICK COLORIST
TOM NAPOLITANO LETTERER
KRISTY QUINN EDITOR

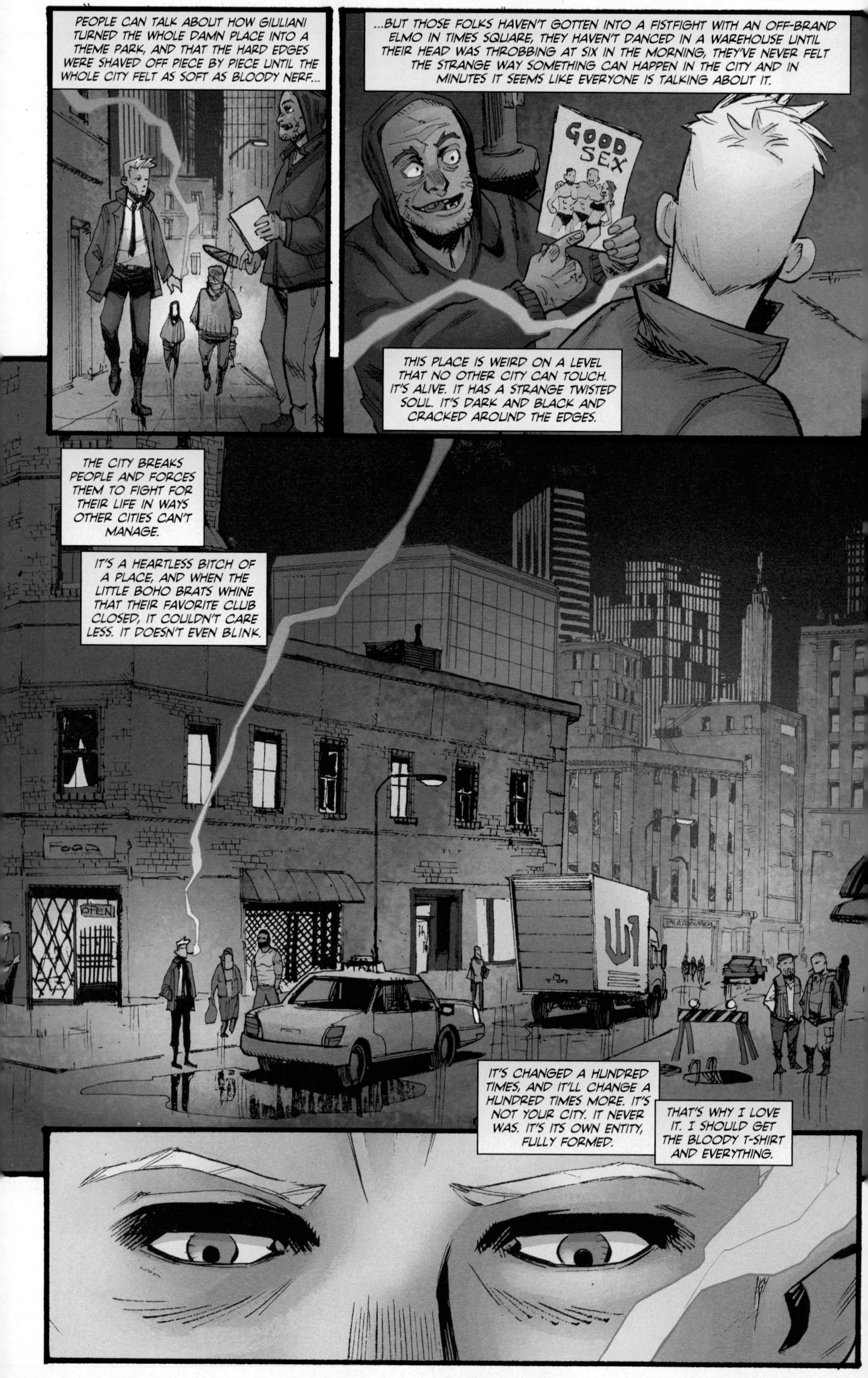
PEOPLE CAN TALK ABOUT HOW GIULIANI TURNED THE WHOLE DAMN PLACE INTO A THEME PARK, AND THAT THE HARD EDGES WERE SHAVED OFF PIECE BY PIECE UNTIL THE WHOLE CITY FELT AS SOFT AS BLOODY NERF...
...BUT THOSE FOLKS HAVEN'T GOTTEN INTO A FISTFIGHT WITH AN OFF-BRAND ELMO IN TIMES SQUARE, THEY HAVEN'T DANCED IN A WAREHOUSE UNTIL THEIR HEAD WAS THROBBING AT SIX IN THE MORNING, THEY'VE NEVER FELT THE STRANGE WAY SOMETHING CAN HAPPEN IN THE CITY AND IN MINUTES IT SEEMS LIKE EVERYONE IS TALKING ABOUT IT.
GOOD SEX
THIS PLACE IS WEIRD ON A LEVEL THAT NO OTHER CITY CAN TOUCH. IT'S ALIVE. IT HAS A STRANGE TWISTED SOUL. IT'S DARK AND BLACK AND CRACKED AROUND THE EDGES.
THE CITY BREAKS PEOPLE AND FORCES THEM TO FIGHT FOR THEIR LIFE IN WAYS OTHER CITIES CAN'T MANAGE.
IT'S A HEARTLESS BITCH OF A PLACE, AND WHEN THE LITTLE BOHO BRATS WHINE THAT THEIR FAVORITE CLUB CLOSED, IT COULDN'T CARE LESS. IT DOESN'T EVEN BLINK.
FOOD
OPEN
IT'S CHANGED A HUNDRED TIMES, AND IT'LL CHANGE A HUNDRED TIMES MORE. IT'S NOT YOUR CITY. IT NEVER WAS. IT'S ITS OWN ENTITY, FULLY FORMED.
THAT'S WHY I LOVE IT. I SHOULD GET THE BLOODY T-SHIRT AND EVERYTHING.

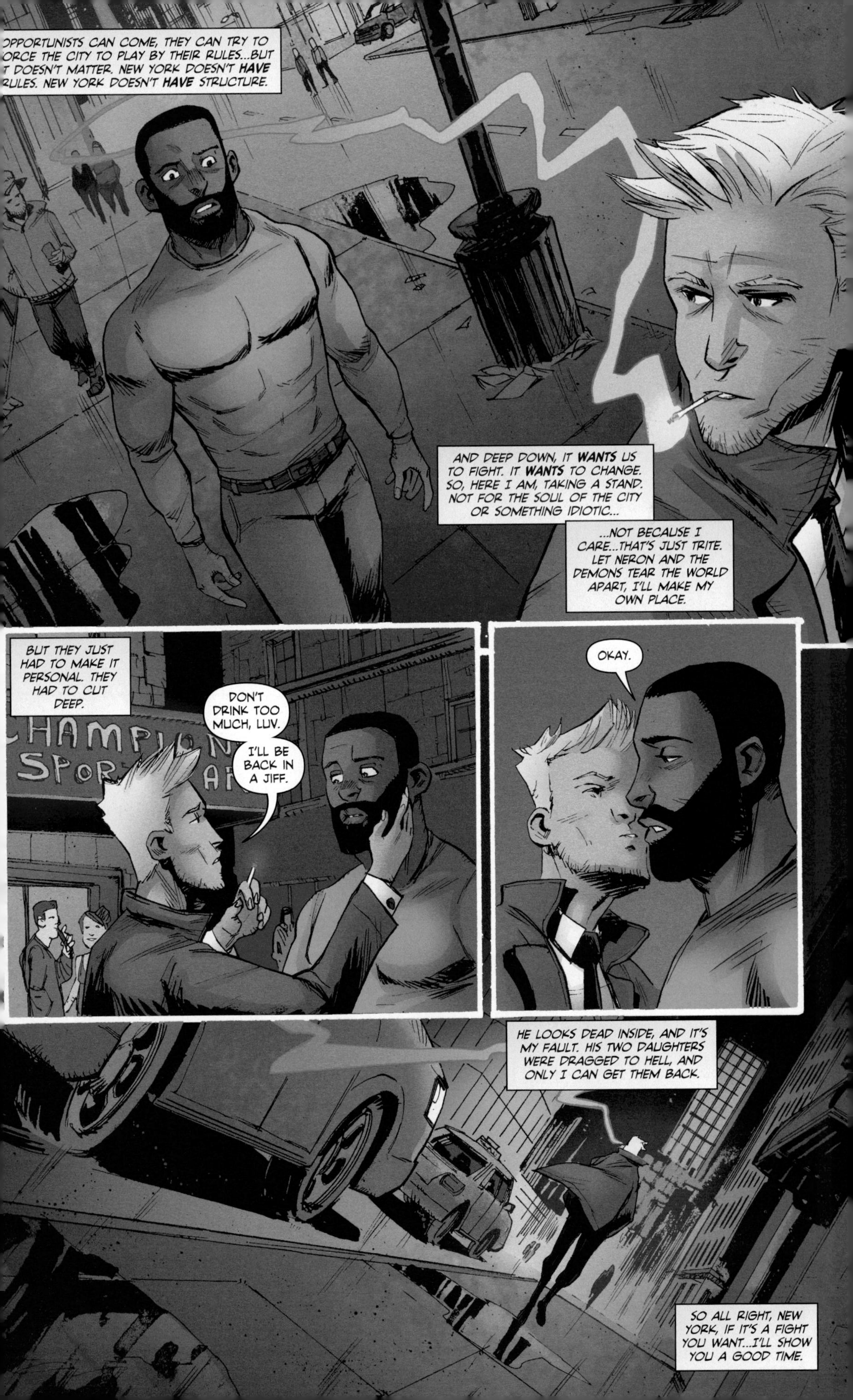
OPPORTUNISTS CAN COME, THEY CAN TRY TO FORCE THE CITY TO PLAY BY THEIR RULES...BUT IT DOESN'T MATTER. NEW YORK DOESN'T HAVE RULES. NEW YORK DOESN'T HAVE STRUCTURE.
AND DEEP DOWN, IT WANTS US TO FIGHT. IT WANTS TO CHANGE. SO, HERE I AM, TAKING A STAND. NOT FOR THE SOUL OF THE CITY OR SOMETHING IDIOTIC...
...NOT BECAUSE I CARE...THAT'S JUST TRITE. LET NERON AND THE DEMONS TEAR THE WORLD APART, I'LL MAKE MY OWN PLACE.
BUT THEY JUST HAD TO MAKE IT PERSONAL. THEY HAD TO CUT DEEP.
DON'T DRINK TOO MUCH, LUV.
I'LL BE BACK IN A JIFF.
OKAY.
HE LOOKS DEAD INSIDE, AND IT'S MY FAULT. HIS TWO DAUGHTERS WERE DRAGGED TO HELL, AND ONLY I CAN GET THEM BACK.
SO ALL RIGHT, NEW YORK, IF IT'S A FIGHT YOU WANT...I'LL SHOW YOU A GOOD TIME.

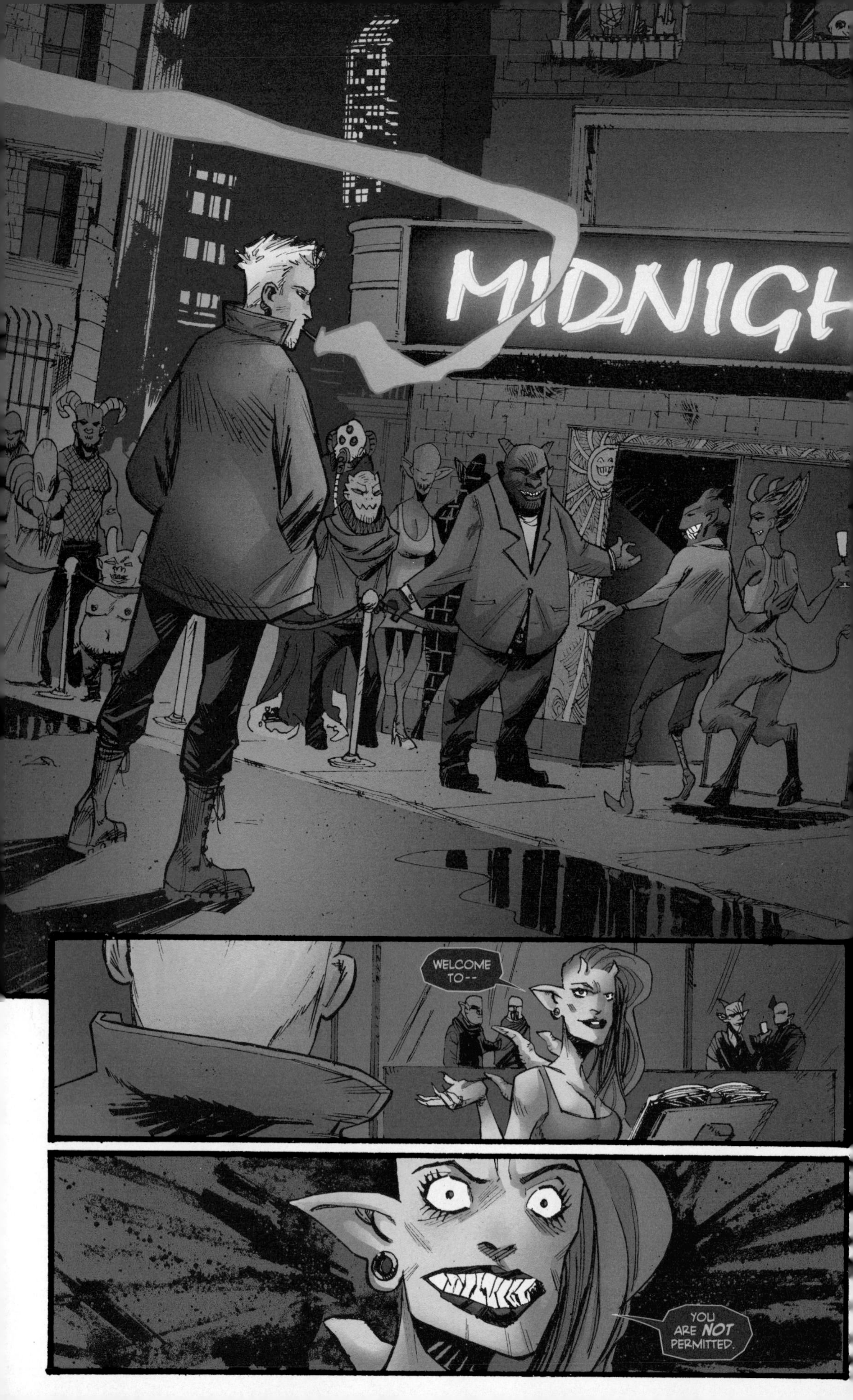
MIDNIGH
WELCOME TO--
YOU ARE **NOT** PERMITTED.

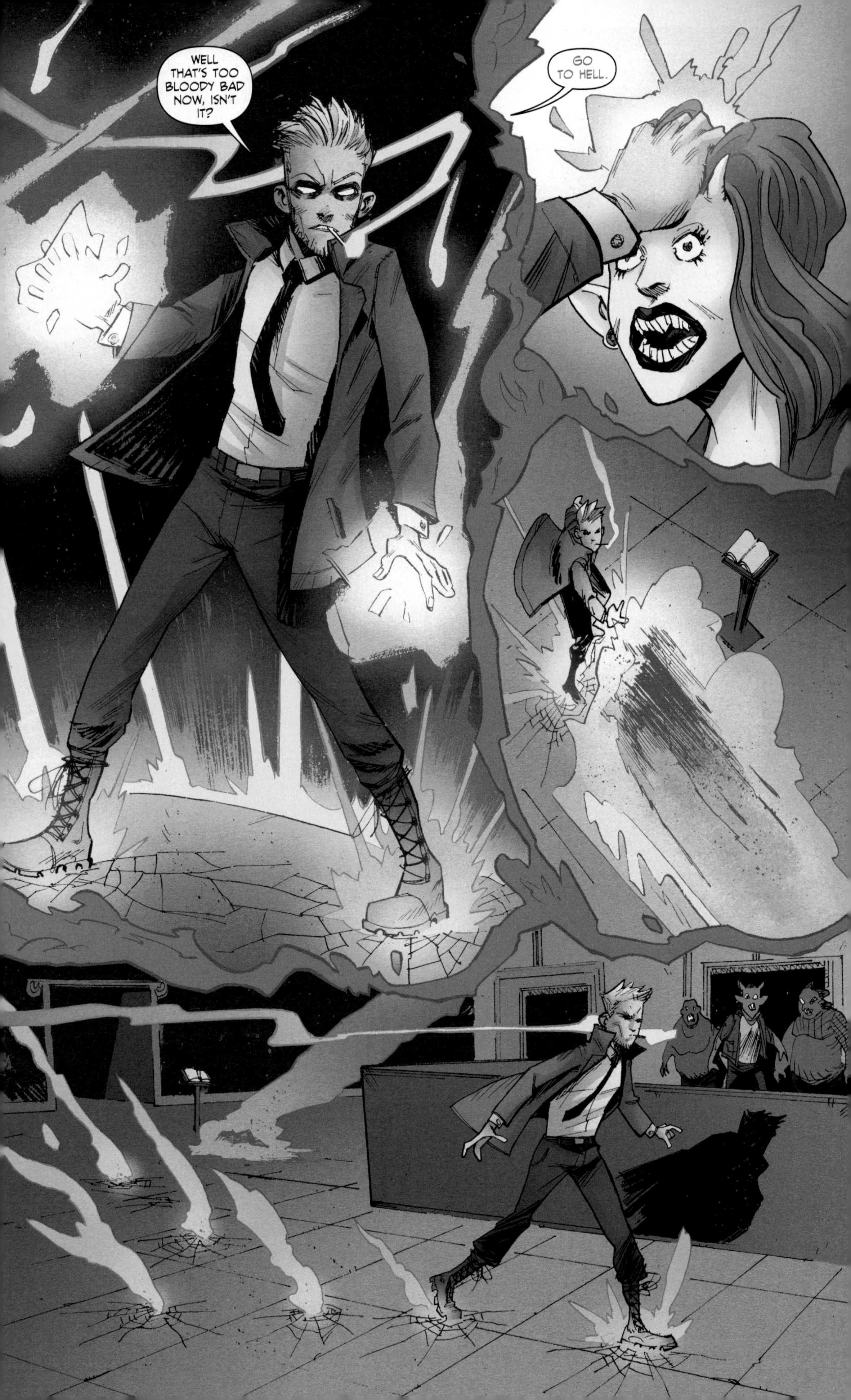
WELL THAT'S TOO BLOODY BAD NOW, ISN'T IT?
GO TO HELL.

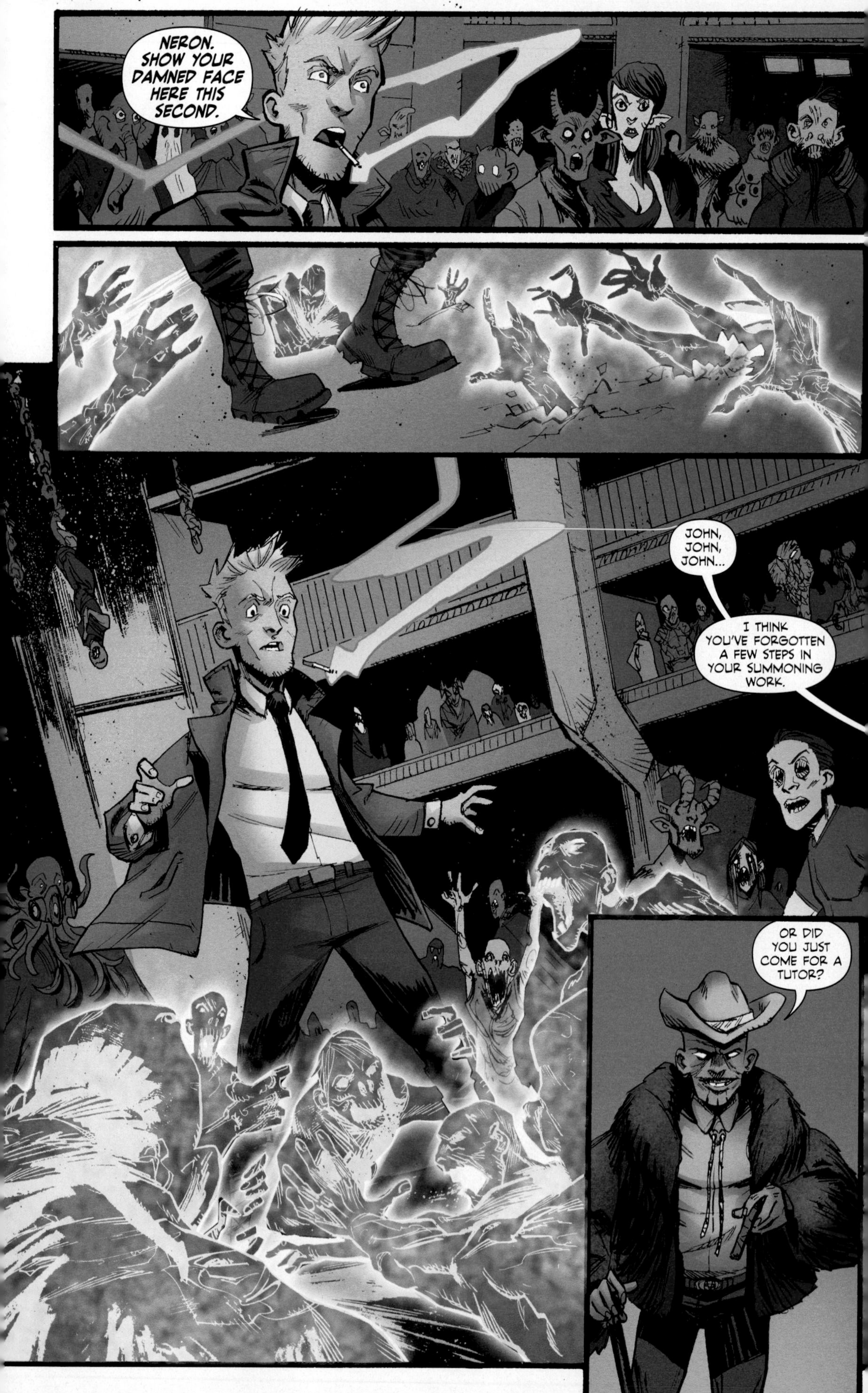
NERON. SHOW YOUR DAMNED FACE HERE THIS SECOND.
JOHN, JOHN, JOHN...
I THINK YOU'VE FORGOTTEN A FEW STEPS IN YOUR SUMMONING WORK.
OR DID YOU JUST COME FOR A TUTOR?

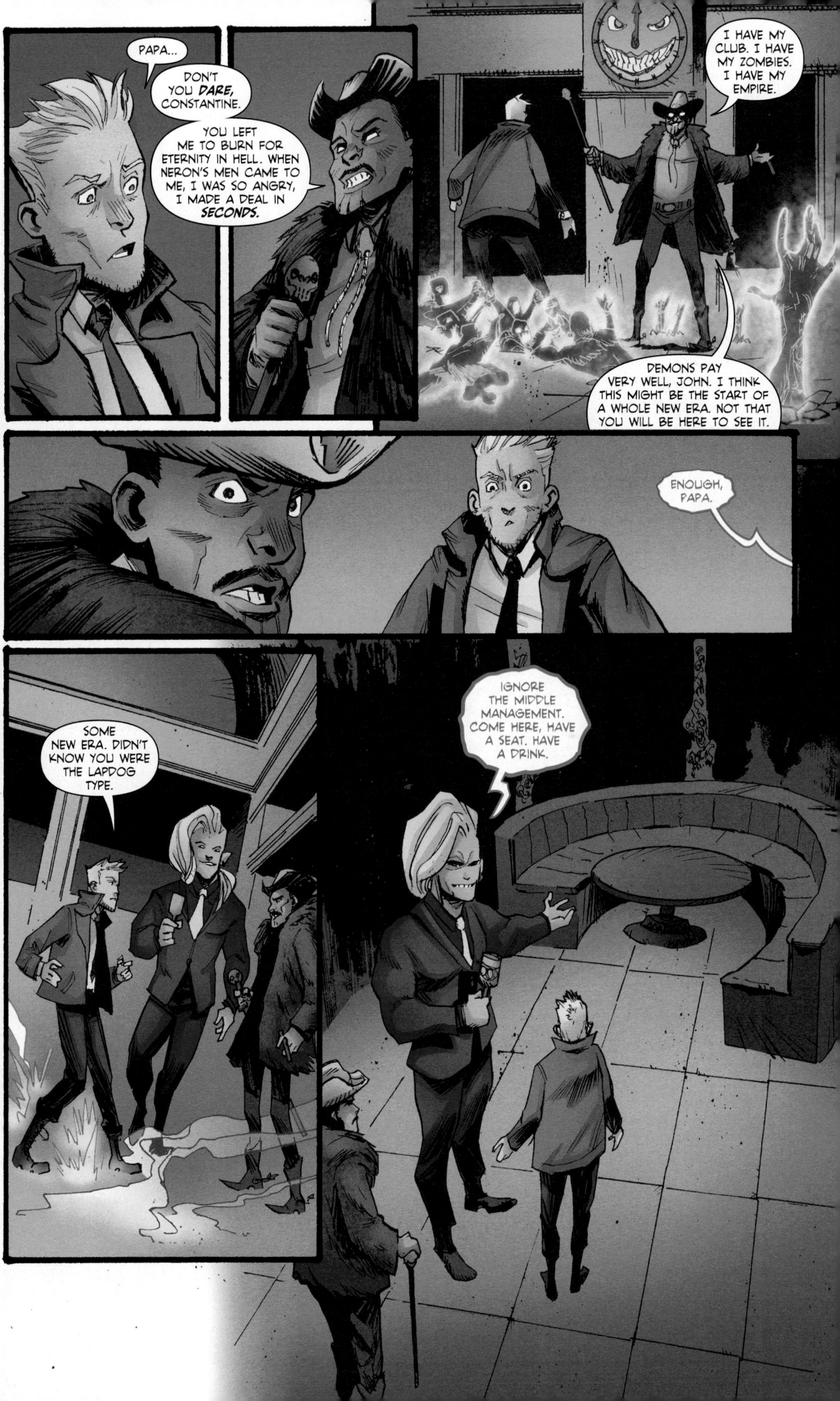
PAPA...
DON'T YOU DARE, CONSTANTINE.
YOU LEFT ME TO BURN FOR ETERNITY IN HELL. WHEN NERON'S MEN CAME TO ME, I WAS SO ANGRY, I MADE A DEAL IN SECONDS.
I HAVE MY CLUB. I HAVE MY ZOMBIES. I HAVE MY EMPIRE.
DEMONS PAY VERY WELL, JOHN. I THINK THIS MIGHT BE THE START OF A WHOLE NEW ERA. NOT THAT YOU WILL BE HERE TO SEE IT.
ENOUGH, PAPA.
SOME NEW ERA. DIDN'T KNOW YOU WERE THE LAPDOG TYPE.
IGNORE THE MIDDLE MANAGEMENT. COME HERE, HAVE A SEAT. HAVE A DRINK.

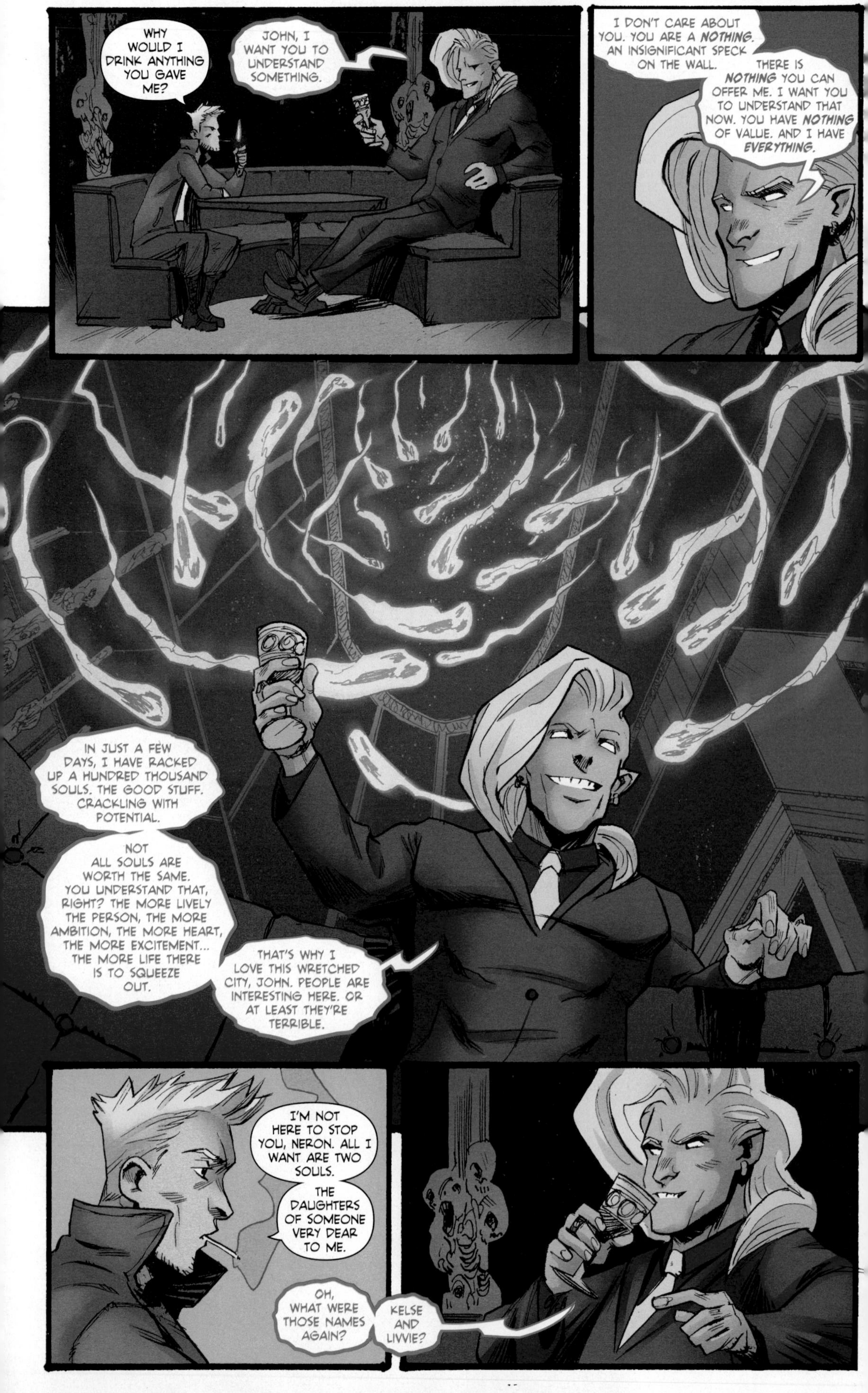
WHY WOULD I DRINK ANYTHING YOU GAVE ME?
JOHN, I WANT YOU TO UNDERSTAND SOMETHING.
I DON'T CARE ABOUT YOU. YOU ARE A NOTHING. AN INSIGNIFICANT SPECK ON THE WALL.
THERE IS NOTHING YOU CAN OFFER ME. I WANT YOU TO UNDERSTAND THAT NOW. YOU HAVE NOTHING OF VALUE. AND I HAVE EVERYTHING.
IN JUST A FEW DAYS, I HAVE RACKED UP A HUNDRED THOUSAND SOULS. THE GOOD STUFF. CRACKLING WITH POTENTIAL.
NOT ALL SOULS ARE WORTH THE SAME. YOU UNDERSTAND THAT, RIGHT? THE MORE LIVELY THE PERSON, THE MORE AMBITION, THE MORE HEART, THE MORE EXCITEMENT... THE MORE LIFE THERE IS TO SQUEEZE OUT.
THAT'S WHY I LOVE THIS WRETCHED CITY, JOHN. PEOPLE ARE INTERESTING HERE. OR AT LEAST THEY'RE TERRIBLE.
I'M NOT HERE TO STOP YOU, NERON. ALL I WANT ARE TWO SOULS.
THE DAUGHTERS OF SOMEONE VERY DEAR TO ME.
OH, WHAT WERE THOSE NAMES AGAIN?
KELSE AND LIVVIE?

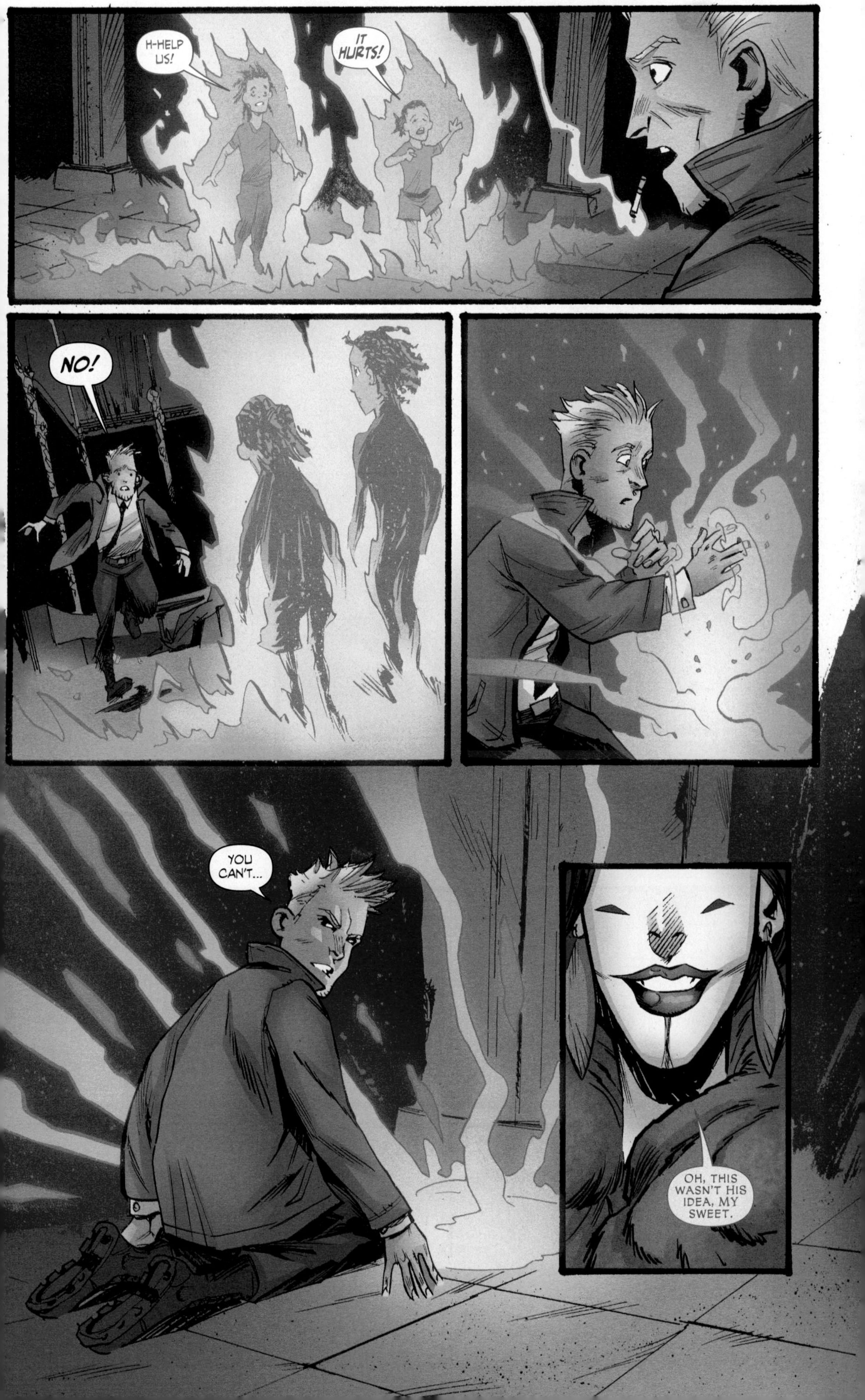
H-HELP US!
IT HURTS!
NO!
YOU CAN'T...
OH, THIS WASN'T HIS IDEA, MY SWEET.

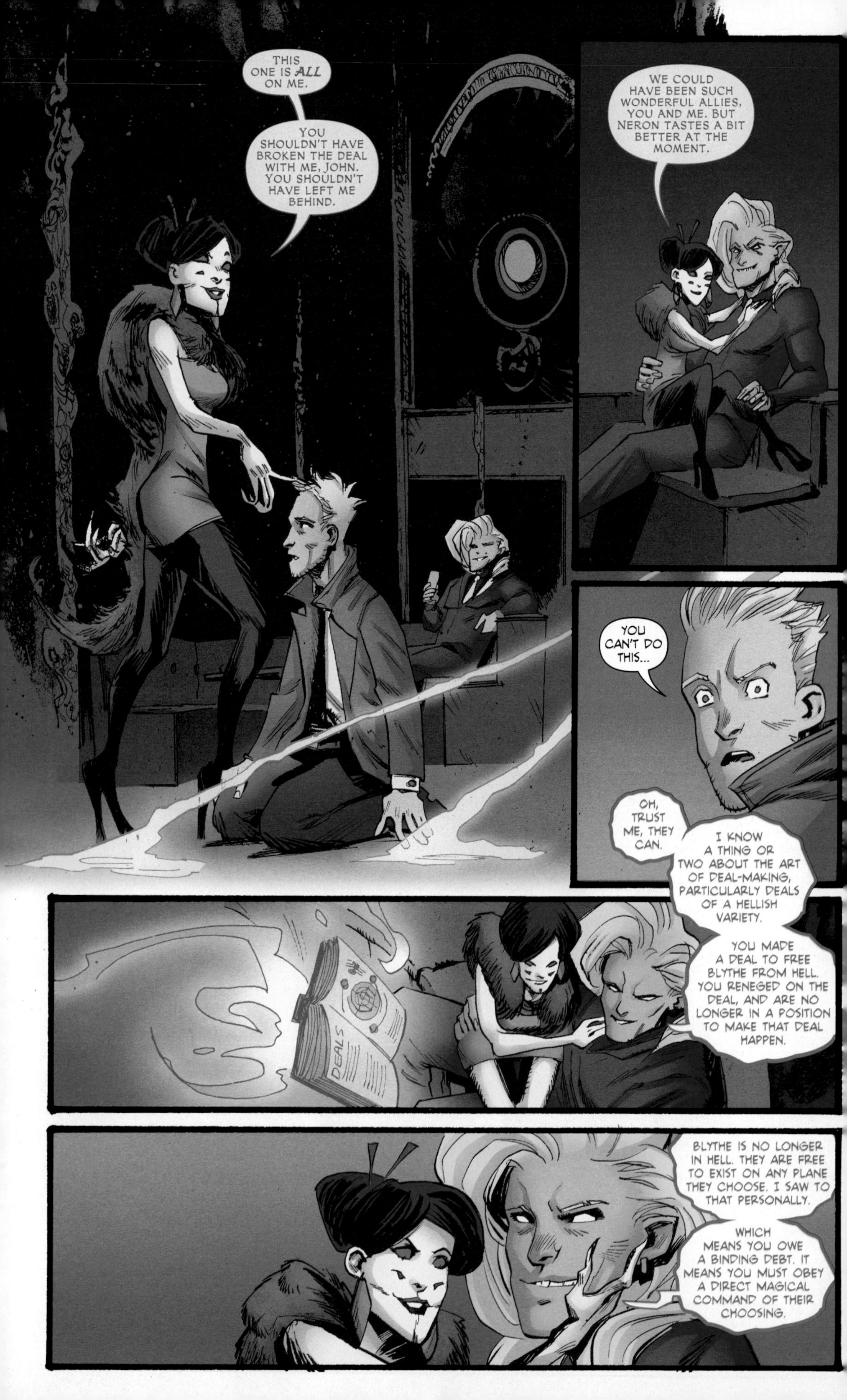
THIS ONE IS ALL ON ME.
YOU SHOULDN'T HAVE BROKEN THE DEAL WITH ME, JOHN. YOU SHOULDN'T HAVE LEFT ME BEHIND.
WE COULD HAVE BEEN SUCH WONDERFUL ALLIES, YOU AND ME. BUT NERON TASTES A BIT BETTER AT THE MOMENT.
YOU CAN'T DO THIS...
OH, TRUST ME, THEY CAN.
I KNOW A THING OR TWO ABOUT THE ART OF DEAL-MAKING, PARTICULARLY DEALS OF A HELLISH VARIETY.
YOU MADE A DEAL TO FREE BLYTHE FROM HELL. YOU RENEGED ON THE DEAL, AND ARE NO LONGER IN A POSITION TO MAKE THAT DEAL HAPPEN.
DEALS
BLYTHE IS NO LONGER IN HELL. THEY ARE FREE TO EXIST ON ANY PLANE THEY CHOOSE. I SAW TO THAT PERSONALLY.
WHICH MEANS YOU OWE A BINDING DEBT. IT MEANS YOU MUST OBEY A DIRECT MAGICAL COMMAND OF THEIR CHOOSING.

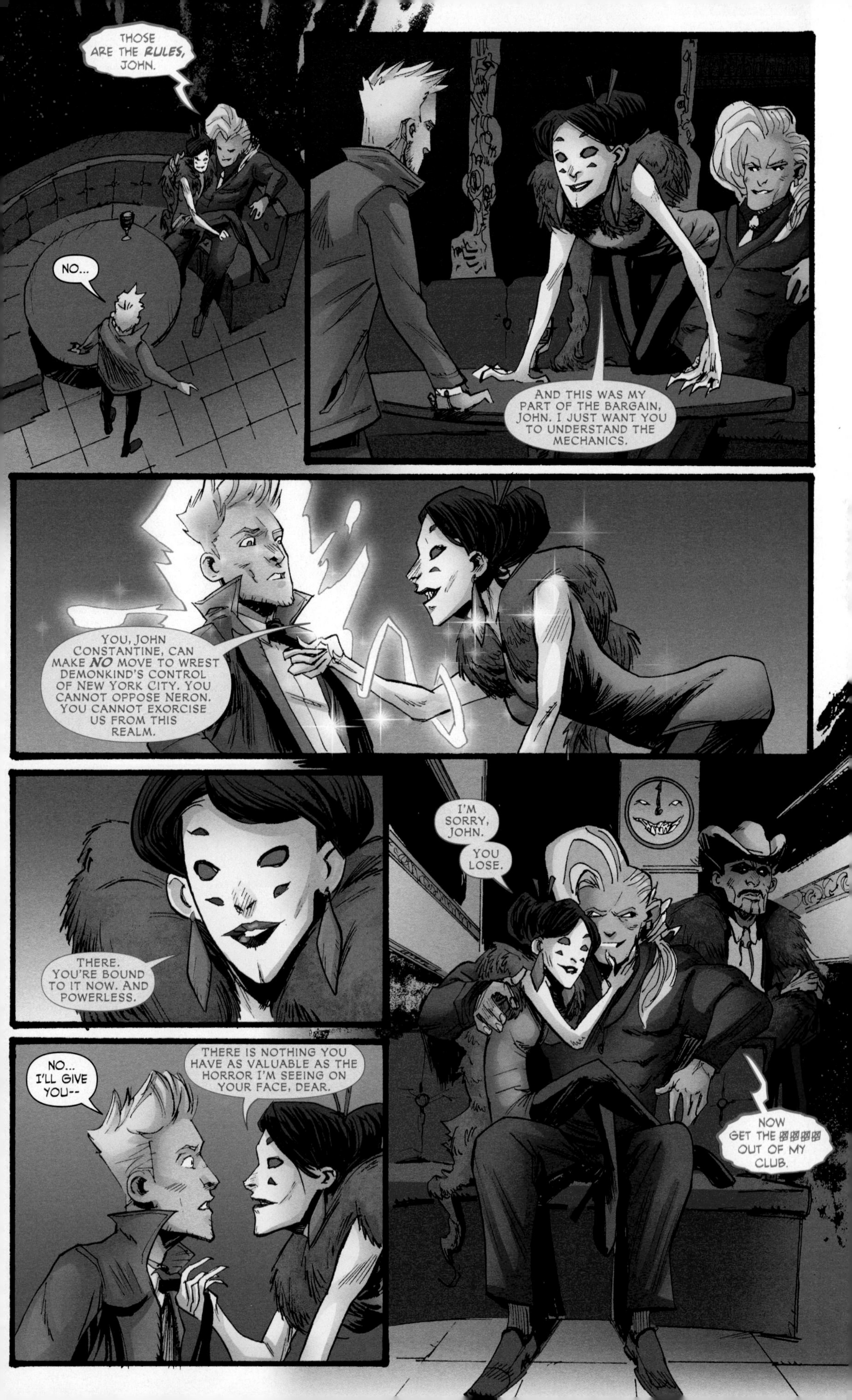
THOSE ARE THE RULES, JOHN.
NO...
AND THIS WAS MY PART OF THE BARGAIN, JOHN. I JUST WANT YOU TO UNDERSTAND THE MECHANICS.
YOU, JOHN CONSTANTINE, CAN MAKE NO MOVE TO WREST DEMONKIND'S CONTROL OF NEW YORK CITY. YOU CANNOT OPPOSE NERON. YOU CANNOT EXORCISE US FROM THIS REALM.
THERE. YOU'RE BOUND TO IT NOW. AND POWERLESS.
NO... I'LL GIVE YOU--
THERE IS NOTHING YOU HAVE AS VALUABLE AS THE HORROR I'M SEEING ON YOUR FACE, DEAR.
I'M SORRY, JOHN.
YOU LOSE.
NOW GET THE ▩▩▩▩ OUT OF MY CLUB.

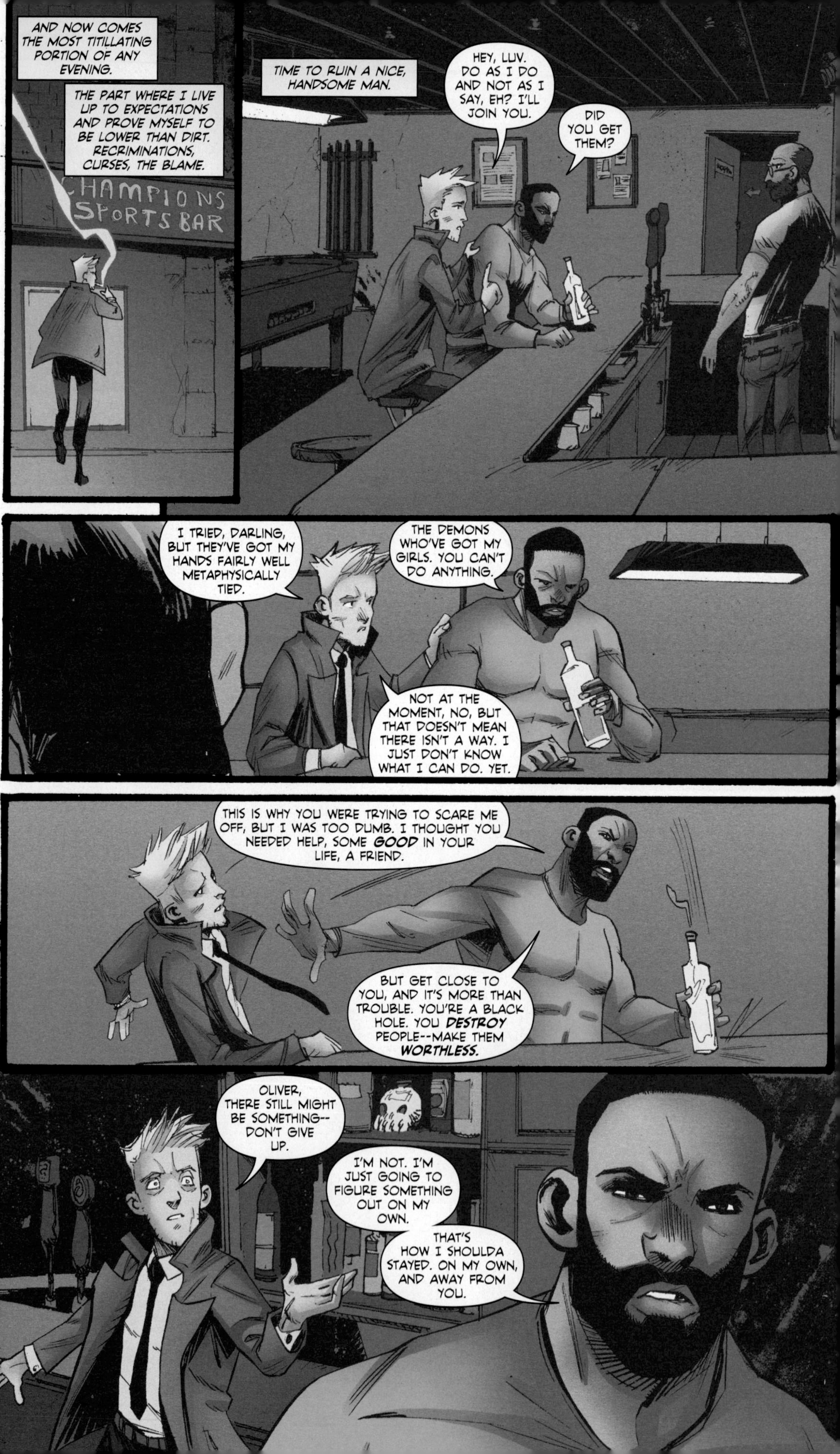
AND NOW COMES THE MOST TITILLATING PORTION OF ANY EVENING.
THE PART WHERE I LIVE UP TO EXPECTATIONS AND PROVE MYSELF TO BE LOWER THAN DIRT. RECRIMINATIONS, CURSES, THE BLAME.
CHAMPIONS SPORTS BAR
TIME TO RUIN A NICE, HANDSOME MAN.
HEY, LUV. DO AS I DO AND NOT AS I SAY, EH? I'LL JOIN YOU.
DID YOU GET THEM?
I TRIED, DARLING, BUT THEY'VE GOT MY HANDS FAIRLY WELL METAPHYSICALLY TIED.
THE DEMONS WHO'VE GOT MY GIRLS. YOU CAN'T DO ANYTHING.
NOT AT THE MOMENT, NO, BUT THAT DOESN'T MEAN THERE ISN'T A WAY. I JUST DON'T KNOW WHAT I CAN DO. YET.
THIS IS WHY YOU WERE TRYING TO SCARE ME OFF, BUT I WAS TOO DUMB. I THOUGHT YOU NEEDED HELP, SOME GOOD IN YOUR LIFE, A FRIEND.
BUT GET CLOSE TO YOU, AND IT'S MORE THAN TROUBLE. YOU'RE A BLACK HOLE. YOU DESTROY PEOPLE--MAKE THEM WORTHLESS.
OLIVER, THERE STILL MIGHT BE SOMETHING--DON'T GIVE UP.
I'M NOT. I'M JUST GOING TO FIGURE SOMETHING OUT ON MY OWN.
THAT'S HOW I SHOULDA STAYED. ON MY OWN, AND AWAY FROM YOU.

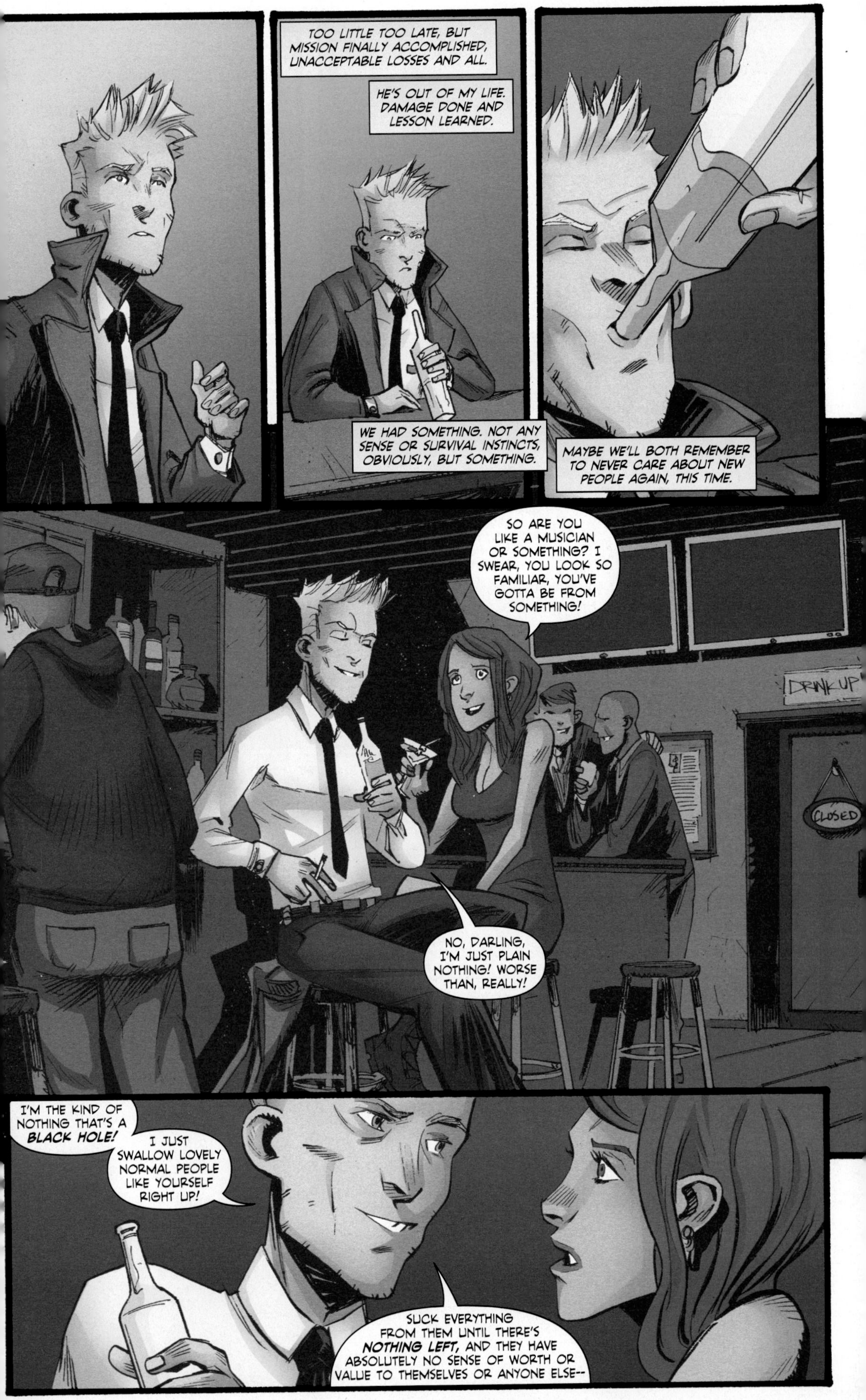
TOO LITTLE TOO LATE, BUT MISSION FINALLY ACCOMPLISHED, UNACCEPTABLE LOSSES AND ALL.
HE'S OUT OF MY LIFE. DAMAGE DONE AND LESSON LEARNED.
WE HAD SOMETHING. NOT ANY SENSE OR SURVIVAL INSTINCTS, OBVIOUSLY, BUT SOMETHING.
MAYBE WE'LL BOTH REMEMBER TO NEVER CARE ABOUT NEW PEOPLE AGAIN, THIS TIME.
SO ARE YOU LIKE A MUSICIAN OR SOMETHING? I SWEAR, YOU LOOK SO FAMILIAR, YOU'VE GOTTA BE FROM SOMETHING!
DRINK UP
CLOSED
NO, DARLING, I'M JUST PLAIN NOTHING! WORSE THAN, REALLY!
I'M THE KIND OF NOTHING THAT'S A BLACK HOLE!
I JUST SWALLOW LOVELY NORMAL PEOPLE LIKE YOURSELF RIGHT UP!
SUCK EVERYTHING FROM THEM UNTIL THERE'S NOTHING LEFT, AND THEY HAVE ABSOLUTELY NO SENSE OF WORTH OR VALUE TO THEMSELVES OR ANYONE ELSE--

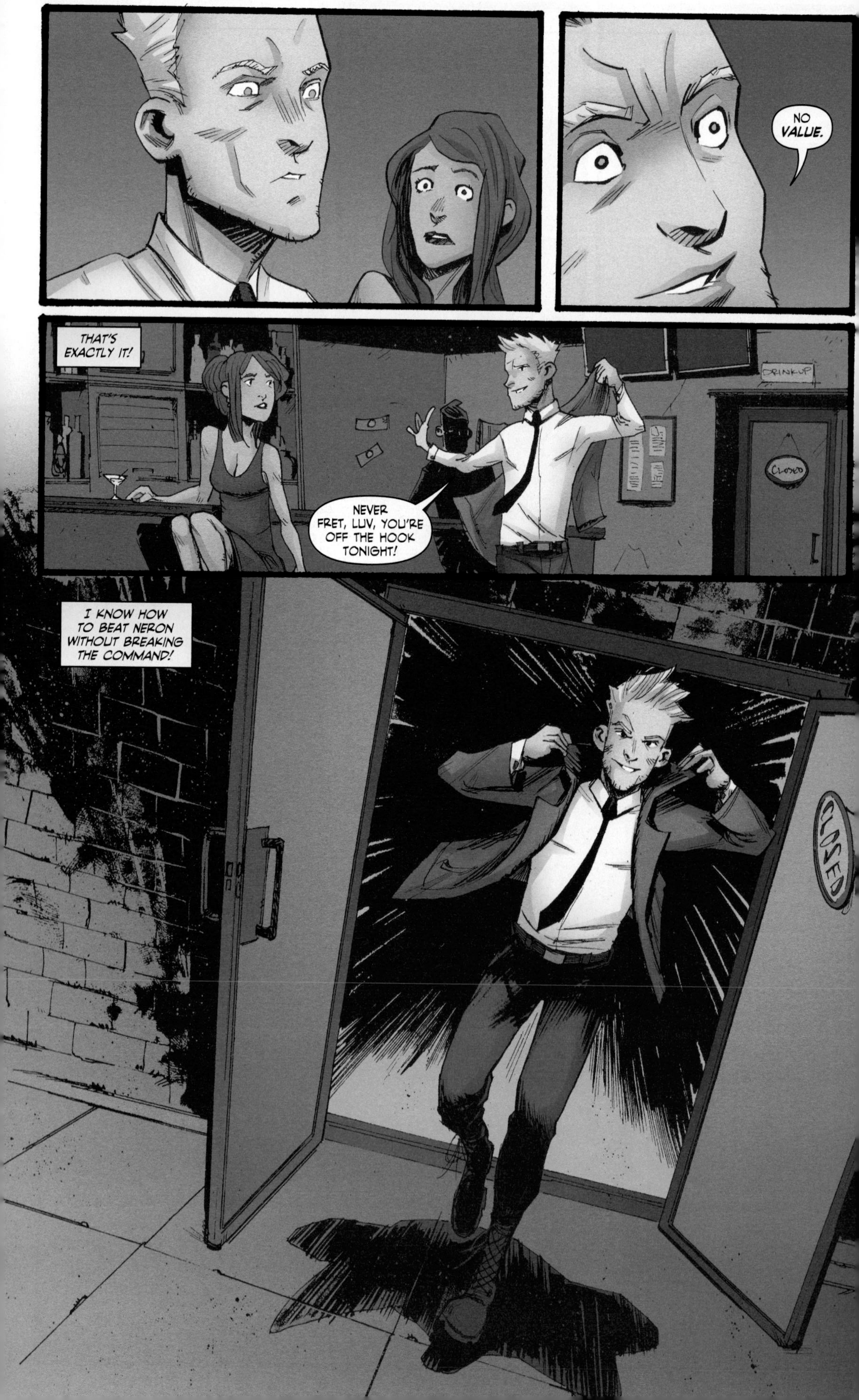
NO VALUE.
THAT'S EXACTLY IT!
DRINK UP
CLOSED
NEVER FRET, LUV, YOU'RE OFF THE HOOK TONIGHT!
I KNOW HOW TO BEAT NERON WITHOUT BREAKING THE COMMAND!
CLOSED

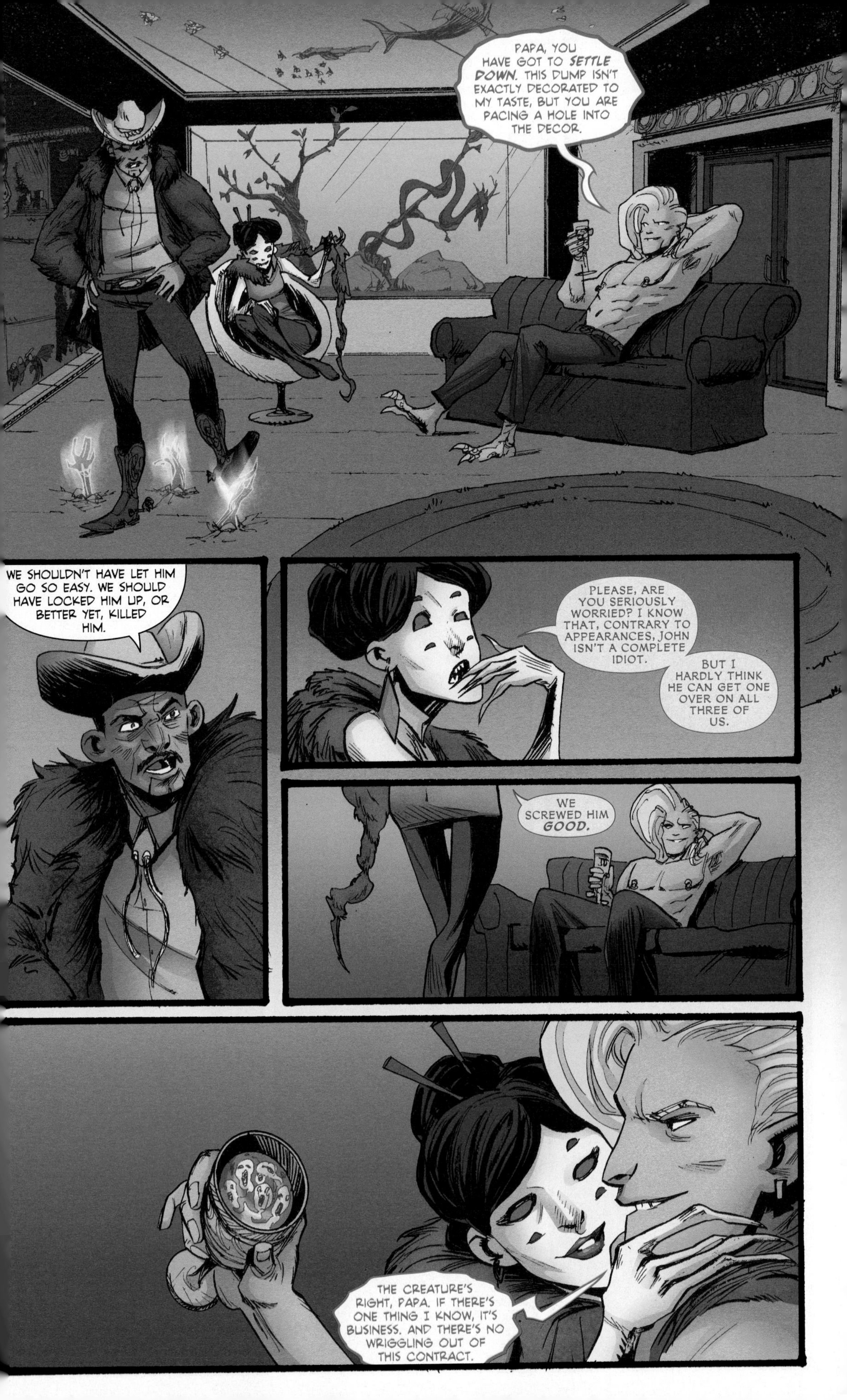
PAPA, YOU HAVE GOT TO SETTLE DOWN. THIS DUMP ISN'T EXACTLY DECORATED TO MY TASTE, BUT YOU ARE PACING A HOLE INTO THE DECOR.
WE SHOULDN'T HAVE LET HIM GO SO EASY. WE SHOULD HAVE LOCKED HIM UP, OR BETTER YET, KILLED HIM.
PLEASE, ARE YOU SERIOUSLY WORRIED? I KNOW THAT, CONTRARY TO APPEARANCES, JOHN ISN'T A COMPLETE IDIOT.
BUT I HARDLY THINK HE CAN GET ONE OVER ON ALL THREE OF US.
WE SCREWED HIM GOOD.
THE CREATURE'S RIGHT, PAPA. IF THERE'S ONE THING I KNOW, IT'S BUSINESS. AND THERE'S NO WRIGGLING OUT OF THIS CONTRACT.

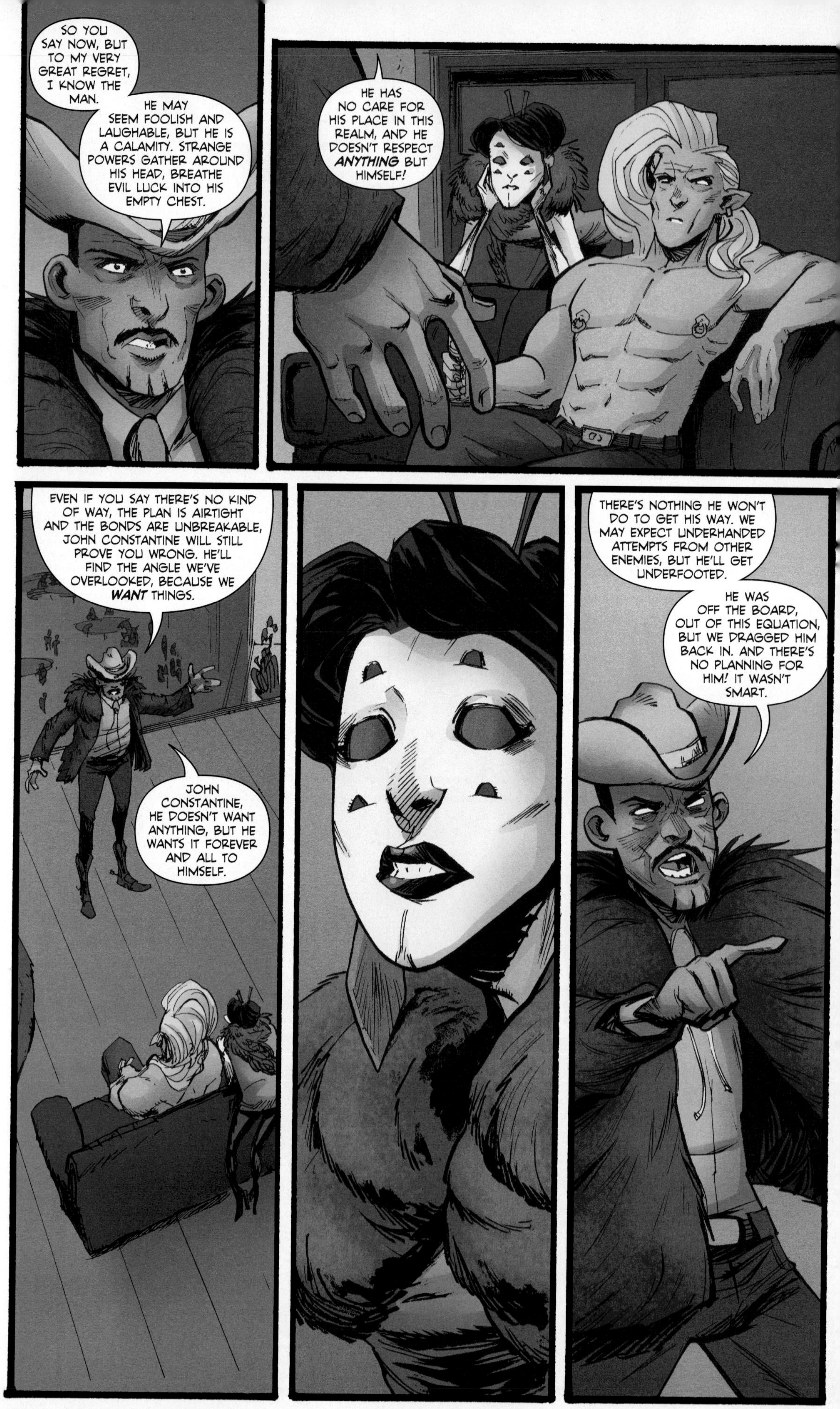
SO YOU SAY NOW, BUT TO MY VERY GREAT REGRET, I KNOW THE MAN.
HE MAY SEEM FOOLISH AND LAUGHABLE, BUT HE IS A CALAMITY. STRANGE POWERS GATHER AROUND HIS HEAD, BREATHE EVIL LUCK INTO HIS EMPTY CHEST.
HE HAS NO CARE FOR HIS PLACE IN THIS REALM, AND HE DOESN'T RESPECT ANYTHING BUT HIMSELF!
EVEN IF YOU SAY THERE'S NO KIND OF WAY, THE PLAN IS AIRTIGHT AND THE BONDS ARE UNBREAKABLE, JOHN CONSTANTINE WILL STILL PROVE YOU WRONG. HE'LL FIND THE ANGLE WE'VE OVERLOOKED, BECAUSE WE WANT THINGS.
JOHN CONSTANTINE, HE DOESN'T WANT ANYTHING, BUT HE WANTS IT FOREVER AND ALL TO HIMSELF.
THERE'S NOTHING HE WON'T DO TO GET HIS WAY. WE MAY EXPECT UNDERHANDED ATTEMPTS FROM OTHER ENEMIES, BUT HE'LL GET UNDERFOOTED.
HE WAS OFF THE BOARD, OUT OF THIS EQUATION, BUT WE DRAGGED HIM BACK IN. AND THERE'S NO PLANNING FOR HIM! IT WASN'T SMART.

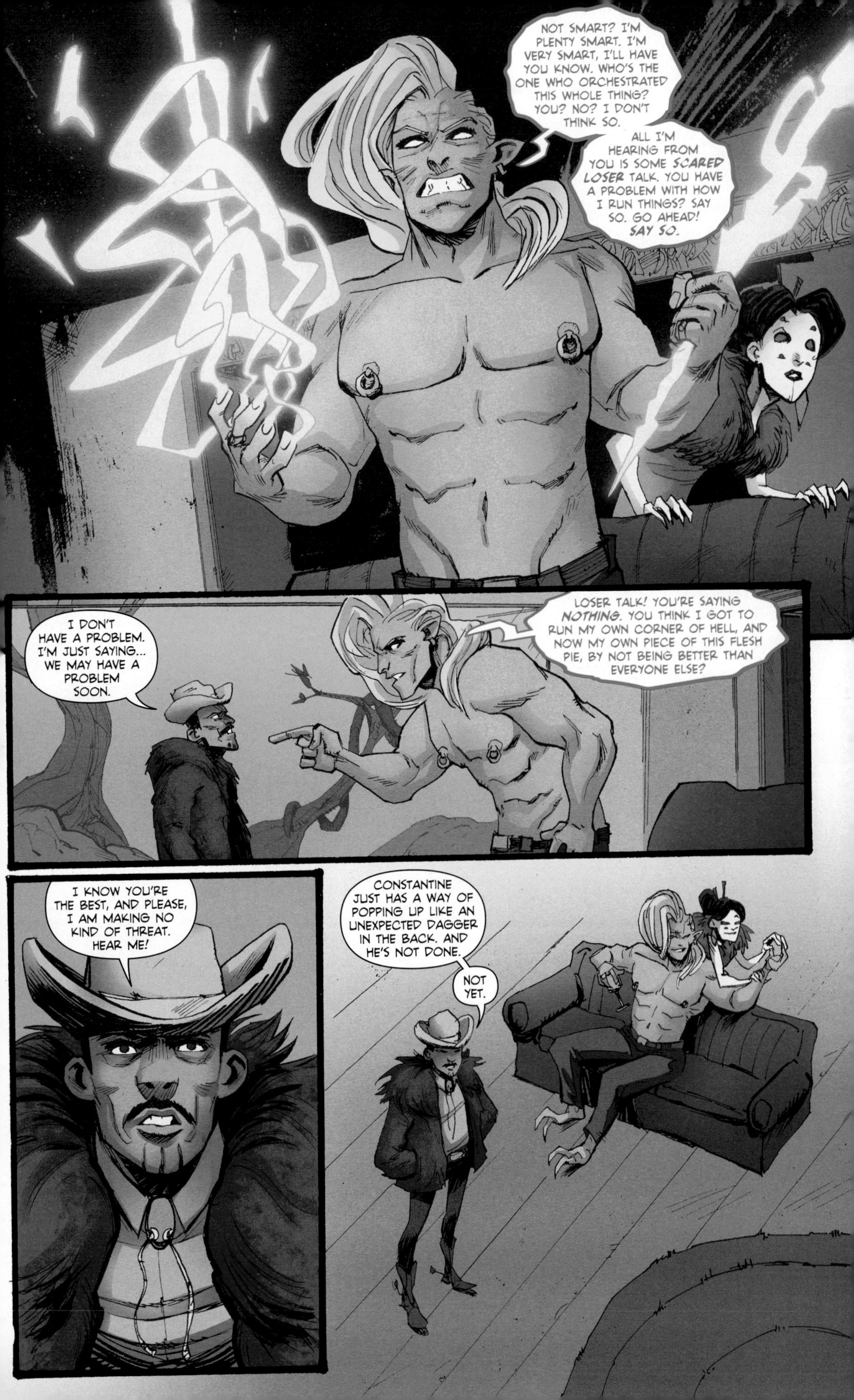
NOT SMART? I'M PLENTY SMART. I'M VERY SMART, I'LL HAVE YOU KNOW. WHO'S THE ONE WHO ORCHESTRATED THIS WHOLE THING? YOU? NO? I DON'T THINK SO.
ALL I'M HEARING FROM YOU IS SOME SCARED LOSER TALK. YOU HAVE A PROBLEM WITH HOW I RUN THINGS? SAY SO. GO AHEAD! SAY SO.
I DON'T HAVE A PROBLEM. I'M JUST SAYING... WE MAY HAVE A PROBLEM SOON.
LOSER TALK! YOU'RE SAYING NOTHING. YOU THINK I GOT TO RUN MY OWN CORNER OF HELL, AND NOW MY OWN PIECE OF THIS FLESH PIE, BY NOT BEING BETTER THAN EVERYONE ELSE?
I KNOW YOU'RE THE BEST, AND PLEASE, I AM MAKING NO KIND OF THREAT. HEAR ME!
CONSTANTINE JUST HAS A WAY OF POPPING UP LIKE AN UNEXPECTED DAGGER IN THE BACK. AND HE'S NOT DONE.
NOT YET.

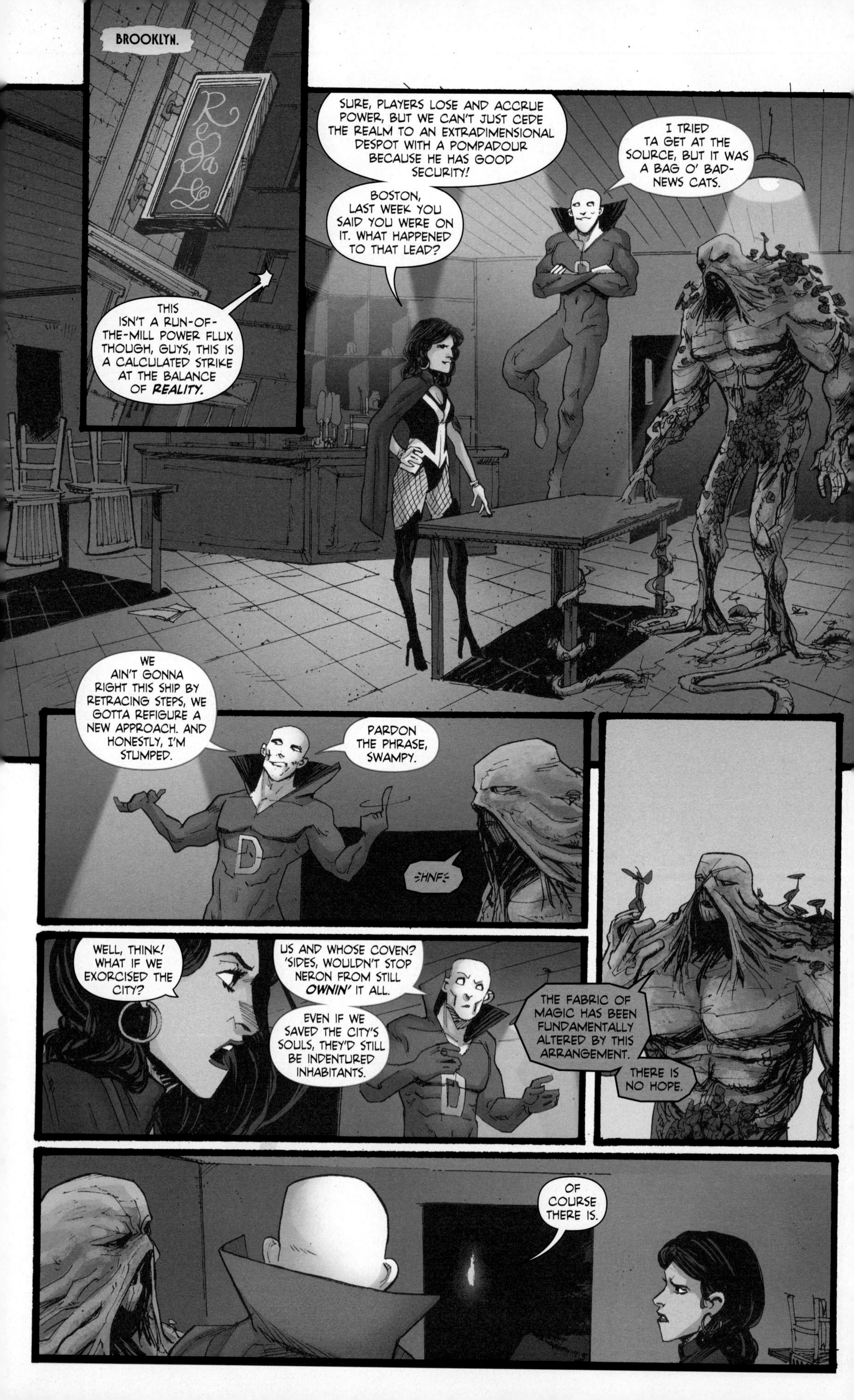
BROOKLYN.
THIS ISN'T A RUN-OF-THE-MILL POWER FLUX THOUGH, GUYS, THIS IS A CALCULATED STRIKE AT THE BALANCE OF REALITY.
SURE, PLAYERS LOSE AND ACCRUE POWER, BUT WE CAN'T JUST CEDE THE REALM TO AN EXTRADIMENSIONAL DESPOT WITH A POMPADOUR BECAUSE HE HAS GOOD SECURITY!
BOSTON, LAST WEEK YOU SAID YOU WERE ON IT. WHAT HAPPENED TO THAT LEAD?
I TRIED TA GET AT THE SOURCE, BUT IT WAS A BAG O' BAD-NEWS CATS.
WE AIN'T GONNA RIGHT THIS SHIP BY RETRACING STEPS, WE GOTTA REFIGURE A NEW APPROACH. AND HONESTLY, I'M STUMPED.
PARDON THE PHRASE, SWAMPY.
HNF
WELL, THINK! WHAT IF WE EXORCISED THE CITY?
US AND WHOSE COVEN? 'SIDES, WOULDN'T STOP NERON FROM STILL OWNIN' IT ALL.
EVEN IF WE SAVED THE CITY'S SOULS, THEY'D STILL BE INDENTURED INHABITANTS.
THE FABRIC OF MAGIC HAS BEEN FUNDAMENTALLY ALTERED BY THIS ARRANGEMENT.
THERE IS NO HOPE.
OF COURSE THERE IS.

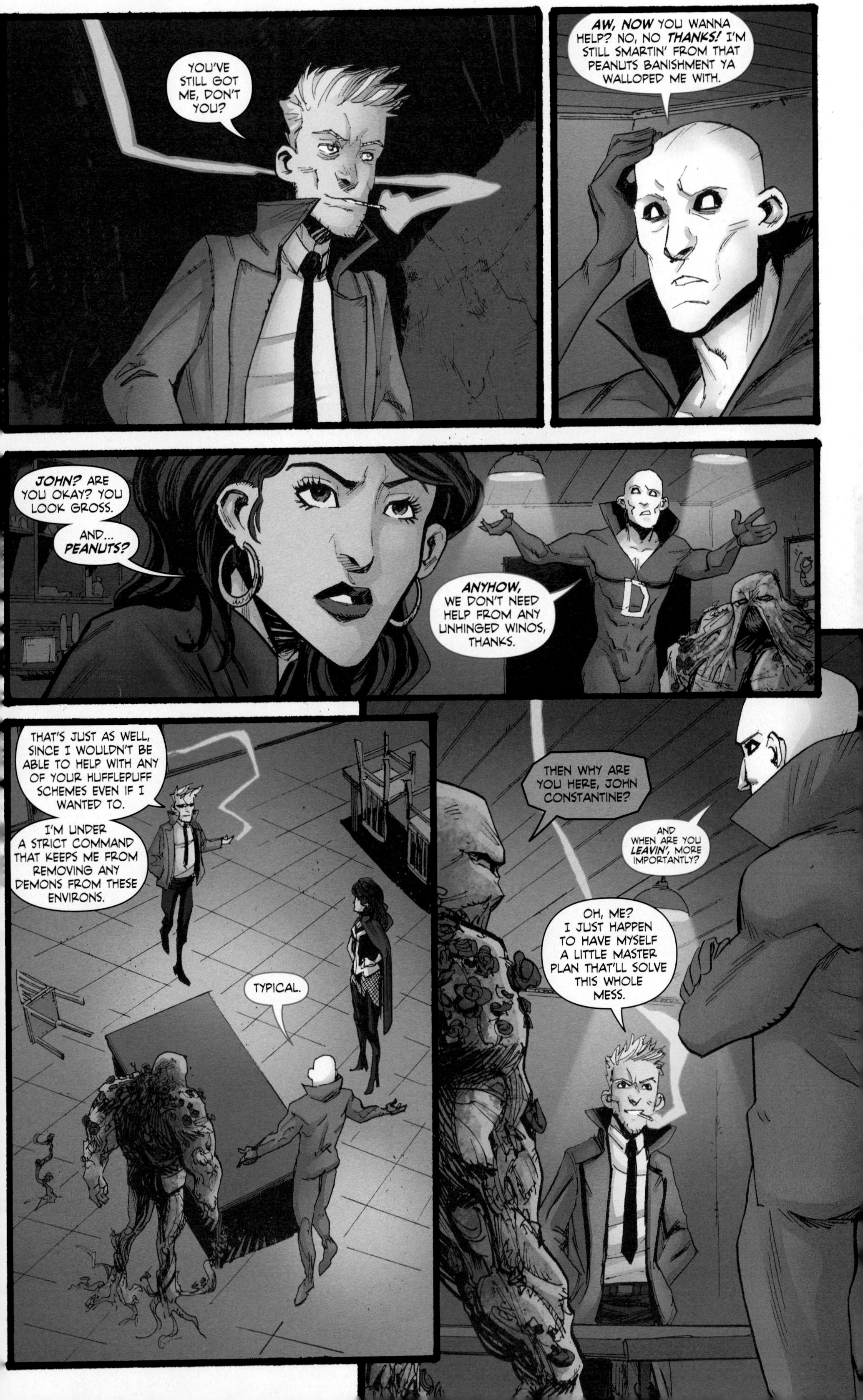
YOU'VE STILL GOT ME, DON'T YOU?
AW, NOW YOU WANNA HELP? NO, NO THANKS! I'M STILL SMARTIN' FROM THAT PEANUTS BANISHMENT YA WALLOPED ME WITH.
JOHN? ARE YOU OKAY? YOU LOOK GROSS.
AND... PEANUTS?
ANYHOW, WE DON'T NEED HELP FROM ANY UNHINGED WINOS, THANKS.
THAT'S JUST AS WELL, SINCE I WOULDN'T BE ABLE TO HELP WITH ANY OF YOUR HUFFLEPUFF SCHEMES EVEN IF I WANTED TO.
I'M UNDER A STRICT COMMAND THAT KEEPS ME FROM REMOVING ANY DEMONS FROM THESE ENVIRONS.
TYPICAL.
THEN WHY ARE YOU HERE, JOHN CONSTANTINE?
AND WHEN ARE YOU LEAVIN', MORE IMPORTANTLY?
OH, ME? I JUST HAPPEN TO HAVE MYSELF A LITTLE MASTER PLAN THAT'LL SOLVE THIS WHOLE MESS.

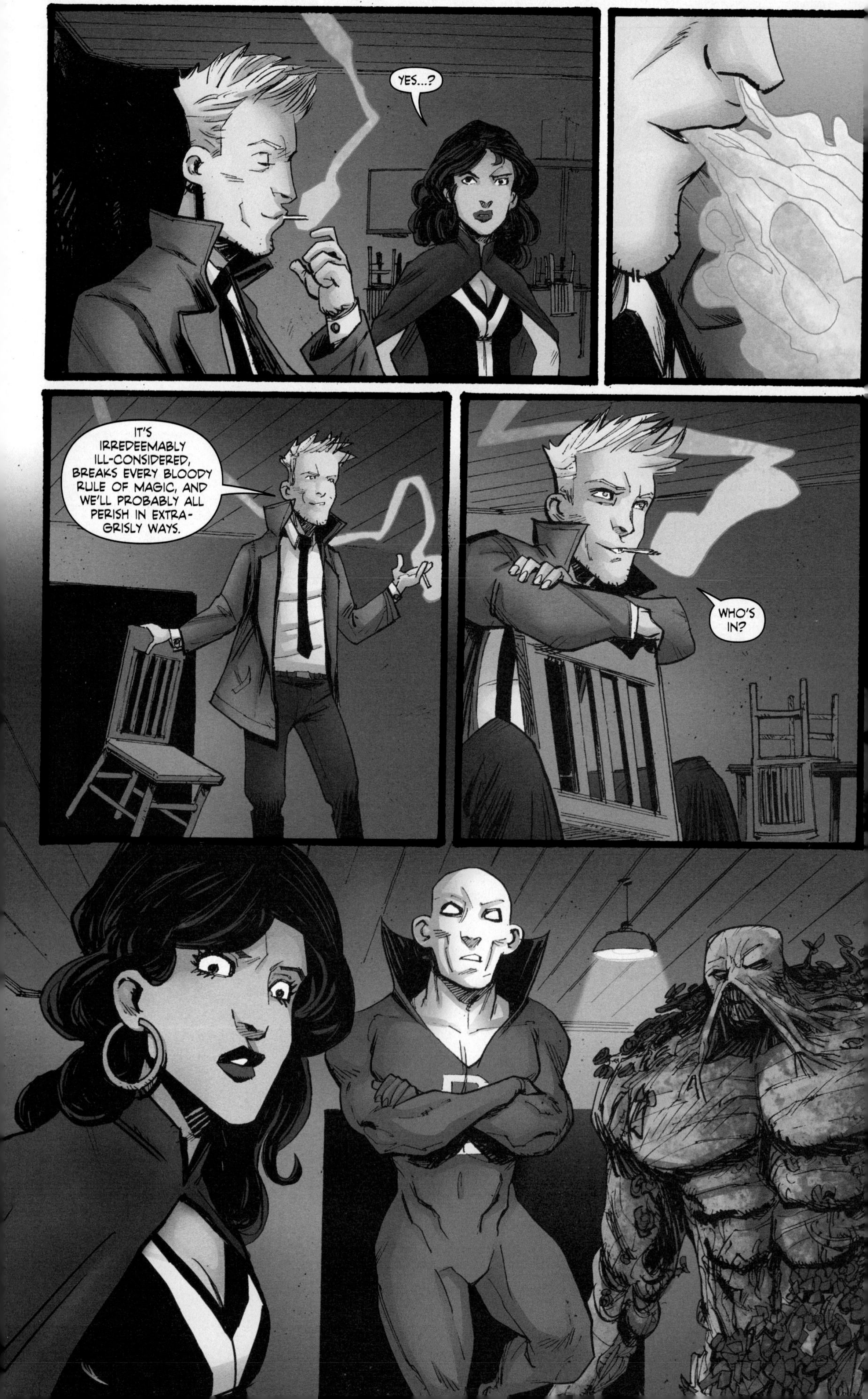
YES...?
IT'S IRREDEEMABLY ILL-CONSIDERED, BREAKS EVERY BLOODY RULE OF MAGIC, AND WE'LL PROBABLY ALL PERISH IN EXTRA-GRISLY WAYS.
WHO'S IN?

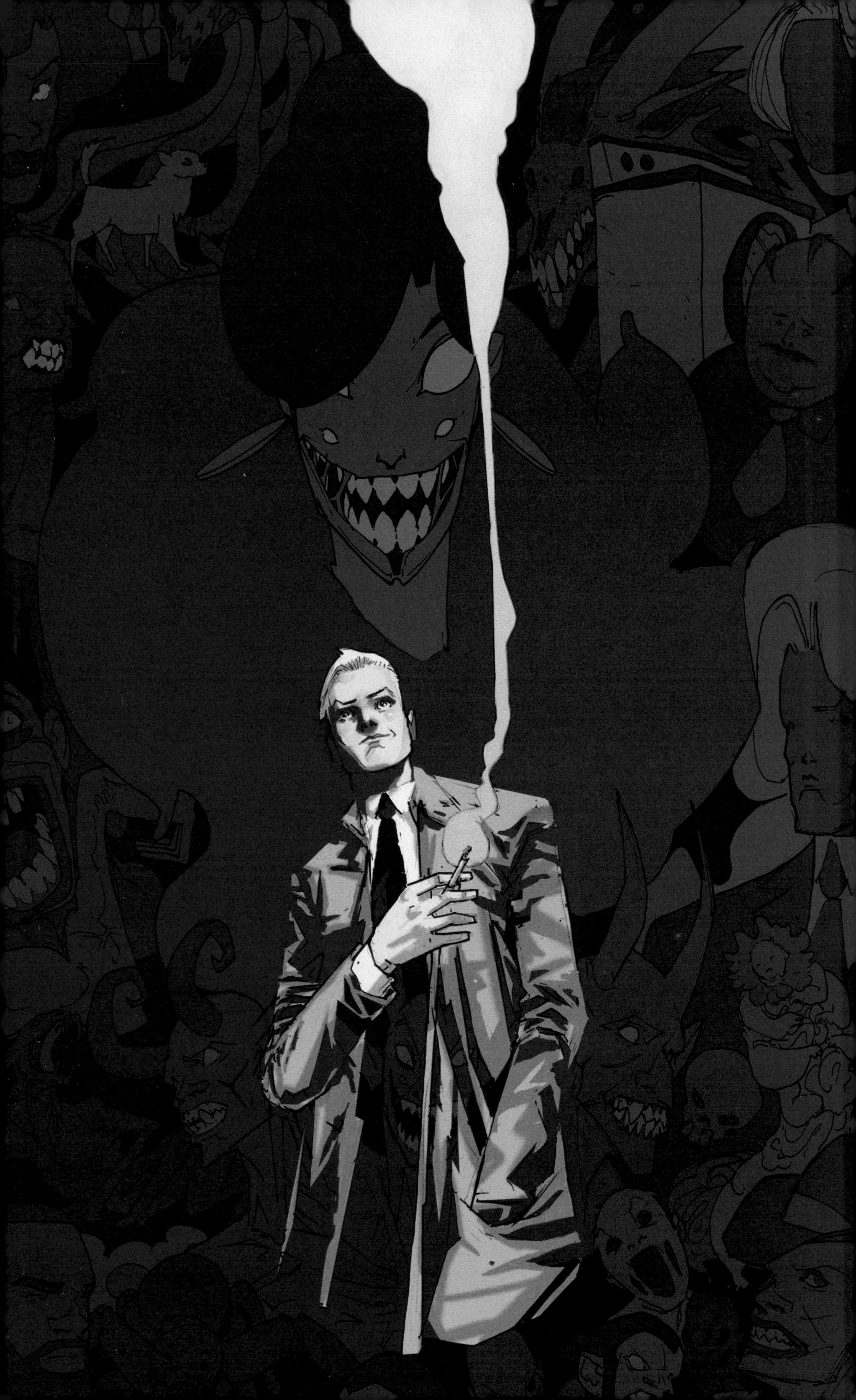

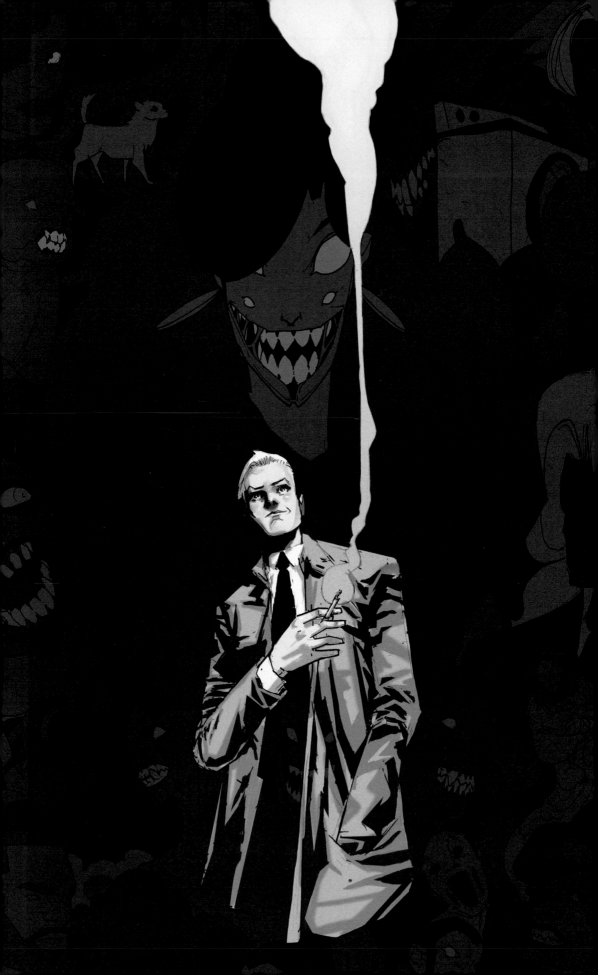

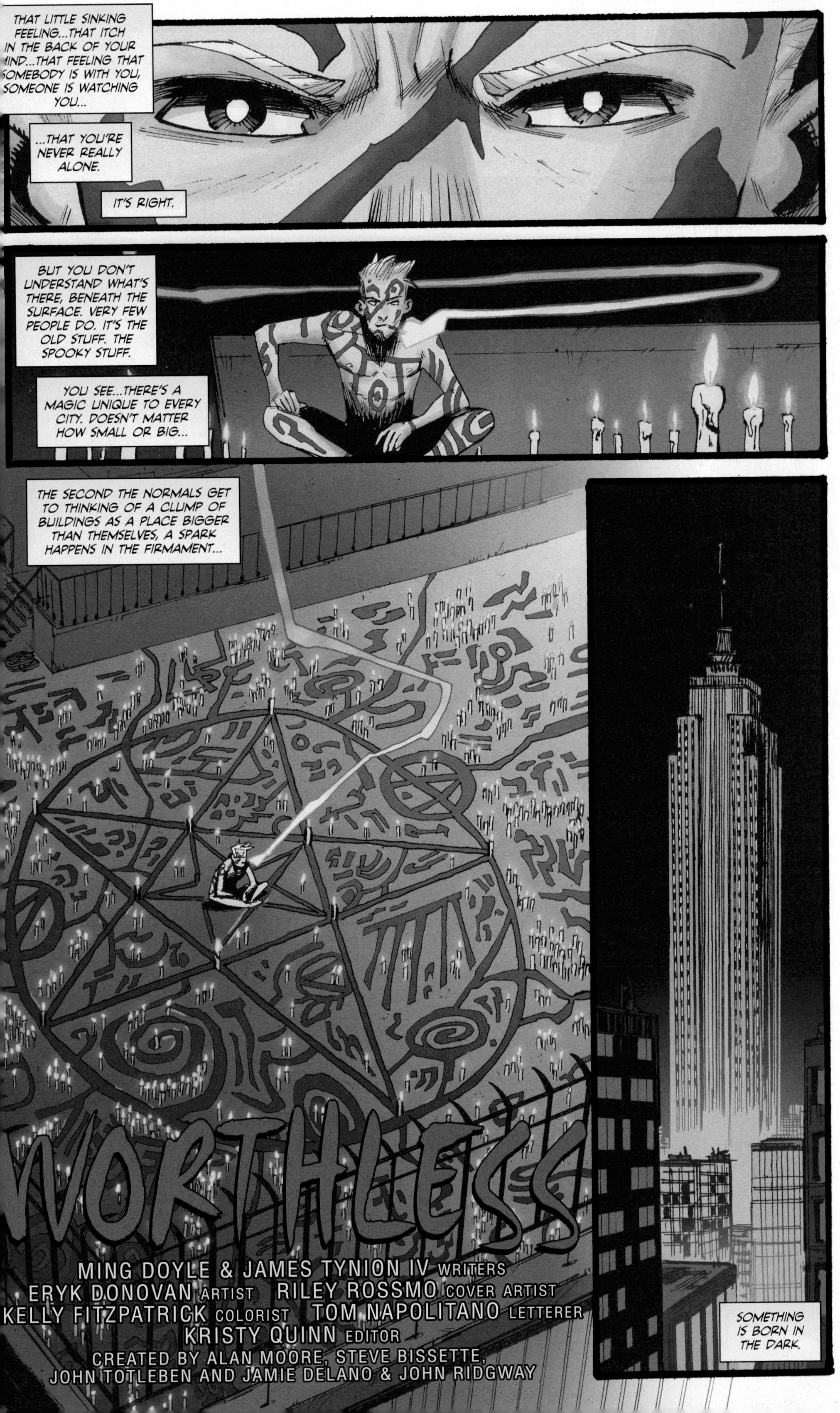

THAT LITTLE SINKING FEELING...THAT ITCH IN THE BACK OF YOUR MIND...THAT FEELING THAT SOMEBODY IS WITH YOU, SOMEONE IS WATCHING YOU...
...THAT YOU'RE NEVER REALLY ALONE.
IT'S RIGHT.
BUT YOU DON'T UNDERSTAND WHAT'S THERE, BENEATH THE SURFACE. VERY FEW PEOPLE DO. IT'S THE OLD STUFF. THE SPOOKY STUFF.
YOU SEE...THERE'S A MAGIC UNIQUE TO EVERY CITY. DOESN'T MATTER HOW SMALL OR BIG...
THE SECOND THE NORMALS GET TO THINKING OF A CLUMP OF BUILDINGS AS A PLACE BIGGER THAN THEMSELVES, A SPARK HAPPENS IN THE FIRMAMENT...
WORTHLESS
MING DOYLE & JAMES TYNION IV WRITERS
ERYK DONOVAN ARTIST RILEY ROSSMO COVER ARTIST
KELLY FITZPATRICK COLORIST TOM NAPOLITANO LETTERER
KRISTY QUINN EDITOR
CREATED BY ALAN MOORE, STEVE BISSETTE, JOHN TOTLEBEN AND JAMIE DELANO & JOHN RIDGWAY
SOMETHING IS BORN IN THE DARK.

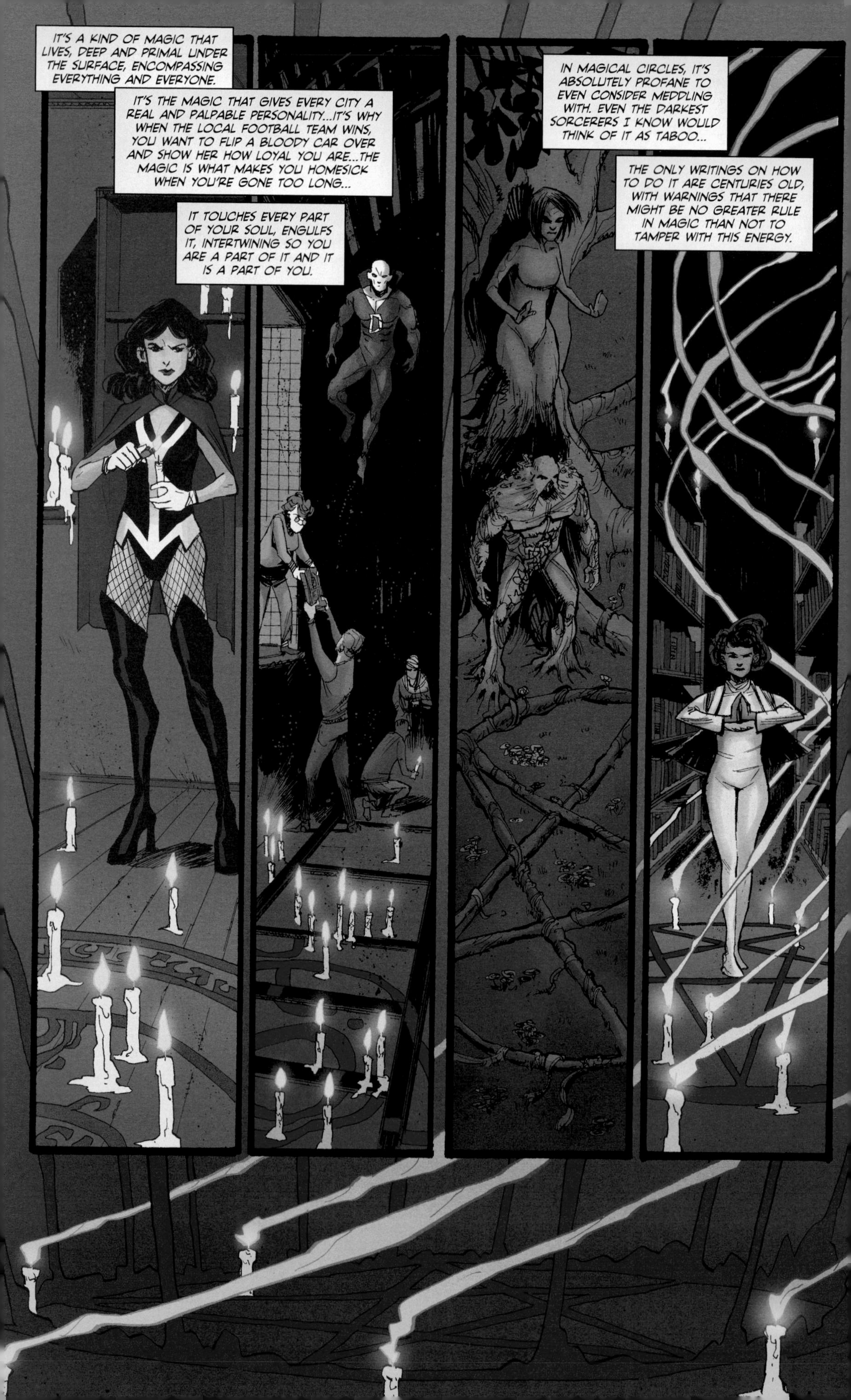
IT'S A KIND OF MAGIC THAT LIVES, DEEP AND PRIMAL UNDER THE SURFACE, ENCOMPASSING EVERYTHING AND EVERYONE.
IT'S THE MAGIC THAT GIVES EVERY CITY A REAL AND PALPABLE PERSONALITY...IT'S WHY WHEN THE LOCAL FOOTBALL TEAM WINS, YOU WANT TO FLIP A BLOODY CAR OVER AND SHOW HER HOW LOYAL YOU ARE...THE MAGIC IS WHAT MAKES YOU HOMESICK WHEN YOU'RE GONE TOO LONG...
IT TOUCHES EVERY PART OF YOUR SOUL, ENGULFS IT, INTERTWINING SO YOU ARE A PART OF IT AND IT IS A PART OF YOU.
IN MAGICAL CIRCLES, IT'S ABSOLUTELY PROFANE TO EVEN CONSIDER MEDDLING WITH. EVEN THE DARKEST SORCERERS I KNOW WOULD THINK OF IT AS TABOO...
THE ONLY WRITINGS ON HOW TO DO IT ARE CENTURIES OLD, WITH WARNINGS THAT THERE MIGHT BE NO GREATER RULE IN MAGIC THAN NOT TO TAMPER WITH THIS ENERGY.

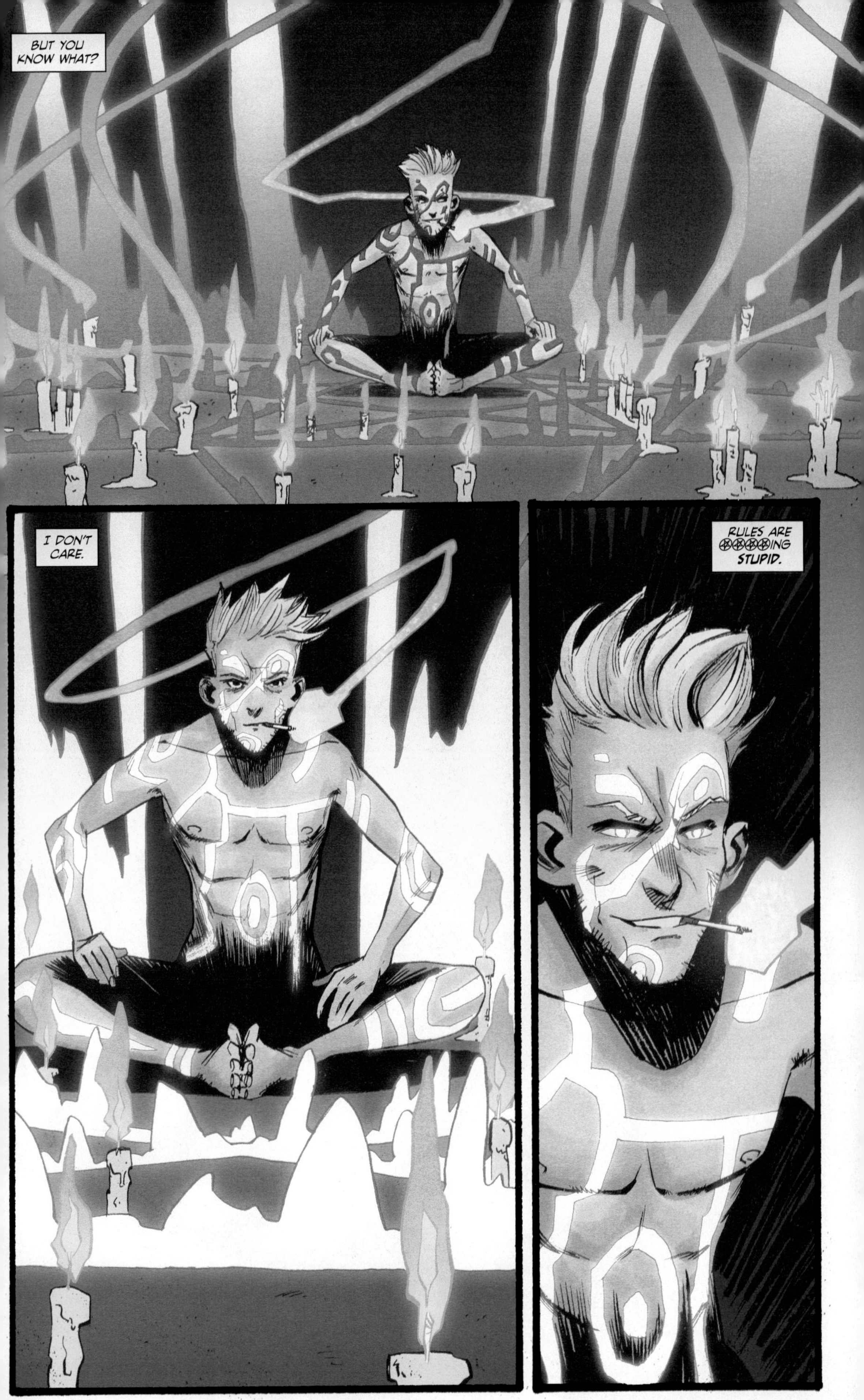
BUT YOU KNOW WHAT?
I DON'T CARE.
RULES ARE ✪✪✪✪ING STUPID.

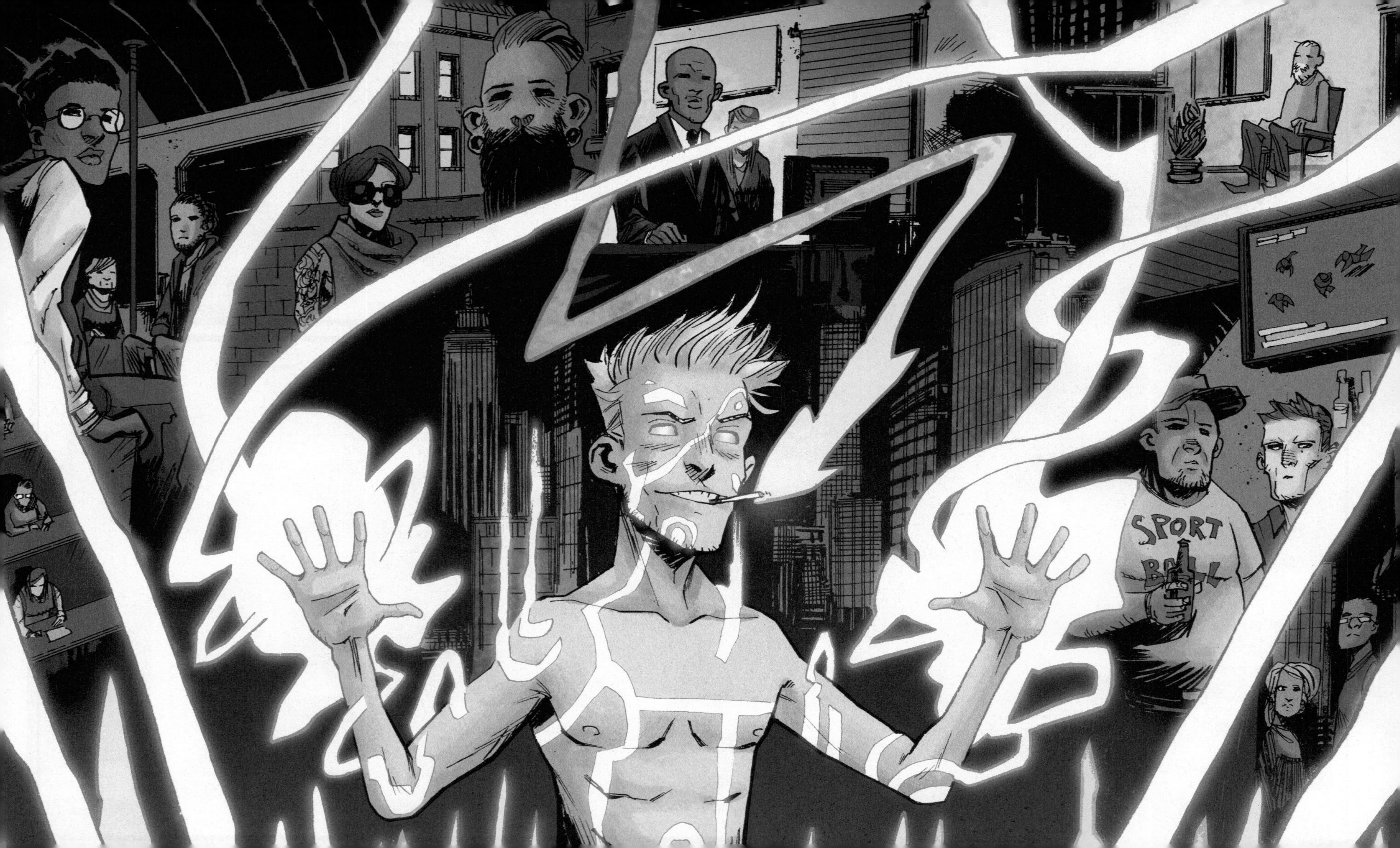
SPORT

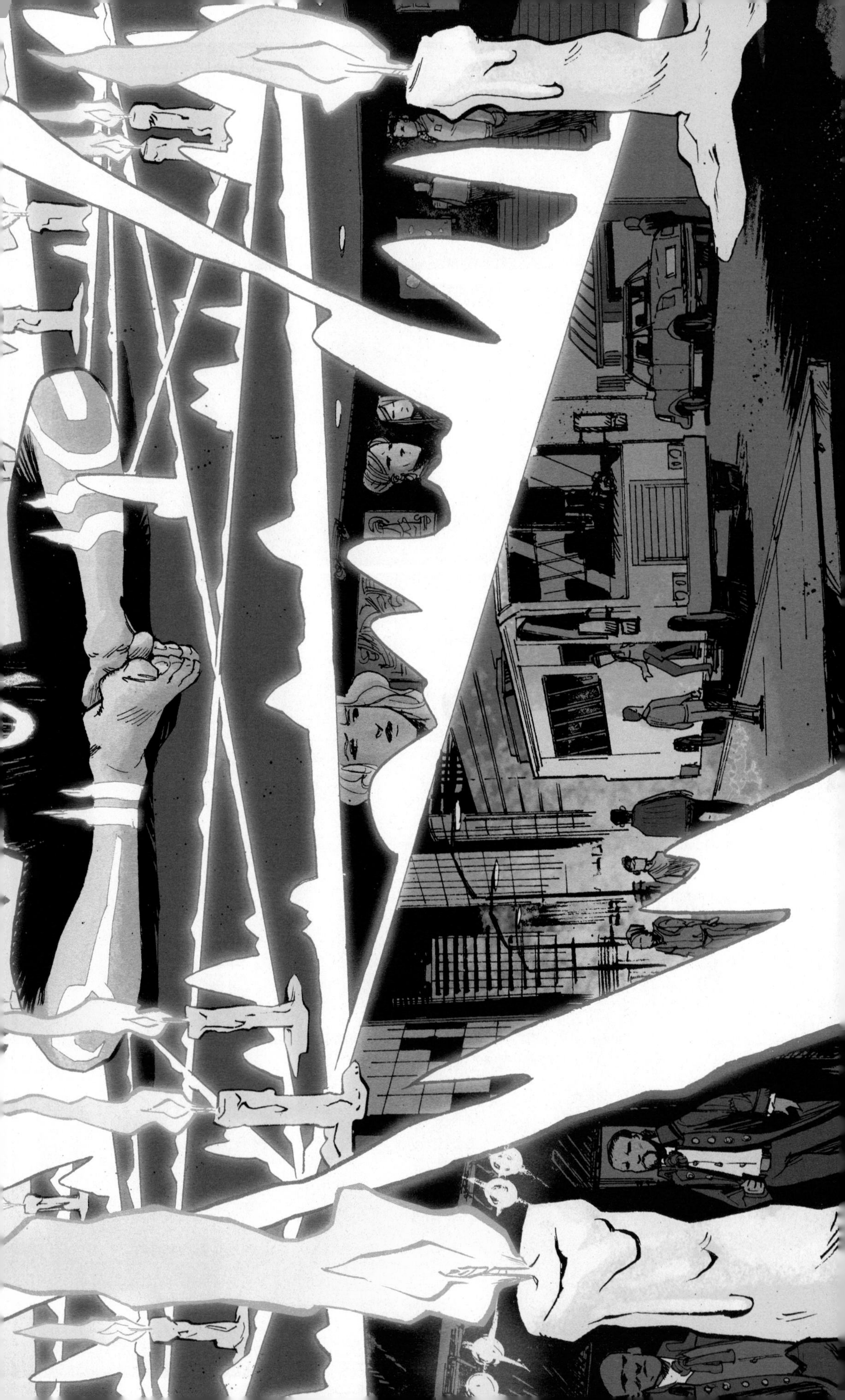

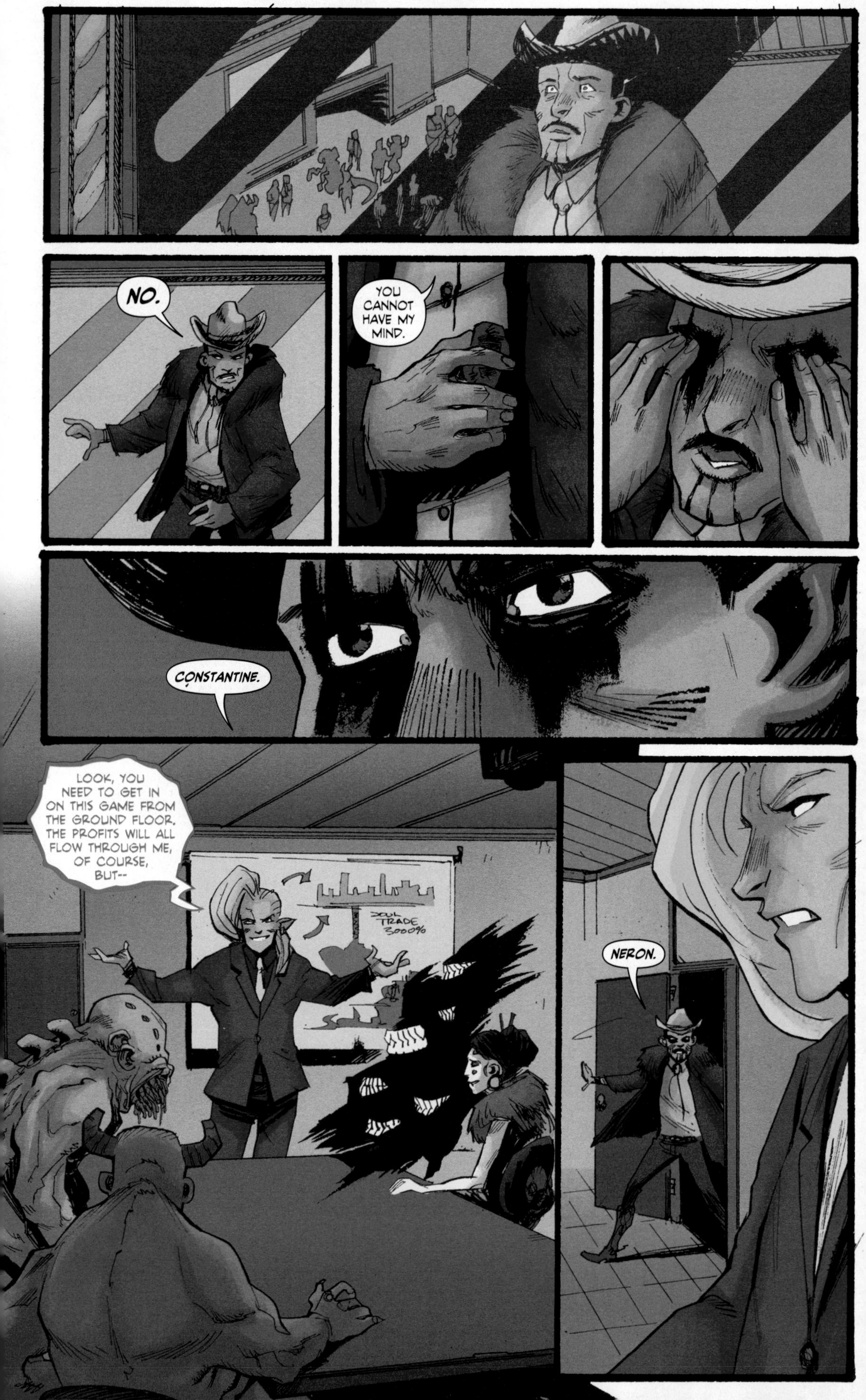
NO.
YOU CANNOT HAVE MY MIND.
CONSTANTINE.
LOOK, YOU NEED TO GET IN ON THIS GAME FROM THE GROUND FLOOR. THE PROFITS WILL ALL FLOW THROUGH ME, OF COURSE, BUT--
SOUL TRADE 3000%
NERON.

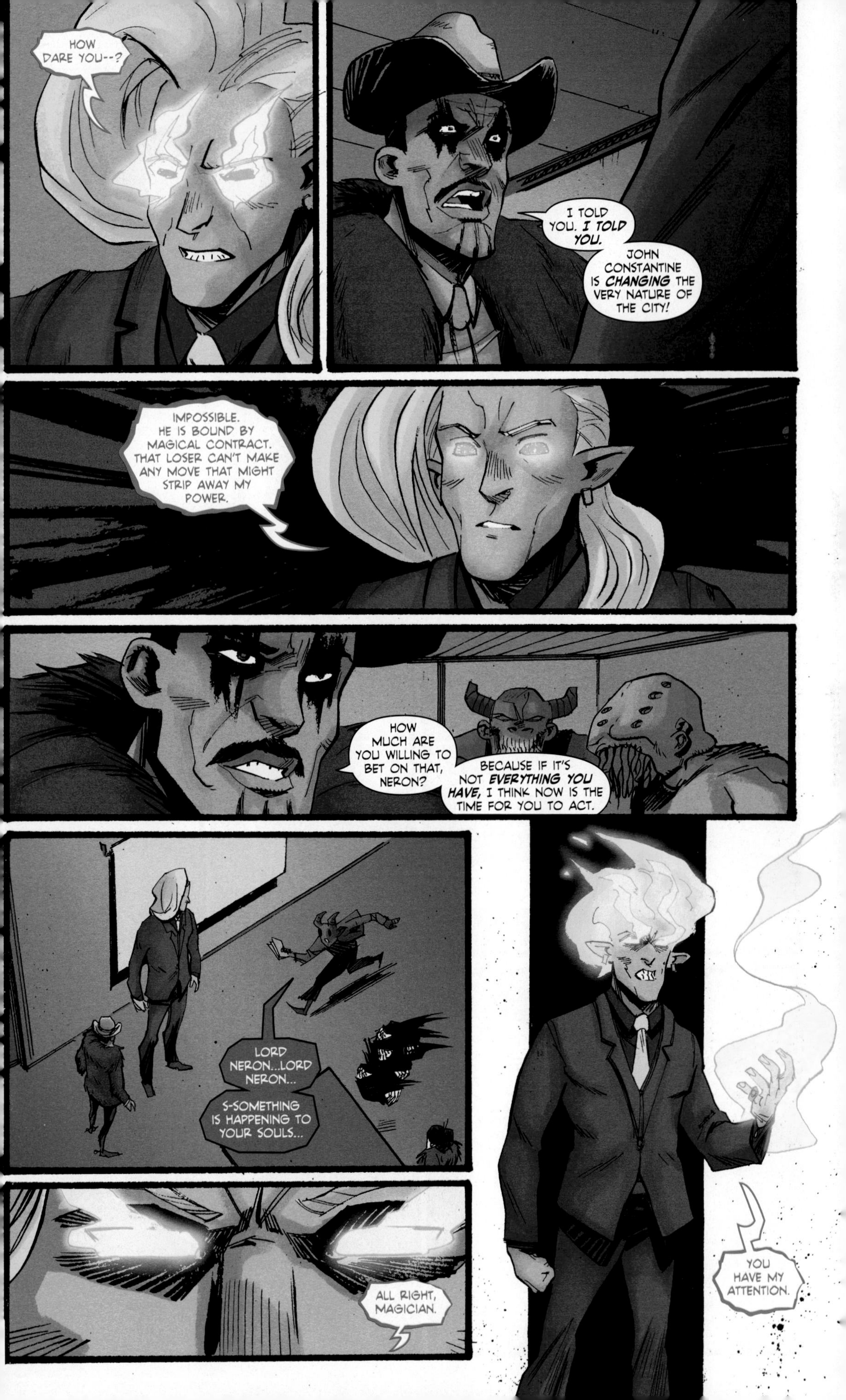
HOW DARE YOU--?
I TOLD YOU. I TOLD YOU.
JOHN CONSTANTINE IS CHANGING THE VERY NATURE OF THE CITY!
IMPOSSIBLE. HE IS BOUND BY MAGICAL CONTRACT. THAT LOSER CAN'T MAKE ANY MOVE THAT MIGHT STRIP AWAY MY POWER.
HOW MUCH ARE YOU WILLING TO BET ON THAT, NERON?
BECAUSE IF IT'S NOT EVERYTHING YOU HAVE, I THINK NOW IS THE TIME FOR YOU TO ACT.
LORD NERON...LORD NERON...
S-SOMETHING IS HAPPENING TO YOUR SOULS...
ALL RIGHT, MAGICIAN.
YOU HAVE MY ATTENTION.

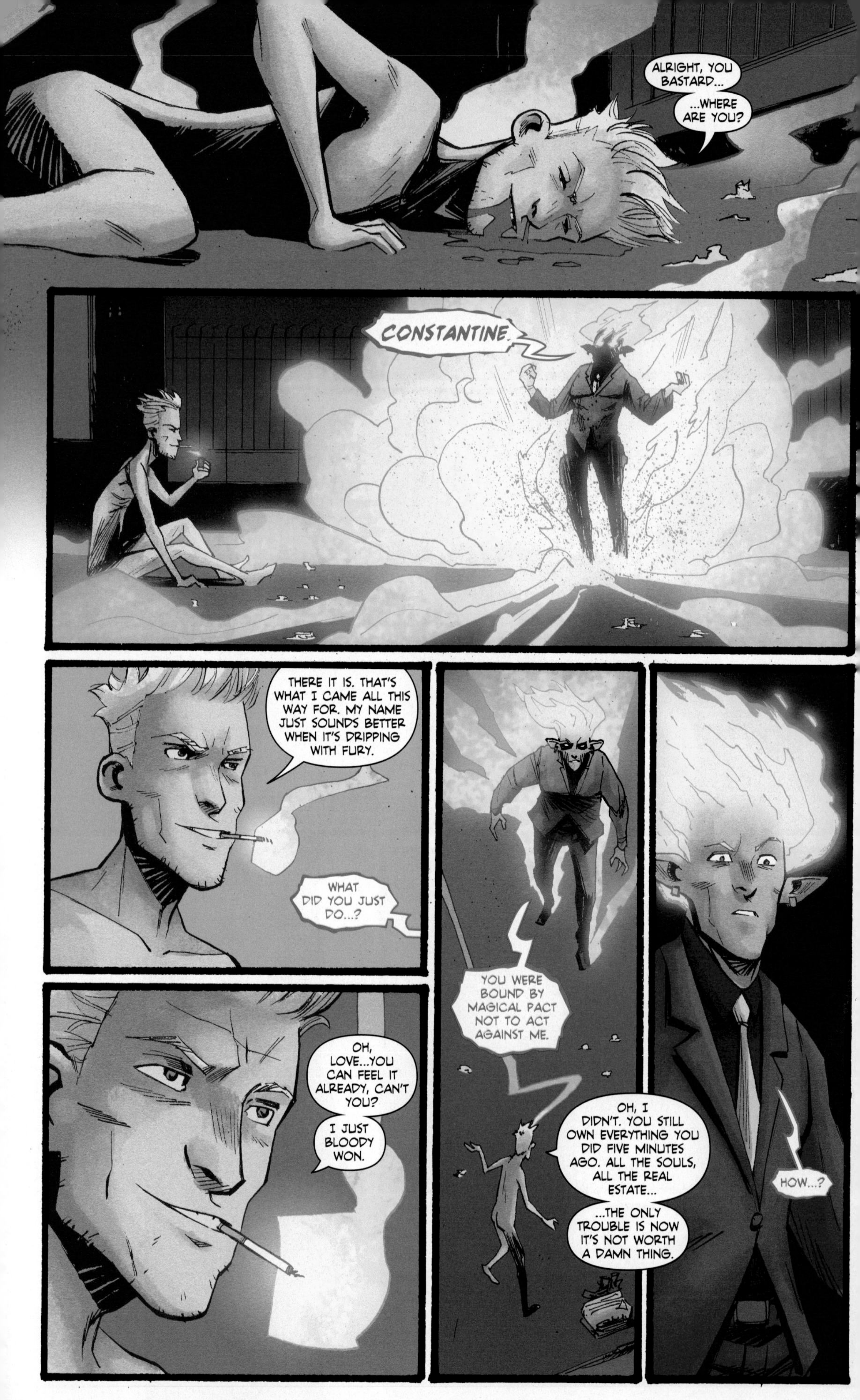
ALRIGHT, YOU BASTARD...
...WHERE ARE YOU?
CONSTANTINE.
THERE IT IS. THAT'S WHAT I CAME ALL THIS WAY FOR. MY NAME JUST SOUNDS BETTER WHEN IT'S DRIPPING WITH FURY.
WHAT DID YOU JUST DO...?
OH, LOVE...YOU CAN FEEL IT ALREADY, CAN'T YOU?
I JUST BLOODY WON.
YOU WERE BOUND BY MAGICAL PACT NOT TO ACT AGAINST ME.
OH, I DIDN'T. YOU STILL OWN EVERYTHING YOU DID FIVE MINUTES AGO. ALL THE SOULS, ALL THE REAL ESTATE...
...THE ONLY TROUBLE IS NOW IT'S NOT WORTH A DAMN THING.
HOW...?

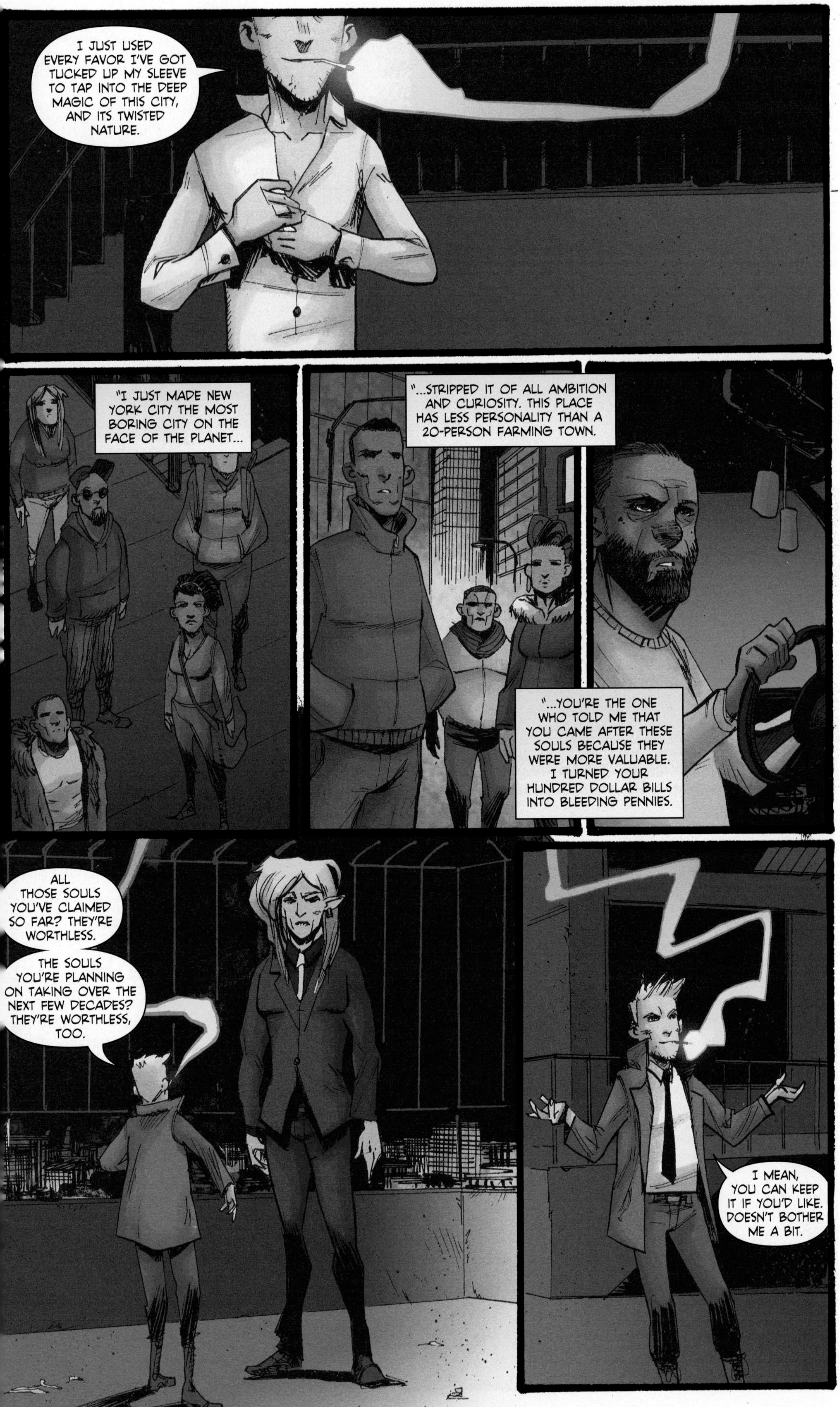

I JUST USED EVERY FAVOR I'VE GOT TUCKED UP MY SLEEVE TO TAP INTO THE DEEP MAGIC OF THIS CITY, AND ITS TWISTED NATURE.
"I JUST MADE NEW YORK CITY THE MOST BORING CITY ON THE FACE OF THE PLANET...
"...STRIPPED IT OF ALL AMBITION AND CURIOSITY. THIS PLACE HAS LESS PERSONALITY THAN A 20-PERSON FARMING TOWN.
"...YOU'RE THE ONE WHO TOLD ME THAT YOU CAME AFTER THESE SOULS BECAUSE THEY WERE MORE VALUABLE. I TURNED YOUR HUNDRED DOLLAR BILLS INTO BLEEDING PENNIES.
ALL THOSE SOULS YOU'VE CLAIMED SO FAR? THEY'RE WORTHLESS.
THE SOULS YOU'RE PLANNING ON TAKING OVER THE NEXT FEW DECADES? THEY'RE WORTHLESS, TOO.
I MEAN, YOU CAN KEEP IT IF YOU'D LIKE. DOESN'T BOTHER ME A BIT.

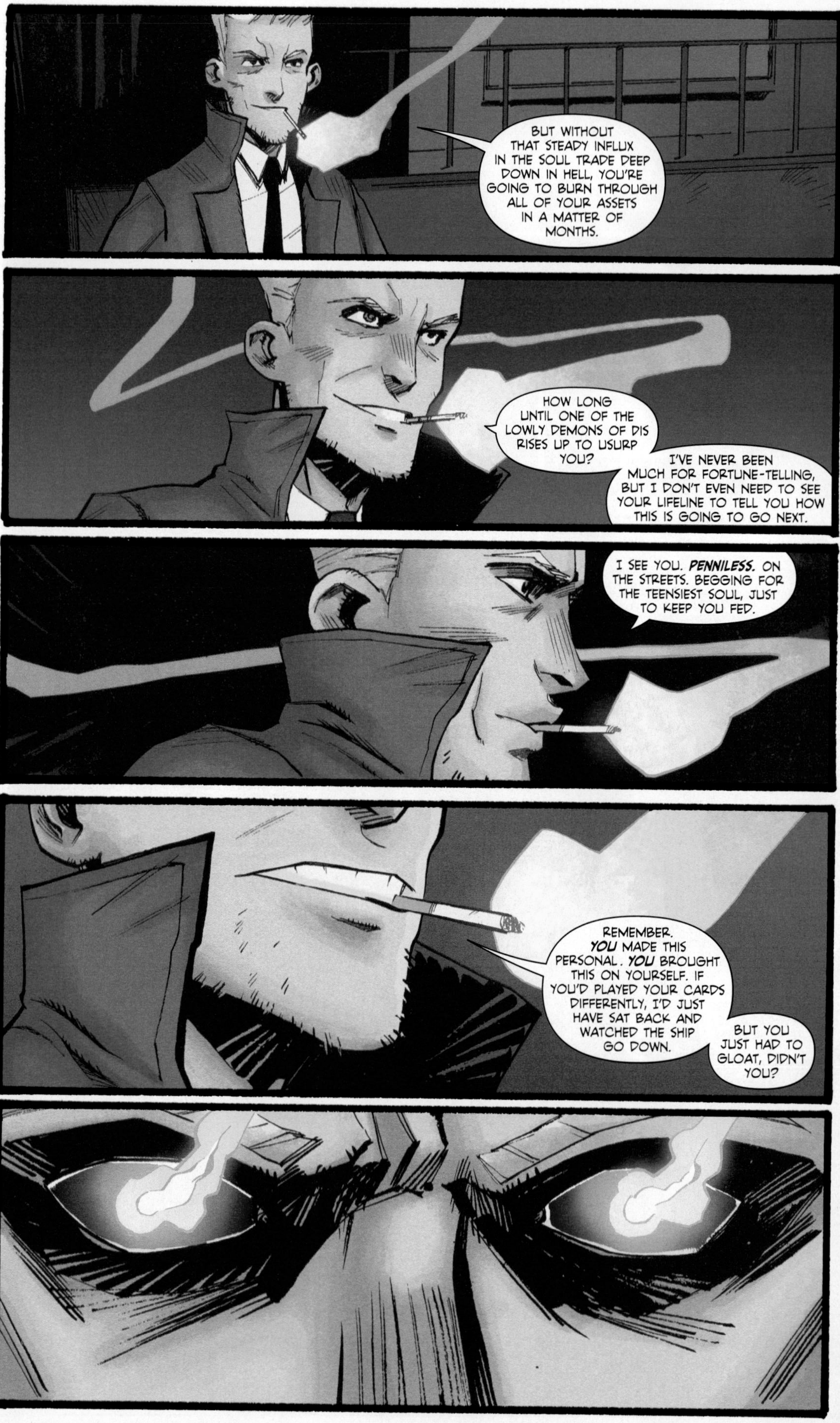
BUT WITHOUT THAT STEADY INFLUX IN THE SOUL TRADE DEEP DOWN IN HELL, YOU'RE GOING TO BURN THROUGH ALL OF YOUR ASSETS IN A MATTER OF MONTHS.
HOW LONG UNTIL ONE OF THE LOWLY DEMONS OF DIS RISES UP TO USURP YOU?
I'VE NEVER BEEN MUCH FOR FORTUNE-TELLING, BUT I DON'T EVEN NEED TO SEE YOUR LIFELINE TO TELL YOU HOW THIS IS GOING TO GO NEXT.
I SEE YOU. PENNILESS. ON THE STREETS. BEGGING FOR THE TEENSIEST SOUL, JUST TO KEEP YOU FED.
REMEMBER. YOU MADE THIS PERSONAL. YOU BROUGHT THIS ON YOURSELF. IF YOU'D PLAYED YOUR CARDS DIFFERENTLY, I'D JUST HAVE SAT BACK AND WATCHED THE SHIP GO DOWN.
BUT YOU JUST HAD TO GLOAT, DIDN'T YOU?

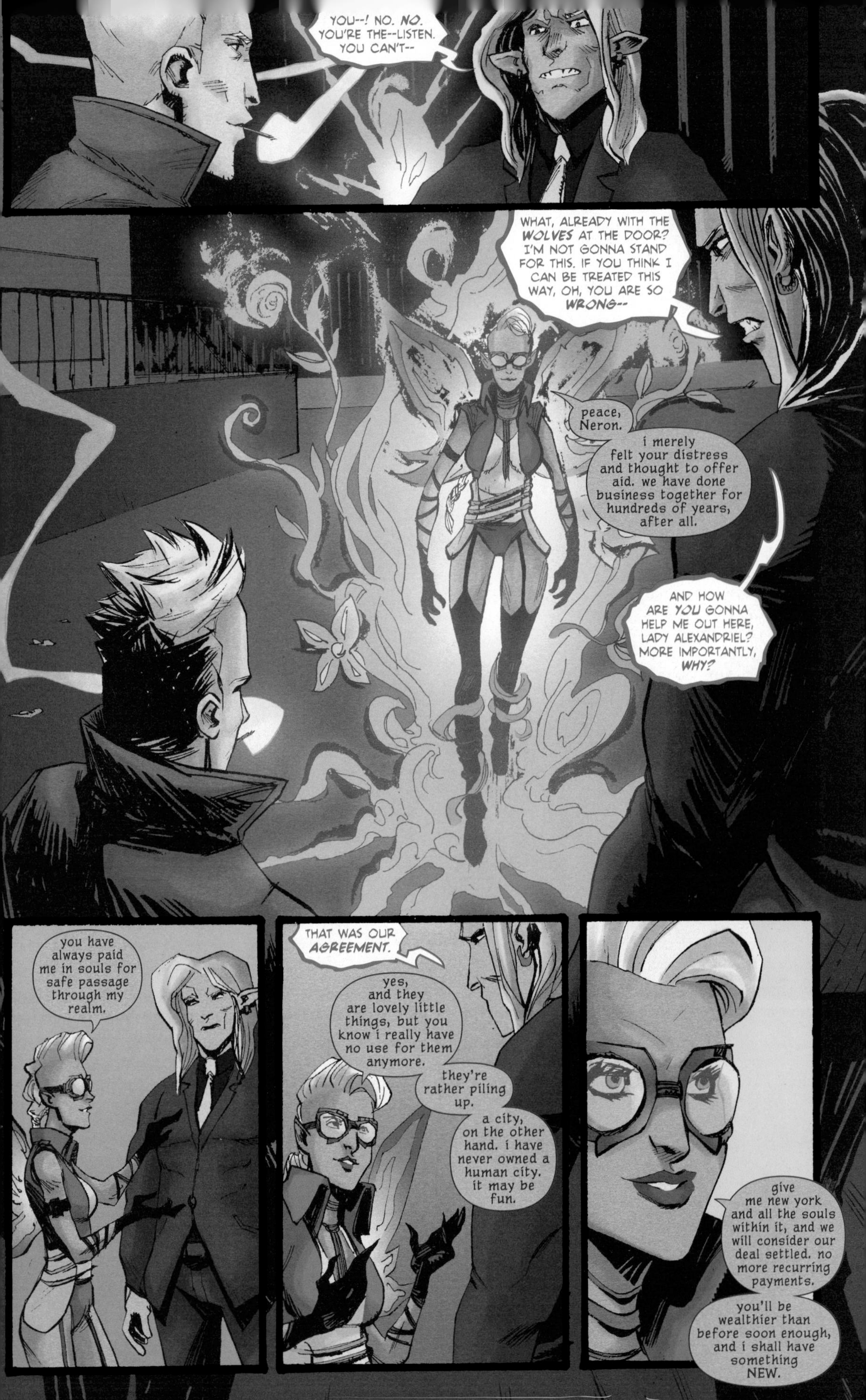

YOU--! NO. NO. YOU'RE THE--LISTEN. YOU CAN'T--
WHAT, ALREADY WITH THE WOLVES AT THE DOOR? I'M NOT GONNA STAND FOR THIS. IF YOU THINK I CAN BE TREATED THIS WAY, OH, YOU ARE SO WRONG--
peace, Neron.
i merely felt your distress and thought to offer aid. we have done business together for hundreds of years, after all.
AND HOW ARE YOU GONNA HELP ME OUT HERE, LADY ALEXANDRIEL? MORE IMPORTANTLY, WHY?
you have always paid me in souls for safe passage through my realm.
THAT WAS OUR AGREEMENT.
yes, and they are lovely little things, but you know i really have no use for them anymore.
they're rather piling up.
a city, on the other hand. i have never owned a human city. it may be fun.
give me new york and all the souls within it, and we will consider our deal settled. no more recurring payments.
you'll be wealthier than before soon enough, and i shall have something NEW.

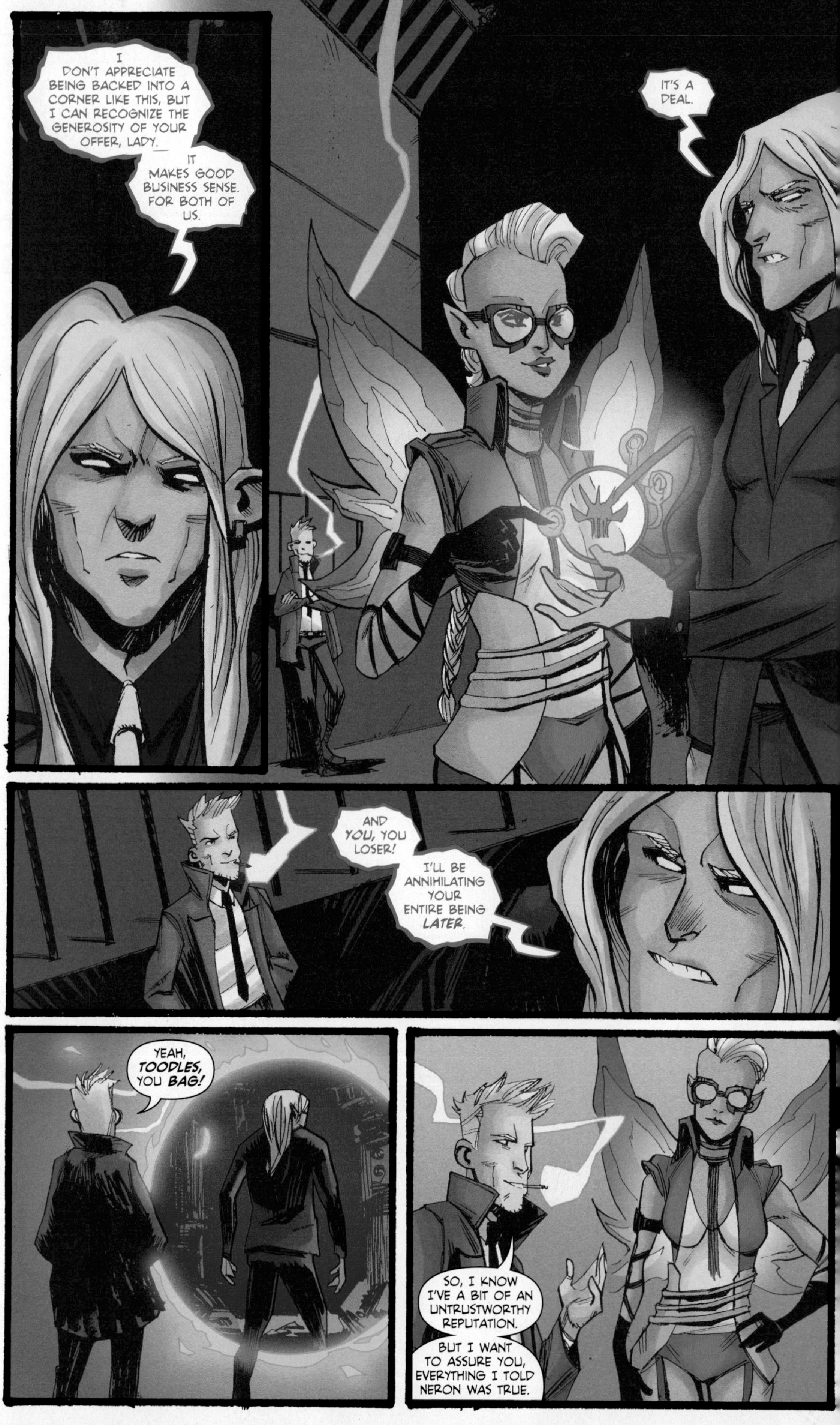
I DON'T APPRECIATE BEING BACKED INTO A CORNER LIKE THIS, BUT I CAN RECOGNIZE THE GENEROSITY OF YOUR OFFER, LADY.
IT MAKES GOOD BUSINESS SENSE. FOR BOTH OF US.
IT'S A DEAL.
AND *YOU*, YOU LOSER!
I'LL BE ANNIHILATING YOUR ENTIRE BEING *LATER*.
YEAH, *TOODLES*, YOU *BAG*!
SO, I KNOW I'VE A BIT OF AN UNTRUSTWORTHY REPUTATION.
BUT I WANT TO ASSURE YOU, EVERYTHING I TOLD NERON WAS TRUE.

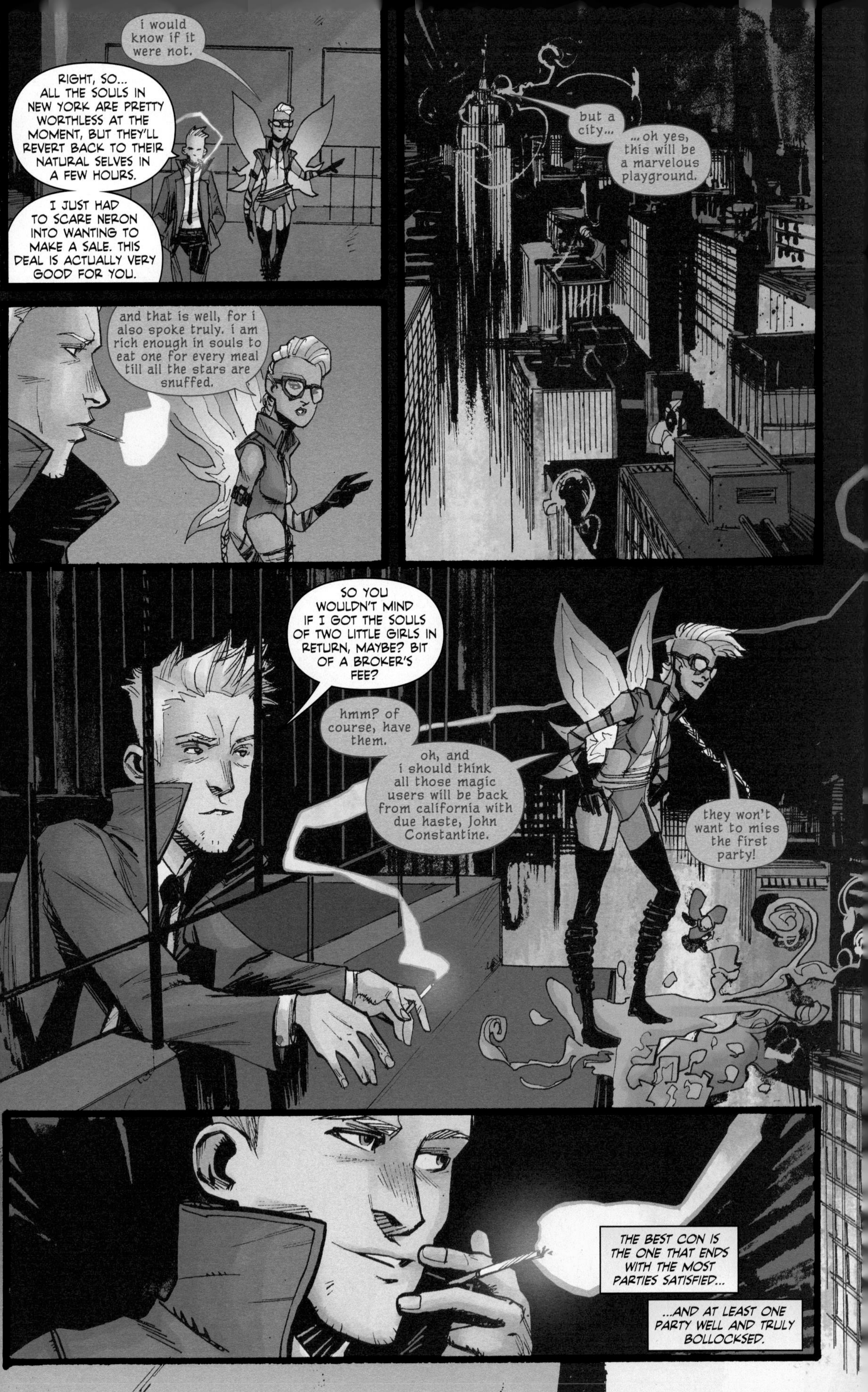
i would know if it were not.
RIGHT, SO... ALL THE SOULS IN NEW YORK ARE PRETTY WORTHLESS AT THE MOMENT, BUT THEY'LL REVERT BACK TO THEIR NATURAL SELVES IN A FEW HOURS.
I JUST HAD TO SCARE NERON INTO WANTING TO MAKE A SALE. THIS DEAL IS ACTUALLY VERY GOOD FOR YOU.
and that is well, for i also spoke truly. i am rich enough in souls to eat one for every meal till all the stars are snuffed.
but a city...
...oh yes, this will be a marvelous playground.
SO YOU WOULDN'T MIND IF I GOT THE SOULS OF TWO LITTLE GIRLS IN RETURN, MAYBE? BIT OF A BROKER'S FEE?
hmm? of course, have them.
oh, and i should think all those magic users will be back from california with due haste, John Constantine.
they won't want to miss the first party!
THE BEST CON IS THE ONE THAT ENDS WITH THE MOST PARTIES SATISFIED...
...AND AT LEAST ONE PARTY WELL AND TRULY BOLLOCKSED.

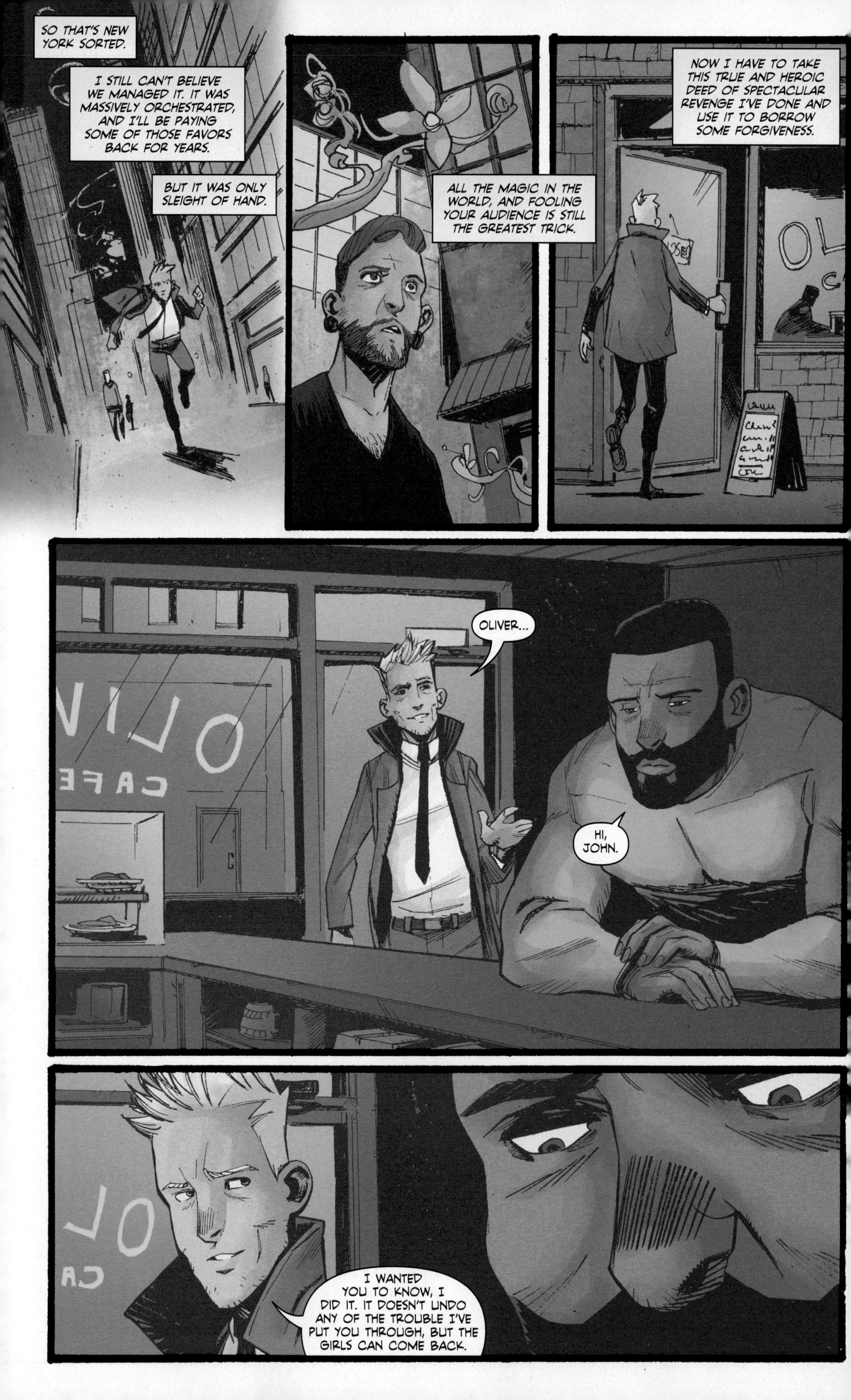
SO THAT'S NEW YORK SORTED.
I STILL CAN'T BELIEVE WE MANAGED IT. IT WAS MASSIVELY ORCHESTRATED, AND I'LL BE PAYING SOME OF THOSE FAVORS BACK FOR YEARS.
BUT IT WAS ONLY SLEIGHT OF HAND.
ALL THE MAGIC IN THE WORLD, AND FOOLING YOUR AUDIENCE IS STILL THE GREATEST TRICK.
NOW I HAVE TO TAKE THIS TRUE AND HEROIC DEED OF SPECTACULAR REVENGE I'VE DONE AND USE IT TO BORROW SOME FORGIVENESS.
OLIVER...
HI, JOHN.
I WANTED YOU TO KNOW, I DID IT. IT DOESN'T UNDO ANY OF THE TROUBLE I'VE PUT YOU THROUGH, BUT THE GIRLS CAN COME BACK.

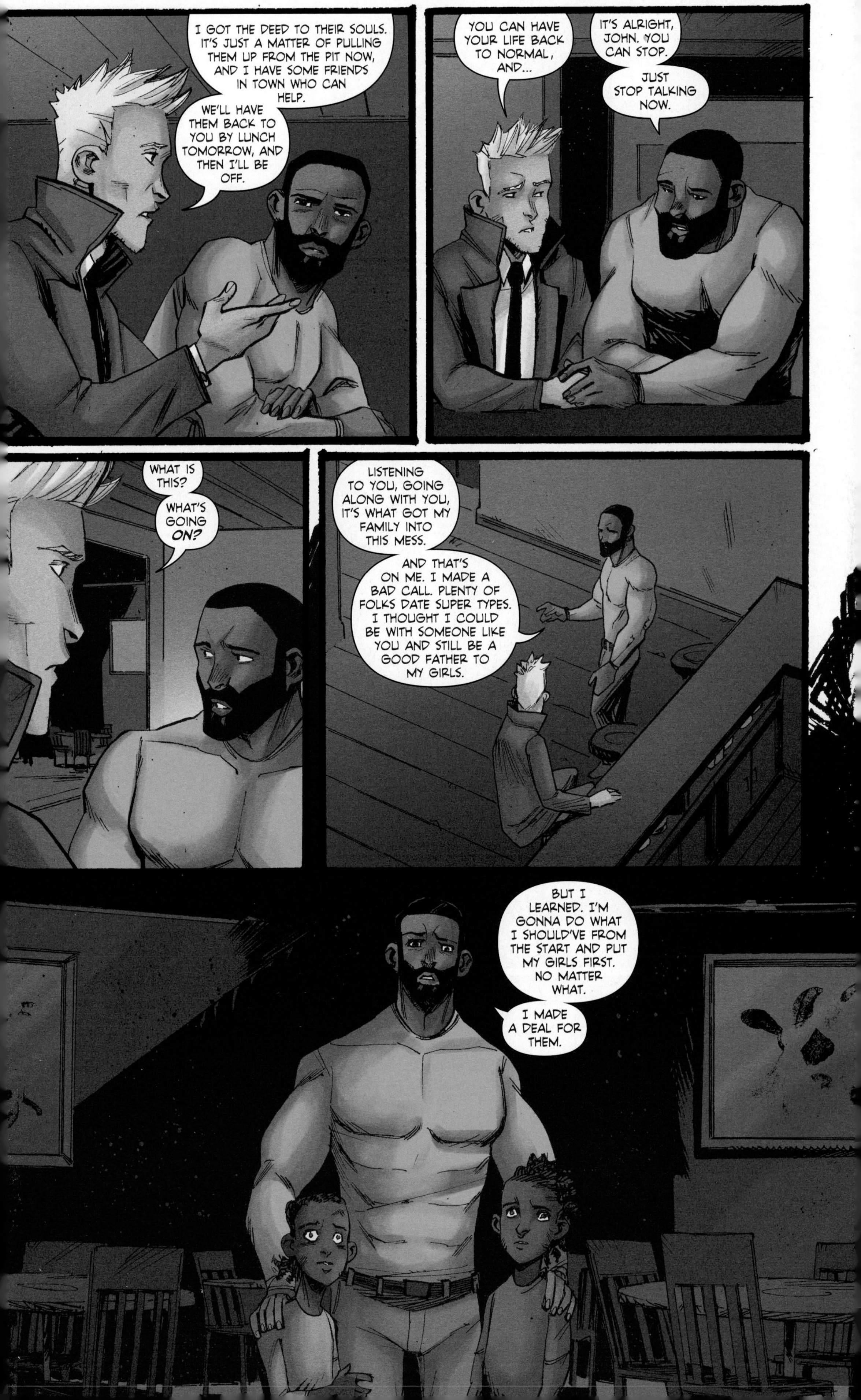
I GOT THE DEED TO THEIR SOULS. IT'S JUST A MATTER OF PULLING THEM UP FROM THE PIT NOW, AND I HAVE SOME FRIENDS IN TOWN WHO CAN HELP.
WE'LL HAVE THEM BACK TO YOU BY LUNCH TOMORROW, AND THEN I'LL BE OFF.
YOU CAN HAVE YOUR LIFE BACK TO NORMAL, AND...
IT'S ALRIGHT, JOHN. YOU CAN STOP.
JUST STOP TALKING NOW.
WHAT IS THIS?
WHAT'S GOING *ON?*
LISTENING TO YOU, GOING ALONG WITH YOU, IT'S WHAT GOT MY FAMILY INTO THIS MESS.
AND THAT'S ON ME. I MADE A BAD CALL. PLENTY OF FOLKS DATE SUPER TYPES. I THOUGHT I COULD BE WITH SOMEONE LIKE YOU AND STILL BE A GOOD FATHER TO MY GIRLS.
BUT I LEARNED. I'M GONNA DO WHAT I SHOULD'VE FROM THE START AND PUT MY GIRLS FIRST. NO MATTER WHAT.
I MADE A DEAL FOR THEM.

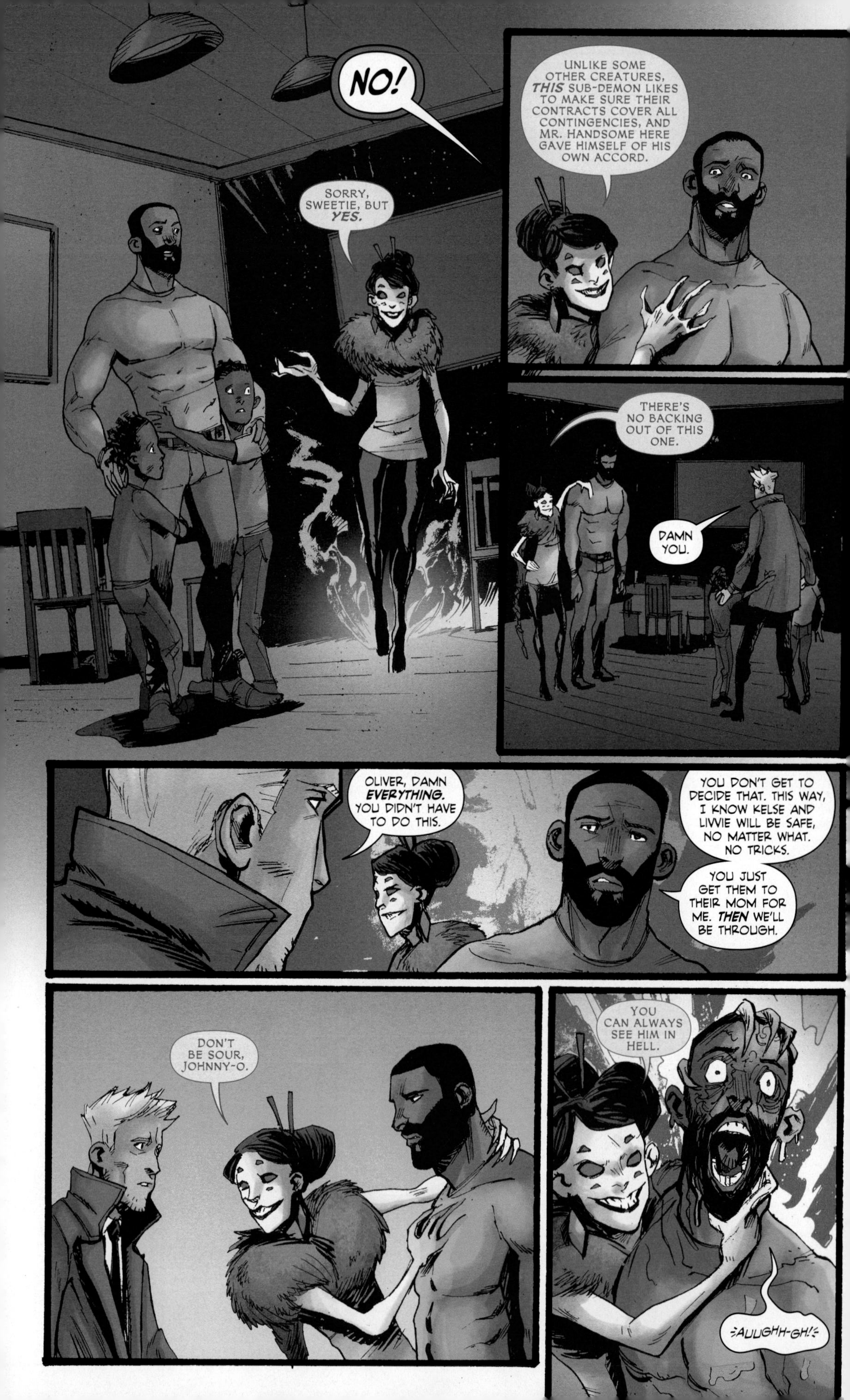
NO!
SORRY, SWEETIE, BUT YES.
UNLIKE SOME OTHER CREATURES, THIS SUB-DEMON LIKES TO MAKE SURE THEIR CONTRACTS COVER ALL CONTINGENCIES, AND MR. HANDSOME HERE GAVE HIMSELF OF HIS OWN ACCORD.
THERE'S NO BACKING OUT OF THIS ONE.
DAMN YOU.
OLIVER, DAMN EVERYTHING. YOU DIDN'T HAVE TO DO THIS.
YOU DON'T GET TO DECIDE THAT. THIS WAY, I KNOW KELSE AND LIVVIE WILL BE SAFE, NO MATTER WHAT. NO TRICKS.
YOU JUST GET THEM TO THEIR MOM FOR ME. THEN WE'LL BE THROUGH.
DON'T BE SOUR, JOHNNY-O.
YOU CAN ALWAYS SEE HIM IN HELL.
AUUGHH-GH!

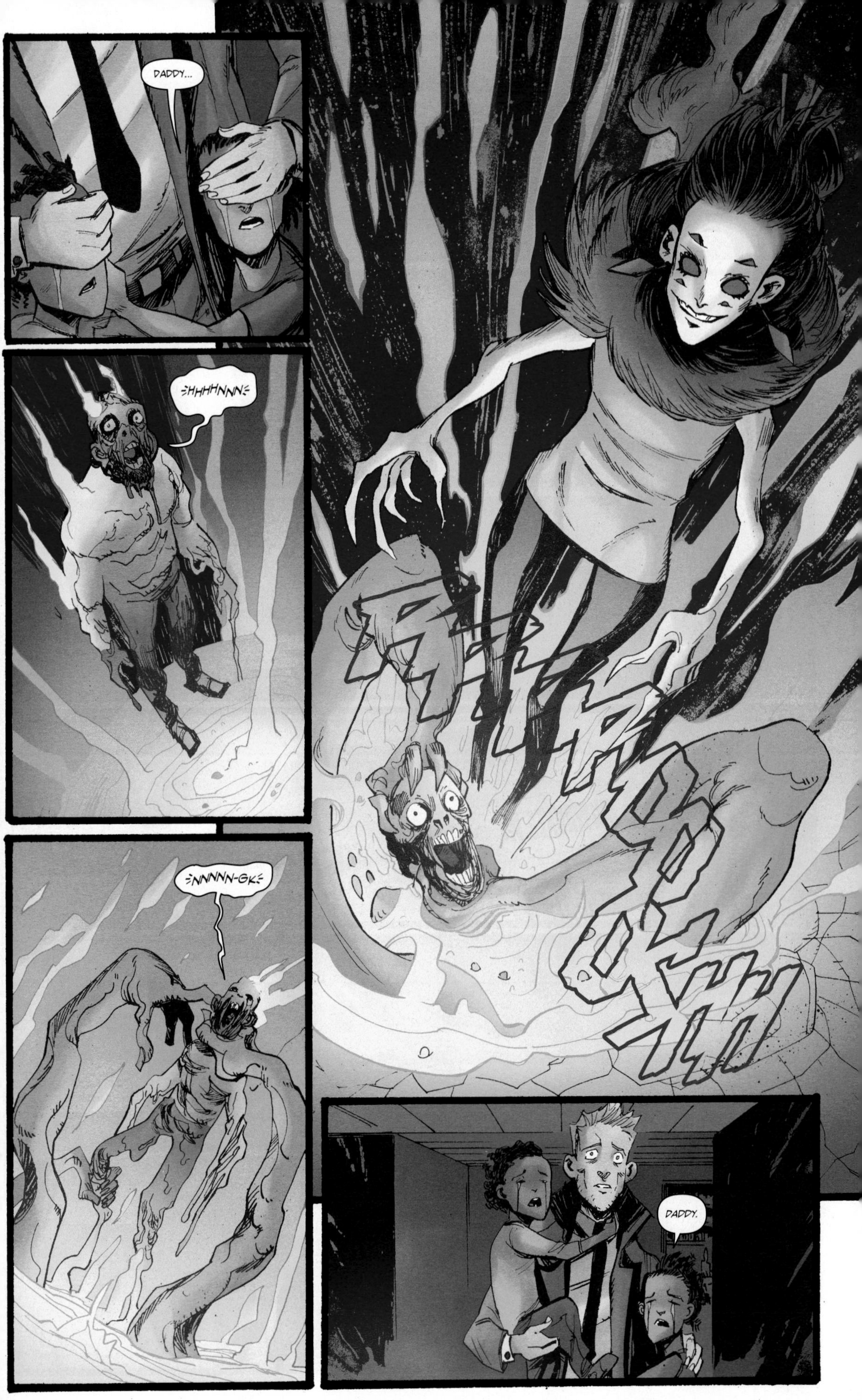
DADDY...
HHHHNNN
NNNNN-GK
DADDY.

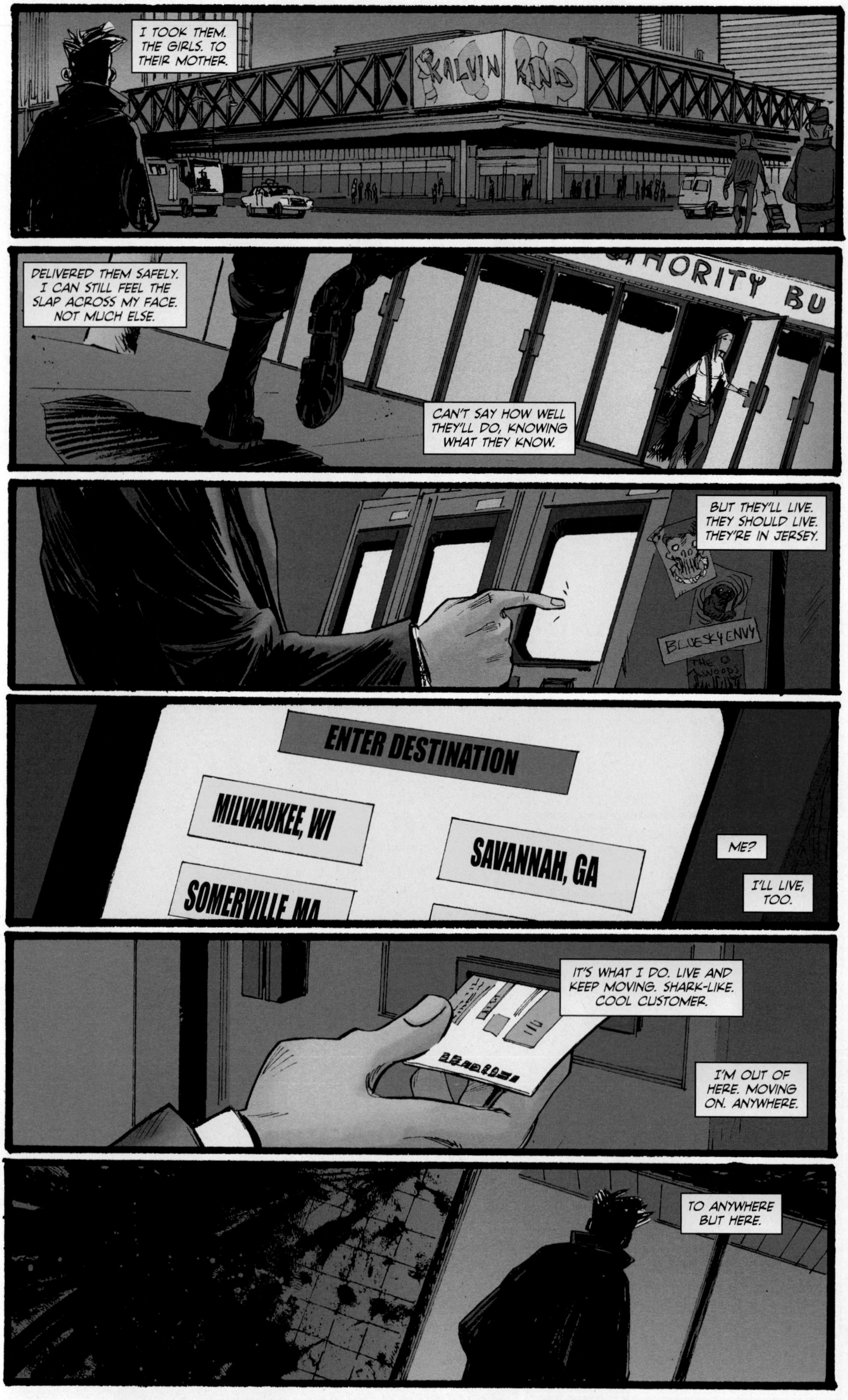
I TOOK THEM. THE GIRLS. TO THEIR MOTHER.
KALVIN KIND
DELIVERED THEM SAFELY. I CAN STILL FEEL THE SLAP ACROSS MY FACE. NOT MUCH ELSE.
HORITY BU
CAN'T SAY HOW WELL THEY'LL DO, KNOWING WHAT THEY KNOW.
BUT THEY'LL LIVE. THEY SHOULD LIVE. THEY'RE IN JERSEY.
BLUESKY ENVY
ENTER DESTINATION
MILWAUKEE, WI
SAVANNAH, GA
SOMERVILLE MA
ME?
I'LL LIVE, TOO.
IT'S WHAT I DO. LIVE AND KEEP MOVING. SHARK-LIKE. COOL CUSTOMER.
I'M OUT OF HERE. MOVING ON. ANYWHERE.
TO ANYWHERE BUT HERE.

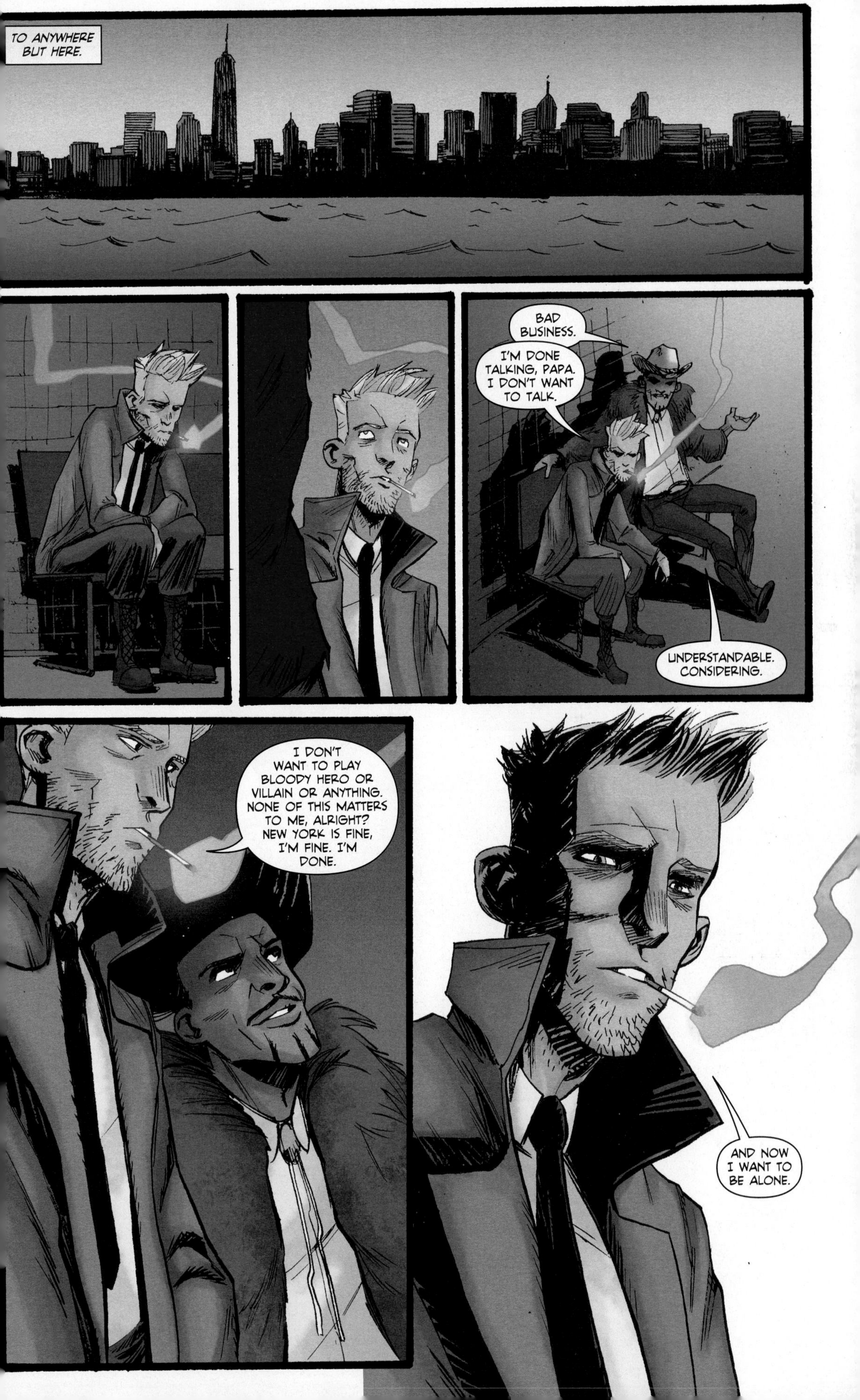
TO ANYWHERE BUT HERE.
BAD BUSINESS.
I'M DONE TALKING, PAPA. I DON'T WANT TO TALK.
UNDERSTANDABLE. CONSIDERING.
I DON'T WANT TO PLAY BLOODY HERO OR VILLAIN OR ANYTHING. NONE OF THIS MATTERS TO ME, ALRIGHT? NEW YORK IS FINE, I'M FINE. I'M DONE.
AND NOW I WANT TO BE ALONE.

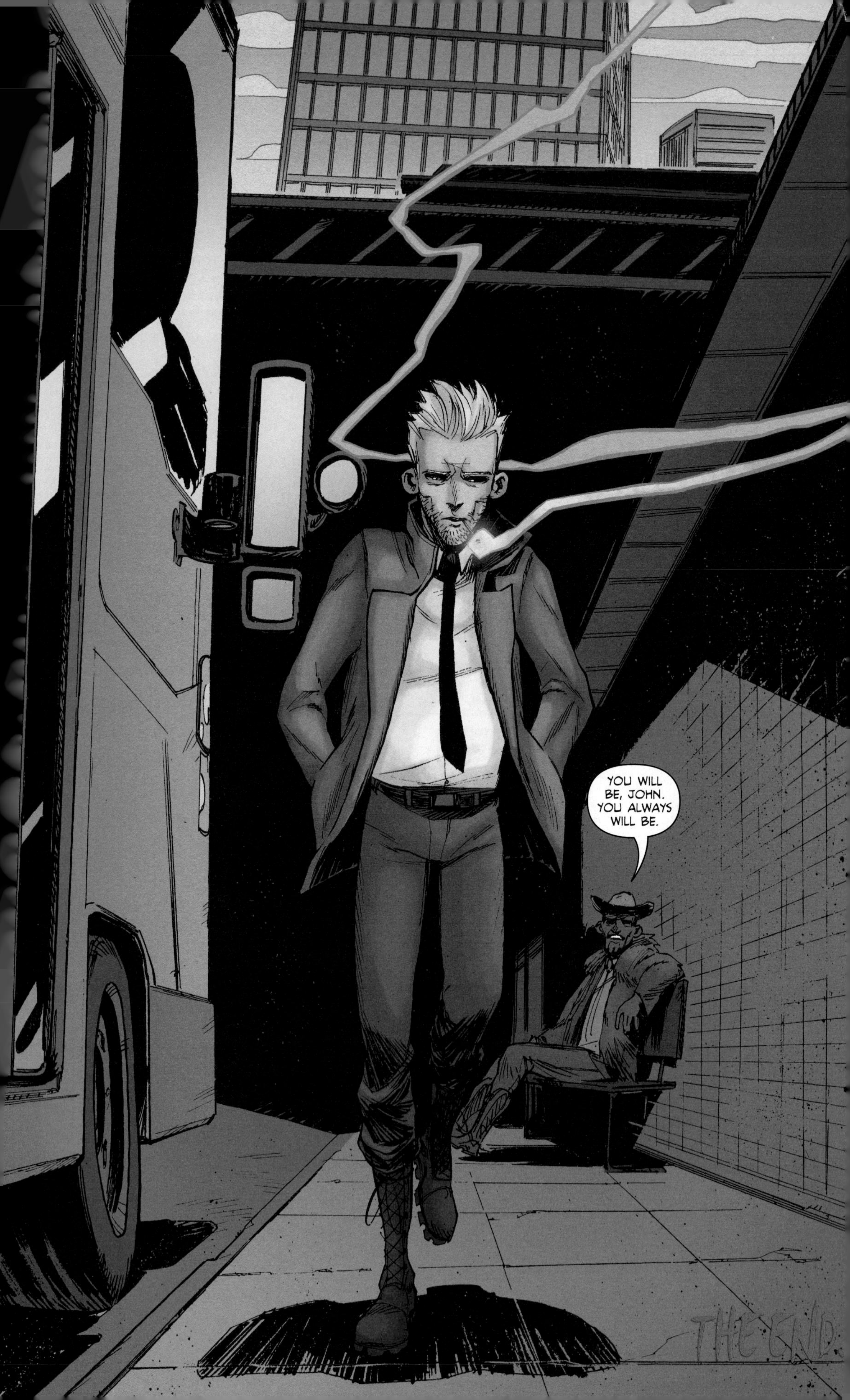
YOU WILL BE, JOHN. YOU ALWAYS WILL BE.
THE END.

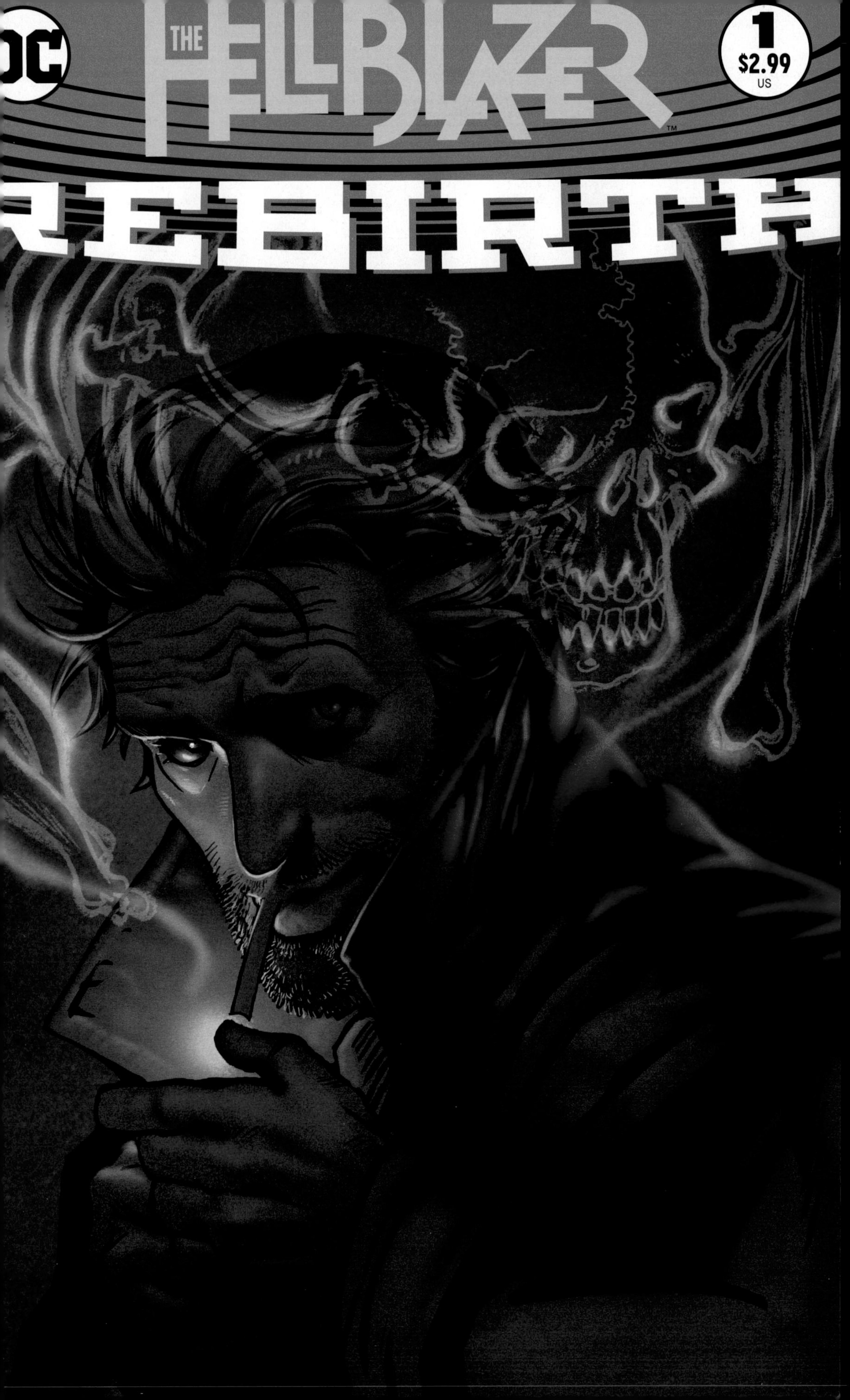
THE HELLBLAZER
1
$2.99
US
REBIRTH

The future (and past) of the DC Universe starts with DC UNIVERSE: REBIRTH!

Explore the changing world of John Constantine in this special preview of **HELLBLAZER: REBIRTH #1.**

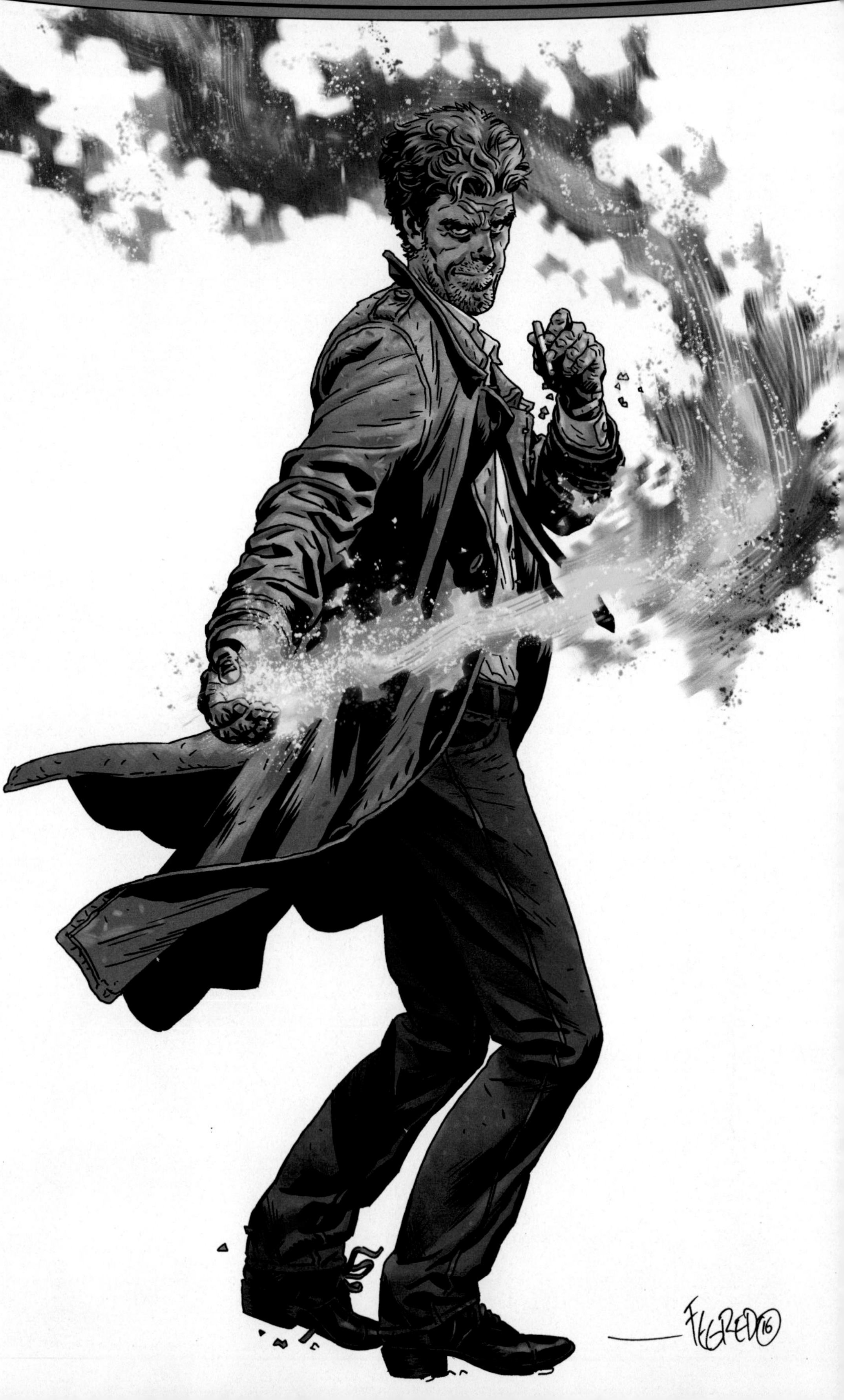

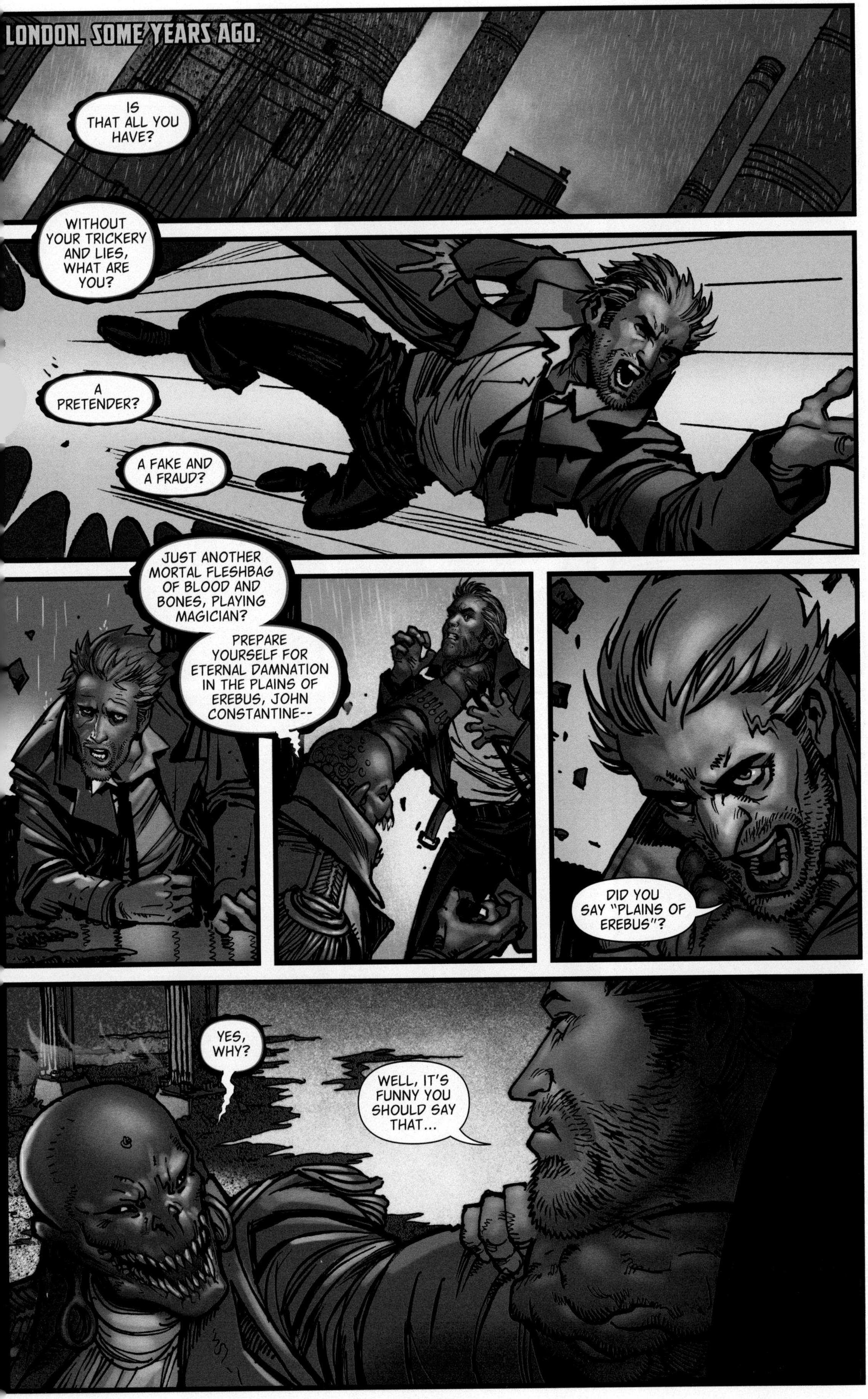
LONDON. SOME YEARS AGO.
IS THAT ALL YOU HAVE?
WITHOUT YOUR TRICKERY AND LIES, WHAT ARE YOU?
A PRETENDER?
A FAKE AND A FRAUD?
JUST ANOTHER MORTAL FLESHBAG OF BLOOD AND BONES, PLAYING MAGICIAN?
PREPARE YOURSELF FOR ETERNAL DAMNATION IN THE PLAINS OF EREBUS, JOHN CONSTANTINE--
DID YOU SAY "PLAINS OF EREBUS"?
YES, WHY?
WELL, IT'S FUNNY YOU SHOULD SAY THAT...

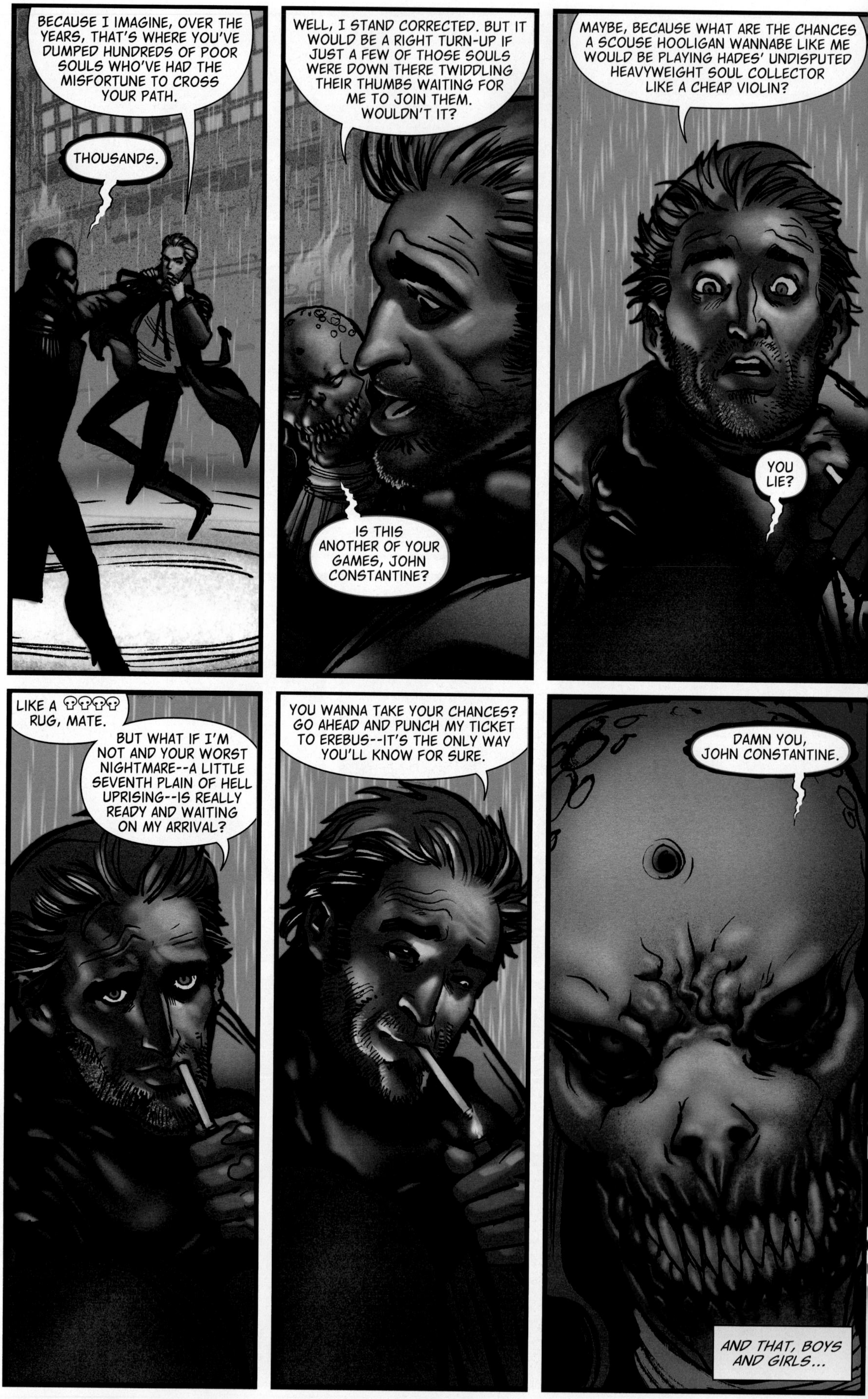
BECAUSE I IMAGINE, OVER THE YEARS, THAT'S WHERE YOU'VE DUMPED HUNDREDS OF POOR SOULS WHO'VE HAD THE MISFORTUNE TO CROSS YOUR PATH.
THOUSANDS.
WELL, I STAND CORRECTED. BUT IT WOULD BE A RIGHT TURN-UP IF JUST A FEW OF THOSE SOULS WERE DOWN THERE TWIDDLING THEIR THUMBS WAITING FOR ME TO JOIN THEM. WOULDN'T IT?
IS THIS ANOTHER OF YOUR GAMES, JOHN CONSTANTINE?
MAYBE, BECAUSE WHAT ARE THE CHANCES A SCOUSE HOOLIGAN WANNABE LIKE ME WOULD BE PLAYING HADES' UNDISPUTED HEAVYWEIGHT SOUL COLLECTOR LIKE A CHEAP VIOLIN?
YOU LIE?
LIKE A RUG, MATE.
BUT WHAT IF I'M NOT AND YOUR WORST NIGHTMARE--A LITTLE SEVENTH PLAIN OF HELL UPRISING--IS REALLY READY AND WAITING ON MY ARRIVAL?
YOU WANNA TAKE YOUR CHANCES? GO AHEAD AND PUNCH MY TICKET TO EREBUS--IT'S THE ONLY WAY YOU'LL KNOW FOR SURE.
DAMN YOU, JOHN CONSTANTINE.
AND THAT, BOYS AND GIRLS...

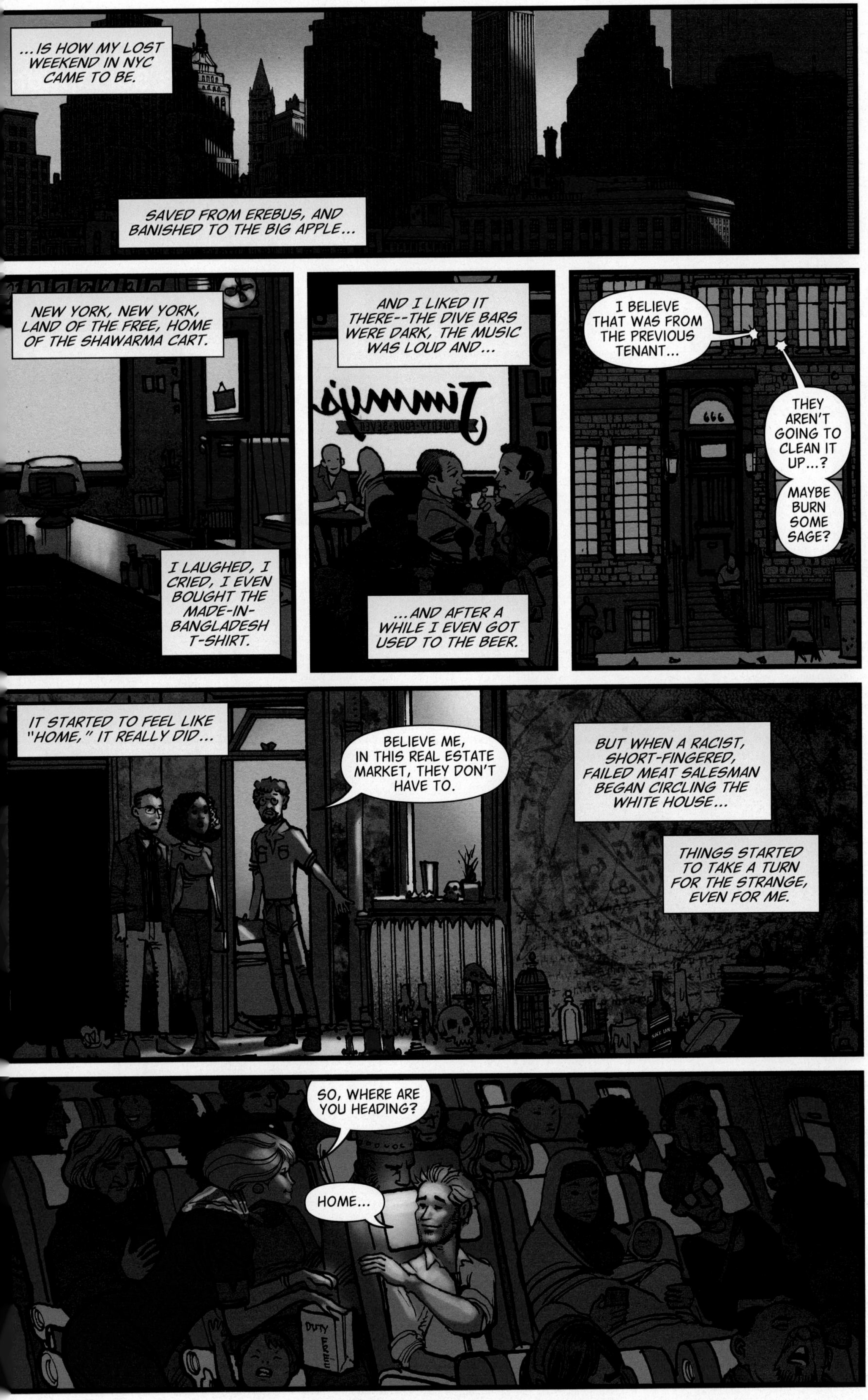
...IS HOW MY LOST WEEKEND IN NYC CAME TO BE.
SAVED FROM EREBUS, AND BANISHED TO THE BIG APPLE...
NEW YORK, NEW YORK, LAND OF THE FREE, HOME OF THE SHAWARMA CART.
I LAUGHED, I CRIED, I EVEN BOUGHT THE MADE-IN-BANGLADESH T-SHIRT.
AND I LIKED IT THERE--THE DIVE BARS WERE DARK, THE MUSIC WAS LOUD AND...
...AND AFTER A WHILE I EVEN GOT USED TO THE BEER.
666
I BELIEVE THAT WAS FROM THE PREVIOUS TENANT...
THEY AREN'T GOING TO CLEAN IT UP...?
MAYBE BURN SOME SAGE?
IT STARTED TO FEEL LIKE "HOME," IT REALLY DID...
BELIEVE ME, IN THIS REAL ESTATE MARKET, THEY DON'T HAVE TO.
BUT WHEN A RACIST, SHORT-FINGERED, FAILED MEAT SALESMAN BEGAN CIRCLING THE WHITE HOUSE...
THINGS STARTED TO TAKE A TURN FOR THE STRANGE, EVEN FOR ME.
SO, WHERE ARE YOU HEADING?
HOME...
DUTY

Writer: Simon Oliver Artist: Moritat
Colorists: Andre Szymanowicz and Moritat Letterer: Sal Cipriano
Cover Artist: Moritat Variant Cover Artist: Duncan Fegredo
Associate Editor: Jessica Chen Editor: Kristy Quinn
John Constantine created by Alan Moore, Steve Bissette, John Totleben and Jamie Delano & John Ridgway

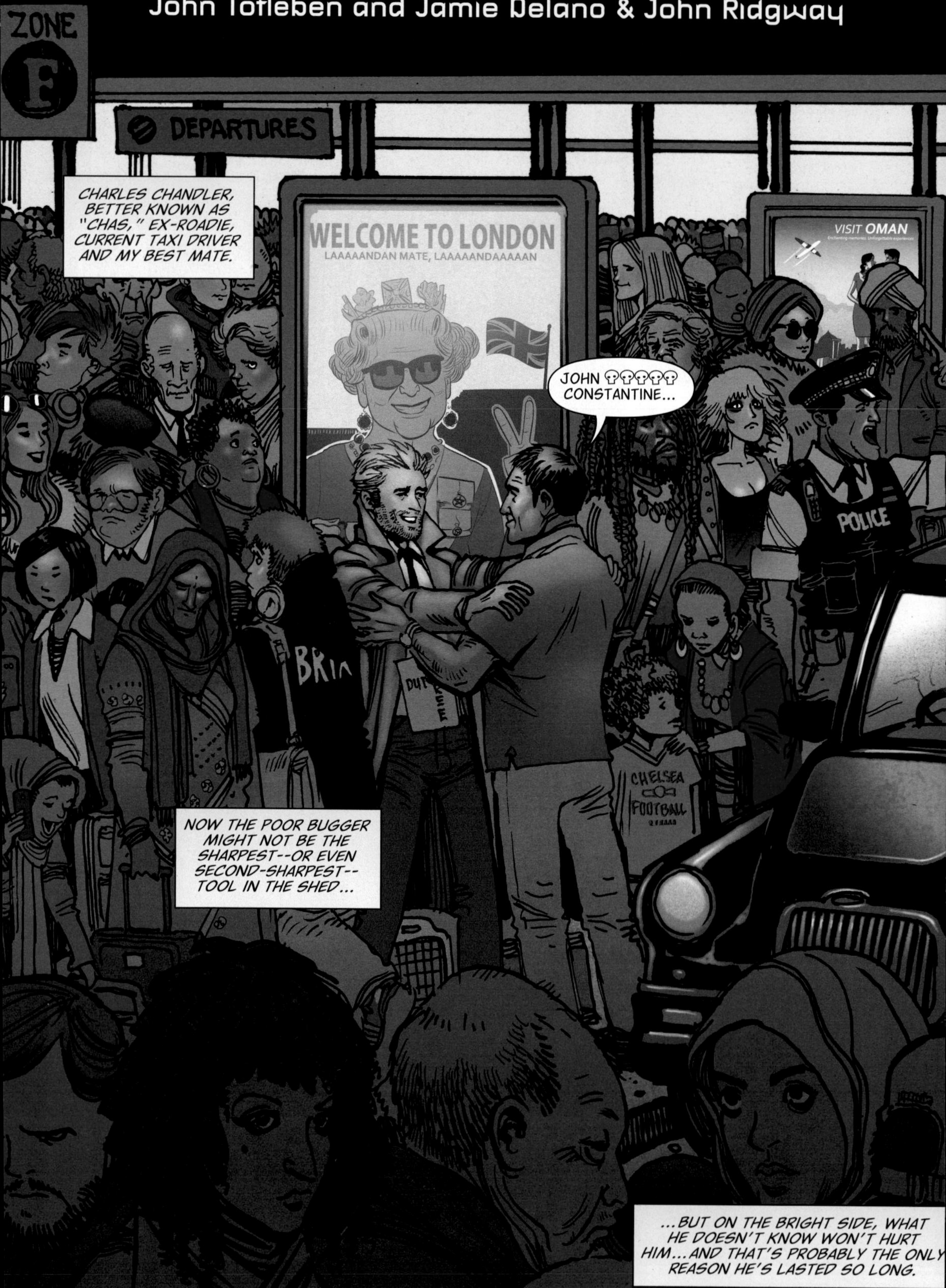
ZONE F
DEPARTURES
CHARLES CHANDLER, BETTER KNOWN AS "CHAS," EX-ROADIE, CURRENT TAXI DRIVER AND MY BEST MATE.
WELCOME TO LONDON
LAAAAANDAN MATE, LAAAAANDAAAAAN
VISIT OMAN
JOHN CONSTANTINE...
POLICE
CHELSEA FOOTBALL
NOW THE POOR BUGGER MIGHT NOT BE THE SHARPEST--OR EVEN SECOND-SHARPEST--TOOL IN THE SHED...
...BUT ON THE BRIGHT SIDE, WHAT HE DOESN'T KNOW WON'T HURT HIM...AND THAT'S PROBABLY THE ONLY REASON HE'S LASTED SO LONG.

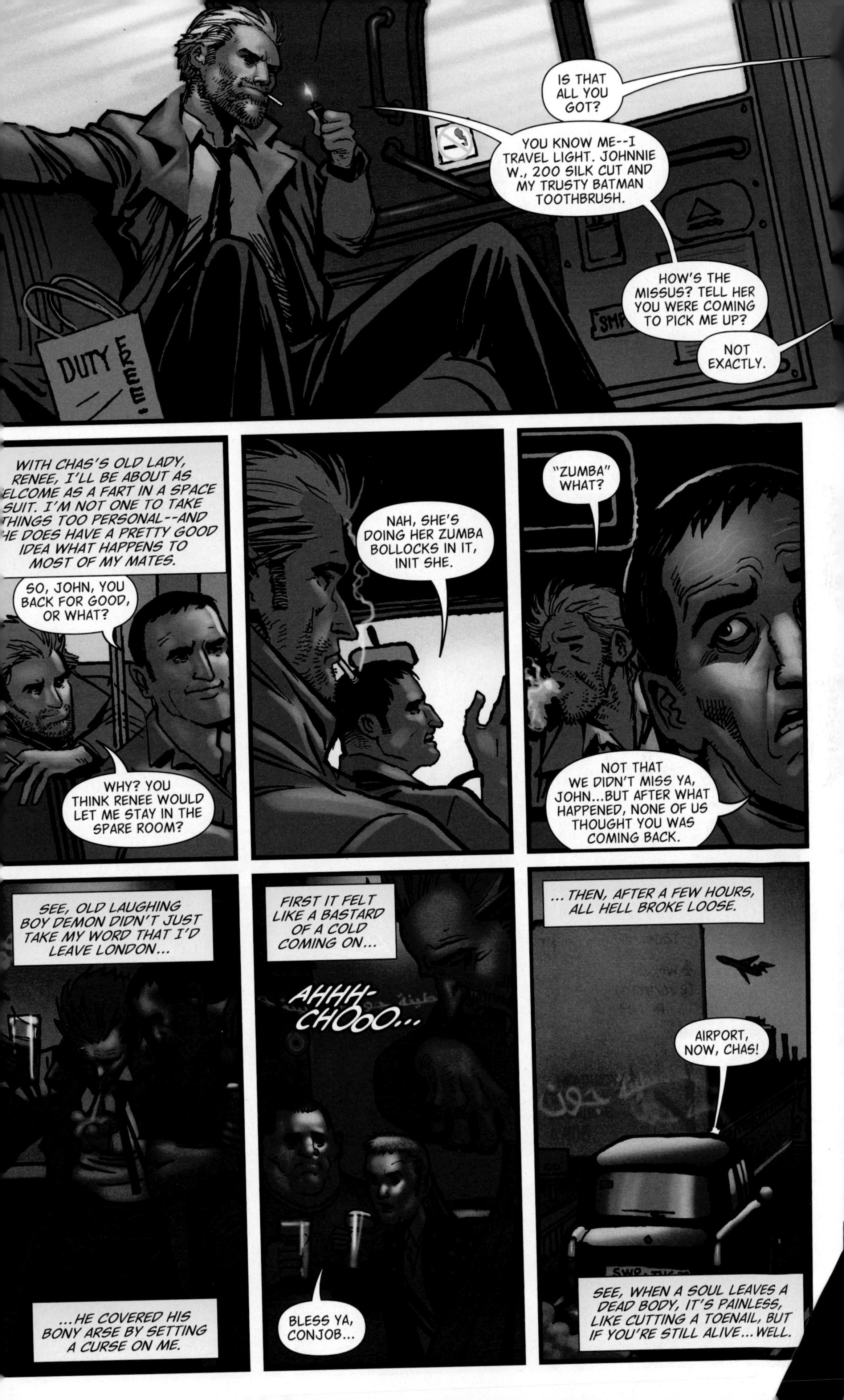
IS THAT ALL YOU GOT?
YOU KNOW ME--I TRAVEL LIGHT. JOHNNIE W., 200 SILK CUT AND MY TRUSTY BATMAN TOOTHBRUSH.
HOW'S THE MISSUS? TELL HER YOU WERE COMING TO PICK ME UP?
NOT EXACTLY.
DUTY FREE
WITH CHAS'S OLD LADY, RENEE, I'LL BE ABOUT AS WELCOME AS A FART IN A SPACE SUIT. I'M NOT ONE TO TAKE THINGS TOO PERSONAL--AND SHE DOES HAVE A PRETTY GOOD IDEA WHAT HAPPENS TO MOST OF MY MATES.
SO, JOHN, YOU BACK FOR GOOD, OR WHAT?
WHY? YOU THINK RENEE WOULD LET ME STAY IN THE SPARE ROOM?
NAH, SHE'S DOING HER ZUMBA BOLLOCKS IN IT, INIT SHE.
"ZUMBA" WHAT?
NOT THAT WE DIDN'T MISS YA, JOHN...BUT AFTER WHAT HAPPENED, NONE OF US THOUGHT YOU WAS COMING BACK.
SEE, OLD LAUGHING BOY DEMON DIDN'T JUST TAKE MY WORD THAT I'D LEAVE LONDON...
...HE COVERED HIS BONY ARSE BY SETTING A CURSE ON ME.
FIRST IT FELT LIKE A BASTARD OF A COLD COMING ON...
AHHH-CHOOO...
BLESS YA, CONJOB...
...THEN, AFTER A FEW HOURS, ALL HELL BROKE LOOSE.
AIRPORT, NOW, CHAS!
SEE, WHEN A SOUL LEAVES A DEAD BODY, IT'S PAINLESS, LIKE CUTTING A TOENAIL, BUT IF YOU'RE STILL ALIVE...WELL.

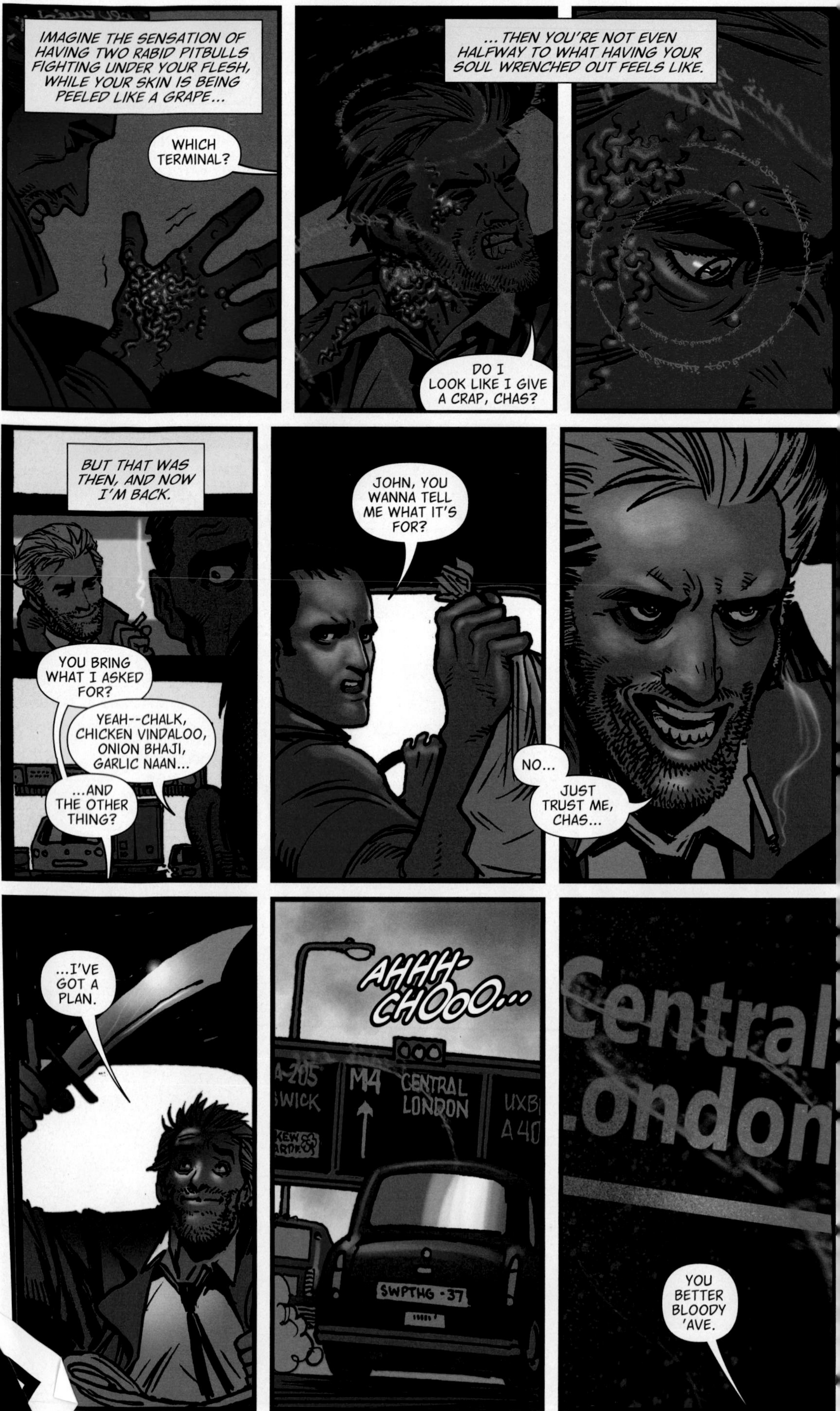
IMAGINE THE SENSATION OF HAVING TWO RABID PITBULLS FIGHTING UNDER YOUR FLESH, WHILE YOUR SKIN IS BEING PEELED LIKE A GRAPE...
WHICH TERMINAL?
...THEN YOU'RE NOT EVEN HALFWAY TO WHAT HAVING YOUR SOUL WRENCHED OUT FEELS LIKE.
DO I LOOK LIKE I GIVE A CRAP, CHAS?
BUT THAT WAS THEN, AND NOW I'M BACK.
YOU BRING WHAT I ASKED FOR?
YEAH--CHALK, CHICKEN VINDALOO, ONION BHAJI, GARLIC NAAN...
...AND THE OTHER THING?
JOHN, YOU WANNA TELL ME WHAT IT'S FOR?
NO...
JUST TRUST ME, CHAS...
...I'VE GOT A PLAN.
AHHH-CHOOOO...
M4
CENTRAL LONDON
SWPTHG-37
Central London
YOU BETTER BLOODY 'AVE.

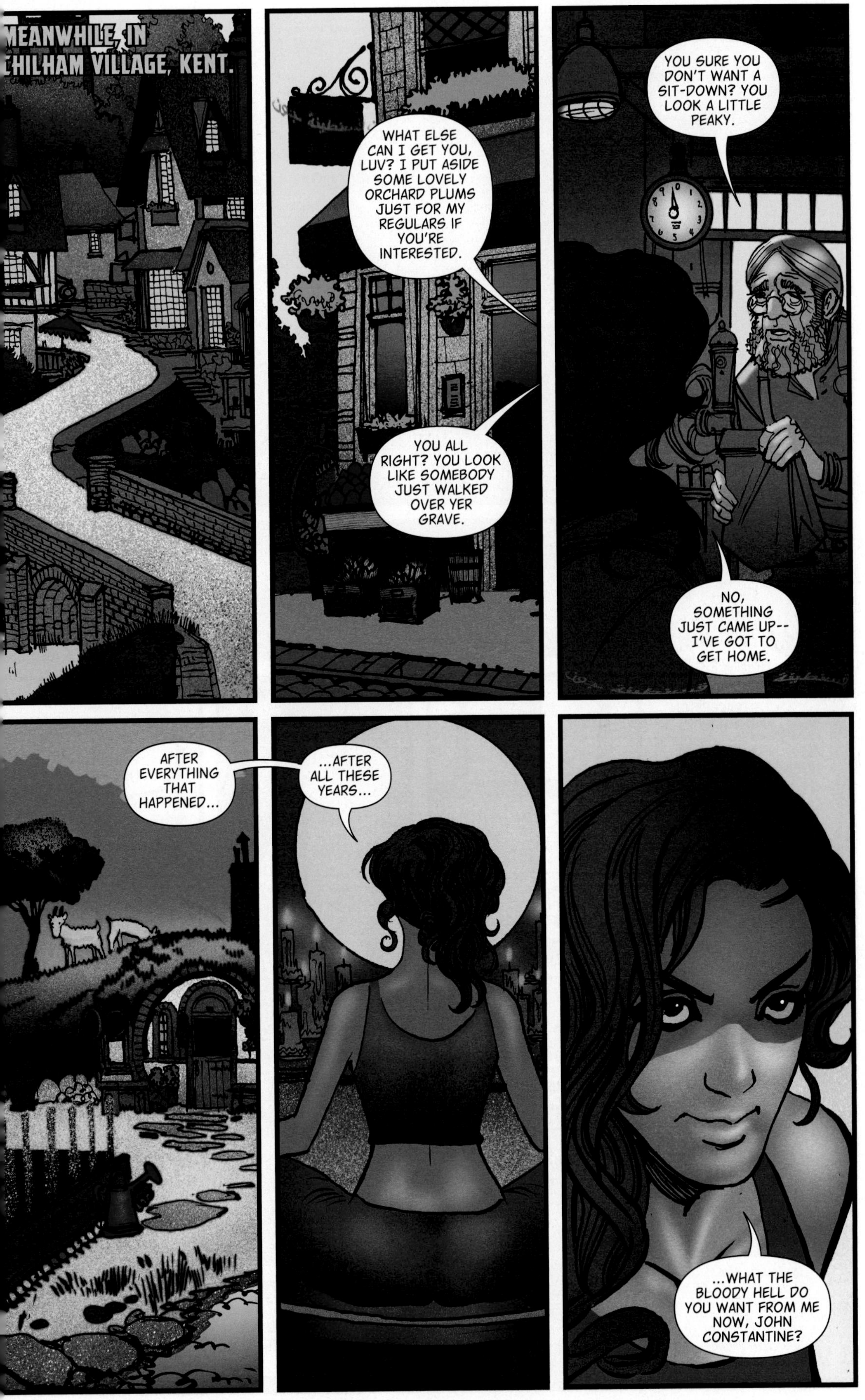
MEANWHILE, IN CHILHAM VILLAGE, KENT.
WHAT ELSE CAN I GET YOU, LUV? I PUT ASIDE SOME LOVELY ORCHARD PLUMS JUST FOR MY REGULARS IF YOU'RE INTERESTED.
YOU ALL RIGHT? YOU LOOK LIKE SOMEBODY JUST WALKED OVER YER GRAVE.
YOU SURE YOU DON'T WANT A SIT-DOWN? YOU LOOK A LITTLE PEAKY.
NO, SOMETHING JUST CAME UP-- I'VE GOT TO GET HOME.
AFTER EVERYTHING THAT HAPPENED...
...AFTER ALL THESE YEARS...
...WHAT THE BLOODY HELL DO YOU WANT FROM ME NOW, JOHN CONSTANTINE?

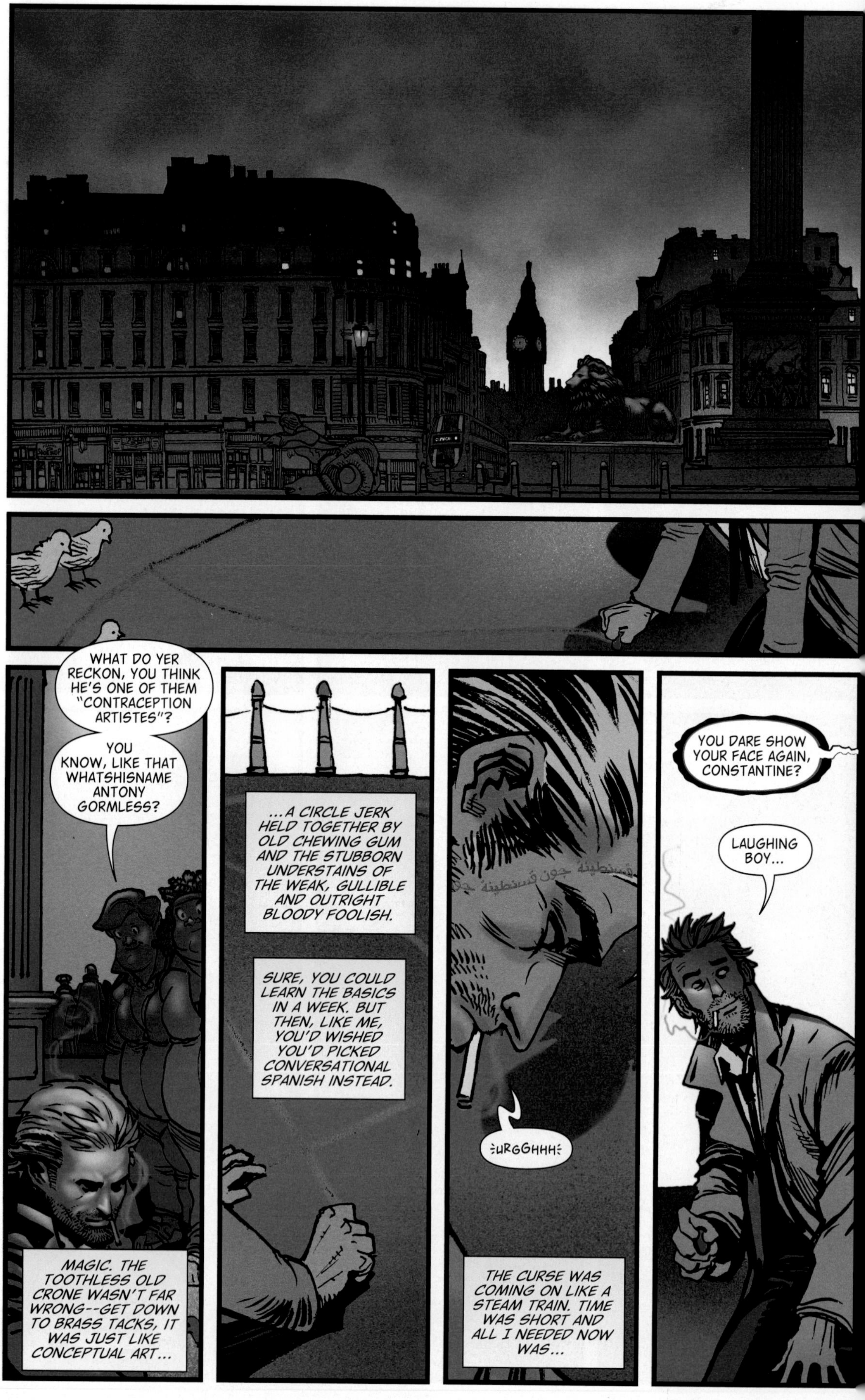

WHAT DO YER RECKON, YOU THINK HE'S ONE OF THEM "CONTRACEPTION ARTISTES"?
YOU KNOW, LIKE THAT WHATSHISNAME ANTONY GORMLESS?
MAGIC. THE TOOTHLESS OLD CRONE WASN'T FAR WRONG--GET DOWN TO BRASS TACKS, IT WAS JUST LIKE CONCEPTUAL ART...
...A CIRCLE JERK HELD TOGETHER BY OLD CHEWING GUM AND THE STUBBORN UNDERSTAINS OF THE WEAK, GULLIBLE AND OUTRIGHT BLOODY FOOLISH.
SURE, YOU COULD LEARN THE BASICS IN A WEEK. BUT THEN, LIKE ME, YOU'D WISHED YOU'D PICKED CONVERSATIONAL SPANISH INSTEAD.
URGGHHH
THE CURSE WAS COMING ON LIKE A STEAM TRAIN. TIME WAS SHORT AND ALL I NEEDED NOW WAS...
YOU DARE SHOW YOUR FACE AGAIN, CONSTANTINE?
LAUGHING BOY...

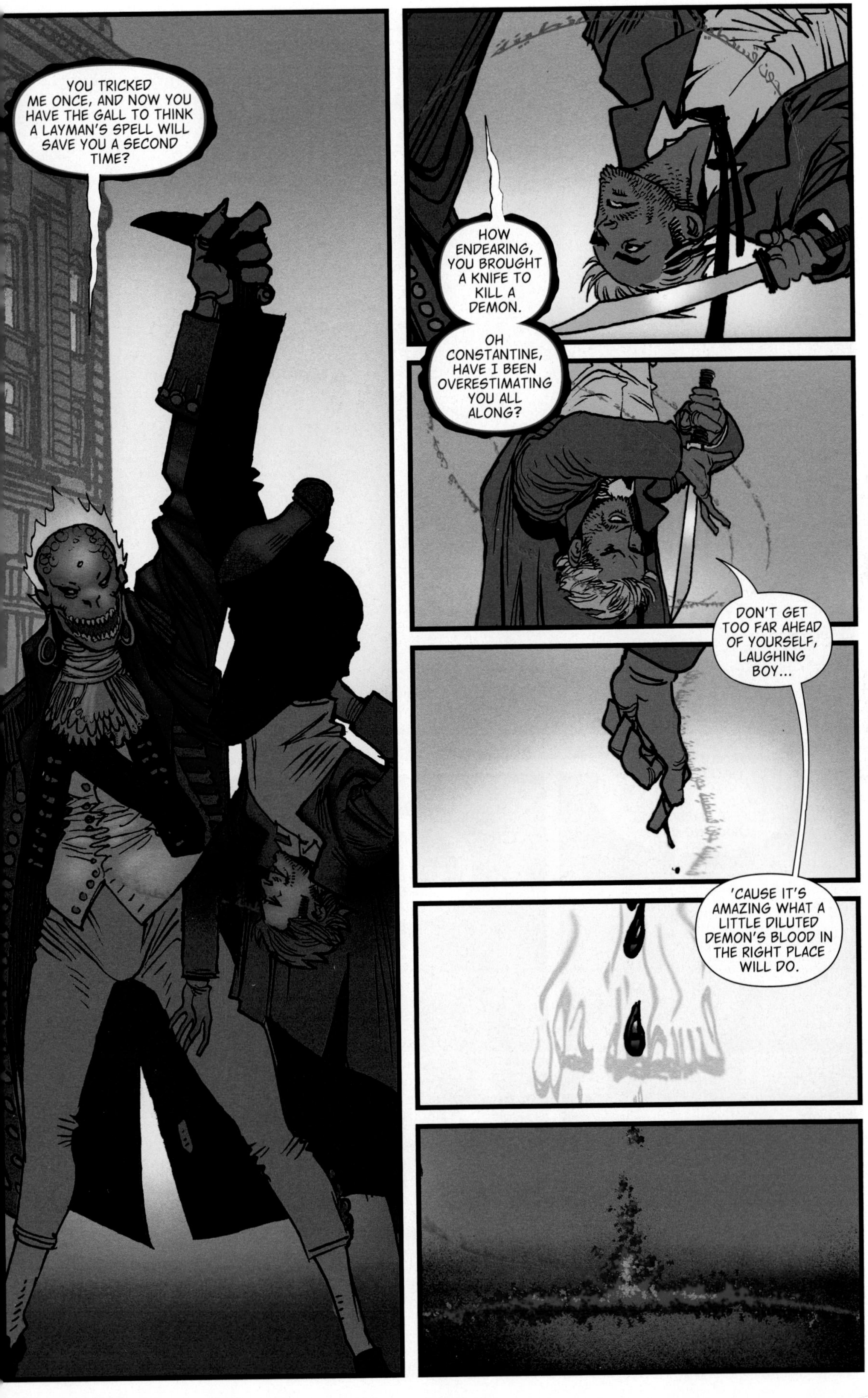
YOU TRICKED ME ONCE, AND NOW YOU HAVE THE GALL TO THINK A LAYMAN'S SPELL WILL SAVE YOU A SECOND TIME?
HOW ENDEARING, YOU BROUGHT A KNIFE TO KILL A DEMON.
OH CONSTANTINE, HAVE I BEEN OVERESTIMATING YOU ALL ALONG?
DON'T GET TOO FAR AHEAD OF YOURSELF, LAUGHING BOY...
'CAUSE IT'S AMAZING WHAT A LITTLE DILUTED DEMON'S BLOOD IN THE RIGHT PLACE WILL DO.

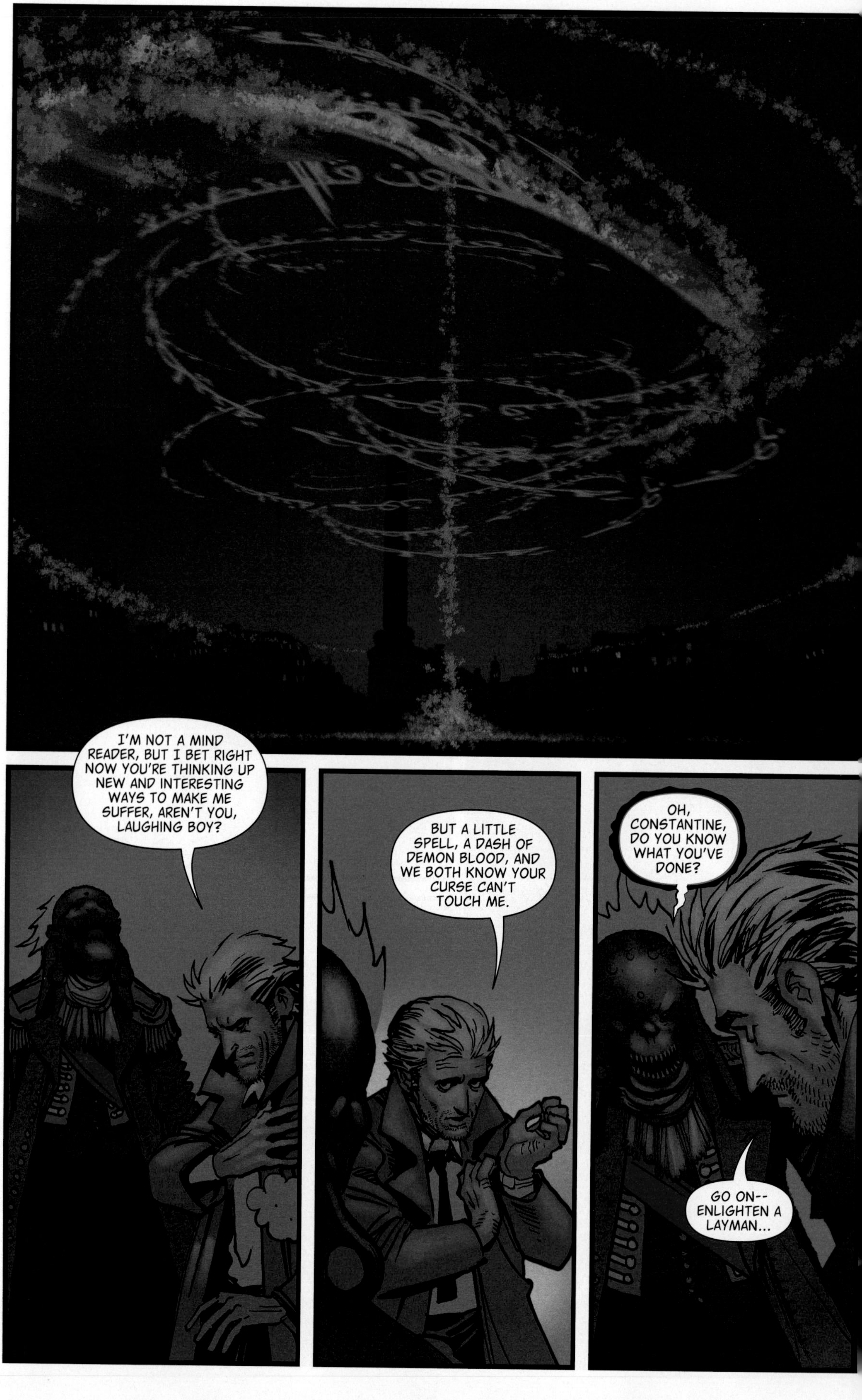
I'M NOT A MIND READER, BUT I BET RIGHT NOW YOU'RE THINKING UP NEW AND INTERESTING WAYS TO MAKE ME SUFFER, AREN'T YOU, LAUGHING BOY?
BUT A LITTLE SPELL, A DASH OF DEMON BLOOD, AND WE BOTH KNOW YOUR CURSE CAN'T TOUCH ME.
OH, CONSTANTINE, DO YOU KNOW WHAT YOU'VE DONE?
GO ON-- ENLIGHTEN A LAYMAN...

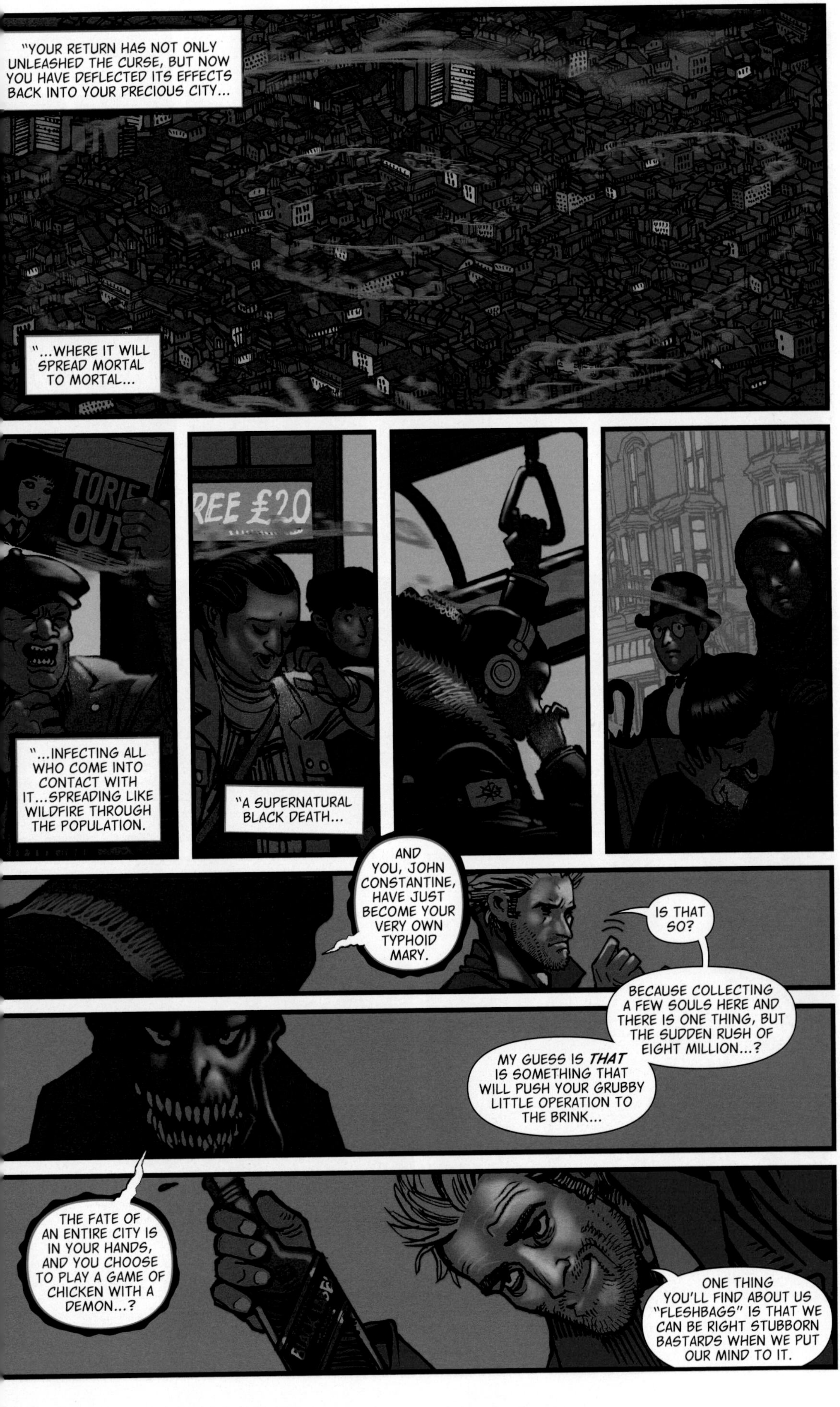
"YOUR RETURN HAS NOT ONLY UNLEASHED THE CURSE, BUT NOW YOU HAVE DEFLECTED ITS EFFECTS BACK INTO YOUR PRECIOUS CITY...
"...WHERE IT WILL SPREAD MORTAL TO MORTAL...
TORIE OUT
"...INFECTING ALL WHO COME INTO CONTACT WITH IT...SPREADING LIKE WILDFIRE THROUGH THE POPULATION.
REE £20
"A SUPERNATURAL BLACK DEATH...
AND YOU, JOHN CONSTANTINE, HAVE JUST BECOME YOUR VERY OWN TYPHOID MARY.
IS THAT SO?
BECAUSE COLLECTING A FEW SOULS HERE AND THERE IS ONE THING, BUT THE SUDDEN RUSH OF EIGHT MILLION...?
MY GUESS IS *THAT* IS SOMETHING THAT WILL PUSH YOUR GRUBBY LITTLE OPERATION TO THE BRINK...
THE FATE OF AN ENTIRE CITY IS IN YOUR HANDS, AND YOU CHOOSE TO PLAY A GAME OF CHICKEN WITH A DEMON...?
ONE THING YOU'LL FIND ABOUT US "FLESHBAGS" IS THAT WE CAN BE RIGHT STUBBORN BASTARDS WHEN WE PUT OUR MIND TO IT.

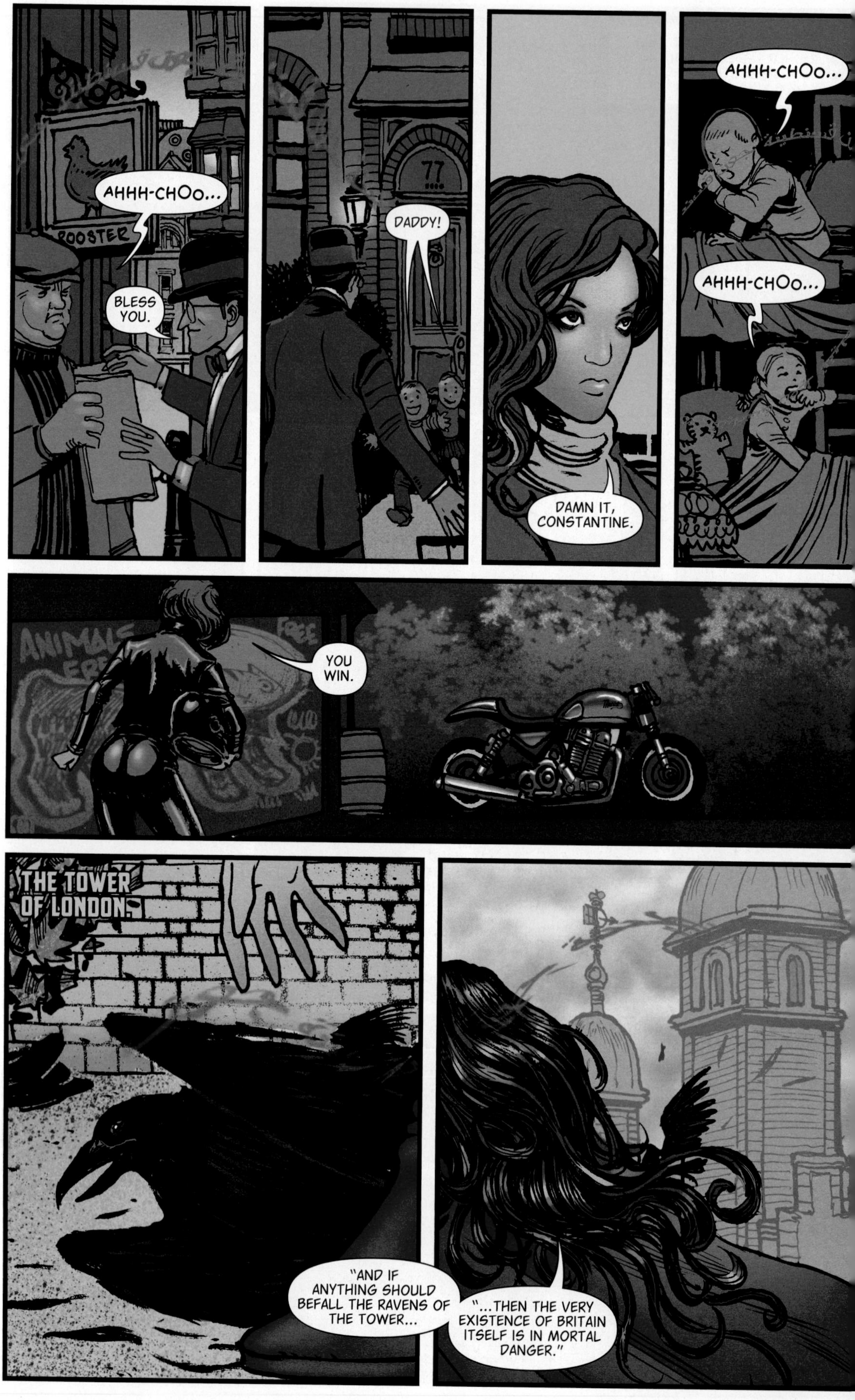
ROOSTER
AHHH-CHOo...
BLESS YOU.
77
DADDY!
DAMN IT, CONSTANTINE.
AHHH-CHOo...
AHHH-CHOo...
ANIMALS FREE
FREE
YOU WIN.
THE TOWER OF LONDON.
"AND IF ANYTHING SHOULD BEFALL THE RAVENS OF THE TOWER...
"...THEN THE VERY EXISTENCE OF BRITAIN ITSELF IS IN MORTAL DANGER."

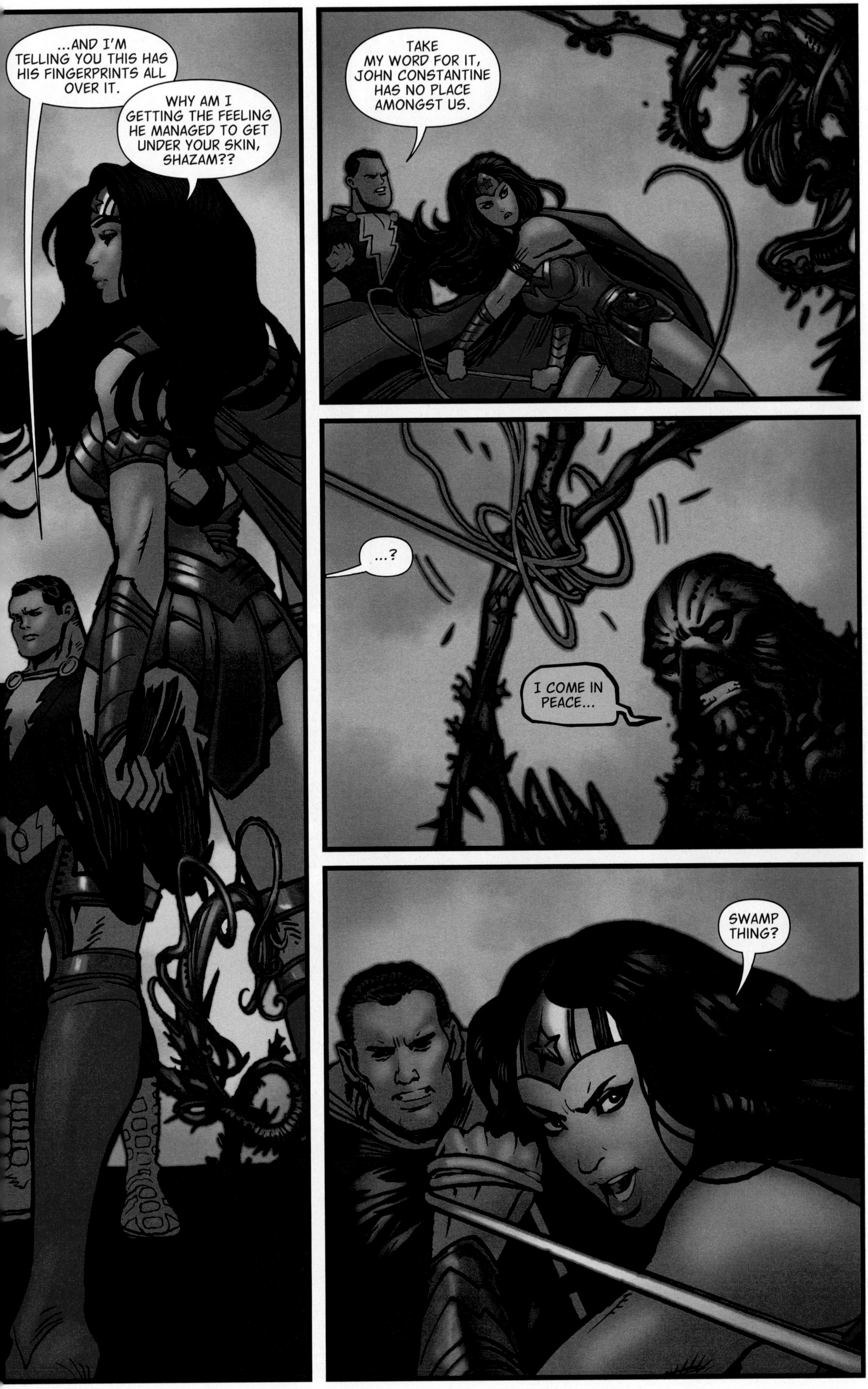
...AND I'M TELLING YOU THIS HAS HIS FINGERPRINTS ALL OVER IT.
WHY AM I GETTING THE FEELING HE MANAGED TO GET UNDER YOUR SKIN, SHAZAM??
TAKE MY WORD FOR IT, JOHN CONSTANTINE HAS NO PLACE AMONGST US.
...?
I COME IN PEACE...
SWAMP THING?

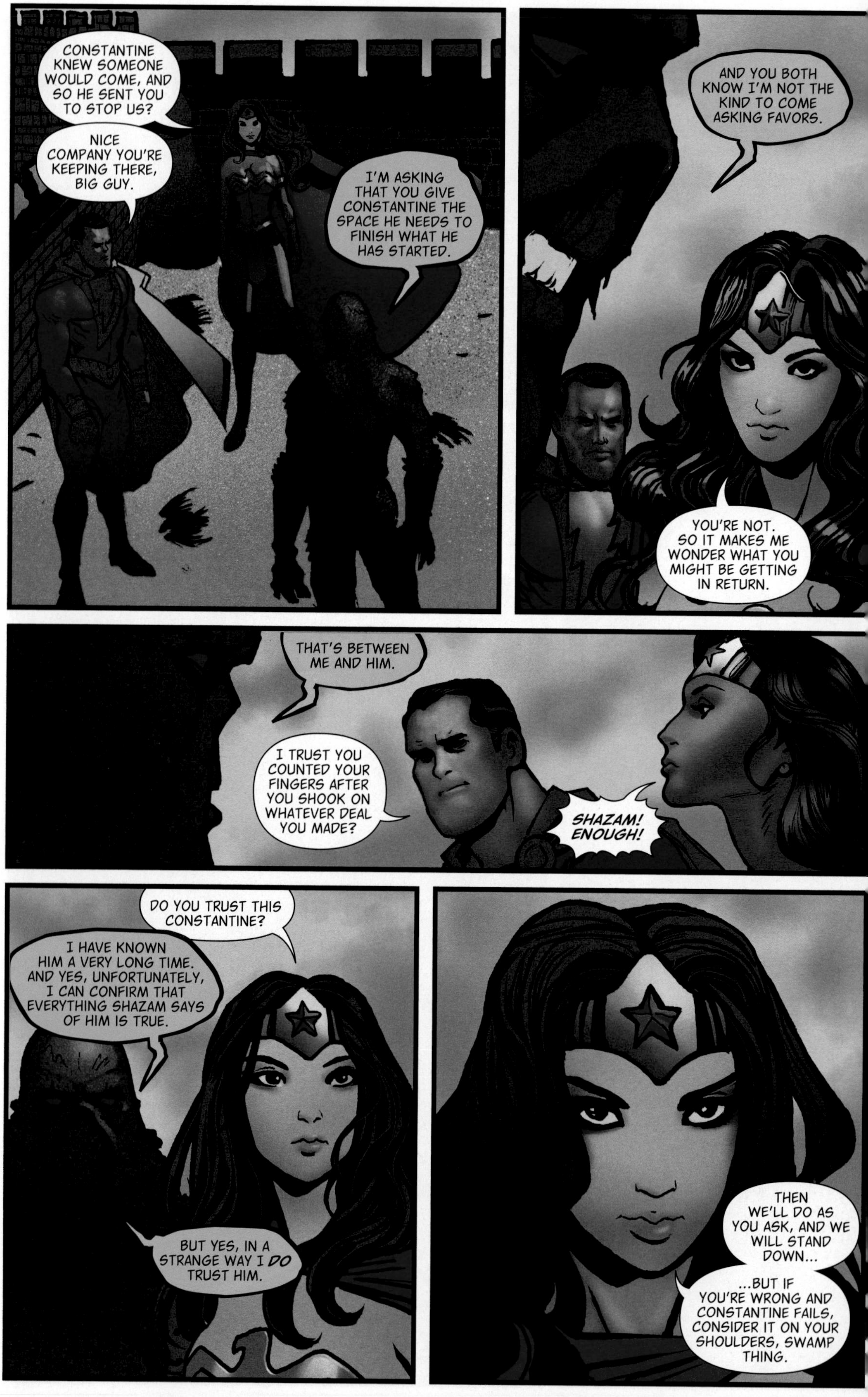

CONSTANTINE KNEW SOMEONE WOULD COME, AND SO HE SENT YOU TO STOP US?
NICE COMPANY YOU'RE KEEPING THERE, BIG GUY.
I'M ASKING THAT YOU GIVE CONSTANTINE THE SPACE HE NEEDS TO FINISH WHAT HE HAS STARTED.
AND YOU BOTH KNOW I'M NOT THE KIND TO COME ASKING FAVORS.
YOU'RE NOT. SO IT MAKES ME WONDER WHAT YOU MIGHT BE GETTING IN RETURN.
THAT'S BETWEEN ME AND HIM.
I TRUST YOU COUNTED YOUR FINGERS AFTER YOU SHOOK ON WHATEVER DEAL YOU MADE?
SHAZAM! ENOUGH!
DO YOU TRUST THIS CONSTANTINE?
I HAVE KNOWN HIM A VERY LONG TIME. AND YES, UNFORTUNATELY, I CAN CONFIRM THAT EVERYTHING SHAZAM SAYS OF HIM IS TRUE.
BUT YES, IN A STRANGE WAY I DO TRUST HIM.
THEN WE'LL DO AS YOU ASK, AND WE WILL STAND DOWN...
...BUT IF YOU'RE WRONG AND CONSTANTINE FAILS, CONSIDER IT ON YOUR SHOULDERS, SWAMP THING.

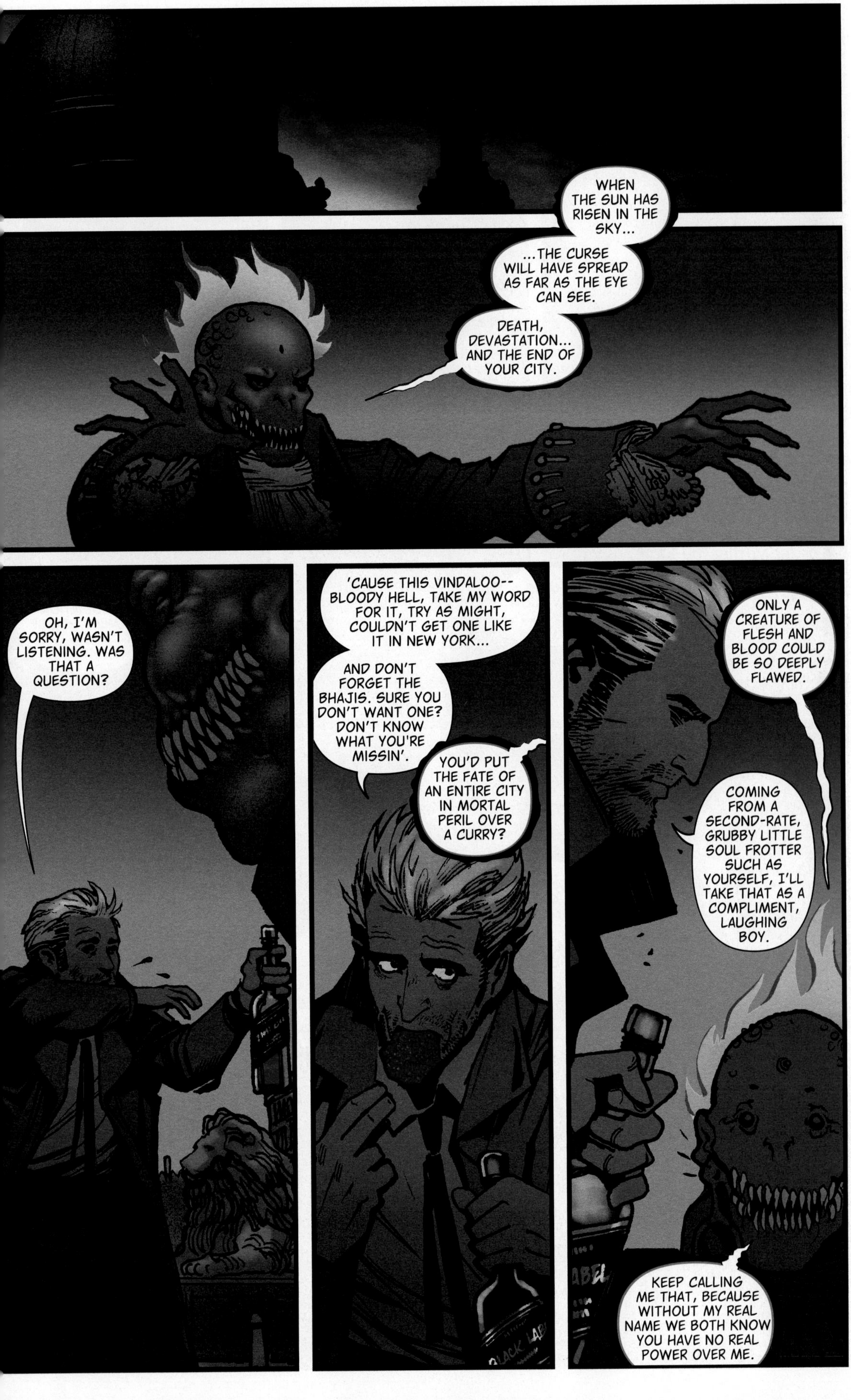
WHEN THE SUN HAS RISEN IN THE SKY...
...THE CURSE WILL HAVE SPREAD AS FAR AS THE EYE CAN SEE.
DEATH, DEVASTATION... AND THE END OF YOUR CITY.
OH, I'M SORRY, WASN'T LISTENING. WAS THAT A QUESTION?
'CAUSE THIS VINDALOO-- BLOODY HELL, TAKE MY WORD FOR IT, TRY AS MIGHT, COULDN'T GET ONE LIKE IT IN NEW YORK...
AND DON'T FORGET THE BHAJIS. SURE YOU DON'T WANT ONE? DON'T KNOW WHAT YOU'RE MISSIN'.
YOU'D PUT THE FATE OF AN ENTIRE CITY IN MORTAL PERIL OVER A CURRY?
ONLY A CREATURE OF FLESH AND BLOOD COULD BE SO DEEPLY FLAWED.
COMING FROM A SECOND-RATE, GRUBBY LITTLE SOUL FROTTER SUCH AS YOURSELF, I'LL TAKE THAT AS A COMPLIMENT, LAUGHING BOY.
KEEP CALLING ME THAT, BECAUSE WITHOUT MY REAL NAME WE BOTH KNOW YOU HAVE NO REAL POWER OVER ME.

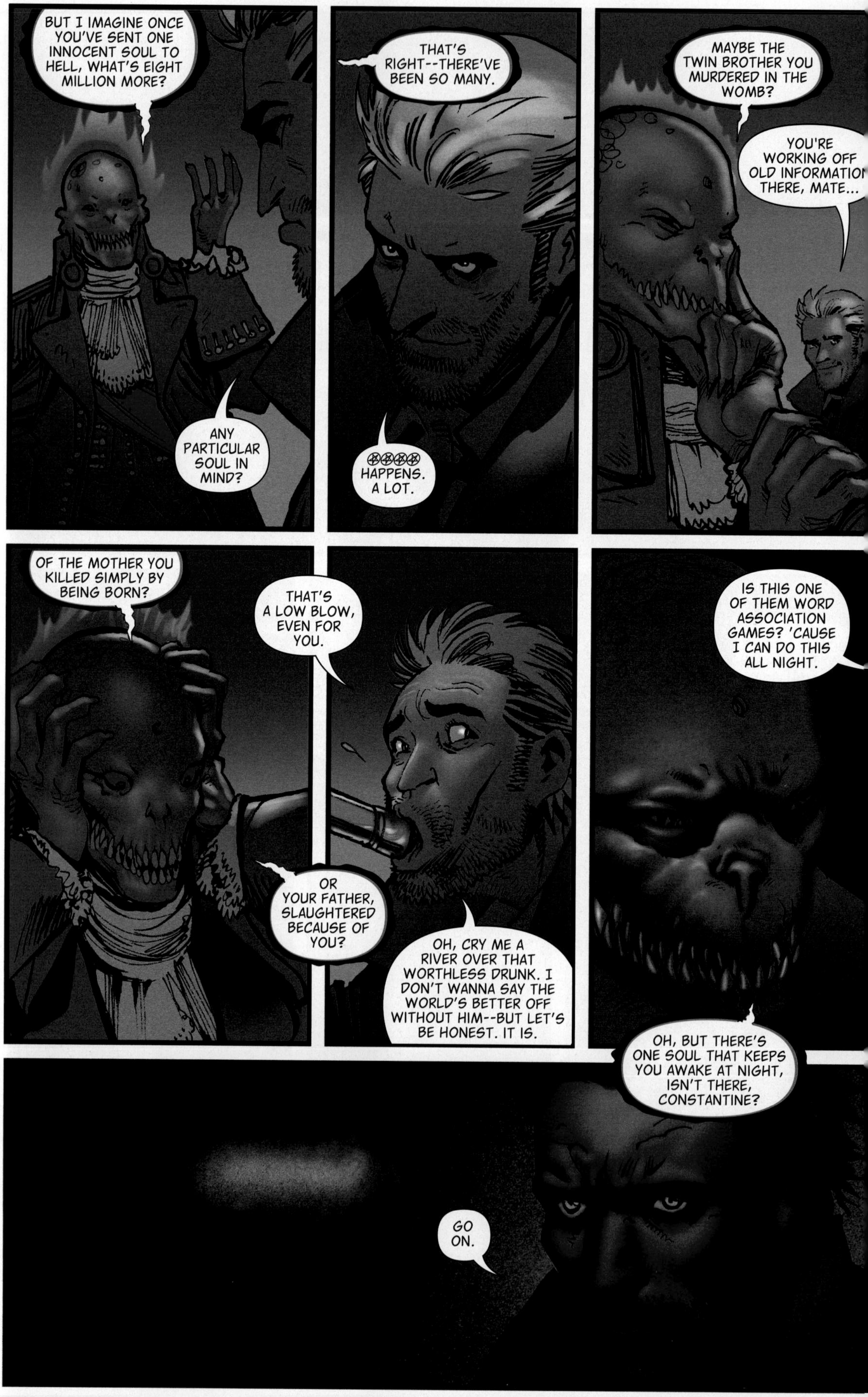
BUT I IMAGINE ONCE YOU'VE SENT ONE INNOCENT SOUL TO HELL, WHAT'S EIGHT MILLION MORE?
ANY PARTICULAR SOUL IN MIND?
THAT'S RIGHT--THERE'VE BEEN SO MANY.
HAPPENS. A LOT.
MAYBE THE TWIN BROTHER YOU MURDERED IN THE WOMB?
YOU'RE WORKING OFF OLD INFORMATION THERE, MATE...
OF THE MOTHER YOU KILLED SIMPLY BY BEING BORN?
THAT'S A LOW BLOW, EVEN FOR YOU.
OR YOUR FATHER, SLAUGHTERED BECAUSE OF YOU?
OH, CRY ME A RIVER OVER THAT WORTHLESS DRUNK. I DON'T WANNA SAY THE WORLD'S BETTER OFF WITHOUT HIM--BUT LET'S BE HONEST. IT IS.
IS THIS ONE OF THEM WORD ASSOCIATION GAMES? 'CAUSE I CAN DO THIS ALL NIGHT.
OH, BUT THERE'S ONE SOUL THAT KEEPS YOU AWAKE AT NIGHT, ISN'T THERE, CONSTANTINE?
GO ON.

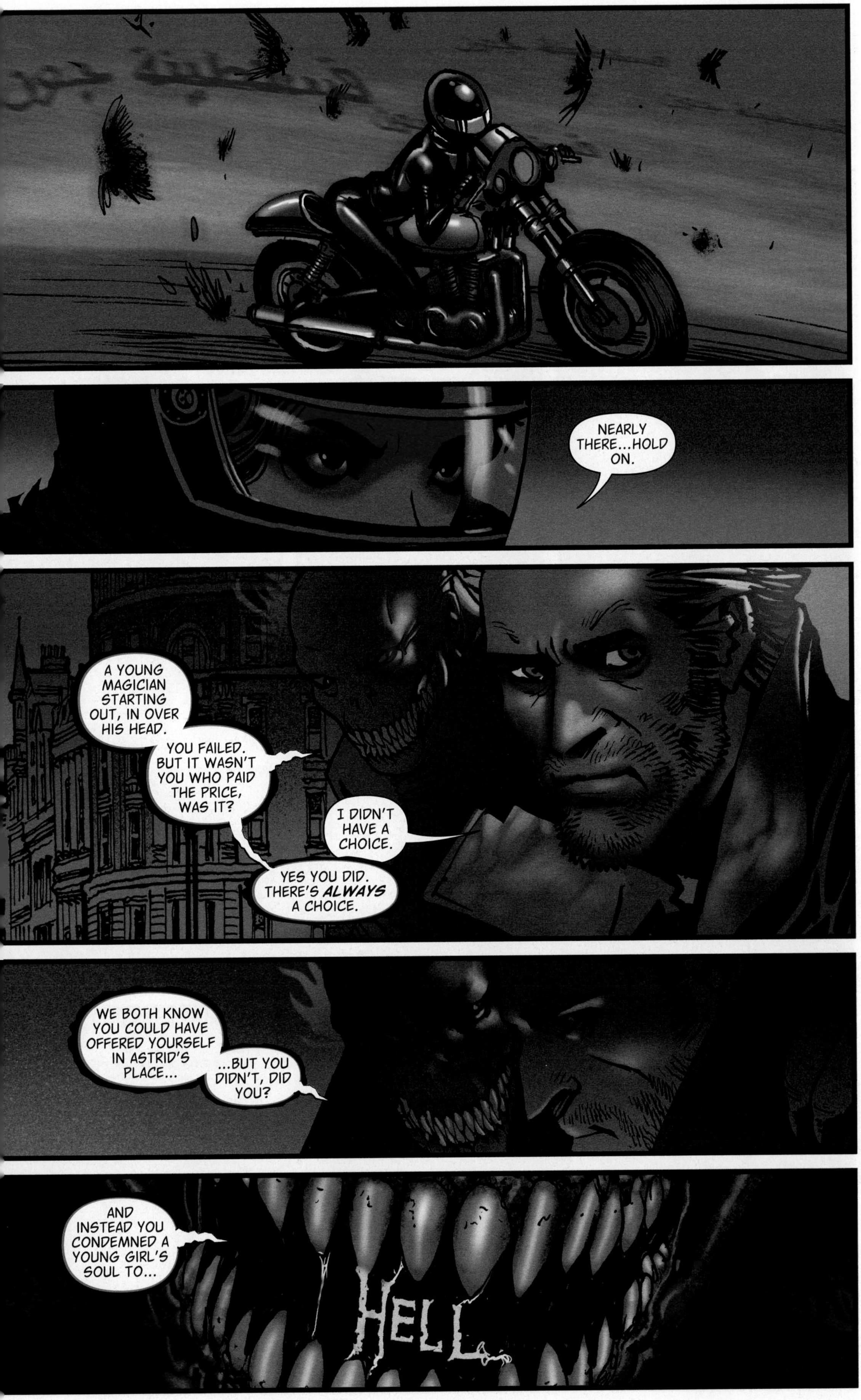
NEARLY THERE...HOLD ON.
A YOUNG MAGICIAN STARTING OUT, IN OVER HIS HEAD.
YOU FAILED. BUT IT WASN'T YOU WHO PAID THE PRICE, WAS IT?
I DIDN'T HAVE A CHOICE.
YES YOU DID. THERE'S *ALWAYS* A CHOICE.
WE BOTH KNOW YOU COULD HAVE OFFERED YOURSELF IN ASTRID'S PLACE...
...BUT YOU DIDN'T, DID YOU?
AND INSTEAD YOU CONDEMNED A YOUNG GIRL'S SOUL TO...
HELL

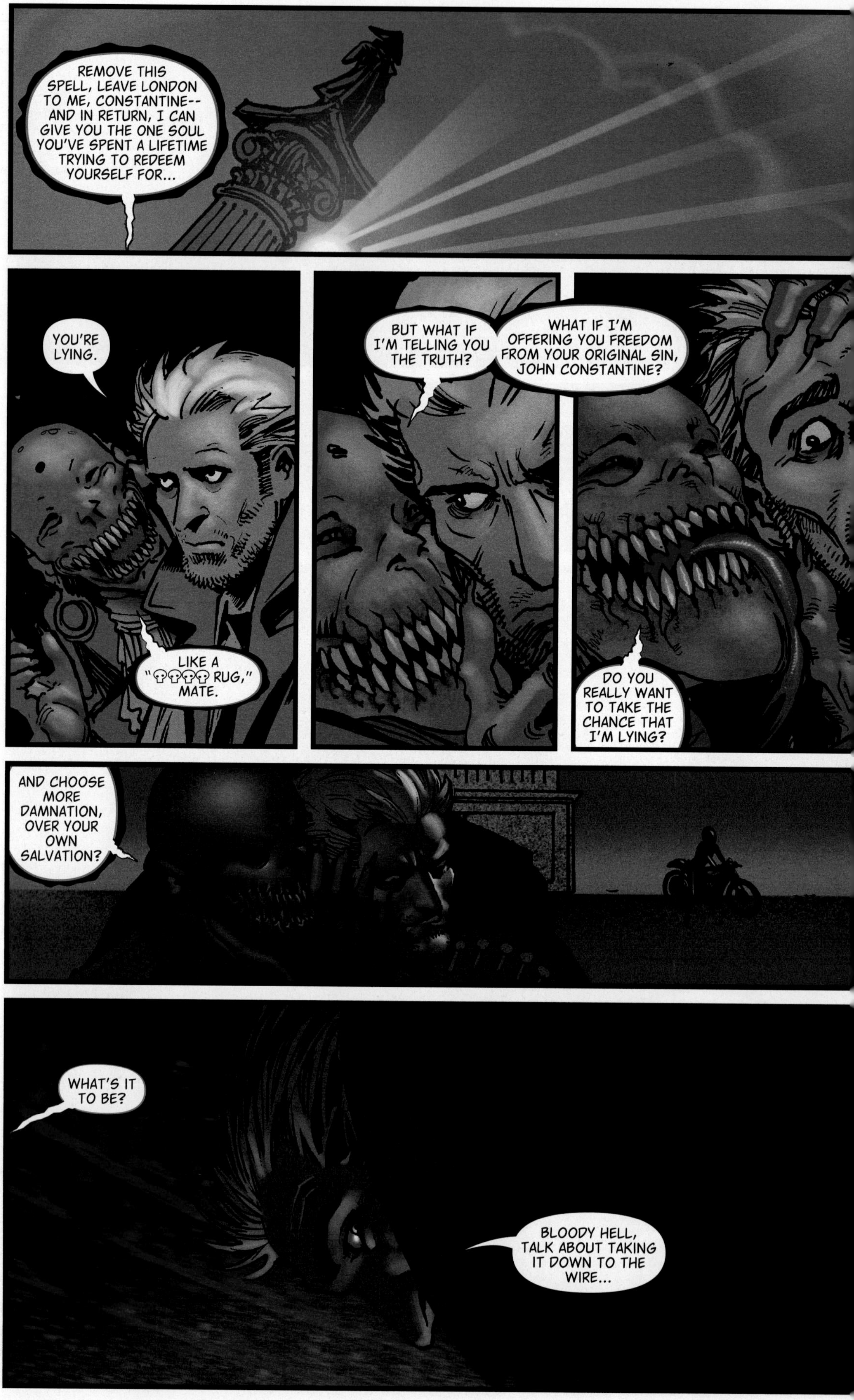
REMOVE THIS SPELL, LEAVE LONDON TO ME, CONSTANTINE-- AND IN RETURN, I CAN GIVE YOU THE ONE SOUL YOU'VE SPENT A LIFETIME TRYING TO REDEEM YOURSELF FOR...
YOU'RE LYING.
LIKE A "💀💀💀💀 RUG," MATE.
BUT WHAT IF I'M TELLING YOU THE TRUTH?
WHAT IF I'M OFFERING YOU FREEDOM FROM YOUR ORIGINAL SIN, JOHN CONSTANTINE?
DO YOU REALLY WANT TO TAKE THE CHANCE THAT I'M LYING?
AND CHOOSE MORE DAMNATION, OVER YOUR OWN SALVATION?
WHAT'S IT TO BE?
BLOODY HELL, TALK ABOUT TAKING IT DOWN TO THE WIRE...

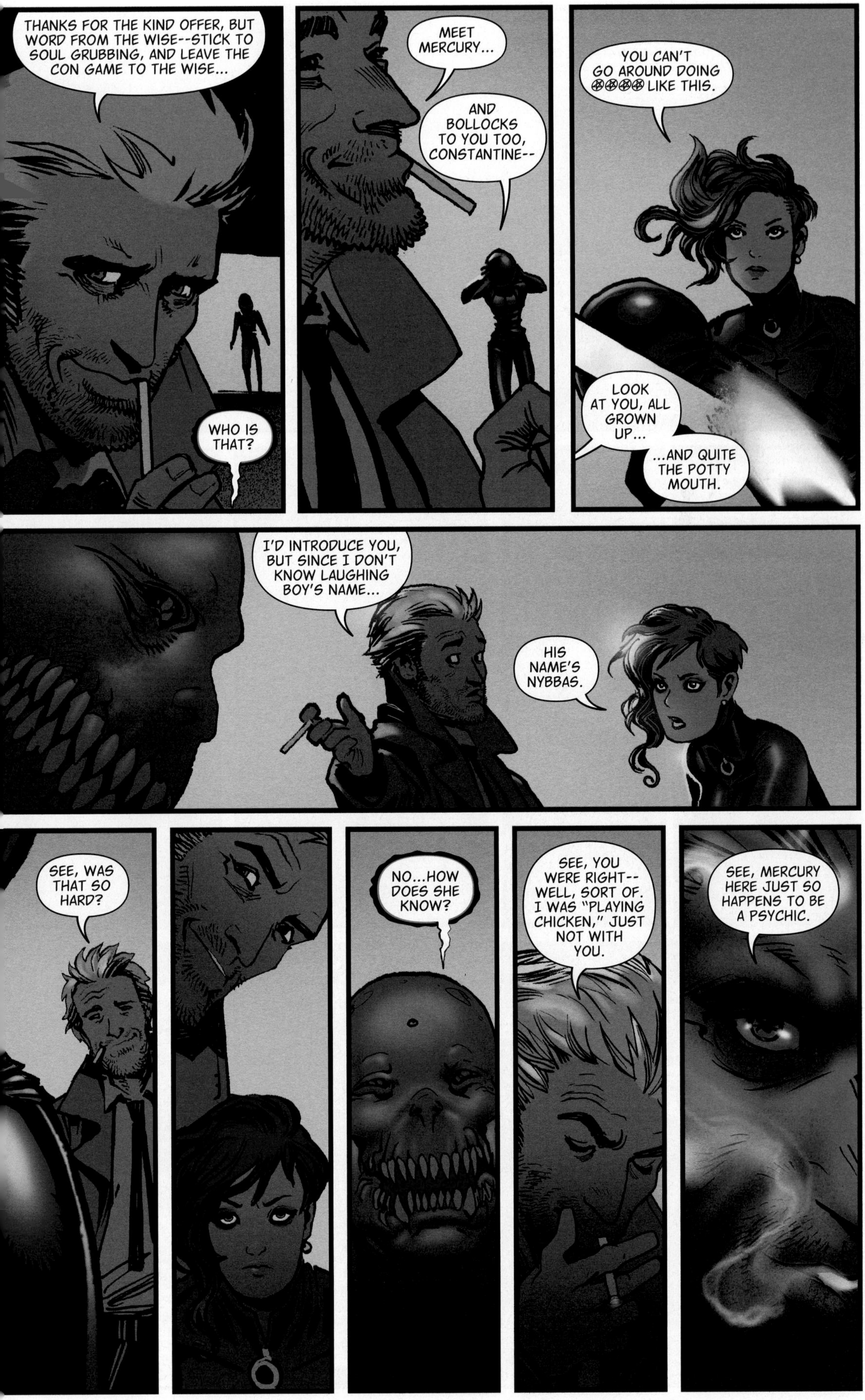
THANKS FOR THE KIND OFFER, BUT WORD FROM THE WISE--STICK TO SOUL GRUBBING, AND LEAVE THE CON GAME TO THE WISE...
WHO IS THAT?
MEET MERCURY...
AND BOLLOCKS TO YOU TOO, CONSTANTINE--
YOU CAN'T GO AROUND DOING ✖✖✖✖ LIKE THIS.
LOOK AT YOU, ALL GROWN UP...
...AND QUITE THE POTTY MOUTH.
I'D INTRODUCE YOU, BUT SINCE I DON'T KNOW LAUGHING BOY'S NAME...
HIS NAME'S NYBBAS.
SEE, WAS THAT SO HARD?
NO...HOW DOES SHE KNOW?
SEE, YOU WERE RIGHT-- WELL, SORT OF. I WAS "PLAYING CHICKEN," JUST NOT WITH YOU.
SEE, MERCURY HERE JUST SO HAPPENS TO BE A PSYCHIC.

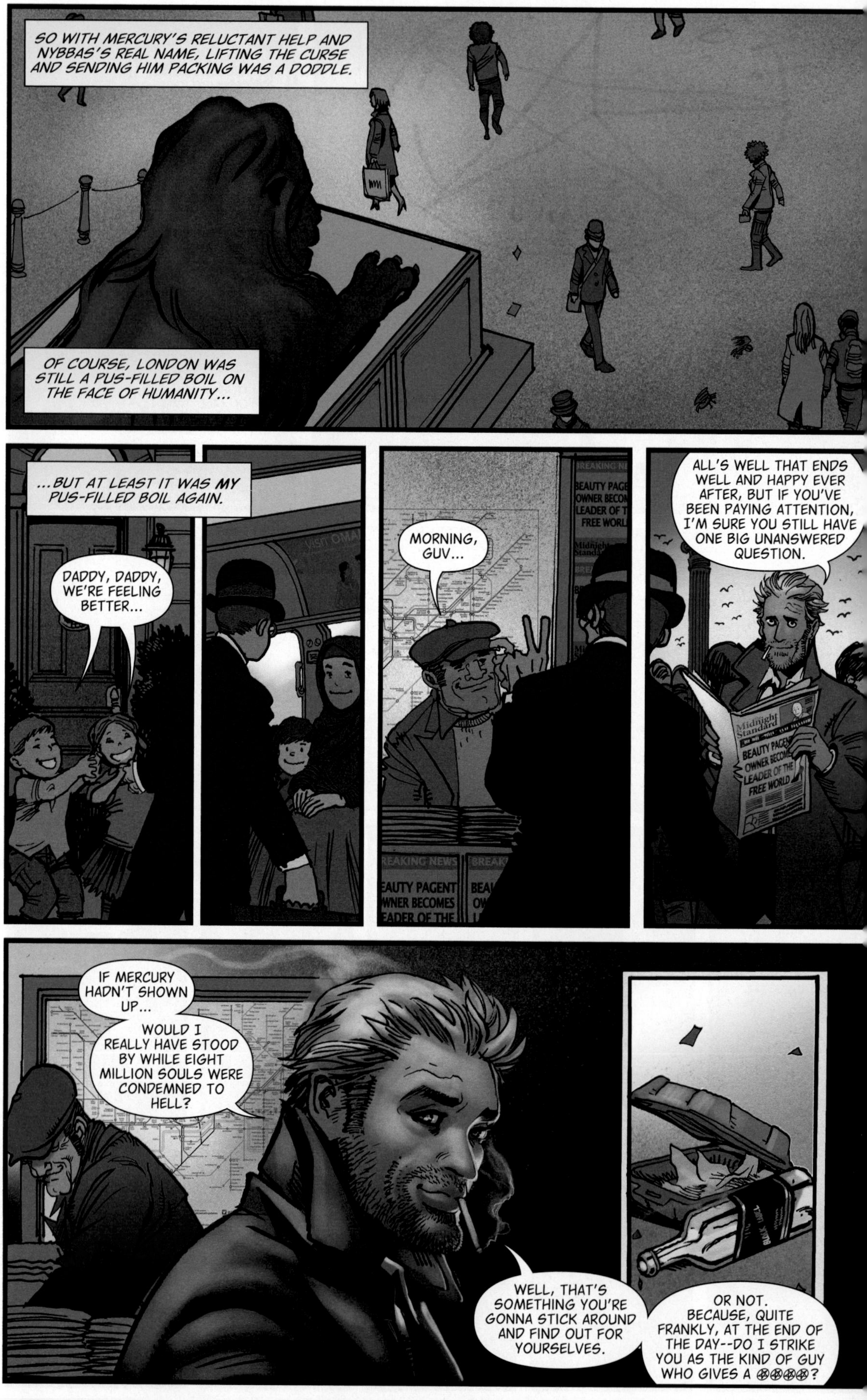
SO WITH MERCURY'S RELUCTANT HELP AND NYBBAS'S REAL NAME, LIFTING THE CURSE AND SENDING HIM PACKING WAS A DODDLE.
OF COURSE, LONDON WAS STILL A PUS-FILLED BOIL ON THE FACE OF HUMANITY...
...BUT AT LEAST IT WAS *MY* PUS-FILLED BOIL AGAIN.
DADDY, DADDY, WE'RE FEELING BETTER...
MORNING, GUV...
ALL'S WELL THAT ENDS WELL AND HAPPY EVER AFTER, BUT IF YOU'VE BEEN PAYING ATTENTION, I'M SURE YOU STILL HAVE ONE BIG UNANSWERED QUESTION.
Midnight Standard
IF MERCURY HADN'T SHOWN UP...
WOULD I REALLY HAVE STOOD BY WHILE EIGHT MILLION SOULS WERE CONDEMNED TO HELL?
WELL, THAT'S SOMETHING YOU'RE GONNA STICK AROUND AND FIND OUT FOR YOURSELVES.
OR NOT. BECAUSE, QUITE FRANKLY, AT THE END OF THE DAY--DO I STRIKE YOU AS THE KIND OF GUY WHO GIVES A ⊗⊗⊗⊗?

# FROM THE WRITER OF *ANIMAL MAN*
# JAMIE DELANO
## with JOHN RIDGWAY, ALFREDO ALCALA and others

**JOHN CONSTANTINE, HELLBLAZER VOL. 2: THE DEVIL YOU KNOW**

with DAVID LLOYD, MARK BUCKINGHAM and others

**JOHN CONSTANTINE, HELLBLAZER VOL. 3: THE FEAR MACHINE**

with MARK BUCKINGHAM, RICHARD PIERS RAYNER and others

**JOHN CONSTANTINE, HELLBLAZER VOL. 4: THE FAMILY MAN**

with GRANT MORRISON, NEIL GAIMAN and others

JOHN CONSTANTINE
**Hellblazer**
ORIGINAL SINS

VERTIGO

Jamie Delano    John Ridgway
Alfredo Alcala    Rick Veitch    Tom Mandrake

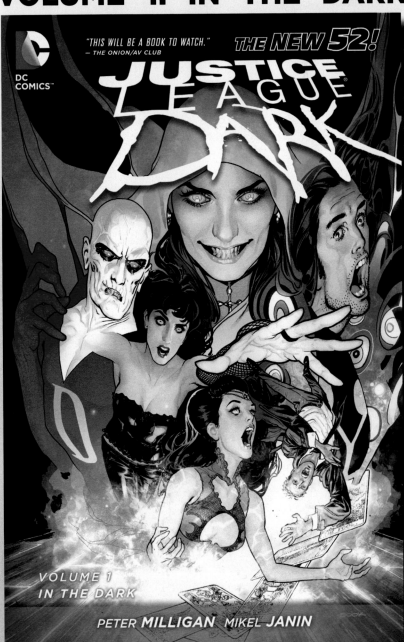